THE DECLINE AND FALL OF
THE MEDIEVAL PAPACY

THE
DECLINE AND FALL
OF THE
MEDIEVAL PAPACY

L. ELLIOTT BINNS

BARNES
&NOBLE
BOOKS
NEW YORK

This edition published by Barnes & Noble, Inc.

1995 Barnes & Noble Books

ISBN 1-56619-849-6

Printed and bound in the United States of America

M 9 8 7 6 5 4 3 2 1

INTRODUCTION

IN the Introduction to my volume on Innocent III, published in 1930, I expressed the hope that, in due season, I should be able to produce a large-scale *History of the Papacy from the Concordat of Worms to the Great Schism*. The present volume, I need hardly say, is not the realisation of that hope. I would have it looked upon as being in the nature of a preliminary study; for the survey of a wider period has given me the opportunity of clearing my mind on not a few points of significance. But this was not my only reason for undertaking the task. It has long appeared to me that Gibbon, in describing the rise of the modern nations, for that was his real subject, not only failed to recognise the great merits of the Byzantines, but also to realise that the true successor of the Western Empire was the Papacy. My volume is therefore to be regarded definitely as a supplement to *The Decline and Fall of the Roman Empire*, and, in particular, of its final volume, where the treatment is inclined to be hurried and superficial, and where a number of small errors occur, which even Bury's comprehensive learning has failed to eliminate.

In dealing with my subject I have adopted, though by no means slavishly, the chronological method. This method may be condemned by some as a mere arithmetical device; it has, however, distinct advantages in tracing out a decline and fall. In the various chapters a uniform treatment has not been attempted. Certain of them demanded more detail than others. It also seemed worth while to include in some, the Northern Renaissance for example, fruits of special studies in the shape of material useful to other students and not easily accessible. In the Conciliar Period I have made

full use of Finke *Acta Concilii Constantiensis* (1896-1928)—
I think that this is the first time that an English writer has
done so—and also Haller *Studien und Quellen zur Geschichte
des Konzils von Basel* (1896-1926).

The mention of these volumes may well introduce a word
of apology for the absence of a Bibliography. An adequate
one would have swollen to vast proportions, and is no longer
necessary, as lists of books are easily accessible in the various
volumes of the *Cambridge Medieval History* and in Paetow's
Guide to the Study of Medieval History. In a number of instances, however, I have noticed, in the footnotes, monographs
which I have come across, especially such as are of recent
date and not included in published Bibliographies. I must
apologise, further, for not having used, in every case, the latest
edition of original authorities ; for the most part I have relied
on texts in the great collections and on works in my own possession. Of Muratori I can say, as Gibbon did (vii. p. 216) :
" that treasure is in my library " ; it has been for many
years " an amusement ", as well as " a duty, to consult " its
various parts. I also possess St. Bernard in Mabillon's edition,
and my references have been made to it. So also in the case
of the works of Continental scholars I have only, in a few
instances, added the page of the English Translation where
such exists. I trust that this procedure will not merit the
accusation of having sacrificed too freely the convenience of
the reader to my own necessities.

To observe the rise, development, and partial decline and
fall of a great institution ; to note the various influences,
racial and cultural, as well as definitely religious, which
affected it ; cannot fail to be an enthralling pursuit. In the
case of the Papacy it is doubly so, for here we have an institution which exhibits a distinct life of its own ; so much so,
indeed, that the individual Popes, that is the best of them,
seem not so much the temporary directors of its destinies,
as the incarnation of its spirit.

But if enthralling, the task is also arduous. If I have
failed adequately to fulfil it, the cause must be assigned to

lack of the appropriate qualities, and not to blindness to the responsibilities involved. I was, indeed, first moved to undertake it by reading, in the *Recollections* of Lord Morley (i. p. 12), of Cotter Morison's desire for the coming of the historian who " would depict with sweeping brush the Decline and Fall of Theological, as Gibbon did of Imperial, Rome ". The historian of the Decline and Fall of the Medieval Papacy must endeavour to produce a work which will be stamped with the seal of largeness. It is not enough for him to explain single events and particular transactions; he must, in addition, disentangle the main thread in its various manifestations, as it is carried hither and thither by the sweeping revolutions of the changing years; and since in religion, as in politics, tendencies are often more potent than doctrines, he must observe, in connexion with each epoch, those secret dispositions which prepare the way for great changes. In a word, he must realise the difference between the Papacy at different stages of its development, and yet, beneath the ever-varying scene, retain his consciousness of its identity. This demands continual wariness against straying down tempting by-paths. It demands, also, severe restraint upon the writer's own views and prejudices; for no student of the Medieval Papacy can hope to understand it, unless he is willing, not only to lay aside such personal proclivities, but even to forget, for the moment, any merely provincial loyalties. He must attempt to breathe the wide air of European culture. For the story belongs, until its closing chapters, to an age when Canterbury was one with Rome, and Wittenberg had not yet been heard of.

But what, it may be asked, has been the result of the enquiry? What were the causes of the Decline and Fall of the Medieval Papacy? I must confess that the longer I have pondered over this question the more complex has it become, and the more numerous the answers which might be given to it. But behind them all there seems to have lain a single, fundamental cause. This was—secularisation. From this root sprang all the other causes; they were, to change the figure, symptoms of one, universal disease.

For the secularisation of the Papacy, however, there is much to be said by way of excuse. At the beginning of its history the Church was faced by a momentous choice. Was it to keep itself apart entirely from the world and remain a small, and probably decaying, sect ? Or was it to undertake a world-wide mission ? The Church accepted the latter alternative, but in doing so it had to plunge into the Roman social system.[1] That was the first, and necessary, step in the direction of secularisation. Later on, when the Papacy had established its supremacy over the West, it had to solve the problem of combining a strong central government with local initiative ; it failed in this, became over-centralised and self-absorbed. The failure was due, in part, to its basing the spiritual and moral leadership of Christendom on the possession of temporal power. But for this again there was abundant excuse in an age of violence and insecurity. To maintain the Papal States armed forces were necessary ; this, and the upkeep of the papal court, required ample financial resources ; to supply them taxation, on an ever increasing scale, was imposed. Such taxation was resented, and helped to swell the volume of national and racial feeling.

But the emergence of national and racial feeling had other consequences. The Papacy was, I believe, founded on the older Rome ; and a foundation not only supports a building, it gives to it its main outline. So the Papacy, in its virtues and in its defects, was surprisingly similar to the Republic and the Empire.[2] This similarity did not make for understanding by other peoples, especially those which had never borne the yoke of Rome. By the end of the fifteenth century the Church was coming to be regarded, in the North, as Italian rather than Catholic. Furthermore, the Papacy had failed, as the Empire had failed, because it was no longer able to produce men capable of guiding and ruling it. It failed, moreover, again like the Empire, because it had become too large and cumbrous ; the centre was out of touch

[1] Cf. Harnack *Monasticism* pp. 26 sq.
[2] Parallels have been noted from time to time in the course of the narrative.

with the extremities. The Popes had had too great a burden of responsibility thrust upon them :

" they had conspired to outreach
their own ambition, winning dominions too wide
for domination ".[1]

Then at the beginning of the sixteenth century a new situation arose. The Eastern Empire, by this time, had disappeared, and the Western was but a shadow ; a grave blow to old traditional institutions. On the horizon new continents were looming to unsettle and excite men's minds. Humanism was spreading everywhere and bringing with it an atmosphere that was alien and enervating; it brought also new ideas and the wider diffusion of knowledge. In face of a changing world the Papacy held close to the old ways. The Church may, at times, be impervious to new ideas; it seldom fails to exhibit readiness in finding fresh expedients for defending the old. So in the previous century it had turned back the Conciliar Movement and other efforts after reform. The truth was that the abuses had become so interwoven with the structure, that to abolish them seemed tantamount to the demolition of the whole building. Moreover the Papacy was, by this time, a decaying institution, without the necessary vigour and energy, so it seemed, to reform itself. In the end it invited the fate of the man who, as Balzac somewhere says, repairs the roof of an outhouse by the light of his own burning homestead.

In conclusion I wish to acknowledge the help of various scholars. I am indebted, above all, to Dr Whitney, the Dixie Professor of Ecclesiastical History in my own University. Dr Whitney has, on many occasions, allowed me to discuss with him the plan of my volume ; he has, also, recommended to me works which I might otherwise have missed. I have, in addition, received valuable advice from Professor Ernest Barker and Dr Coulton. Certain chapters have been submitted, in

[1] Bridges *The Testament of Beauty* I. ll. 767 sqq.

proof, to Dr A. J. Macdonald, Professor G. R. Potter, and Mr H. O. Evennett. I have to thank them for kindly criticisms and suggestions. I ought to add that none of the above is in any way responsible for the views set forth in the following pages ; for them the sole burden must rest upon the author.

L. ELLIOTT BINNS

GREAT HALLINGBURY RECTORY
Festival of the Epiphany 1934

CONTENTS

CHAPTER V

THE GREAT SCHISM OF THE WEST

CHAPTER VI

THE CONCILIAR MOVEMENT

CHAPTER VII

THE PAPAL TRIUMPH

CHAPTER VIII

THE FALL OF THE EASTERN CHURCH

CHAPTER IX

THE RENAISSANCE

CHAPTER X

THE POPES AS ITALIAN PRINCES

CHAPTER XI

THE NORTHERN RENAISSANCE

CHAPTER XII

THE TEUTONIC REVOLT

CHAPTER XIII

THE SACK OF ROME : THE END OF AN EPOCH

ABBREVIATIONS

E.T.	English Translation.
MGH.	*Monumenta Germanicae Historica* in various series.
PG.	Migne *Patrologiae Cursus Completus*—Series graeco-latina.
PL.	,, ,, ,, ,, —Series latina.
RIS.	Muratori *Rerum Italicarum Scriptores.*
RS.	Rolls Series (*Rerum Britannicarum Medeii Aevi Scriptores*).
Rot. Parl.	*Rotuli Parliamentorum.*
SS.	*Scriptores.*

FULL TITLES OF WORKS REFERRED TO BY NAME OF AUTHOR

Gibbon *Decline and Fall of the Roman Empire* (ed. Bury).
Hardt, Van der *Magnum Oecumenicum Constantiense Concilium.*
Hefele *Conciliengeschichte nach den Quellen bearbeitet.*
Mansi *Sacrorum Conciliorum nova et amplissima Collectio.*
Raynaldus *Annales Ecclesiastici* (references under year).

CHAPTER I

INTRODUCTORY: THE GROWTH OF PAPAL POWER TO INNOCENT III

IT has recently been stated by a sympathetic critic that Introduction "To the ordinary cultivated student of civilisation the genesis of a Church is of little interest, and at all events we must not confound the history of a Church with its spiritual meaning." [1] This may well be true; but it is surely equally true that to understand the spiritual meaning of a Church some knowledge of its origins and development is essential. Certainly any study of the decline and fall of the Medieval Papacy requires as a preliminary a brief review of its rise.

The first impression imposed by such a study is one of Character-istics of Growth wonder at the extensive part played by the accidental and the contingent. Whether this contingent element is less fortuitous than it seems is a question for the theologian rather than the historian, and in any event it is probably not so important as the first glance would suggest, for above the accidental and fortuitous as an explanation of the progress of the Roman Church in the early ages of Christianity stands out its amazing ability to profit by the opportunities which came its way. As in the case of the Roman people before it,—that people of whom it has been said that they might lose battles but would never surrender an acre of soil,—its progress was due more to patience and steadfastness, to stubbornly holding on to what had been already won, than to the brilliant execution of any pre-conceived and far-reaching plan. [2] In other words it was a free historical development,

---

[1] T. S. Eliot *For Lancelot Andrewes* p. 15.

[2] The methods of the Papacy might well have been suggested by the advice which, according to Livy V. vi. 8, Appius Claudius gave to the Romans some five centuries before the birth of the founder of Christianity; "Nec finem ullum alium belli quam victoriam noverit nec impetu potius bella quam perseverantia gerat."

brought about by a series of innumerable acts and decisions, and not a premeditated evolution.[3]

The Papacy, to rate it no higher, is perhaps the most interesting manifestation of the human spirit in its strivings after self-expression, not only in individual men, but even more in great institutions. The striving of the Papacy after self-expression involved it in a double set of relations ; on the one hand to the Church as a whole, on the other to the Empire. Its activities in these two spheres find a close parallel in the efforts of an individual personality to gain inner harmony as well as to adjust itself to externals. During the critical period of early development the Papacy was groping half blindly, amidst distractions and dangers, towards maturity and cohesion. The sustaining power in its long and arduous struggle was a belief in its divine mission, a belief so strong that any question of the righteousness and value of its ambitious purposes was precluded ; a vision had been vouchsafed, the task of the Popes was to make it actual.

The method by which the men of the middle ages sought to bring their ideals into relation with the' actual world was by fashioning an institution in which they might become concrete. Hence the Churchman sought to establish a visible Church, a great society embracing within it all the manifold activities of the human spirit and claiming to be the highest expression of its purpose.[4] This society was to be, above all, the realisation of the divine *respublica* upon earth. For this ideal he schemed and fought and suffered as step by step it drew nearer, until the great days of Innocent III seemed to bring it almost within his grasp.[5]

Two aspects of Christendom. But the Papacy was not the equivalent of the visible Church, nor did it exhaust the meaning of Christendom. Christendom had two aspects, represented by the Pope and the Emperor respectively. It was a single community founded upon the will of God, and since so founded, having as its most cherished characteristic that unity which was the constitutive principle of the universe. The division into Papacy and Empire was not a breach of the ideal

---

[3] Cf. Eucken *The Life of the Spirit* p. 163.

[4] Gerbert (Sylvester II) once described the Church as " sanctissima societas humani generis " : *Epist.* LXXIX.

[5] See below p. 35 sq.

unity, for it met the two-fold nature and destiny of man himself, and was, moreover, provided for in our Lord's own words.[6] At the same time the need for a higher unity was felt, though the different points of view of papalist and imperialist made no general agreement possible as to where this was to be found.[7]

It is not without interest to notice that this dual aspect of Christendom corresponded to two great conceptions which the middle ages had inherited from the ancient world ; the idea of a universal Empire and the idea of a universal religion. Furthermore it is to be noticed that these two, the Roman Empire and Christianity, both had their origin within a single reign, that of Augustus.[8] But in spite of this correspondence there was a vast difference of outlook between the ancient world and the middle ages.   Under the pagan Empire the centre of unity had been political, the paramount authority that of the Emperor himself ; so long as the supremacy of the state was recognised [9] men might hold many different kinds of creeds and philosophies.   The middle ages developed on exactly opposite lines ; its centre of unity was religious, the Roman Church ; whilst alongside this religious unity there might go any number of political variations.

But the ideal of unity had to face an anomaly and, if possible, to avoid a practical evil.   In the first place the claim of the Roman Church, through its bishops, to represent Christendom as a whole seemed futile owing to the schism between East and West.   The Eastern Church had older traditions than those of the West and it steadfastly refused to recognise either the Pope or the Head of the Holy Roman Empire.   That, in spite of this refusal, men should have gone

Schism of East and West

---

[6] Matt. xxii. 21.   " Render therefore unto Caesar . . . and unto God, etc."
See further Rivière *Le Problème de l'Église et de l'État* p. 1.

[7] The middle ages, with their fondness for figures, represented Christendom as a pyramid ; in the papal scheme the apex was the supreme pontiff ; in the imperial, God was the apex, with Pope and Emperor on a level below Him.

[8] This fact was used by the apologist, Melito of Sardis, in appealing to Marcus Aurelius,—twin growths ought to be at peace with one another : see Eusebius *Hist. Eccles.* IV. xxvi.   Later Prudentius regarded the work of pagan Rome as a preparation for the Church ; " The Scipios worked for Christ."

[9] In the ancient world the citizen saw in the state the supreme object of service and in obedience to its commands the height of moral virtue.

on clinging to the ideal was only possible by reason of the cleavage between East and West.[10]

The evil arose from the undue subordination of the individual to the institution which the papal theory demanded. The Roman Church was the heir of the Roman people—and the Roman people, like the Greeks before them, in their political thinking aimed at conformity as the basis of stability.[11] That a number of differing forms of Christianity should exist side by side without bringing down the whole religious structure, would have been to them an impossible conception. Hence there was an emphasis on the importance of unity, which under the increasing prestige of Rome and the growth of the Canon Law tended to become uniformity. The individual lost his value at the expense of the institution, an unfortunate consequence, for from it there is only a short step to regarding power as more important than justice, to a general policy of subordinating means to ends.

The notion of subordinating the individual to the community is, of course, a commonplace in Plato, though less marked in Aristotle who had not Plato's belief in the compensations which personal survival might bring in another sphere. But Plato, seeing all things in the light of eternity, regarded the sacrifice of the temporal interests of individuals as allowable for the good of the whole. The Roman Church might have made the same defence had it been necessary.

Thus the Papacy had before it the ideal of Christendom as a single community united in a visible head, and like the Roman state regarded its problems from the standpoint of society.[12] The realisation of the ideal involved, as we have seen, a double task. First, the establishment of the papal supremacy throughout the Western Church—the East for practical purposes had virtually to be ignored—and secondly,

[10] Gibbon has pointed out that a similar cleavage between Greeks and Romans existed in earlier times in literature. The East ignored the Latins ; "There is not, I believe, from Dionysius to Libanius, a single Greek critic who mentions Virgil or Horace. They seem ignorant that the Romans had any good writers." I. p. 38. So too Plutarch ignored, and was ignored by, the Latin writers of his day.

[11] An interesting example of the growing recognition of the need for stability can be found in St Augustine (*De Civ. Dei* II. xxi.) where he modifies Cicero's definition by substituting ' concord ' for ' justice ' as the essence of a state.

[12] Cf. Westcott *The Gospel of the Resurrection* p. 85.

the achievement of freedom from the Empire by the attainment of a position of admitted superiority. The necessity of this latter task soon became evident, and it was undertaken, not merely for its own sake, but in the effort to achieve mastery over the Church. In a similar manner the Roman people, again to notice an instructive parallel, acquired their empire; for, as Mommsen contends, originally they had cherished no deliberate design of universal dominion, they sought merely the hegemony of Italy; but in order to secure this they were led to undertake one conquest after another.[13]

We must now turn to a detailed study of the means by which this task was carried to a successful issue, and in doing so we must remember that the Papacy is not to be regarded as an artificial creation but as a living organism; the events which led up to its final position of pre-eminence are not isolated happenings but factors in the gradual realisation of a great, though not fully formulated, conception. Stage by stage the separate elements of which the visible Church is made up were incorporated within it, " molten into the great stiffening alloy of Rome," as Robert Bridges puts it.[14] But the alloy of Rome was not quite so ' stiff ' as some have imagined, if by stiffness we mean rigidity; in this again Rome was a living organism and no mere machine; as the circumstances demanded, in those early days, it could change, could cast off what was old and impeding, could renew what was of abiding worth.

The history of the Roman Church, like the history of the Roman people, did not begin in Rome. This is a truism, but it serves to remind us that any review of the growth of the Papacy must go back to Palestine and the first records of the Christian Church. At this stage, and for generations afterwards, there was nothing to suggest the later papal monarchy; on the contrary there seems to have been the possibility of a kind of Caliphate establishing itself with the headship of the Church vested in a single family, that of the Messiah.[15]

The Church in the New Testament

---

[13] *History of Rome* II. p. 176.

[14] *The Testament of Beauty* I. *l.* 770.

[15] So far as I know, this idea was first suggested by Renan in his famous Hibbert Lectures. It certainly receives some confirmation from the recognition of the headship of James in the Clementine Romances where Peter is but the Apostle of the Gentiles. Gwatkin says that " but for the catastrophe of

At all events so far as the New Testament is concerned no single, definite form of government has emerged or found universal acceptance; the Catholic Church of the future exists as a number of small groups bound loosely together by the possession of a single faith and a common tradition rather than by a rigid organisation. But this society was a developing society, and indeed when first we come across the Church its earliest stages have already been left behind, a statement which applies to doctrine as well as to organisation. The Church was to follow " the same course of evolution as the ancient Roman state, passing gradually from a modified democracy into a centralised despotism." [16]

The Church in the Pagan Empire   The period which elapsed between the close of the New Testament and the adoption of Christianity by Constantine saw the process of development well on its way. This was not due, as I have already pointed out, to the carrying out of any predetermined policy, it was the inevitable result of the circumstances in which the Church found itself. Here again there was a double struggle to be carried on ; outwardly against persecution, inwardly against heresy and perverted ideas of the gospel. To cope with these threats the Church had to tighten up its organisation and define more exactly its beliefs. In the process the clergy came more and more to be differentiated from the laity—the first step towards the later policy by which it came almost to be identified with the Church.[17]

Ranks among Clergy   But not only was there a growing distinction between clergy and laity, within the order of the clergy itself there was also a gradual discrimination. Above the lower ranks the bishop, as the centre of unity and the guardian of the apostolic faith, became increasingly important ; and above the individual bishops the great sees soon began to stand out, and, in particular, the Bishop of the imperial city was re-

the Roman war, there might, in another generation, have been an attempt to govern the Churches by some sort of Abbaside Khalifate of the Lord's relations at Jerusalem " ; *Early Church History* I. pp. 70 seq.   The same idea has more recently been revived by Canon Streeter *The Primitive Church* p. 40.

[16] Inge *Christian Ethics and Modern Problems* p. 12.

[17] In this exaltation and differentiation of the priesthood the Roman Church was following the example, not of Roman religion, but of the Oriental cults which had become popular in the West : see S. Dill *Roman Society from Nero to Marcus Aurelius* p. 580.

cognised as having some kind of pre-eminence.[18] This did not mean, however, that he was the accepted ruler of the whole Church, as Victor discovered in the controversy over the date of Easter, and Stephen in his dispute with Cyprian.[19]

With the adoption of Christianity by Constantine the Church entered upon a new stage, a stage which was perhaps one of decline rather than progress, for the example of Constantine could not fail to be imitated by his subjects. In the past men and women had embraced the faith of the Church with the ardour of genuine conviction ; too often in the future they would merely acquiesce in a religion which had been distinguished by the favour of the Emperor.

It is difficult to say what motives inspired Constantine when he became the patron of the Church. His statesmanlike mind must have recognised that, after the breakdown of the persecution, the Christians were the strongest, if not the most numerous, body in the state, and it was a natural step for him to enter into an alliance with them.[20] Whether anything beyond the political advantage weighed with him can never be known ; but undue stress should not be laid upon the fact that his baptism was delayed until the end of his life ; such a delay was common in an age when superstitious views of the power of baptism to cleanse from all sins were held. More

[margin note: Constantine]

[margin note: His motives for becoming a Christian]

---

[18] The well-known passage of Irenaeus, written towards the close of the second century is worth quoting in this connexion : " Ad hanc enim ecclesiam propter potentiorem prinipalitatem necesse est omnem convenire ecclesiam." *Adv. Haer.* III. iii.   Canon Streeter, whilst recognising that " both a special pre-eminence and a special responsibility belonged to the churches in the three capitals which could also claim to be ' Apostolic Sees '—Antioch, Ephesus, and Rome " considers that " in the earliest period the authority . . . resided rather in the metropolitan church as such than in the person of its bishop." *Op. cit.* pp. 257 seq.

[19] An appeal was made to Cyprian against the decision of Stephen in the matter of the Bishops of Leon and Merida ; he did not hesitate to reverse it on the ground that the Bishop of Rome had been deceived through ignorance of the facts and distance from the scene (*Epist.* LXVII. 5).   Stephen was fond of making a lavish use of excommunication to enforce his wishes ; the result was, as Firmilian of Caesarea pointed out to him, that he excommunicated himself : see Cyprian, *Epist.* LXXV.

[20] Ferdinand Lot, however, considers that Constantine was inspired by religious motives and that his act was dangerous politically, since the army was devoted to the worship of the Sun, and the Christians were weak in the West (*The End of the Ancient World*, pp. 31 seq.).   But may he not have relied on his own personal popularity with his soldiers and hoped by his action to gain adherents, as Clovis did after him, in the territories of his rivals.

decisive, perhaps, is the retention of the title Pontifex Maximus, which made him head of the old pagan religion, as he was in practice of the new Christian Church.[21]

As Head of the Church Constantine's ideas of what was involved in the headship of the Church were entirely pagan and the Church had to submit to all the disadvantages of an established religion without its full privileges.[22] One of the services which it had to render was that of a unifying force within the Empire. But to be a unifying force the Church had to be at unity within itself. This was by no means the case and the attempt to impose uniformity of belief brought in the age of creed-making. At the first great Council held at Nicea the Emperor, who had not even been baptised, was hailed as Bishop of Bishops and given a position of high prominence.

Theological Controversies Most of the disputes which divided the Church were concerned with the doctrine of the Trinity or the person of Christ; but one dispute, the Donatist controversy in North Africa, struck at the doctrine of the Church itself. To this it owed its importance, for the Church had here to face not heresy but schism, and in so doing gained fresh consciousness of its own significance.[23]

Effect on Roman See These controversies had a notable effect on the position of the Roman See, although it was, for the most part, not directly concerned in them. The controversies, so far as they affected doctrine, arose in the East, and in the East they dragged out their tedious span. The Popes, as typical Romans,[24] looked upon doctrinal disputes as annoying interruptions to be settled as speedily as possible. For the East they were of unsurpassed interest and on no account to be hurried. The only real theologian among the Popes was Leo I, and even he by foreclosing discussion with his famous Tome plunged the East into internal schism. Thus the aloofness of Rome from any direct part in controversy

[21] The successors of Constantine down to Gratian imitated his example.

[22] The Church was not, of course, established as the sole religion of the Empire until the days of Theodosius; but as it was the Emperor's religion, it held a privileged place, and was virtually established.

[23] See H. Schmidt "Des Augustinus Lehre von der Kirche" in *Jahrb. für deutsche Theol.* VI. p. 198.

[24] The religion of the Romans has been described as "episodical and unsystematic"; the Etruscan system which influenced it so considerably was much more developed: see Randall-MacIver *The Etruscans* p. 126.

gave it the position of an arbiter; a position which was rendered more imposing by the attitude to the West of the two great rival Eastern schools of Antioch and Alexandria.[25] To the Popes went appeals upon the most varied subjects; not only upon dogma, but upon Church order and even upon justice to individuals. In addition Rome was a kind of city of refuge for persecuted Catholics during disturbances in the East.[26] It has to be remembered that the Roman Church, in its earlier days especially, was a link between East and West, for until well into the second century it was as much Greek as Latin.[27]

For some years before the triumph of Constantine over his rivals the Empire had had no fixed capital. He now proceeded to build one on the banks of the Bosphorus; thus transferring the seat of Empire from West to East. This transfer had consequences of vast import for the Church. The mere command of an Emperor could not eradicate from the mind of the West instincts which had been the slow growth of centuries; in spite of Constantine's action men still looked to Rome as the centre of the civilised world—they saw there no longer an Emperor but a bishop. The little settlement on the Palatine had developed into the capital of a world Empire; it was now to enter upon a fresh stage of its eternal career by becoming the seat of a universal Church. The Roman genius was about to take to itself an ecclesiastical form. In days gone by political importance had often followed religious centralisation as at Nippur, Babylon, and Jerusalem itself. Rome was unique in that its religious importance followed political decline. *Foundation of Constantinople*

It was not until 392 that the pagan temples were finally closed by Theodosius I and a period of transition brought to an end. During the eighty years or so which had elapsed since the Edict of Milan had placed paganism and Christianity on more or less equal terms, the former had been steadily *The End of Paganism*

---

[25] Practically every heretic in the second and third centuries found his way, soon or late, to Rome : an embarrassing testimony to its importance.

[26] Even as early as 170 A.D. Rome was noted in the East for its charity ; see Dionysius of Corinth's Letter to the Romans in Eusebius *Hist. Eccles.* IV. 28 ἐξ ἀρχῆς γὰρ ὑμῖν ἔθος ἐστὶν τοῦτο, πάντας μὲν ἀδελφοὺς ποικίλως εὐεργετεῖν.

[27] " Almost every document connected with the Roman church before the Nicene age was written in Greek " : Gwatkin *Early Church History* II. p. 214.

decaying, the latter as uniformly gaining new strength and new adherents ; men saw that the struggle between them was virtually decided and wished, if no higher motive influenced them, to be found on the winning side.

Pagan influence on Christianity
Christianity thus triumphed, but it was almost entirely transformed in the course of the contest—a fate which seems to attend all parties, political and religious alike, as almost a condition imposed by life itself upon antagonists. It ' stooped to conquer ' and its victory was due to that power of assimilation which is so evident at every stage of the history of Rome, whether as Republic, as Empire, or as Church. The Romans might become Christians, but, in the words of a learned Roman Catholic writer, " they took over . . . the language, the ritual, the yearly observances, the festal adornments, and even the artistic symbols to which they had been brought up." [28] Paganism was indeed to perish, but its passing was not without dignity—one thinks of that noble group around the Altar of Victory [29]—and in dying it left to its supplanter no inconsiderable legacy, for the breach was intellectual rather than moral. It remains still a factor in the life of Europe, a deeper paganism indeed than that of Rome ; for beneath civilisation itself, concealed merely by a superficial veneer, profound elemental forces and racial qualities, Celtic, Teutonic, Italian, Slavonic, are potent still and liable to emerge.

The Growth of Papal Power
During this last century of the Western Empire the position of the Popes was becoming ever stronger, and when the Theodosian Code legalised the privileges of the Church and clergy, taking as the standard of belief that faith which had been delivered to St Peter, it merely gave imperial sanction to what had already become customary. The Law of Valentinian in 445 in recognising the Roman supremacy gave three reasons for so doing ; the merits of St Peter, the dignity of Rome,[30] and the authority of Councils. But the authority

[28] Barry *The Papal Monarchy* p. 11. The list might be greatly enlarged.
[29] For a sympathetic account of the last age of paganism see Dill *Roman Society in the last Century of the Western Empire.*
[30] At a later period the extreme papalists were careful to guard against the supposition that the Popes owed anything to Rome. Alvaro Pelayo, early in the fourteenth century, declares '' locus non sanctificat homines, nec Roma papam, quae res inanimata est '' : see *Collyrium adv. hereses* in Scholz *Unbekannte Kirchenpol. Streitschrifte* X. p. 507

of the Roman See had grown up in independence of the
Empire ; hence it came about that the fall of the Empire
in the West took no whit from the prestige of the Papacy.[31]
In fact the transfer completed the work of Constantine.
When there was no longer an Emperor in the West and the
link with the East was but slender, papal Rome took the place
of imperial Rome.   Rome was indeed eternal and the Latin
mind has always refused to put a term to its rule.   It was
therefore a strange misunderstanding of the course of history
which impelled St Jerome, on hearing of the fall of the city
before the Goths, to proclaim from the safe refuge of his cell
at Bethlehem that " the city once the head of the universe
is the sepulchre of the Roman people." [32]   But Jerome was
no true Latin, merely a barbarian from Dalmatia, and he
underrated the powers of revival and adaptation which were
latent in the Roman people.   The insight of the poet made
Prudentius see more clearly, and he had no doubt that the
civilising mission of Rome had not ceased.   There were not
many in that age who combined, as he did, intense Christian
fervour with a patriotic love for Rome and a profound knowledge of her history.

If the barbarian peoples who crowded into the Empire had
not such a knowledge of its past as Prudentius, they had
at least caught something of its spirit, and during the long
years of tutelage had learned to honour its ancient glories.
Before they overcame Rome they had been largely
Romanised.[33]   This was especially true of the Goths who
displayed unabated energy in propping up and restoring
the old imperial edifice which was crumbling away on every
side.[34]   Amid this decay there was one stable institution,
one power which could link them up to the older world which

The Barbarians and Rome

---

[31] Christianity survived when the Empire fell because its organisation had
been hammered out in an age of persecution.   The apocalyptic teaching had
also prepared it for a time of catastrophe : see F. C. Burkitt in *Cambridge
Biblical Essays* p. 207.

[32] The same error was repeated four centuries later by Paul the Deacon :
" (Roma) quae caput orbis *erat* " :   *Carm.* xxv. 9 in MGH. Poet. I. p. 60.

[33] The love of Rome is seen in the poem of Rutilius Namatianus, a Romanised Gaul, *De reditu suo* (ed. Keene).   The influence of Christianity had already
spread beyond the frontiers of the Empire : e.g. Ambrose corresponded with
Fritigil, a Marcomanni queen who had been converted by an Italian trader :
see *Vita Ambrosii* XXXVI.

[34] L. Halphen *Les Barbares* p. 77.

was perishing, and with that institution they came at length to make their peace. There was indeed no other bond of union for the West save in the Church. It is true that the invaders were to a man Arians [35]—but sooner or later, as the generations succeeded one another, the Catholic faith displaced its rival. The strong people of the Franks alone were pagan and as such offered virgin soil; when in 496 Clovis was baptised the reproach that Catholicism was the religion of the conquered was removed and its final triumph assured.

The Church and the Eastern Empire   The end of the Western Empire did not mean, at any rate in theory, that the West was independent; Constantinople still ruled over it.[36] In practice, however, that rule was often ignored and the Church developed with very little interference from the civil power; room was thus given for the development of Latin, as distinct from Greek or Eastern, Christianity. In the seventh century the rise of Islam further increased the gap between East and West; and it is probable that it was the example of the Moslems, who scorned idol worship, which led to the attempt of the Eastern Emperors to abolish images, an attempt which provoked a controversy only ended by schism and the complete emancipation of the Popes from the Eastern Empire.

Power of the Clergy   During the centuries which followed the barbarian invasions the power of the clergy over their flocks steadily increased. The greater part of them were drawn from the vanquished who were as superior to the newcomers in culture and civilisation as they were inferior in strength and valour. In the course of time they found themselves, by a natural development, entrusted not only with education, but with statecraft and administration as well. An immense power was theirs in consequence and in some parts they were the real rulers.[37] Among the survivors of the vanquished the clergy had equally high status, for even under the Empire

---

[35] According to Orosius and Socrates the Burgundians were originally Catholics : see Hauck *Kirchengeschichte Deutschlands* I. p. 101.

[36] Theoderic, for example, did not wish to found a separate Empire. Writing to Anastasius, he says : " Romani regni unum velle, una semper opinio sit " : see Cassiodorus *Variae* I. 1 (P.L. LXIX. col. 505).

[37] Hauck has collected some interesting material for their position in Gaul : *Kirchengeschichte Deutschlands* I. pp. 131 sq. and 171 n. It should not be forgotten that the barbarians before their conversion had been accustomed to recognise the authority of their priests even in secular matters.

the Christians had often preferred the judgement of their bishops in cases of dispute to that of the corrupt imperial officials. This process was naturally continued under barbarian rulers.

When the Empire was transferred to Constantinople there were numerous peoples beyond its confines in the West over whom the genius of Rome was destined to exert its influence. The task of drawing them into the Church was first attempted in the days of Gregory the Great, a man of wide vision with a statesmanlike power of transmuting vision into serious purpose. In him the old Roman virtues seemed to find fresh manifestation. It was Gregory, ' as every schoolboy knows ', who sent St Augustine to England and thus began a connexion which was to have momentous consequences for the Roman See. From England and the sister isle missionaries soon began to cross to the peoples of Germany; Columbanus, Willibrord, Winfrith and their fellows went forth to win new lands for the Roman allegiance.[38] *Missions to Heathen*

But the eyes of Gregory were not only on the ends of the earth ; whilst his agents were extending the sphere of Rome's influence he himself was increasing its power at the centre. The great object of his pontificate was the exaltation of his See and, as he said, the enforcement of justice.[39] There was need indeed, especially in Gaul, for insistence upon papal rights. St Avitus, Bishop of Vienne, in the early sixth century, might declare that " to question the authority of the Pope of Rome is to overthrow not one bishop but all," but such an attitude did not continue ; for the bishops of Gaul, finding themselves in the presence of a weak secular power, became little monarchs [40] and looked askance at the distant pontiff across the Alps. It was left to Boniface, with the sympathetic support of Charles Martel and Pepin, to reform the Frankish Church and to restore respect for Rome. Under Charlemagne it expanded, with the expansion of the nation, into a species of imperial Church.[41] *Gregory the Great*

The consideration of the relations of the Papacy and *Consolidation of Papacy*

[38] Winfrith, better known as Boniface, was the first transalpine Bishop to take the oath of obedience to the Pope.

[39] " Ut possit florere cum libertate justitia " ; *Epist.* I. 61.

[40] See Fustel de Coulanges *La Monarchie Franque* pp. 522 seq.

[41] Cf. Hauck *op. cit.* II. pp. 71 seq. " So wurde die Landeskirche zur Reichskirche."

Charlemagne, who now came to dominate the scene, will receive attention later.[42]   Under his weak or pious successors the Papacy had the opportunity, which it was not slow to seize, of enforcing its power over Christendom.[43]   Ranke goes so far as to suppose that at this epoch it entered upon a definite campaign for the overthrow of the powers of metropolitans and the immediate subjection of all bishops to itself.[44] By the time of Nicholas I [45] its supremacy over the West had been established, and it was well for Europe that the Papacy had thus consolidated its position, for the break-up of the Carolingian Empire shewed clearly to all who had eyes to perceive the significance of the times that upon it depended the unity of Christendom.

The " False Decretals "   One great means towards the establishing of papal prestige was the collection of Decretals attributed to Isidore of Seville, but known to history as the ' False Decretals.' [46]   This collection had been put forth in order to strengthen the local bishops against their metropolitans and among its forgeries were a number of genuine documents.   There is nothing to suggest that the Popes were accomplices in the crime save the fact that they above all others were to benefit from it.

Forgeries and Legends   The case of the False Decretals provokes the observation that legend and imposture played a very large part in the development of papal power as in the shaping of the middle ages in general.   These legends were often the reading back into the past of the conditions of the time in which they arose ; and after all in an ultra-conservative age the only way of progress often consists in the invention of precedents.   Sometimes, too, they were based on a foundation of fact, such was the case of the well-known legend of Leo I and Attila, and even the so-called Donation of Constantine.   This last document is a good example of a quite common type of fabrication by which the possession of certain rights or territories is

[42] See pp. 20 sq.

[43] There were occasional protests as that by Claudius, Bishop of Turin (d. 839) who held that St Peter did not hand on his primacy and that his successors would do well to copy his manner of life.

[44] *Deutsche Gesch. im Zeitalter der Reformation* I. p. 7.

[45] On this Pope see Rocquain *La Papauté au Moyen Âge* pp. 54 sqq.   In view of his great importance a study of his pontificate in English is much needed.

[46] On the ' False Decretals ' see P. Fournier *Étude sur les Fausses Decretales* (1907) and *Hist. des Collections Canoniques en Occident, &c.* (1931) pp. 127 sqq.

supported by the invention of a legend. Such legends were frequent, not only in the middle ages, but also in ancient Greece, and even if without any foundation of fact, they mirrored the history of the times.[47] Thus they have vital significance, as proclaiming fresh ideals and provoking men vehemently to action in their behalf.[48]

To realise that an institution so venerable as the Papacy had developed as the result of forgeries is at first a little startling; but the modern reader has to remember that literary conventions differ in different ages. This is well known to the student of both the Old and the New Testaments as well as to the classical scholar; no one, for example, supposes that the speeches in Thucydides or in the Acts of the Apostles were delivered exactly as they are recorded. Piety in all ages has found itself able to make astounding assumptions. Perhaps the most naïve of such cases is that of Agnello of Ravenna who, in compiling lives of the early bishops of that see, filled up any gaps from his own imagination assisted by the prayers of the brethren.[49]

To carry out its various schemes of expansion and con-solidation, the Papacy, like every other institution, had need of a complex organisation. At first the government of the Church had been modelled on that of the Empire and in the early middle ages it continued to develope on the lines of a secular power. A writer of the ninth century draws out the parallels between the Emperor who governed the world and the Pope who governed the Church; as the former has under him kings and counts and lesser nobles, so the latter has archbishops and bishops and inferior clergy.[50] The problems of the two institutions were similar; the relation of

Government of the Church

---

[47] Cf. Milman *History of Latin Christianity* II. p. 82; "History to be true must condescend to speak the language of legend; the belief of the times is part of the record of the times."

[48] The history of Islam furnishes an exact parallel to the False Decretals for the rights and privileges of the Quraysh, the dominant faction, were supported by forged traditions concerning the prophet.

[49] "Ubi Historiam non inveni, aut qualiter eorum Vita fuisset, nec per annosos, et vetustos homines . . . ne intervallum Sanctorum Pontificum fieret . . . vestris orationibus me Deo adjuvante, illorum vitam composui." *Vita Sancti Exuperantii* ii. in RIS. II. p. 62. Muratori himself draws attention to the passage in the Introduction (p. 4).

[50] See Walafrid Strabo *Liber de exordiis et incrementis* (ed. Knöpfler) pp. 98 sqq.

the central power to the local administration, the question of rival jurisdictions, and even such mundane matters as the relation of landlord and tenant.

Decline of Papacy in the Ninth Century   The flourishing state of the Papacy in the middle of the ninth century was unfortunately followed by a period of decline, and for nearly two centuries its prestige sank lower and lower under the weight of continual scandals almost unrelieved by efforts after better things. This loss of prestige was naturally accompanied by a loss of effective authority, and although the Pope was still the final court of appeal for Christendom, and although archbishops still received from him, as a sign of their authority, the sacred pallium, his headship of the Church, outside Italy, became merely nominal.[52] An interesting illustration of the independence of the local Churches is to be found in the contention of the French bishops that they were not bound to obey Damasus II because he had been elected without their consent.[53]

Reforming Movement: Cluny   Long before this a reforming movement had arisen in the monastic world, of which the chief inspiration came from the famous house of Cluny and its dependencies.[54] The spirit soon spread among the secular clergy, especially in Lorraine; and, through the union of the Kingdom of Arles with the Empire under Conrad II, into Germany itself. In France the reformed clergy received the support of the king, who saw in them useful allies in his struggle against the feudal nobles. A remarkable feature of the movement in its earlier stages was the extent to which the lay rulers co-operated with the metropolitans and bishops. The next stage was to see the elimination of both these factors.

Emperors as Reformers   By the efforts of the Saxon and Franconian Emperors the Papacy was purified and freed from the control of the local nobles;[55] new life seemed to come into it and a new

[52] In the early eleventh century Burchard of Worms emphasised the power of the bishops and seemed to assign to the Pope little more than the right of the feudal overlord who was not to interfere in the affairs of his vassal except in unusual circumstances. See P. Fournier " Le Décret de Burchard de Worms " in *Rev. d'hist. ecclés.* XII. p. 473. This incidentally was exactly the position of William I and Lanfranc in England.

[53] See *De Ordinando Pont.* in MGH. Lib. de Lite I. p. 11.

[54] The centralising of monastic power in Cluny led the way to effective centralising of the Western Church. Cluny itself only accepted the protection of Rome " ad tuendum ".

[55] The first occasion of their interference was on the death of Paul I in 767 : see Hegel *Geschichte der Städteverfassung in Italien* I. p. 212.

enthusiasm. Foremost in this development was Leo IX 1048-54. under whose wise and statesmanlike rule the Papacy began to gain the control of the reforming movement. In his choice of cardinals he was careful to elevate only those who would support his efforts in that direction. Furthermore, by a series of progresses through the transalpine lands Leo did much to restore papal authority and prestige. He also made a lavish use of legates who were given full powers of action and so were a means of bringing metropolitans and bishops into subordination.

The subordination of the episcopate, although it was a Pope and the prominent feature in the reforming work of the Papacy, was Bishops not viewed in too favourable a light by many ardent reformers. It had the effect of robbing the bishops of necessary authority in their own dioceses. This point of view was most forcibly expressed by St Bernard in his famous treatise *De Consideratione* as well as in a letter to Innocent II himself.[56] He accuses the Pope and the curia of allowing appeals from the bishops and thus putting them to shame, since the final verdict so often depended on bribery and secret influence. The virtuous bishops are in despair, he writes, the evil know only too well how to make use of the system. All this is bringing scandal upon the Papacy.

We have in this effort at centralising the government of the Church the beginnings of one of the most potent causes of the decline and fall of the medieval Papacy. Undue weight was placed on the centre which was unable to bear it, for the centre so frequently was the least worthy portion of the Church. That this process was the work of sincere and earnest reformers, who saw in it the only means of restoring and maintaining the Church's purity, adds to its tragic irony.

The Popes, when challenged either by metropolitans or The Canon by lay rulers jealous for the independence of their bishops, Law had a complete defence by appealing to the Canon Law which from the second half of the eleventh century began to obtain great prominence.[57] The Canon Law was indeed an immense

---

[56] Bk. IV. (*Opera* I. coll. 425 sqq.) and *Epist.* CLXXVIII. (*Opera* I. coll. 174 sq.).

[57] The use of the Canon Law by the Popes has been well worked out, mainly in relation to England, by Z. N. Brooke in his Birkbeck Lectures *The English Church and the Papacy 1066-1200*.

2

help to the Papacy for by collecting decretals every little incidental triumph became a precedent and the basis for further advance. The Popes never made the mistake of regarding a temporary halting place as the far-off bourne of their journeyings. They were not like the more ignorant of the Crusaders who imagined that each city they approached was Jerusalem itself.

Different Opinions of Papal Power   The attitude of the bishops and the Church in general was by no means unanimous in the eleventh and early twelfth centuries. At one extreme there were men like Anselm who regarded obedience to the Pope as a supreme duty and disobedience as equivalent to disobeying God Himself.[58] At the other there was the anonymous author of *Tractatus Eboracenses* who claimed that the Pope had no power over other bishops, but that, by a species of episcopal congregationalism, each bishop was supreme in his own diocese.[59] This writer stood practically alone. At the same time the idea that the power of the Pope was limited was frequently found. Deusdedit, writing at the end of the eleventh century, holds that the Pope is but one patriarch among several and that he has no right to alter what has been decided in the past.[60]

A practical exhibition of the limits to papal power was furnished in 1112 by the action of the bishops in compelling Paschal II to withdraw the concessions which he had made to Henry V. The bishops might have justified their action along the lines previously suggested by Godfrey, Abbot of Vendôme, who held that whilst an evil-living Pope had to be tolerated, one who like Paschal was threatening to do damage to the Church might suffer the loss of allegiance.[61]

Papacy and Empire   The great contest between the Papacy and the Empire which arose in the second half of the eleventh century had its

[58] *Epist.* iii. 65 and iv. 13.

[59] MGH. Lib. de Lite III. coll. 642 sqq.

[60] He has in mind the decree of Nicholas II which provided for the notification to the Emperor of the election of a Pope prior to his election ; see *Libellus contra invasores et symoniacos* i. 11 ; quoted by Carlyle *Hist. of Med. Political Theory in the West* IV. pp. 90 sqq.

[61] " Tolerandus quidem est pastor, ut canones dicunt, pro reprobis moribus : si vero exorbitaverit a fide, iam non est pastor, sed adversarius, a quolibet peccatore tantum catholico detestandus." *Libellus* i. in MGH. Lib. de Lite II. coll. 676 sqq.

origin, strangely enough, in those efforts to reform the Church in which lay rulers had co-operated. Before, however, we enter into the details of the contest it will be well to retrace our steps and review very briefly the relations of the Papacy to the civil power from its commencement.

The Church, as we have seen, grew up apart from and yet within the Empire under which it came to birth ; and it was not until Constantine at the beginning of the fourth century, recognising the value of the Church, became its patron, that there was any close relationship between them. The successors of Constantine followed his policy of patronising the Church. Some of the nobler spirits among the Catholics began to resent this situation, especially when the Emperor tacitly claimed the right to control the Church. Hosius of Cordova, for example, warned Constantius that he must not intrude into sacred matters nor give commands concerning them ; just as the kingdom had been entrusted by God to the Emperor so had the Church to the bishops, it was for him to learn of them in spiritual things. St Athanasius and St Ambrose shewed a similar independence when occasion required. For the most part, however, the headship of the Emperor was accepted as a natural thing.[62]

After the transfer of the Empire the Popes were under the suzerainty of the Eastern Emperors until in 731 Gregory II began a new policy.[63] For the greater part of this time the power of Constantinople was little more than nominal, though elections to the Papal See had to be confirmed by the Emperor, and occasionally Popes, Silverius and Martin I for example, found themselves roughly handled. Justinian, through his generals, made the power of the Eastern Empire real in Italy for a generation, and by his organisation of society encouraged the clergy in claiming exemption from secular jurisdiction, as well as in taking a large share in secular matters. But his assertion of the rights of the Byzantines involved the

Papacy and the Eastern Empire

---

[62] Cf. the statement of Optatus of Miletus (PL. II. p. 999) " cum super imperatorem non sit nisi solus Deus ".

[63] Gibbon (V. pp. 257 sqq.) misunderstood the attitude of Gregory. He was opposed, indeed, to the religious policy of Leo III, but was at the same time loyal to the Empire, as he saw that the only alternative was Lombard rule. When rebellion came it was due to over-taxation rather than to theological differences.

fall of the Goths.[64]   This in turn led to the Lombard invasion.

The Lombards   The invasion of the Lombards was of great significance for the future of both Italy and the Papacy.   To Italy they brought new life and strength, just as the Franks had done to Gaul and the Anglo-Saxons to Britain.   But they were not so favourably disposed to the older civilisation as the Goths, and the terror of their coming is reflected even in their own historians.[65]   Furthermore they had no respect for the Roman Church and its rights.   This led to open disagreement between the civil and religious governments of the country —a foretaste of later struggles [66]—and eventually to the beginning of political relations between the Papacy and the Franks who came in to defend Rome from Lombard threats.

The Franks   The Franks were to receive their reward for this intervention.   The feeble Childeric, the last of the Merovingians, was dethroned, after the Pope had been consulted on the impropriety of having the nominal rule and the actual power in different hands ; [67]   and in his place Pepin, the first of the Carolingian line, was crowned as king.[68]   Although the actual transfer of the crown was the work of the Franks themselves the appeal to the Papacy is of great importance as a very early instance of its being invoked to act as a supernational power.   A still greater mark of papal favour was shewn when on Christmas Day 800 Leo III crowned Charles as Emperor and then did homage to his new lord.   This act finally freed the West from the rule of the Byzantine Emperors and ideally was a revival of that Empire which had been ended by the transfer of power to Constantinople in 476.   The exact meaning of the Pope's act gave matter

[64] H. A. L. Fisher thinks that it destroyed an interesting attempt to found a new Italian kingdom out of Gothic and Latin elements and so led direct to the rise of the states of the Church ; *Med. Emp.* I. p. 20.   Others would hardly allow that the Goths and Latins had sufficiently assimilated to encourage such hopes ; cf. Previté-Orton *Outlines of Med. Hist.* p. 67.

[65] See the eighth century writer Paul the Deacon *De Gestis Langobardorum* in RIS. I. pt. i. pp. 106 sqq.

[66] I owe this thought to Villari *Le Invasioni barbariche in Italia* pp. 273 sq.

[67] See *Ann. Laur.* under May 749 ; " Interrogando de regibus in Francia, qui illis temporibus non habentes regalem potestatem, si bene fuisset an non." Quoted by Hauck *Kirchengeschichte Deutschlands* II. pp. 12 sq.

[68] In return Pepin granted to the Papacy the lands held in Italy by the Byzantines : see Caspar *Pippin und die römische Kirche* (Berlin 1914).

for dispute during many centuries.[69] By what right had
Charles received the imperial crown ? By conquest ? By
the acclamation of the Roman crowds ? By the papal
power to transfer the crown from the degenerate East ? [70]

Charles, whatever debt he may have owed towards Leo, *Charlemagne*
did not regard himself as in any way subject to the Pope. *and the*
The Empire was his by the power of his sword and, as a *Papacy*
practical statesman and soldier, he saw that on this basis
alone it must be maintained. The Pope's part was to pray
for him as Moses had prayed for Joshua.[71] So far there had
been little speculation as to the respective rights and dignities
of Pope and Emperor ; [72] both were much too busy in bringing
order out of chaos to have time for such a pursuit. The famous
ruling of Gelasius, that each was independent in his own sphere
and dependent in the sphere of the other, satisfied men's
minds.[73]

The attempt to revive the ancient glories of the Empire *Emperors as*
of the Caesars was sadly premature and under the feeble *Reformers*
successors of Charles both Empire and Papacy sank into
weakness and contempt. A strong line of German Emperors
at length brought relief to both institutions and saved Europe
from barbarism. Their efforts at revival involved them in
acts which savoured of undue interference in the spiritual
sphere. There was nothing new in lay rulers stepping in
to correct spiritual irregularities, such a course had even

[69] The important passages for the Coronation of Charlemagne are (1)
Einhard *Vita Caroli Magni* xxvii. sq. ; (2) *Annales regni Francorum* ad ann.
801 ; (3) *Ann. Laureshamenses* in MGH. SS. I. p. 38 ; (4) *Vita Leonis* xxiii sq.
in Duchesne *Lib. Pont.* II. p. 7.

[70] An interesting rider to the coronation of Charles is the request of
Manuel Comnenus to Alexander III in 1166 that he would dethrone Frederick
Barbarossa and elect him instead. He supported his request by large bribes.
The Pope was doubtless flattered by this recognition from such an unexpected
source ; none the less after much counsel he returned the bribes and informed
the Greek Emperor that the question was too complicated : see *Vita Alex.
III.* in RIS. III. pt. i. pp. 460 sq.

[71] See Jaffé *Bibliotheca Rerum Germanicarum* IV. p. 356.

[72] See G. Kissling *Das Verhältnis zwischen Sacerdotium und Imperium . . .
von Leon I bis Gelasius I.*

[73] *Tract.* IV. 11 and *Epist.* XII. 3.   Cf. also Fulgentius of Ruspe (467-532)
" Quantum pertinet ad huius temporis vitam constat quia in ecclesia nemo
pontifice potior, et in seculo Christiano nemo imperatore celsior invenitur."
(PL. LXV. col. 647 D).   On the importance of Fulgentius, especially in the
Carolingian age, see M. L. W. Laistner in *Mélanges Hrouchevsky* (Ukrainian
Academy of Sciences), pp. 445 sqq.

been approved, for example, by Sedulius Scotus in the middle of the ninth century,[74] but since the days of Charles no attempt on any large scale had been made.

But the intervention of lay rulers was made easier by the fact that at the end of the tenth century many bishops and abbots were vassals either of the Emperor or of some lesser ruler ; to this extent they were subject to feudal jurisdiction. Thus when Conrad I exiled three Lombard bishops the only protest was raised on the ground that he ought, before taking action, to have brought them before the proper court.[75]

Papal Elections   It was in connexion with the election of Popes that the greatest and most notable innovations took place. During the tenth and the greater part of the eleventh centuries it was generally recognised that the Emperor had some kind of indefinite rights in the matter, but such rights did not mean that the Pope was subordinate to him. The Pope was actually chosen by the bishops and clergy of Rome, in the presence of the imperial representatives, whose functions included the preservation of order and the securing of a free election. The Pope-elect was not to take any oath which would cause scandal to the Church or any diminution of imperial rights.[76]

Imperial Interference   During the next century and a half several Popes were removed and their successors appointed by the Emperor. There was, however, a recognition that the conditions were exceptional and that strong and unusual measures were called for in dealing with them. This came out clearly when Otto I was called upon to depose John XII in 963.[77] Leo VIII, the next Pope, insisted that in future no Pope was to be elected without the consent of the Emperor.[78]

Otto III took a deep interest in ecclesiastical affairs and in 996 appointed Bruno, his kinsman and chaplain, to be Pope.[79]

[74] See *De rectoribus Christianis* p. 86 in the new edition by Hellmann (Munich 1906).

[75] See Wippo *Vita Chuonradi* (PL. CXLII. p. 1245).

[76] See the Canons of the Council of Rome held under John IX in 898 in Mansi XVIII, A. p. 225.

[77] The clergy and people of Rome explained that " inauditum vulnus inaudito est cauterio exurendum " : see Liudprand of Cremona *De Rebus Gestis Ottonis* § 15 in MGH. SS. III.

[78] See *Vita Rom. Pont.* in RIS. III. pt. ii. col. 329 D.

[79] Cf. *op. cit.* col. 336 D ; " Bruno erat consanguineus Ottonis ad cuius instantiam ipse in Papam fuerat electus."

As Bruno was the first non-Italian Pope for some two hundred and fifty years Otto's action may have saved the Papacy from becoming localised. On the death of Bruno, who had taken the name of Gregory V, the famous Gerbert was elected as Sylvester II and thus began that historic partnership with Otto which seemed to realise the ideal relationship of Pope and Emperor. They made it their object to restore the fortunes of the Empire which they regarded as their joint responsibility. But Otto, though he knew it not, was really playing into the hands of the extreme papal party and lowering imperial prestige.

Perhaps the most famous instance of imperial interference was the deposition of Gregory VI by Henry III at Sutri in 1046. This action was welcomed by ardent reformers like St Peter Damian and Cardinal Humbert, who in their enthusiastic campaign against simony, did not stop to enquire into the legality of the Emperor's action.[80] Even the Cluniacs gave their approval.[81] Other Churchmen, however, were not so complacent, and such drastic methods of dealing with the ills of the Church were by no means to their taste. When Clement II died in 1047 Henry wrote to Wazo of Liège asking for his advice as to a successor ; Wazo refused to admit that there was any vacancy whilst Gregory the true Pope was still alive. He did not conceal his opinion that the Pope was responsible to God alone and could not be deposed by an Emperor.[82]

In this period the method of papal election seems to have been that the Emperor himself actually made the choice, on the advice of the bishops and great men around him and with the consent of the Roman people. This was apparently the procedure adopted in the election of Leo IX in 1048, Imperial Rights

[80] St Peter Damian affirmed that it was the divine will that none should be made Pope without the Emperor's authority ; see MGH. Lib. de Lite I. p. 71.

[81] The older view was that Cluny was always opposed to any kind of imperial interference, but this cannot any longer be held in face of the letter of Odilo recently discovered by Sackur and printed in *Neues Archiv*. XV. p. 119. Odilo says of the consecration of Clement II, the successor of Gregory, " In cuius sacra unctione praesens adstitit, dans gloriam Deo qui Romanum imperium electo iustissir~o presule et catholico reipublice principe sedatis malorum turbinibus robe .re voluerit."

[82] See MGH. Lib. de Lite I. p. 11. The same doctrine had been enunciated a little earlier by Thietmar of Merseburg *Chronicon* II. p. 18.

although the accounts are not quite clear. According to one version the Romans informed Henry of the death of Damasus II and asked him to appoint a successor. The Emperor, after consulting the bishops and magnates, appointed Bruno of Toul, who proceeded to Rome for his enthronement.[83] The other version states that Bruno was elected by the bishops and magnates in the presence of the Emperor, but only accepted the Papacy on condition that the choice was approved by the clergy and people of Rome.[84]

In the epoch-making decree of Nicholas II in April 1059, which placed the papal election on a new basis, the leading position is given to the cardinal bishops and other cardinals, whilst there is a vague recognition of the rights of the Emperor;[85] the historic privileges of the Roman people are quietly ignored.[86] The importance of this decree can scarcely be exaggerated, for it freed the election, theoretically at least, from the control of the local nobles as well as from undue imperial interference.

Relation of Pope and Emperor up to Eleventh Century The position up to the outbreak of the quarrel in the later eleventh century may be summarised as follows. Each party respected the rights of the other in its proper sphere; but it was recognised that exceptional circumstances might arise which would demand exceptional methods of treatment. There had, of course, been disputes before the days of Hildebrand; but for the most part these had not been serious or prolonged, and had been concerned with practical difficulties rather than great principles. But it was just at this point that serious trouble was bound eventually to arise. Both Empire and Papacy were in reality attempting the same

---

[83] Anselm *Hist. dedicationis Eccles. S. Remigii* in PL. CXLII. coll. 1420 sq.

[84] Wibert *Vita Leo. IX.* in PL. CXLIII. col. 487. His actual words are " ea conditione, si audiret totius cleri ac Romani populi communem esse sine dubio concensum."

[85] Fisher points out that this clause is omitted in the Papal Letter publishing the decrees (*Med. Empire* II. p. 207 n. 1). The text of the Decrees is printed in Hugo of Flavigny in MGH. SS. VIII. p. 408, and MGH. Leges IV. Constit. No. 382 I. pp. 538 sqq. See further Whitney *Hildebrandine Essays* p. 18.

[86] There was a similar usurpation of the rights of the Roman people in classical times. Gibbon, after referring to Cicero *De Leg.* iii. 3 states that " The election of consuls, of generals, and of magistrates, however it had been recently usurped by the senate, was the ancient and undoubted right of the Roman people." I. p. 105.

great task and overlapping was constant. Conscientious lay rulers were bound to insist that ecclesiastics in their dominions should attend to their duties in a reasonably efficient manner ; on the other hand the spiritual authorities found many occasions when they felt compelled to intervene in secular affairs. Thus sooner or later conflict was inevitable.

It arose at length over the question of Church reform. At first the Papacy had allowed a good deal of license to reforming rulers ; it could bide its time, for reform in the long run meant recognition of papal claims. The extent to which even Gregory VII could go in this matter is remarkable.[87] But the new life surging up within the Church made it resent all restraint by lay powers. This feeling was further strengthened by the apparent support which in some cases such powers were giving to old abuses.

The reform of the Church in the eleventh century followed a double track—for the individual it was a way of renunciation, for the Church a way of assertion. The way of renunciation expressed itself in the monastic revival of the time, and in the renewed attempt to impose celibacy upon the secular clergy. This attempt, which was successful only in theory, had as one of its objects the prevention of ecclesiastical benefices going the same way as secular, and becoming hereditary possessions.[88] The English clerics, as they were notorious for disregarding the rule of celibacy, were notorious also for these successions. As late as 1221 sons were regularly succeeding to fathers in parts of Yorkshire.[89]

Church Reform in the Eleventh Century

In carrying out this reform the Church and the lay rulers came into no conflict. But it was far different with the other aspect of reform, the way of ecclesiastical assertion. By this the Church insisted on permanently retaining all its temporal rights and possessions. The extent to which this sentiment prevailed can be estimated by the universal outcry which followed the proposed arrangement between

[87] His dealings with William I of England are especially noteworthy : see Z. N. Brooke *The Eng. Church and the Papacy* p. 144.

[88] Such successions were not unknown in the early Church. An interesting example is the case of St Gregory Nazianzen who was born during his father's tenure of the see which he himself was later to hold ; see Gibbon III. pp. 143 sq.

[89] See *Cal. Pap. Letters* I. 84 and 90 and Wilkins *Concilia* I. p. 653.

Pascal II and Henry V by which the Church, in return for the surrender of its temporal possessions, except tithes and so forth, was to enjoy complete liberty in spiritual matters. The point, however, at which the conflict was most bitter **Simony** was in connexion with simony.[90] During the minority of Henry IV his guardians, the Archbishop of Bremen and Count Werner, had put up every office for sale, and when he himself came of age there was little improvement. The secular power was thus standing in the way of reform. But an even worse form of simony in the eyes of some of the more ardent reformers, such as St Peter Damian,[91] was taking service in the imperial court. This course of action was especially common in the eleventh century when the backbone of the government was found in bishops, abbots and royal chaplains. Such servants were a salutary check on local and particular interests and were almost indispensable to their masters. That they should find their reward or their stipend in holding important ecclesiastical positions was, to the ruler, quite natural. But such appointments did not always serve the best interests of the Church.

It will thus be seen that there was plenty of material to feed the flame of any combustion which might break out; and that the reformers had a good case from their own standpoint. The exaltation of the *sacerdotium* over the *regnum* was, to many of them, the only way of securing reform for the Church and of preserving its independence.

Outbreak of Quarrel The contest when it came was marked by that bitterness which seems inseparable from struggles over great principles. Both sides were tempted to put forth exaggerated claims, knowing that concessions would be called for and wishing to have something with which to bargain. On the side of the Papacy there was in addition the enthusiasm which comes from the conscious allegiance to a great cause; men in these circumstances are apt to "talk strong" and to magnify their office. The fact that both sides had good arguments and

---

[90] As successions in feudal benefices were acknowledged by the payment of a 'relief' it was easy for lay rulers to accept payment for spiritual successions. In Germany benefices were largely regarded as private property: see U. Stutz *Die Eigenkirche als Element des mitteläIt.-german. Kirchenrechtes.*

[91] Cf. *Epist.* I. xiii. (PL. CXLIV. coll. 218 sqq.) where he condemns those who owe their office to bribery or what is even worse, service at court—" quod damnabilius est per curialis obsequii famulatum."

worthy supporters did not minimise the difficulties of the situation nor render the conflict less intense.

The Churchman feared that lay control of the Church would become so stringent that all elections would be in the hands of rulers, and that political considerations would have predominant weight in making appointments. There was also the possibility that the possessions of the Church might be alienated. It is hardly probable that the reformers from the first contemplated taking from lay rulers all share in ecclesiastical appointments, that would have been too great a breach with custom, but to this position they seem gradually to have tended until, by the decrees of the Lenten Synod of 1075, Gregory VII prohibited all 'investiture' by laymen.[92] Before this date Manegold of Lautenbach had argued that bishops ought to be elected by the clergy and people and not be thrust upon them, willy-nilly, by the appointment of their rulers. He emphasised the absurdity of the use by the secular prince of the ring and staff which were symbols, not of the possession of the temporalities of the see, but of the spiritual mysteries.[93] There was certainly much force in this last plea which, however, was merely a matter of procedure. Another strong advocate of the papal cause, Deusdedit, insisted that by tradition elections were to be free ; he further pointed out that princes are the real cause of simony ; at the same time he is careful to respect imperial rights and has no desire to diminish them.[94]

The position of the Churchman

The imperialists for their part began by distinguishing between the spiritual and the secular authority of the bishop ; they claimed that so long as prelates had political importance, held fortresses and controlled military resources, the prince must insist on their doing homage. This is a very strong

The position of the Imperialists

[92] It is possible that the term is not used in its strict sense of appointment but refers only to the actual ceremony of investing.

[93] *Ad Gebehardum* in MGH. Lib. de Lite I. pp. 300 sqq.   Cf. Rangerius *Liber de Anulo et Baculo* in MGH. Lib. de Lite II. p. 860 ;

> " Anulus et baculus in sacra signa datur.
> Anulus, ut sponsum se noverit et sibi iunctam,
> Non sibi, sed Christo, diligat ecclesiam.
> At vero baculus, ut Christi servet ovile
> Et caveat sevos terrificetque lupos."

[94] *Libellus contra invasores et symoniacos* in MGH. Lib. de Lite II. pp. 292 sqq.

argument and is well stated by Wido of Ferrara.[95]   In many ways the imperialists were more moderate in their claims than their opponents and never sought to usurp spiritual authority or the whole right of appointment.   Even when Henry V forced his own terms on Pascal II all that he demanded was the power to veto an unacceptable candidate —*episcopo vel abbate libere electo . . . assensu regis.*

The Appeal to Scripture   Both sides sought to find support in the Scriptures and some very mystical interpretations were forced upon the sacred text.   Here again the imperialists had the best of it—judged by modern standards—for they could bring forward the very relevant case of Moses who was a layman and yet received the law and organised the priesthood.   They naturally made free use of the Old Testament in general as well as the Books of Maccabees where there are numerous examples of the superior status of kings when compared with priests.   The papal party had to fall back on isolated texts and allegorical interpretation ;   the keys of St Peter and the two swords (Luke xxii. 38) were worked for all they were worth.[96]   In connexion with the latter text it is interesting to notice that arguments which had served their purpose in demonstrating the supremacy of the Pope over the Church were used again in the contest with the Empire.[97]

The Office of King   It should not be forgotten that both sides agreed that the office of king was not a purely secular one, as the coronation ceremony shewed.   The more extreme writers on the imperial side could thus claim that since the prince was like

---

[95] *De scismate Hildebrandi* in MGH. Lib. de Lite I. pp. 564 sqq.

[96] Early writers allowed one sword to the temporal power ; but St Bernard and others of later date were not so generous and claimed both for the Pope, who wielded the spiritual sword in person, the secular he entrusted to the prince : see *Epist.* CCLVI. and cf. *De Consideratione* IV. 3.   John of Salisbury explains the reason—" Hunc ergo gladium de manu ecclesiae accipit princeps, cum ipsa tamen gladium sanguinis omnino non habeat " ;   *Policraticus* iv. 3 (Ed. Webb I. p. 337 or PL. CXCIX. p. 516).   Some interpreted the swords in a spiritual manner of the papal powers of excommunication and restoration—" Potestas spiritualiter occidendi et potestas spiritualiter vivificandi " : see Alvaro Pelayo *De Statu et Planctu Ecclesiae* II. art. 57.

[97] A good example is the well-known saying of St Peter Damian—" qui beato vitae aeternae clavigero terreni simul et caelestis imperii iura commisit " ; *Opusc.* V. in PL. CXLV. p. 91.   The saying was originally aimed at the Milanese : see Rivière *Le Problème de l'Église et de l'État* pp. 387 sqq.   He points out that Hauck, by an unusual lapse, in *Der Gedanke der päpst. Weltherrschaft* pp. 33-36 (cf. p. 44 n. 3) attributes the saying to Eugenius III.

Christ, both priest and king, the royal power was superior to the sacerdotal.[98]

One important principle was first adumbrated during the conflict by Gregory's deposition of Henry IV. This action was significant in itself; but the grounds upon which it was justified by Manegold were still more so. He held that the sovereign was a responsible being and if he failed in his responsibilities he was liable to removal. Sovereignty was based on contract and the Emperor had failed to fulfil his part. It is noteworthy that Henry had actually been crowned by Gregory himself; but the Old Testament furnished a precedent for had not Samuel rejected Saul, whom he had anointed, and chosen David. *The Principle of Responsibility*

After the death of both Gregory and Henry IV the fierceness of the conflict abated a little. A body of opinion grew up which had common sense enough to recognise that there was much to be said for both sides. The imperialists in particular came to see that the exact form in which homage was done was not really important. The action of Henry V in wringing concessions from the unwilling Paschal II might have ushered in a fresh stage of bitterness, but the mediating spirit was strong enough to prevent it. Both sides realised how much they depended upon each other.[99] The Concordat of Worms in 1122 put an end to the struggle for the time, but it was at best a compromise. By its provisions the Emperor was to retain the right of investing with the temporalities by means of the sceptre, not by the gift of the ring and crozier. In Germany itself the investiture was to precede the consecration—this provision, if taken literally, gave the Emperor the power of veto—in the rest of the Empire it was to follow. The Emperor or his representative had the right to be present at all elections,[100] and certain powers fell to him in the event of a disputed election. *Compromise*

[98] The sacred character of the kingly office had been acknowledged from early times; St Augustine (? Ambrosiaster) even declared that " the king has the image of God as the bishop that of Christ " : *Quest. veteris et novi Test.* XXXV. See further A. J. Macdonald *Authority and Reason* pp. 115 sq. and cf. Wyclif *De officio regis* pp. 14 and 197 who sees the king as the representative of the divinity of Christ, the priest of His humanity.

[99] This is well brought out by Ivo of Chartres *Epist. ad Hugonem* in MGH. Lib. de Lite II. pp. 640 sqq ; " Videmus . . . divisum regnum et sacerdotium, sine quorum concordia res humanae nec incolumes esse possunt nec tutae."

[100] The presence of the Emperor or his representative might seem to threaten the freedom of the electors as in the case of the vacancy in the see of Mainz in 1200 ; Hauck *Kirchengesch. Deutschlands* IV. p. 761.

The Church's Gain   This agreement seems to the modern historian a fair one ; but to contemporary opinion the victory was decidedly with the Papacy.   In an age when men attached vast significance to symbols they saw that the Emperor no longer made use of the ring and crozier, and they drew their own conclusions. But if the dreams which the more advanced reformers had cherished of a Church freed from all secular control had not been fulfilled—for while there was homage there might be simony—the Church's essential freedom had been secured. The actual terms of the settlement also helped to make clear the distinction between the secular and the spiritual side of the office of bishop.   That a bishop was also in many cases a baron constituted a real danger in view of the growth of the feudal system which almost threatened to swallow up Church and Empire alike.   The Concordat saved the spiritual side from absorption.[101]

Clerics and Laity   But if one result of the struggle was thus to distinguish between the secular and the spiritual in the activities of the bishop it also made more sharp the division between the clergy as a body and the laity, and encouraged the tendency to identify the Church with the clergy.[102]   This had its good side, for there was grave danger that the cleric might become confounded with the layman when both were living lives so similar and performing functions which in many cases were identical.[103]   The distinction also made it more difficult for rulers to rely upon the ecclesiastics in their service ;   the double allegiance was a source of conflict and for the minister often enough a question of loyalties.   From this time onwards there is a growing reluctance to employ ecclesiastics ;   a tendency which was encouraged by the rise of the new class of ' ministeriales '.

Papal Interference   From the Concordat of Worms to the reign of Innocent III the Emperors, with one exception, were striving to re-

[101] Cf. the case of Odo of Bayeux arrested, not as a bishop, but as a baron. This was done by the advice of Lanfranc : see Ordericus Vitalis *Hist. Eccles.* VII. viii.   Another notorious case was that of Philip, Bishop of Beauvais, captured in armour by Richard I : see Matthew Paris *Chron. Major* II. p. 422 (RS.).   When Celestine III protested to the king he sent him the armour with the query ;   " Is this thy son's coat or not ? "   The Pope saw the point and withdrew his protest.

[102] Gregorovius considers that a new period of history begins from the division which followed ;   *Die Stadt Rom. etc.* I. p. 1014.

[103] Monasticism also helped to preserve the distinction ; see below p. 92.

gain some of their lost power, or at least to preserve what remained. But the process of social development was against them, and such triumphs as they enjoyed were neither lasting nor extensive. The same was true of the lesser rulers in their sphere. The history of England in this epoch gives a good illustration. A strong ruler like William I might refuse to do homage to the Pope, might even forbid his subjects to make journeys or appeals to Rome without royal permission; but his weaker successors allowed papal influence once more to creep in; whilst the struggles of Henry II to recover lost ground were thwarted by the obstinacy and the heroism of Becket.

The break in the continuous efforts of the Empire, to which Lothar III reference has just been made, followed the election of Lothar III in 1125. He owed his throne to a combination of Churchmen with a body of nobles who were afraid of the establishment of the hereditary principle. Lothar has sometimes been accused of sacrificing the true interests of the Empire for the sake of small political gains and in order to obtain the favour of the Church. But this is hardly a fair indictment. His policy of placing Germany before Italy may have weakened the Empire in the peninsula but it enabled Germany to prosper. He certainly missed a great opportunity during the schism between Innocent II and Anacletus of acting as arbitrator,[104] or at least of gaining concessions in return for his support. Such attempts as he made were only half-hearted and, like stronger men than himself, he was carried away by the eloquence of St Bernard into support of Innocent.[105] He left it to the astute and unprincipled Roger of Sicily to resist the saint's powers of persuasion and to play off one claimant against the other, and so to found that Sicilian kingdom which was to be for so long a thorn in the side of the Papacy. Lothar, towards the end of his life, seems to have been on less

[104] Ordericus Vitalis *Hist. Eccles.* XIII. xiv. says that Lothar ordered both to submit to the judgement of a council; Anacletus agreed, but Innocent refused.

[105] There is a story that St Norbert also resisted demands made by Lothar; see *Vita Norberti* XXI. in MGH. SS. XII. pp. 700 sq. At Liège Lothar tried to extort concessions but St Bernard rendered the attempt abortive: see Ernaldus *In vit. Bern.* II. i. n. 5. The student of the Old Testament will be reminded of the stories told apparently of both Elijah and Elisha: cf. Binns *From Moses to Elisha* p. 229.

friendly terms with the Pope and if death had not cut him off might well have anticipated the part played by his great-grandson, Otto IV. None the less his reign marks a break in the continuity and the beginnings of the Guelf party in Italy.[106]

The next Emperor, Conrad III, distracted by internal troubles in Germany and by the abortive Second Crusade, contributed little to the struggle. It was left for his nephew to inaugurate the final stage of the contest for the recovery of imperial power.

Frederick I (Barbarossa)
Frederick I, surnamed Barbarossa, " the best and bravest and mightiest of the German Caesars," as Stubbs called him,[107] was in every way a worthy champion of the cause to which he devoted himself so unreservedly. The Empire to him was a great ideal, a divine kingdom set above all earthly governments. This ideal was nourished by his habit of constantly reading the story of the past, and found sanction in the support of the growing school of Roman lawyers which Bologna was then training. From these two sources, history and law, Frederick derived his conception of the rights and powers of those Roman Emperors whom he held to be his own predecessors.

The Emperor was in no hurry to begin actual hostilities. He probably felt that his material resources were so extensive that he could take his time and gain more by the gradual exercise of the powers which he claimed than by an open breach. So when he entered Italy for his coronation he had no objection to doing Adrian IV the small service of handing over to him the revolutionary, Arnold of Brescia.[108] But this favour was followed by a misunderstanding which might have brought matters to a head at once. The Emperor

---

[106] Lothar accepted the lands of Countess Matilda from the Pope for life and took the feudal oath for them. This probably led to the legend which lies behind the picture in the Lateran in which Lothar at the Pope's feet is receiving the imperial crown and below is written ;

" Rex stetit (venit) ante fores iurans prius urbis honores
Post homo fit papae, sumit quo dante coronam."
Rahewin *Gesta Frid. imp.* III. 10.

The picture was effaced by Adrian IV at the request of Frederick Barbarossa.
[107] *Germany in the Early Middle Ages* p. 212.
[108] There is a recent study of this important character *Arnold of Brescia* by G. W. Greenaway.

failed to perform the office of squire to the Pope, and the Pope
and his cardinals became excited and alarmed. Next day,
however, Frederick goodnaturedly submitted to hold the
Pope's stirrup and so the difficulty was smoothed over.[109]

Before his coronation Frederick was approached by the **Rebuffs the**
Roman people, as Conrad had been,[110] and like his uncle **Romans**
he rebuffed them. This refusal seems a mistaken policy,
for a Roman republic on the Capitol under imperial protection
would have been an admirable check upon the pretensions
of the Lateran, and might well have prevented the growth of
the temporal power of the Papacy. But Frederick was a
man of his age and that age, whilst recognising ancient institutions such as the Empire and the Papacy, had lost all
recollection, save in Rome itself, of the still more ancient
institution which the Romans were trying to revive. In
any case the republic had been pagan and, moreover, the
ambitions of its supporters must have savoured too strongly
of the similar ambitions of the Lombard communes for the
Emperor to regard them with any sympathy. The Empire
and the Papacy were old antagonists, they must have no
dealings with upstarts, so Frederick may have argued in his
grand way ; the Papacy was much more practical, and was
not hampered by fine feelings and so did not scruple to find
allies where it could.

This happened in 1155. Two years later open disagree- **The Meaning**
ment was again narrowly avoided at a Diet at Besançon **of**
Beneficium
when the papal representative, Cardinal Bandinelli, seemed
deliberately to provoke hostilities by his conduct after the
Germans had protested against the ambiguous use of the
word *beneficium*. Used in its technical sense of fief it would
have reduced the Emperor to a papal vassal. The cardinal
demanded from whom the Empire was held if not from the
Pope, and but for the intervention of Frederick himself
might not have escaped alive from the enraged imperialists.

---

[109] Gerhoh of Reichersberg (c. 1150) blames the Pope for thus insisting on
a custom which was degrading to the Emperor, and contrasts the attitude of
the Patriarch of Constantinople to the Eastern Emperor : *De inventione
Anti-christi* pp. 174 sqq. (ed. Scheibelberger).

[110] The terms in which the overtures to Conrad were made are important
and were possibly inspired by Arnold of Brescia ; they are printed in RIS.
IX. pp. 663 sq.

3

The time, however, was not yet ripe for the conflict and Adrian's explanations were accepted.[111]

Accession of Alexander III   When in 1159 Cardinal Bandinelli himself ascended the papal throne as Alexander III the strife was quickly opened, for those cardinals who had imperial sympathies at once elected an anti-pope, who took the style of Victor IV. Frederick hoped to make use of the situation to increase imperial prestige by acting as arbitrator. But Alexander refused to attend the council which was called to discuss the schism, and by so doing avoided the trap and established a valuable precedent for his successors. Although driven to take refuge in France the Pope stuck to his position, and at length succeeded in bringing Frederick to submission. This was after his disas-

May 29, 1176 trous defeat at Legnano when the German chivalry, weakened it is true by the absence of Henry the Lion, found themselves unable to overcome the stout Milanese burghers. Peace was finally ratified at Venice in August 1177, a peace which was a greater triumph for the Papacy than the more spectacular submission of Henry IV at Canossa exactly a century before. By it Frederick in effect renounced his rights over the Patrimony, gave up his anti-pope and his attempt to dominate the Papacy. It was a definite admission of the

Frederick's Recovery   failure of his ambitions. But Venice was not all loss, for it enabled the Emperor to cultivate more friendly relations with the Lombards, and when Frederick succeeded in marrying his son Henry to Constance, the heiress of Sicily, it was in Milan that the wedding took place. This was a double threat to the Papacy which thus found itself in danger of being crushed between the Empire and Sicily, whilst the Lombards who were the natural barrier to the North were acting in a dubious manner.

When Henry ascended the imperial throne in 1190, it seemed that at last the Empire was to become predominant. But a sudden illness cut down the ambitious Emperor and all his schemes fell to the ground, vast schemes which had included the conquest of the Eastern Empire,[112] and the subdual of France.[113]

[111] See Rahewin *Gesta Frederici I*. III. 8-10, 16 in MGH. SS. XX. pp. 420 sqq. and Adrian *Epist*. CLXXXI. in PL. CLXXXVIII. pp. 1556 sq.

[112] Such ambitions he may well have taken over from his wife's Norman ancestors : but cf. Cohn *Das Zeitalter der Hohenstaufen in Sizilien* for criticisms of the view that he contemplated a conquest of the East.

[113] See A. Lane Poole in *Essays presented to R. L. Poole* pp. 262 sq.

The death of Henry was followed by a schism in the Empire. Schism in During his lifetime he had succeeded in persuading the German the Empire princes to accept as his successor the infant Frederick, his son by Constance ; but the situation demanded an effective ruler and the Hohenstaufen party put forward Philip, the dead Emperor's brother. Their opponents chose Otto of Brunswick, the son of Henry the Lion and Matilda of England.

This schism gave Innocent III, who had just become Pope, the opportunity of mediating, and at the same time of setting forth his own conception of the relative dignities of Pope and Emperor. He claimed that the Empire derived its origin from the Pope, since a Pope had transferred it from the East— a reference to the coronation of Charlemagne—and each Emperor at his coronation received his authority from the Pope who crowned him. In case of schism the Pope must decide which is the lawful candidate, and in any event he has a right of veto, since otherwise he might be called upon to crown a heretic or an idiot.[114]

Innocent, after a short delay, gave his decision in favour Innocent III of Otto ; but in spite of papal support the latter made no and Otto IV headway, and was only saved from complete disaster by the murder of Philip in 1208.[115] In order to prevent further disputes the German princes thereupon recognised Otto. But the latter, once he had the supreme power, soon quarrelled with the Papacy and Innocent found himself obliged to de- nounce and finally to excommunicate ' his beloved son ' ; choosing in his place Frederick, the son of Henry, now grown to manhood. By this choice, a daring piece of policy in any case, he succeeded in defeating the designs of Otto ; but he ushered in for future Popes a period of desperate strife and danger.

During the reign of Innocent III the medieval Papacy Seeds of probably reached its point of highest influence and power ; Decay yet even in its triumph there lurked the possibility of future trouble. If, as Dr Coulton claims, it was " in one sense the

[114] See further my *Innocent III*. pp. 47 sqq. and Carlyle *Hist. Med. Politi- cal Theory in the West* V. pp. 151 sqq.

[115] Papal interventions were but rarely successful unless supported by public opinion, as in the case of John of England. But interventions when they did succeed gave the Papacy a delusive sense of power and when a century later Boniface VIII tried to take the same line against national sympathies the result was disaster.

greatest of medieval achievements ", in another it was " the greatest of medieval failures ".[116]   In spite of the loftiest pretensions and ideals, already the seeds had been sown of practices which were ultimately to prove the bane of the Papacy,[117] and since these abuses arose in part from the attempt of the Popes to establish a visible kingdom upon earth, it will be well at this point to go a little further into the matter of the temporal power of the Papacy.

The Temporal Power

By writers of different standpòints the temporal power is viewed in different lights ; the great Roman Catholic historian, Pastor, can claim that the Pope " in order to fulfil his high office must be a monarch and not a subject " ; [118] on the other hand the Anglican, A. L. Smith, writes of " the whole fateful legacy left by Innocent III, to gather temporal sway into spiritual hands ", and in even more drastic terms he declares that " The Papal States were a veritable body of death to the true spiritual life of the greatest institution in human history ".[119]

That spiritual power should seek to clothe itself in earthly panoply, and the kingdom of God set itself out as a secular state seems hard to reconcile with the principles of the gospel, and " the priestly Caesar of the Vatican " is certainly a strange " representative of the Gallilean prophet ".[120]   But the history of the Church provides some explanation of the process by which this contradiction arose even if it does not entirely excuse it.

Ancient Rome had been a military power, and to the modern spectator of its byegone majesty this aspect of its greatness is brought home most vividly by the *Via Sacra* along which the victorious general pursued his triumphal way.   The Popes treading a far different *Via Sacra* came to believe that they too could only maintain themselves by military and political weapons.   In some sense the temporal power was part of the imperial legacy.   In another sense, however, it was due to the weakness of imperial power ; had the Eastern Empire, for example, been strong enough to keep the Lombards out of Italy, would there have been any tem-

---

[116] *Five Centuries of Religion* II. p. 18.
[117] See *Innocent III* pp. 199 sqq.
[118] *History of the Popes* I. p. 20.
[119] *Church and State in the Middle Ages* pp. 192 and 210.
[120] Inge *Christian Ethics etc.* p. 15.

poral power of the Papacy at all ?   Or again had the Papacy in the early middle ages not been left at the mercy of the Saracens and the unruly nobles of the Campagna, not to mention the turbulent citizens of Rome itself, would there have been need of military force ?   Gebhart has well put the matter when he writes that " in the feudal state secular greatness was the Church's only guarantee of integrity ".[121] Perhaps too the real donation of Matilda of Tuscany had the effect which was attributed to the false Donation of Constantine, for the desire to retain or recover what were felt to be the possessions of the Papacy must have gone a long way to encourage the appeal to arms.

From the earliest times, however, the corrupting effect **Its Evil Con-** of striving after temporal power can be traced.   Perhaps **sequences** one of the most significant examples is the case of Bruno of Toul, who as Leo IX was one of the greatest of the Popes. When elected to his office, according to one account,[122] he refused to hold it until convinced that the Roman clergy and people desired him, and he entered the city in humble guise and with none of the pomp of a pope-elect.   Yet this same man, drawn away by the need to protect or extend the temporal interests of the Papacy, went on an expedition against the Normans—with disastrous results.

To the higher minds among the Catholics this growing reliance upon material resources and the steadily accumulating wealth of the Church were matters for disquiet, and many shared the views of St Bernard, who longed to see the Church as it was in Apostolic days, fishing not for gold and silver, but for the souls of men.   To them a Pope who strove for temporal power was the successor, not of Peter, but of Constantine.[123]

[121] *Mystics and Heretics in Italy* p. 87.
[122] See above, pp. 23 sq.
[123] " In his successisti, non Petro, sed Constantino " wrote St Bernard in *De Consideratione* IV. iii. 6 (*Opera* I. coll. 487 sq.).

CHAPTER II

THE TRIUMPH OVER THE EMPIRE

Fall of both Empires

THE Eastern Empire fell before the treacherous attack of the Crusaders in 1204 ; the same century was to see the fall of the Western Empire also.   Neither of them was in any real sense to be revived, though both were to have nominal Emperors, and the East was once again to have a ruler in Constantinople.[1]

Opening of the Struggle   The struggle between the Empire and the Papacy, which came to a head in the middle years of the thirteenth century, was perhaps the most significant happening of the middle ages, for no department of man's life was left unaffected by it. The opening of the campaign, which was to end in the triumph of the Papacy, followed on the death of Henry VI ; [2] for, as we have seen, Innocent III was then able to make preparations for future aggressive action.   It was not, however, until the accession of Honorius III, and the manhood of Frederick II, that the struggle began seriously to be undertaken.   Even then it developed gradually ; for Honorius was too timid to push things to extremes, and, in the following pontificate, although there were some fierce passages of arms, Gregory IX found Frederick too useful to provoke a decisive conflict ; at the end of his life, however, matters were tending in that direction.   With the accession of Innocent IV the struggle approached its final stages—the serpent's brood must be exterminated.

Character of Frederick II   We begin then with Frederick II, as it was in some sense his policy which precipitated the inevitable conflict.   History presents few characters more difficult to fathom than

[1] The fall of the Abbasids in 1258 on the capture of Baghdad by the Mongols brought yet another Empire to an end in this century.   There was, it is true, an Abbasid line in Egypt until 1517, but it was not sufficiently important to rank as imperial.

[2] See Fisher *The Mediaeval Empire* II. pp. 40 sq. and 249 for its effects.

that of the Wonder of the World as his contemporaries called him.[3] Ultimately he was, I suppose, a universal genius of the order of Leonardo and Goethe; but here was a genius who occupied a throne and had at his disposal means which were denied to the others. The reaction to such a character is always intense and varied, and so, whilst some looked upon Frederick as half-divine and saw in his birth-place a second Bethlehem;[4] to others he was another Lucifer attempting to raise his throne above the stars of heaven.[5] Hence the accounts of him are strongly prejudiced and to find a balance between them is almost impossible. Here was a man who was on the one hand enquiring and sceptical, on the other romantic and mystical almost to excess; one who in his patronage of letters anticipated the princes of the Renaissance and at the same time could give his mind to statecraft and warfare, as indeed many of them also did. His own culture had been acquired by the sheer desire for knowledge, as the circumstances of his early life had not been such as to render its acquisition at all easy. But his curiosity was universal and tireless, and all things drew his attention. His love for things oriental was no doubt in part a heritage from his native Sicily, in part the result of his brief sojourn in the East. It took forms repulsive to Western minds, which could not be expected to approve of his harem and eunuchs, though his menagerie might provoke their astonishment.[6] Frederick was a strange product of the races which bore him, and both the Swabian Frederick and the Norman Roger, the grandfathers from whom he took his names, might have found it hard to recognise in him a descendant.[7] In some ways he was surprisingly

---

[3] For an estimate of the character of Frederick see Niese " Zur Gesch. des geist. Lebens am Hofe K. Friedrichs II " in *Hist. Zeit.* CVIII. pp. 473 sqq. and the recent highly imaginative study by E. Kantorowicz.

[4] This was Jesi " ubi nos diva mater nostra eduxit in lucem ": see Huillard-Bréholles *Hist. Diplom. Frid. II* V. p. 378.

[5] See Huillard-Bréholles *Vie et Corr. de Pierre de la Vigne* p. 196; also *Vita Greg. IX* in RIS. III. pt. i. p. 585.

[6] It is easy to exaggerate the amount of Arabic influence in his court; it was hardly greater than that in the court of Alfonso VI who captured Toledo in 1085. On the subject of Frederick's culture see Niese *op. cit.* p. 492 and Cohn *Das Zeitalter der Hohenstaufen in Sizilien* pp. 196 sqq.

[7] Roger, however, had a taste for oriental life and made use of Moslem troops.

modern in his outlook, he preferred diplomacy for example
to warfare,—perhaps because he was only a moderate general
and had no love of fighting—and in another sphere he recognised the value of experiment in the search after truth.[8]

His religious views   Before describing the policy of Frederick it will be well
to sketch, so far as it is possible to discover them, his religious
views.   Here the difficulties are just as great as in the case
of his character in general.   Many regard him as a modern man
of the world with no real convictions beyond the things of
sense.[9]   Others, going to the opposite extreme, would explain
him as a religious revolutionary.[10]   Between these two atti-
tudes the truth must lie and in the endeavour to find it three
important facts must be borne in mind.   The first is that
all manner of extraordinary beliefs were attributed to Frederick
and that he himself was capable, not always in suitable company, of indulging in exceedingly ironical and incautious
utterances.   It is significant that the accusation of Gregory
IX, that he had declared that the world had been deceived
by three imposters—Christ, Moses, and Mohammed [11]—
was quietly dropped by Innocent IV.   Again it is remarkable
that at the end of his life, when Frederick was under excommunication, he never lost the regard of two exceedingly pious
monarchs, Louis IX of France and our own Henry III.
This seems a guarantee for the substantial orthodoxy which
he himself always professed.   Lastly his expressed desire
to take in hand the reform of the Church seems to point to
some kind of appreciation of the value of religion ; it was
more than a piece of policy.   Even when faced with a rival
in the Empire he refrained from electing an anti-pope.[12]
Possibly his religion was a species of Caesaro-papalism, the
absorption of the Church by the State.[13]   He certainly envied

[8] It has been said that his study *De Arte venandi cum avibus* marks a
turning point in European scientific thought.

[9] So Hampe *Deutsche Kaisergeschichte im Zeitalter der Salier und Staufer*
p. 222.

[10] This is the view of what may be called the Huillard-Bréholles school,
and it is supported by Davidsohn in his *Geschichte Florenz* II.

[11] See MGH. Epp. Saec. XIII I. p. 653.   Frederick himself indignantly
denied the charge : Huillard-Bréholles *Hist. Dipl.* V. p. 348.

[12] This is pointed out by Huillard-Bréholles *Hist. Dipl.* VI. pp.
CDLXXXV. sqq.

[13] As Rivière has put it " Sans cesser d'être une puissance politique,
l'impérialisme est devenu un dogme religieux " : see *Le Problème de l'Église, etc.*
p. 43.

the religious peace of the East where the power of the ruler
was supreme and the ministers of religion were restricted
to the care of the sanctuary.[14] His proclamation that he
wished to reduce the Church to its primitive poverty, though
welcome enough to many fanatics,[15] was a mistake in tactics,
since it enabled Innocent IV to accuse him of wishing to seize
ecclesiastical property. Frederick also held that even in a
just cause the pontiff was denied the use of force against the
Emperor.[16]

The limits which Frederick set to his ambitions can only His
be surmised ; Brunetto Latini declared that the one desire ambitions
of his heart was to be master of the world,[17] and perhaps such
a vision, with the Sultan of Cairo and the Emperor of Nicea
as his vassals, did float before his eyes. After the marriage
with Yolande, the heiress of John of Brienne, the acquisition
of the kingdom of Jerusalem was a real object of his policy.
But the ambition which he declared was a narrower and more
reasonable one—Italy was his patrimony,[18] so he claimed,
and he desired to enforce his power through its length and
breadth and so to rule from Germany in the North to Sicily
in the South with no intervening barriers. The chief
obstacles to the realisation of this aim were the Lombard
cities and the Papal States. It was when Frederick realised
that the temporal power of the Papacy was inconsistent with
his conception of the Empire that, so far as he was concerned, the fight had to be fought to a finish. The Popes on
their side were not slow to accept his challenge, for to them
the matter was equally vital.

In earlier days the Popes had found in Sicily, under its Sicily and
Norman rulers, a set-off to the power of the Emperor.[19] The the Empire
marriage of Henry VI to Constance had placed Sicily in the
possession of the German kings, but his death and the minority
of Frederick had checked any dangerous developments.

---

[14] Huillard-Bréholles op. cit. VI. p. 685.
[15] The Spiritual Franciscans and their predecessors held such views ; whilst
a league of French nobles formed in 1246 also welcomed them ; see Huillard-
Bréholles op. cit. VI. p. 467.
[16] See Huillard-Bréholles op. cit. VI. p. 391.
[17] Li Livres dou Trésor p. 92 (ed. Chabaille)
[18] Huillard-Bréholles op. cit. IV. pt. ii. p. 881.
[19] Their spiritual yoke sat but lightly upon the South, the effect of Byzantine and then of Norman rule.

Innocent III, when he summoned the young prince to be the papal candidate for the Empire against the rebellious Otto, was careful to insist that his infant son, Henry, should be invested with Sicily, and that the Empire should be held separately. This safeguard was to prove a poor protection, and Frederick, when once Otto was out of the way and Innocent dead, soon obtained control of both realms. In April 1220 Henry was actually elected King of the Romans and thus the union of the two states was to be perpetuated. This made it all the more necessary for the Popes to prevent imperial power becoming supreme in the rest of Italy. They wished to keep the Emperors north of the Alps, the natural boundary between the two countries which was never really to be overpassed. Further to check them, they endeavoured to strengthen the political barrier of the Lombard cities, and behind them Guelfic Tuscany. It is clear that no Pope desired to destroy the Empire; its protection was useful at times, and even the Papacy valued the common link with earlier times. But to render the Empire powerless in Italy and to subject it to the spiritual authority they were prepared to take tremendous risks.

The question of a Crusade When Honorius III ascended the papal throne in July 1216 there were two points on which disagreement with the Emperor seemed likely, the union of the Empire and Sicily, and Frederick's participation in a Crusade. The latter question arose from the promise, which Frederick had made in a moment of enthusiasm, to serve in the East. Now he found that his presence was needed in his ancestral kingdom which he wished to consolidate as a step towards the realisation of wider ambitions. At all costs he must have time for his immediate task. Fortunately Honorius was anxious to keep on good terms, and after the Emperor, at his coronation in November 1220, had renewed his vow, the Pope allowed himself to be put off with vague promises and excuses.

Frederick's Concessions in Germany The task of consolidating Sicily, however, needed not only the friendship of the Papacy, which Frederick managed to preserve during the reign of Honorius,[20] but also the

---

[20] Among other things he handed over to the Papacy the lands he had promised to restore at Eger in 1213. This is gratefully acknowledged by Honorius in a letter of Feb. 18, 1221 ; see MGH. Epp. Epis. Saec. XIII I. p. 165.

neutrality of the German princes. This might have proved
a harder matter, but Frederick was so determined to carry out
his plans that he sacrificed imperial prerogatives in Germany.
Thus at the time when he was crushing feudalism in Sicily
the rights of the feudatories in the North were being enlarged.
Considerable concessions were made, especially to ecclesiastical princes, in 1220 ; later Frederick was compelled to accept
those wrung from the incapable King Henry. By them At Worms
the princes were left practically supreme in their own 1231
territories [21] ; whilst the rights of the towns were also severely
limited in their favour. As, however, the towns were no
party to such grants and were well able to look after their
own interests these last concessions proved ultimately of
small value.

Into the details of Frederick's Sicilian policy it is not His Sicilian
necessary to enter.[22] It will be sufficient to point out that policy
it left him absolute in the kingdom, with the feudal system
entirely broken and the power in the hands of the royal
officials. The proud descendants of the Norman conquerors
were compelled to give up their castles, and even the towns
had to receive Frederick's governors. The Churchmen were
not let off more lightly ; their jurisdiction was restricted
and even their right to inherit property, whilst they were
brought under the direct rule of the crown and made subject
to taxation.

Meanwhile Honorius waited patiently for the fulfilment of Death and
Frederick's vow. The Emperor had agreed to sail in 1225, character of
but the Lombards had blocked the passes against the German Honorius III
crusaders whose arms they feared might be turned against
their liberties. So there was further delay, and when the
Pope died on March 18, 1227 nothing had been done.
Honorius, as we have said, was mild and conciliatory, not at
all a fit adversary for the vigorous and skilful Frederick.
But his forbearance had postponed the struggle ; whilst
his work before he became Pope, had he but known it, was

[21] See *Statutum in Favorem Principum* printed in Altman and Bernheim
Ausgewählte Urkunde pp. 18 sqq.

[22] Full details will be found in Cohn *Das Zeitalter der Hohenstaufen in
Sizilien* and in Kantorowicz *Frederick the Second* pp. 112 sqq. (E.T.). Frederick
was able to build on the foundations laid by Roger II who had studied Byzantine methods of organisation.

to prove invaluable in a conflict which came more and more to depend on economic resources.[23]

Gregory IX   The next Pope, Gregory IX, although an old man, was not so easily mollified, and a term was speedily put to all prevarication and procrastination on the part of Frederick, whose measure he had, no doubt, already taken. Perhaps he went too far in the other direction in refusing to consider excuses which may well have been genuine.

Sept. 8, 1227
Frederick
sails and
returns   At last the imperial fleet set sail from Brindisi, but it soon turned back ; plague had broken out among the crusaders owing to the delay and confinement in insufficient quarters. That there was reason behind this action seems to be proved by the death of the Landgrave of Thuringia soon after landing. But Gregory would not listen to any arguments, and as Frederick had sworn to sail by 1227 at any cost he was technically liable to excommunication. This penalty the Pope at once proceeded to enforce.

His success-
ful Crusade   The fact that he was excommunicate did not prevent Frederick from continuing an enterprise which, for his own ends, he was determined to carry out. He finally sailed in June 1228 and succeeded, in face of disunion and treachery,[24] not by force of arms but by diplomacy, in gaining more than any previous leader of a Crusade, since the first, had done. His agreement with Sultan Kamil gave the Christians all that they could reasonably require, short of full sovereignty. But the pious were shocked by a treaty which recognised the right of the Moslems to a mosque on the Temple site, and by the Emperor's pledge to see that peace was kept for ten years. The friendship between Frederick and Kamil was a further source of suspicion, but precedent abundantly justified it, for had not Charlemagne and Haroun-ar-Rashid been friends,[25] whilst Richard Lionheart himself had caused

---

[23] He had been the compiler of the *Liber Censuum*, the Church's tax-book, and so had helped to organise the finances of the Papacy. It had been produced in the last year of Celestine III (1198) and the MSS. still exists as Cod. Vat. 8486 ; see Fabre and Duchesne *Étude sur le Liber Censuum*.

[24] Kantorowicz cites an instance in which the Templars " apparently at the direct instigation of the Pope " informed the Sultan of an opportunity of taking Frederick prisoner. The Sultan gave the Christians a lesson in chivalry, by no means the first or last, and sent their letter to the Emperor : see *op. cit.* p. 189.

[25] See Einhard *Vita Caroli* xvi. Gibbon states that Oriental writers know nothing of this friendship : V. p. 290 n.

scandal by his diplomatic dealings with the Saracen.[26] In
the intervals of the various Crusades the feeling between the
Christians and Moslems resident in Syria was, on the whole,
quite friendly ; the latter indeed often looked upon the
summons to a Holy War as " an annoying interruption disturbing the ordinary course of wars and alliances among
themselves." [27]

In the meantime trouble had broken out at home between Troubles in
Gregory and Rainald of Spoleto, Frederick's vicar in Sicily. Italy
The papal forces were having much the better of things when
the sudden return of Frederick in June 1229 changed the issue
by the mere magic of his name. It was a strange spectacle,
on the one side was the motley host of papal troops under
the banner of the keys, on the other the Saracens and crusaders
of the imperial army.

Peace was agreed upon in the summer of 1230, for both Temporary
Gregory and Frederick had too much on their hands to dis- peace
sipate their resources in fighting one another. The Pope
had held out at first, but the delay was an attempt to save
his face as the Patrimony was open to invasion. He succeeded,
however, in driving a hard bargain,[28] for Frederick not only
promised to surrender territories seized by him, but even to
compensate the Pope for his expense in defending them.
He needed peace and absolution. This he received at Ceprano
in August.

The agreement gave both Pope and Emperor time to con- Frederick in
solidate their positions ; for it was a truce and no final treaty. Germany
Frederick had fresh troubles in Sicily which he suppressed
with cruel fury, and later he had to deal with a rebellion of
his own son, Henry, in Germany. The latter movement
collapsed on the appearance of the Emperor north of the
Alps in 1235. It had never had any real root save among the
lesser nobles and the towns. The luckless Henry was banished
to Apulia where, after some years of imprisonment, he found
release by riding his horse over a precipice.

[26] The Chroniclers endeavoured to explain these relations as due to the
guile of the infidels. Richard had a good answer to any criticism in the
number of Turks he had slain ; the less warlike Frederick was denied this
resource.
[27] G. R. Potter *The Autobiography of Ousama* p. ix.
[28] Some thought the treaty humiliating to Gregory ; see MGH. SS. XXIV.
p. 769. But the Popes were accustomed to humiliation in their dealings with
Sicily.

Punishes the Lombards

Henry had been in agreement with the Lombard cities,[29] and the time had now come to punish their continual opposition. Not only had they again blocked the passes and made the Diet of Cremona in 1226 abortive, but the renewal of their League, inspired no doubt by fears of the extension of the Sicilian despotism, was a direct challenge to the Emperor. Frederick's position was now much stronger since Verona, at the foot of the Brenner, was held by Ezzelino da Romano, one of a group of vigorous Ghibelline nobles whose policy it was to support the Emperor.[30]

Novr. 27, 1237

The decisive battle was fought at Cortenuova when Legnano was avenged and the civic militia ridden down by the German knights. Unfortunately Frederick tried to take advantage of the desperate state of the Lombards by inflicting impossible terms—it is said that Cremona and Pavia advised him in the matter ; seven cities in despair decided to continue their resistance and among them were Milan and Brescia. In the siege of the latter the imperialists met with a check which was in some sense the beginning of Frederick's misfortunes. This was in 1238. The next year Gregory openly took the side of the Lombards and once again excommunicated Frederick.

Is again Excommunicated

The Pope's action was quite unjustified except as a piece of policy. Frederick had given him help in dealing with the rebellious Romans, and the Lombards were obviously offenders against the Empire and had brought punishment on themselves by their disloyalty. In giving reasons for the excommunication Gregory made no mention of the trouble in the North ; but everyone knew that it was the real basis of his action. The Papacy could not at any price allow the Lombard barrier to be swept away.[31]

Position of Rome

After the victory of Cortenuova Frederick had sent the captured *carroccio* of the Milanese as a gift to the Roman people ; thus shewing that he had deserted the consistent

---

[29] Tolosanus *Chron.* CCII and *Mon. Patav. Chron.* in RIS. VIII. col. 674 c.

[30] In the next generation Manfred was to discover that a divergence of policy on their part·was a fatal weakness ; by that time their energies were devoted to carving out principalities for themselves : see Salzer *Ueber die Anfänge der Signorie in Oberitalien* and Jordan *Les Origines dom. Ang.* pp. 54 sq.

[31] For the grounds of the sentence see Huillard-Bréholles *op. cit.* V. pp. 286 sq. Some of these were quite genuine ; but in themselves would hardly have justified excommunication.

policy of previous Emperors which had never allowed them
to favour the citizens even against the Pope. Frederick
had come to realise that Rome was the key to the situation,
in much the same way as the possession of London was to
decide the Civil Wars in England. In the last year of Gregory's
life it seemed as if the city would fall into his hands ; but the
aged Pope made a supreme effort ; he had the relics of the
two apostles carried through the streets, a reminder to the
Romans that from them they derived their importance in
the eyes of Christendom. The appeal to the interests and
the superstitions of the citizens was successful and Frederick
made no attempt to force his way in.

Gregory now proclaimed a crusade against the Emperor The capture
and summoned a council to meet in Rome. Frederick gave of Gregory's
orders that all delegates were to be stopped, and by his council
command of sea and land made it abortive. A large body
of cardinals and bishops, under Genoese escort, did indeed
make the attempt to reach Rome ; but a naval battle left May 3, 1241
them in the hands of Frederick's sailors. They were taken
into Naples, not without terrible hardships, both necessary
and those which came from the brutality of their captors.[32]
It was a bold step to capture a council. Gregory could make
no effective reply and three months later he was dead. As
he died the troops of Frederick were again at the gates of
Rome, and perhaps his death, with the promise of a more
peaceable successor, saved the city from seizure.

After some delay, which included the brief pontificate Election of
of Celestine IV, a new Pope was chosen, the Genoese, Sinibaldo Innocent IV
Fiesco. As he had been friendly to Frederick the latter was June 25, 1243
full of delight at the appointment. But his adoption of the
title of Innocent IV should have warned the Emperor that
such emotion was premature and delusive. Innocent was
to prove the most ruthless of his opponents.

From the first the new Pope realised that the struggle Desperate
must be fought to a finish and that any desire for peace was position of
mere cowardice. To be content to save a remnant of the Papacy
Church's power could lead only to final subjection, a return
to the pre-Hildebrandine status. The position of the Papacy
must be recognised as desperate, and its only chance of recovery to lie in the determination utterly to crush its adversary.

[32] See RIS. VI. col. 486 and G. C. Macaulay in *Eng. Hist. Rev.* VI. pp. 1 sqq.

Innocent flies to Lyons

To gain time Innocent entered into negotiations with the Emperor. But in the midst of them he suddenly fled to Genoa, his own native city and the bitterest of Frederick's foes. Thence he proceeded across the Alps to Lyons. From the security of this city he launched in 1245 a fresh excommunication against Frederick and actually deposed him from the Empire. Such treatment was not to be endured and Frederick set out for the Pope's refuge with a considerable army. Force was to be his main argument.[33]

The revolt of Parma

Then came the sudden revolt of Parma and a Guelf rising in Northern Italy. He turned back and rushed down on the treacherous city determined to destroy it and in its place to build the new city of Vittoria. But though Vittoria might be founded and occupied by his troops, over-confidence on his part and the desperate energy of the besieged proved its undoing. When Frederick was absent hunting, part of the garrison was lured away, and the rest overcome by a sudden sally. The Emperor returned and fought valiantly; but he was too late; Vittoria went up in flames and with it all prospect of a speedy reduction of the rebels.

Conspiracy against Frederick

Vittoria fell in 1248. The following year saw a conspiracy among the Emperor's immediate supporters, in which even Peter, " the chief of the apostles," [34] was involved. This blow, however, was not enough to check Frederick's progress. The blockade of Parma was resumed and the Guelfs slowly brought into subjection. Then came the final, unhealable disaster to the Hohenstaufen cause. In December 1250 the

His death

Emperor was attacked by a sudden illness to which he succumbed. Before his death he had given approval to a will drawn up in his name. By it he arranged the succession and ordered certain restitutions to be made. When all hope of recovery had been abandoned Frederick put on the grey habit of his favourite Cistercians and, having received the last sacrament from Archbishop Berard, made a perfectly good Christian end. But the Pope was merciless in death as in life, and did not attempt to conceal his pleasure at the end of the man who had once been his friend; heaven and earth rejoiced with him he declared.

[33] Lyons was not yet part of the French kingdom. It was to be conquered by Philip IV in 1310.
[34] See Huillard-Bréholles *Pierre de la Vigne* pp. 428 sqq.

By his will Frederick left both Italy and the Empire to Succeeded his legitimate son Conrad who was then in Germany. Until by Conrad IV he could arrive affairs were to be administered by Manfred, the fruit of the union with Bianca Lancia. The struggle with William of Holland, the rival Emperor, detained Conrad for some time, but at last he came south. Innocent, who had already proclaimed a new crusade against the brothers, did the same ; but by slower stages. The Pope seemed afraid to trust himself to the Romans and, though he entered Italy in 1251, it was not until the autumn of 1253 that he reached the city.

Innocent now realised that he could not crush the hated Innocent Hohenstaufen by his own resources. At first he sought for seeks outside help help from France, but the time for that had not yet come. At last Henry III of England agreed to allow his younger son, Edmund, to be a candidate for the throne of Sicily. Then came the sudden death of Conrad in May 1254, leaving a position very like that which ensued on the death of Henry VI. There was an infant heir, a capable uncle, and a Pope in the background to take advantage of the unpopularity of the German captains who formed the chief support of the throne. Manfred's position as regent for the young Conradin was far Manfred from enviable. He was by race and upbringing an Italian, and the Germans never trusted him ; whilst to the Sicilian nobles treachery was second nature and loyalty merely a matter of calculation. Thus he had no certainty of support in any quarter. Moreover the Pope as overlord was a factor which might prove dangerous. Suddenly he decided to work for his own hand, and flying to Lucera he trusted his fortunes to the loyalty of his father's faithful Saracens. Thus at last he found himself his own master, and in pos- session of the treasures of his house which the Saracens handed over to him. Had the Papacy been wise it might have used him to separate Sicily from the Empire. But the hatred of Innocent went too deep for such a scheme to receive consideration.

Manfred did not overtly proclaim himself king of Sicily His prospects until a rumour of Conradin's death became current. He was then crowned at Palermo. His prospects were excellent, for Aug. 1258 Conradin was too young to interfere, and Alexander IV, who had succeeded Innocent in Decr. 1254, was too weak to

cope with his youthful vigour,[35] whilst in Italy the whole
Ghibelline party looked up to him as its leader. Moreover
he was a wise and considerate ruler and it seemed as if the
golden days of Frederick were to be restored. The situation,
however, soon changed, for Alexander died and was followed
by a strong and determined Pope in Urban IV. The rigid
policy of Innocent IV was again to be employed.

Charles of Anjou called in
Urban, passing over any rights which Conradin might
have to Sicily, and even Edmund of England, entered into
negotiations with Charles of Anjou. Charles like so many
of the kingly race of France was driven by wild ambitions,
and his wife, Beatrix, abetted him ; she was jealous of her
three sisters who were all queens ; she also would be a queen.[36]
Men said that Charles was always in earnest, and that across
his face a smile was but seldom allowed to venture.[37] He
certainly shewed ability and determination, for before any
actual agreement had been made he got himself elected
Aug. 1263
senator of Rome. Urban died in October 1264 giving place
to Clement IV, a Frenchman. This smoothed away any
difficulties in the path of Charles who was now called upon
to follow the example of his famous namesake, Charles the
Great, and rescue the threatened Papacy.

Manfred had ample warning of what was to come, but
beyond an unsuccessful attempt to interrupt the negotiations
he did nothing. It is true that in Tuscany his cavalry had
Sept. 1260
helped to win the victory of Montaperto ; but a quarrel
between him and Pisa over the spoils of Lucca weakened
Charles in Rome
the Ghibelline front. In the end Charles, risking his life in
a sea so rough that the watching vessels had stood out from
the shore, managed to land at the mouth of the Tiber. In
Rome he waited for his army to join him from the North.
Central Italy was in the main on his side, for the Popes by
raising judicious loans from Florentine bankers had got them
to support him, and the numbers who came down were
sufficient to overawe any but a considerable resistance.

---

[35] Alexander seems to have regarded the methods of his predecessor with
disquiet, he tried to bring a more Christian spirit into the Papacy.

[36] They were Margaret, wife of Louis IX ; Eleanor, wife of Henry III ;
and Sancia, wife of Richard of Cornwall, King of the Romans.

[37] If the statue which peers mournfully down from the top of the staircase
of the Palazzo dei Conservatori on the Capitoline is a good likeness one can
well believe it.

Manfred had hoped that there would have been at least delay; but he was disappointed, and Charles and his wife were crowned on the Feast of the Epiphany 1266.

In spite of the unfavourable season Charles immediately sought out his rival. Under the sudden attack Manfred's supporters proved very unreliable and his own son-in-law, Richard of Caserta, by either timidity or treachery, allowed Charles to cross the Garigliano. There was nothing for it but a battle, and for that Manfred was now as eager as his rival. *Attacks Manfred*

The two armies met on the field of Benevento. The Provençal footmen were borne down by the fierce charge of the Saracens; but they in turn were scattered by the French knights. The fate of the kingdom hung in the balance. Then Manfred threw in his Germans; but they were too few to check the French advance, for the Apulian nobles who should have supported them had already discreetly taken to flight. Thus all was over and Manfred, having no desire to survive his lost kingdom, in company with his faithful friend, Theobald Annibaldi, flung himself into the thickest of the fight and there found the death which he sought. It was not until some days later that his body was recognised by the captive Ghibelline leaders.[38] The Frenchmen, whatever might be their other failings, knew how to treat a worthy foeman, and his body, although he died excommunicated, was honourably buried. It was left for the Church to shew that malice can outlive the death of its victim. By orders of the Bishop of Cosenza the body was disinterred and cast outside the boundaries of the kingdom. *Defeat and death of Manfred, Feb. 26, 1266*

Charles now took possession of his conquest. But his rigid rule soon turned men's thoughts back to the old ruling house and the boy-king beyond the Alps. Like his grandfather, Frederick II, Conradin was willing to test his fate and with a small following he reached Verona in October 1267. Among them was Rudolph of Habsburg, the future Emperor. But his means were quite unequal to the enterprise and for lack of pay the Germans left him. In spite of all adverse circumstances, however, he pressed on and was rewarded with a brief triumph in Rome. He had won a skirmish over the papal troops on the way and even marched *Conradin in Italy*

[38] Even the Guelf chronicler, Saba Malaspina, can scarce withhold his sympathy : see RIS. VIII. col. 830.

beneath " the tall towers and dead walls " of Viterbo, where
Clement was sheltering. But it could not last. He entered
Rome on July 24, 1268 and left it to seek his foe on August 18.
Within a week he was a fugitive.

His defeat   The fatal battle was fought on August 23 a few miles from
Tagliacozzo, which gave its name to the battle. Things
went well at first for Conradin, and his friend Henry of
Castile, like another Rupert, thinking the victory secure, pursued the beaten enemy from the field. He returned to find
that the crafty Frenchman had brought up concealed re-
serves and that the day was lost. Bravery could do nothing
against fate which had already given its verdict. That
night the grim Frenchman sat in his tent, as after Benevento,
and dictated a message of victory to the anxious Pope.

Flight   Conradin with his friend, Frederick of Austria, fled to
Rome ; but it was impossible to remain there. They then
tried to reach the sea, hoping to get a ship to Sicily or friendly
Pisa. They actually managed to get afloat from Astura,
near Cape Circello, but they were seen from the castle which
guards that lonely shore, pursued, and captured. Their
captor was Giovanni Frangipane, a former supporter of the
Hohenstaufen, but now of dubious loyalty, as he proved by
making a bargain with the victors,[39] and surrendering his
captives.

**And Execu-
tion
Oct. 29, 1268**   In the market place of Naples Conradin and Frederick
of Austria, in the presence of their murderer, were put to
death.[40] The race of the Hohenstaufen in the male line, save
for the imprisoned Enzio,[41] was extinct.

**Interregnum
in the
Empire**   The Empire never recovered from the downfall of this
unhappy dynasty. In 1257 two non-German princes had
been elected to the Kingship of the Romans by rival parties
—Alfonso X of Castile, descended from Philip of Swabia

[39] The Sicilians never forgave this act of treachery and Astura was repeatedly burnt by them. In Sept. 1286 they slew there the son of the betrayer.
Again as late as 1328 King Peter, the son of Frederick II of Sicily, who was
descended from Manfred on the female side, landed and sacked the hated castle.

[40] Charles must bear the whole weight of responsibility for the execution.
The Pope might possibly have prevented it had he realised that it was to
happen ; as it was, he himself only survived the youthful victim of his policy
by a few days. For a discussion of the question see Malgarini *Sulla responsi-
bilità di Clemente IV etc.* (Parma 1902).

[41] He was a natural son of Frederick II and had been captured by the
Bolognese in 1249.

through his mother, and Richard of Cornwall, of the English royal house. Neither of the rivals succeeded in gaining general recognition. Richard, indeed, paid a number of visits to Germany, and lavished vast sums in buying adherents, but he was never more than a phantom king. Alfonso did not even trouble to put in an appearance. There was a real interregnum until the election of Rudolf of Habsburg in 1273. Thus Germany lost the political leadership of Europe, which she had first gained with the Carolingians in the eighth century, and broke up into a number of small states without any effective centre of unity. It remains now to consider the reasons for the papal victory and the effects, for good and evil, which followed.

As opponents the Pope and the Emperor were well matched, Reasons for since each was weak in material resources, and depended Papal triumph upon influence rather than on power. Both were in some sense representatives of artificial creations. The Popes triumphed because, in spite of the claims of the Empire and its advocates, it represented a higher ideal and a more con- Held Higher tinuous tradition. It stood for the spiritual life and the ideal supremacy of the law of Christ. It stood for justice between all men. It stood for the weak against the strong. Because of this it drew to itself the allegiance of great men and their unswerving devotion. Not that the Empire lacked loyal servants ; but with them, too often loyalty coincided with self-interest, and was therefore liable to sudden fluctuations.

The Papacy on the whole also stood for what Dr Carlyle Stood for has termed " the freedom of the moral and spiritual elements spiritual freedom in human society." [42] It had, however, as yet no conception of the modern notion of the liberty of the individual, especially of a liberty which would clash with its own authority. So also it supported municipal freedom up to the close of the struggle with the Empire ; but this was merely policy. The death of Frederick II made a great change. Thereafter the Papacy and the communes had not the same need of each other's support,[43] and the latter had always made it quite clear that they had no wish to exchange the imperial for

[42] *Hist. of Med. Pol. Theory in the West* pp. 438 sq.
[43] It must be remembered that a municipality was itself divided and that any agreement was with the party in power for the time.

the papal yoke.[44]   When Innocent IV returned from Lyons the change of feeling was already evident.   The freedom of the individual and of the municipality alike was ultimately bound to prove obnoxious to a despotic institution.[45]

Had wider recognition   The recognition given to the Papacy was wider than that afforded to the Empire, and its power within the several countries of Europe, with the possible exception of the peculiarly imperial lands of Germany and Italy, was greater. England, for example, always claimed that it had never been part of the Empire after the Christian faith had been accepted by its kings,[46] and though Richard I might have done homage to Henry VI it was under duress.   One most amusing instance of English independence was the refusal to allow Sigismund to land at Dover until he had disclaimed any intention of exercising imperial rights.   The Duke of Gloucester and other nobles actually rode into the sea with drawn swords to meet him.[47]

And better agents   The Papacy was well served by its agents.   If in the early days the bishops and secular clergy were often unreliable, since they had connexions with local politics, the monk and the friar were faithful.   The friars were especially enthusiastic in the service of Gregory IX who as Cardinal Ugolino had been the protector of both the Franciscans and Dominicans.

Use of spiritual weapons   One great advantage the Papacy possessed over the Empire ;   it had spiritual as well as material weapons in its arsenal.   The power of the keys claimed to prevail, not only in this world, but beyond the grave ; and in the unsettlement of the times men turned their gaze more ardently to the unseen world which was to right the wrongs of that in which they lived.   Superstition was all powerful, especially

[44] The action of the citizens of Assisi when their city was handed over to Innocent III is typical ; they pulled down the castle, in spite of the protests of the papal representatives, and built walls with the materials.

[45] Cf. Kantorowicz *op. cit.* p. 152 : " the aristocratic Church of the Middle Ages must of necessity be as hostile as the Emperor to the popular movement."

[46] See Letter of Tunstall to Henry VIII of Feb. 12, 1517 in *Calendar of Letters etc.* I. p. 136.   Wyclif also made a point of England's independence of the Empire : see *De Potestate Papae* p. 227 (Wyclif Soc. ed. 1907).   Even Baldwin II, the feeble Latin Emperor of Constantinople, when he attempted to land at Dover in 1238 was told that he had no right to do so without the king's leave : see Matthew Paris *Chron. Major* III. p. 481 (RS.).

[47] This story was rejected as a sixteenth century invention, but it may well be genuine : see Wylie *Henry V* III. pp. 9 sq.

as life advanced or danger threatened, and the boldest spirits were glad to die in the habit of the monk.[48]

Finally the Papacy might have interregnums, but it was saved from minorities such as those which weakened the Empire. It had not indeed the continuity which comes from hereditary succession; but on the whole the Popes who were elected, especially if a crisis threatened, were men of experience whose virtues could never have been described as " the premature and artificial fruits of a royal education ".[49] What was remarkable was the extraordinary energy shewn by aged Popes; Gregory IX, and Julius II in a later period, were outstanding instances of this. Here and there an individual Pope might have longings after holiness; but if so the saint was quickly outdistanced by the statesman within him. The throne of Peter was no place for a mystic, and as a class the Popes were much less visionary than the Emperors. The ideal of universal dominion floated before the eyes of both, to the one it was a source of weakness and dissipation of power, to the other of strength and concentration. The Churchman was practical and followed practical aims; the imperialist was idealistic and followed ideal aims. This reversal of their expected roles will be strange only to those who are unfamiliar with the thought of the middle ages. *Had no minorities*

The weaknesses of the Emperor came from three sources; the connexion with the Papacy, the link with Rome and Italy, and the double nature of his office as Emperor and as German king. In many ways he was more dependent on the Pope than the Pope on him. The Emperor, indeed, could hardly be said to have any real authority or status until he had received papal recognition and his coronation in Rome. It may be that one reason for the creation of anti-popes was the desire to obtain this coronation. It is true that for a time the Emperors had insisted on their right to confirm papal elections, but that day was long past; the right of the Pope, however, to crown the Emperor was recognized to the very end of the middle ages. But it was not merely in the matter of the coronation that the Emperor was at a disadvantage. The Papacy was a concrete thing; the Empire depended on the person of the Emperor. Time after time, *Imperial weakness from connexion with Papacy,*

[48] John of England and Frederick himself are examples of this custom.
[49] See Gibbon III p. 133 (on the Emperor Gratian).

and not least in the last stages of the conflict, he seemed to be a man fighting an institution.[50]   That was why the death of the Emperor, Henry VI or of Conrad IV for example, played such havoc with the imperial cause.   The Papacy was remarkably fortunate in the deaths of its opponents ; some saw here, not unnaturally, the divine intervention to ' save the bark of Peter from shipwreck '.   The Hohenstaufen, however, were a fated race.   When Barbarossa was swept away his work was done ; but the rest, for the most part, died before reaching their prime.   Italy herself with her deadly climate slew two of them ; one died by the hand of a private assassin ; the last by the executioner's axe.   Manfred alone met a hero's death, Frederick II alone a normal deathbed.

from the connexion with Italy,   We come now to the weakness arising from the connexion with Rome and Italy.   This connexion was ever luring the Emperor away from more pressing duties by its glamour.   Rome added dignity to the imperial office and saved the Emperor from being a mere feudal overlord ; but it brought little else.   Even in the imperial city itself, to which at least once in his lifetime he had to go to receive the traditional hallowing, he and his followers met with mingled hatred and contempt.   Italy and Germany were a strange pair to be linked together, so different in their traditions, their economic and social life, as well as in climate and language.   To rule them both with fairness and justice was impossible ; the one must be sacrificed to the other.   And it was Germany which paid the price.   " Italy was a constant drain of blood and treasure from the year 962 to the year 1866 " ; wrote Stubbs, " nine hundred years of wasted men and money.   It is true that sometimes great good resulted to Italy from German interference ; but never anything but harm resulted to Germany from the Italian dominion." [51]

from double office   But in Germany itself the Emperor found himself weakened

[50] This was reflected in the inadequate central organisation of the Empire when compared with that of the Papacy.

[51] *Germany in the Early Middle Ages* p. 105.   This drain continued even after the abdication of Francis Joseph in 1806.   One is tempted to ask what would have been the history of Europe if Austria, instead of continuing to waste her resources in a vain attempt to preserve the remnants of her power in Italy, had concentrated on her natural mission on the Danube and built up a strong central state in South Germany.   Benjamin Jowett used to say that the balance of power in Europe could best be maintained by such a state to hold Prussia in check.

by the Italian link.   It was not only that his absences tended
in that direction, but his continual need of German support
to carry out his Italian schemes led to the permanent alienation of imperial prerogatives and resources in return for temporary assistance.   The Emperors for generations were
exhausting their capital ; the Popes were wiser, they lived
on the contributions of Christendom.

I pointed out above that the Papacy had to face no Schisms in
minorities.   It also suffered less from contested elections ; the Empire
the days of the Great Schism were yet to come.   But
for the Empire such schisms were frequent and the very
method of election led to the weakening of the office, since the
electors were able to make conditions from which the Emperor,
not having the dispensing power of the Pope, was unable to
extricate himself.   Thus he became steadily weaker in face
of the electoral princes.   The fact, too, that some of the
electors were great ecclesiastics made a difference.   In the
contest with Frederick II these princes were gradually
weaned from their loyalty by the skill with which the papal
envoys played upon their fears or their pride.

The immediate effect of the victory of the Papacy was Effects of
greatly to increase its power in Germany.   The princes were, Papal vic-
as Ranke said, abject in their anxiety to acknowledge that Germany
the Roman Church was the originator of their power.[52]   Whilst
succeeding Emperors, excepting Lewis of Bavaria, were
equally ready to submit.   These acknowledgements were
not allowed to remain idle words by the Papacy, and when
Richard of Cornwall died, Gregory X ordered the princes to
elect an Emperor, warning them that if there was undue delay
he and the cardinals would proceed to nominate him.   So too
the German cities had hesitated to recognise Richard himself
until he had received papal approval.

In Italy the papal victory was so complete that Rudolph in Italy
of Habsburg was willing to give up his claims there.   In
this action he shewed himself to be more statesmanlike and
prudent than his predecessors, for he cut a link which had
been a great source of embarrassment, and left himself free

---

[52] *Deutsche Geschichte im Zeitalter der Reformation* I. p. 28.   He quotes
from the *Tractatus cum Nicholao III Papa*, 1279.   " Romana ecclesia Ger-
maniam decoravit plantans in ea principes tanquam arbores electas " :   see
MGH. SS. IV. p. 421.

to deal with Germany where he speedily laid a firm basis for the future of his house by seizing the Duchy of Austria from his disgruntled rival, Ottocar of Bohemia.[53]

Growth of princely power in Germany

But the power of the princes within Germany had thriven vastly during the contest.[54]   In earlier days the Emperors had tried to play off, with some success, the ecclesiastical against the temporal princes ; but both had been united during the struggle and both gained much in status and actual possessions. Emmanuel Philibert of Savoy held it as a principle that to grant a fief was to create a potential enemy ; if the Emperors recognised the principle the exigencies of their situation compelled them to ignore it.   During the Avignon period the ecclesiastical princes would become less favourable to the Papacy, and both they and the temporal princes were to see a serious diminution of their power before the rise of the lesser nobles (the later knights) and the growing importance of the imperial cities.

Cost of the victory

The Papacy had thus an increase of power in Germany and a free hand in Italy as the result of its strivings.   These were substantial gains, but the price paid for them was too high. Earlier struggles had been in part spiritual, in part secular ; as when Hildebrand fought for freedom from imperial control and Innocent III made possible the future papal states : but this struggle became almost entirely secular and lost the grandeur which would have come from a religious contest. The Papacy in striving to overcome the Empire usurped rights which belonged to the latter.[55]

Loss of spiritual power and influence

Innocent IV had found the Papacy at the height of its influence ; he left it, in spite of some superficial worldly success, on the downward track.   It had become a kingdom of this

[53] Ottocar had appealed to the Pope, because his rights as an elector had been ignored at Rudolph's election : " a quibusdam principibus vocem in electione habentibus . . . sed non a nobis, qui eligendi de jure ac consuetudine jus habemus ".   See Emler *Reg. dip. nec non Epist. Boh. et Moraviae* II. p. 393.

[54] It also witnessed a vast expansion of Germany to the East which was pregnant with great possibilities : see the documents collected by Kötzschke *Quellen zur Geschichte der ostdeutschen Kolonisation im 12 bis 14 Jahrhundert* (Leipzig 1912).

[55] This is admitted by liberal Roman Catholics.   Von Hügel, for example, after justifying the efforts of the earlier Popes to gain their freedom, says that they " were succeeded by the policies of an Innocent IV and Boniface VIII, which largely ignored or directly subordinated, the really different rights specific to the State " : see *Essays and Addresses* I. pp. 245 sq.

world, the centre of an elaborate financial system.   Innocent
has been called a ' consummate man of business ',[56] and he
realised that money was the key to success in the warfare
against the Empire.   The financial burdens which he had to
bear were immense, and some of them had been undertaken
in more honourable causes or at least more spiritual.[57]   To
meet them he sacrificed everything and put everything up
for sale.[58]   Thus the Church lost its moral hold on Christendom
and the respect of men.   Papal claims had been allowed to
grow up almost unchallenged ; but when they came to be
enforced their capacity for abuse and their dangers and
disadvantages were revealed.

The price paid for political victory was thus moral loss. Rise of
But the victory itself was merely a deceptive one, for the fall national
of the Empire led, not to the aggrandisement of the Papacy, Kings
but to the elevation of the national king.   France in particular was to benefit by the weakness of the Emperors.   In
the ninth century the decay of the Carolingian Empire had
left the Papacy the prey of the local nobles, the fall of the
Hohenstaufen left it at the mercy of the French to whom it
owed its triumph.

The truth was that the rival powers had so concentrated Changed
their minds on the conflict that they had failed to realise that attitude to
the world around them was changing.   The tide of faith was both Empire
and Papacy
ebbing, the world which had regarded them as dominant
and unrivalled had passed away, and victor and vanquished
found themselves with vastly diminished prestige.   They
were in effect both politically and morally bankrupt.   It
was a grave disaster for the West that the Church should
have come out of the contest so discredited, for with the
downfall of the Empire it was the sole remaining centre round
which civilisation and culture could gather.   For two centuries the West struggled to find a new order ; then came the
Reformation which, though inevitable, made the whole

[56] See A. L. Smith *Church and State in the Middle Ages* p. 234.
[57] Such as giving aid to the Crusades.   Innocent wrote on one occasion
" Habet ecclesia Romana humeros communibus oneribus assuetos " : see
Rymer *Foedera* I. p. 471.
[58] The middle ages were used to the system of money commutations.
" Feudalism assessed its duties ; the law its list of crimes : religion her grades
of sin.   You could buy off everything . . . up to the offended majesty of the
King, or the wrath of God Himself " : A. L. Smith *op. cit.* p. 181.

situation doubly worse.   Thus the scheme of ruling Western
Europe by the combined Empire and Papacy had broken down.
It had brought upon " the German and Italian people a long
succession of sorrows and humiliations ; and its end, like that
of ancient Rome . . . is among the solemn portents of the
world." [59]

Papal blindness   As one looks back over the course of events one is surprised
that the Popes were so blind to the effect which the fall of
the Empire would have upon their own institution, that
they did not realise the intimate connexion between them.
It was not long, however, before the consequences became
apparent ; Dante is already aware of them.[60]   The Empire
and the Papacy were based on the same foundation and the
principles by which their existence was justified were identical ; hence the weakening of the one involved the weakening
of the other.   Engelbert, the contemporary of Dante, declared that any withdrawal of allegiance from the Empire
would be followed by a similar action towards the Papacy.[61]
It is therefore not a matter for surprise that we find a few
generations later that the suggestion is seriously made that
the Pope is liable to deposition.[62]

   After all Church and Empire were but Western Christendom viewed from different angles ; the same individuals were
members of both.   Like intelligence and will in Hegelian
psychology they might be distinguished by a process of
abstraction, but they could hardly be separated.   In the heat
of the struggle Gregory IX and Innocent IV refused to
the Empire any rights save such as it derived from papal
recognition.   But when the victory was won Gregory X,
with mild condescension, could speak of each having a supreme

---

[59] Acton *Historical Essays and Studies* p. 500.
[60] See *Purgatorio* xvi. 106 sqq.

        " Soleva Roma, che il buon mondo feo,
           Due soli aver, che l'una e l'altra strada
           Facean vedere, e del mondo e di Deo.
           L'un l'altro ha spento ; ed è giunta la spada
           Col pastorale."

[61] *De ortu progressu et fine Romani imperii* in Goldast *Politica* pp. 754 sqq.
[62] Cf. *De Modis Uniendi* I. iv. 75 which after pointing out that a ruler
might be deposed for the good of the state continues " Multo magis unus
Papa unus Praelatus est deponendus qui per electionem Cardinalium fuit
institutus."   This treatise used to be attributed to Gerson : its real author is
unknown.

authority within its own sphere, and expose the evil which
came to the one from the weakness of the other.   Time was
to shew only too clearly the truth of this last judgement.   It
would have been well if it had been borne in mind by his predecessors even in the midst of the struggle ; for the Empire
and the Papacy were to the middle ages what the Roman
Empire and the Persian kingdom had been to an earlier age ;
" the two eyes of the world, which would remain imperfect
and mutilated if either of them should be put out." [63]

With Gregory X a new and more peaceful era in the rela- The new era
tions of the Empire and the Papacy was ushered in.   The strife
was over, another attempt of the Titans to scale the heights
of heaven, to use Figgis's graphic phrase, had been repulsed.
There was, however, one cause for disquiet.   When the
Pope entered Rome there was seen beside him the sinister
figure of Charles of Anjou, the representative and symbol
of the new masters who were to bring the Papacy lower
than any Hohenstaufen.   In the Empire the new stage was
marked by the election of Rudolph of Habsburg, a godson
of Frederick II, who having fought for the Emperors in Italy,
was now glad to admit the superior authority of the Pope
and to recognise the independence of the Papal States and
of Sicily.[64]

The tyranny of Charles was indeed heavy, both in his The rule of
new kingdom and over the power which had given him the Charles
opportunity of gaining it.   The Popes might lay financial
burdens on distant lands and claim that their legates were
superior to kings ; but in Rome, as they had once been at
the mercy of the populace, so were they now at the mercy
of the Angevin.   Nicholas III, a man of strong will, struggled 1277-1280
against this influence with some success.   Martin IV, who 1281-1285
followed, was a Frenchman and a herald of the days of
Avignon ; by him Charles was restored to the office of senator
of Rome which he had lost, whilst important posts in the
papal administration were given to Frenchmen.   But relief The Sicilian
was at hand.   By a sudden rising, a great conflagration lit Vespers ;
Mar. 1282

[63] See the speech of the Persian ambassador to the Emperor Galerius in
Gibbon I. p. 373.
[64] This took place on Feb. 14, 1279 in the reign of Nicholas III.   The
document is printed in MGH. Const. III. p. 213.

as it were by a stray spark, Sicily was freed from her oppressors. Charles' efforts to recover his kingdom were vain, especially after a naval defeat off Naples in 1284, and at the beginning of the next year he died.   The freedom of Sicily had been made possible by the co-operation of Aragon which post-poned its natural task of expelling the Moors from Spain in order to indulge in the adventure.[65]

Thus the vast plans of Charles, which included the sub-jugation of the Eastern Empire, came to naught.   But he had to his credit two great negative achievements ; the end of the Norman rule in Sicily and the exclusion of German influence from Italy.   His death freed the Papacy, for the time, from the Angevin tyranny, as it also saved the East from a serious threat.

Nepotism grows
Between the accession of Gregory X (1271) and that of Celestine V (1294) eight Popes occupied the throne of St. Peter ; they were, with the exception of Nicholas III, men of little note and the chief use which they made of their brief tenure of office was to provide for their families.   Nepotism saw the beginning of its golden age, and not a few of the noble Roman houses of later times could trace their rise to this period.   The Orsini owed much to Nicholas himself,[66] the

1285-1287 1288-1292
Savelli to Honorius IV, and the Colonna to Nicholas IV.

Choice of Celestine V
After the death of the latter Pope there was a long delay and it was not until July 5, 1294 that Celestine V was chosen. His election was one of the strangest in a series which includes some which were strange indeed.   The cardinals, in face of the deadlock, suddenly agreed upon the name of Pietro di Morrone, who was living as a solitary in the mountains near Sulmone in the Abruzzi.   In the early days of monasticism in the East it was not an uncommon thing for a ' reluctant hermit ' to be dragged from his cell and seated upon the epis-copal throne ; [67] but the more practical West did not indulge so freely in such experiments, though the most famous of the early Popes, Gregory the Great, had been forced to leave his monastery to ascend the throne of Peter.   Their experi-

---

[65] Since 1244 Aragon had been cut off from the South by treaties with Castile.

[66] Salimbene says of him that he built up Zion for the benefit of his kins-men ; cf. Dante *Inferno* xix. 69.

[67] See Gibbon IV. p. 63.

ence at the end of the thirteenth century was enough to prevent
its repetition for all time.

Celestine, although not so utterly devoid of experience His
as is generally believed, was quite incapable of bearing the resignation
burden of the Papacy and fell into the hands of Charles II of
Naples in political matters and of Cardinal Gaetani in things
ecclesiastical. The latter, indeed, soon procured his resignation ; there are stories which suggest that he employed a
medieval equivalent of a megaphone by means of which
angelic voices recommended this course to Celestine.

Gaetani was at once elected to fill the vacancy which he Boniface
had created, and he was a strong contrast to his predecessor. VIII
The enemies whom he raised up during his lifetime did not
spare his memory ; but when all allowance has been made it
seems probable that Boniface VIII, as he came to be called,
was in doctrine a sceptic, although entirely devoted to upholding and extending the claims of the office which he held.
With certain modifications, for Boniface was certainly not
incompetent, one might apply to him the lesson which
Lord Morley drew from the failure of George III ; " There
is nothing more fatal . . . than for an incompetent man to
grasp a principle of action which is too big for him ".[68]

Boniface's first step was to leave Naples in order to be High ideas
free of the yoke of Charles II. He made his entry into Rome of papal
on Jan. 17, 1295. From the secure base of the Eternal power
City he then launched his challenge to the lay rulers of
Christendom, and his declaration of the rights of the Papacy.
By the bull *Clericis laicos* [69] clerics were forbidden to pay Feb. 24, 1296
dues to laymen, and laymen who attempt to exact them were
declared to be *ipso facto* excommunicate. The chief effect
of this declaration was a dispute with France which ended
in the Pope explaining away the principles underlying the
bull so as to remove any cause of offence. As a further
concession to French feeling Boniface arranged for the canoni- Aug. 17, 1297
sation of Louis IX.

The emergence of France as the greatest power in Europe Rise of
at this epoch is sufficient justification for a brief digression.[70] France

---

[68] *Early Life and Letters* I. p. 91.
[69] In Raynaldus 1296 No. 23.
[70] France's leadership in politics coincided with the loss of her leadership
in culture and to a less degree in theological learning.

It was the outcome of a long and steady growth and when the Empire fell France was found " concentrated, alert, ambitious, with a dynasty reigning in South Italy ".[71] This growth had been largely the result of harmonious working with the Church and by it the feudal nobles had been checked and their jurisdiction curtailed. In this last achievement the aid of the rising class of lawyers had been of great importance and the insistence on the recognition of Roman law. There have been few, if any, dynasties in history which have enjoyed such an uninterrupted series of direct successions as the Capetian ; it ran from its foundation in 987 to the death of Louis X in 1816. Included among its rulers there had been several able kings who pursued quietly and steadily a consecutive and consistent policy. Perhaps the most successful of them

1180-1223 all was Philip Augustus who recovered Normandy and prepared the way for the inclusion of Languedoc within the

1226-1270 French kingdom. The most famous was, of course, Louis IX to whom reference was made above. He was capable as well as pious ; yet his devotion to the Crusades wasted the resources of his kingdom in visionary enterprises, and although it increased French prestige, a longer continuance of his reign might seriously have impaired her material strength. Evidence is not wanting that his contemporaries by no means regarded his efforts after justice and a purer administration as remarkable for their success.[72]

1285-1814 It was, however, during the long reign of Philip IV, a reign which has left a permanent mark on French life and polity, that the organisation of the administration and the process by which the feudal system was brought into more direct dependence on the king reached its culmination. It

---

[71] Fisher *The Mediaeval Empire* I. p. 9.

[72] John of Garland in his poem *De triumphis ecclesiae* repeatedly bemoans the evils of his day and envies the happy dead and all the past ;

> " O quam felices veteres vixere, sepulti
> Ante dies nostros et populare chaos !
> O quoties fausti sunt hii, feralia facta
> Qui non viderunt quae videt ista dies."

                                                        xi. 21-24.

In another unedited work he even goes so far as to bewail the injustice of kings : " Regum justitia quam levis est et inanis ! " Upon this estimate, L. J. Paetow, to whom I owe the quotation, remarks : " We are shocked by such words applied to the reign of the ' French Justinian ' ". See *The Crusades etc.* pp. 210 sq.

was with this efficient and determined ruler that the Papacy, in the person of Boniface VIII, had to make its account.

In the meantime Boniface had brought upon himself another quarrel, one which was nearer home and less easily settled, and one, moreover, which was to become linked up with the French opposition. Boniface found himself drawn into a dispute with the Colonna family,[73] and gained the hatred of two cardinals of that house. Excommunication followed and then open rebellion and the appeal to arms. Boniface with his habitual lack of any sense of proportion proclaimed a ' crusade ' against the two cardinals, and after a fierce resistance Palestrina, the chief fortress of the Colonna, surrendered and was destroyed, not for the first nor the last time.[74] The cardinals eventually succeeded in finding refuge with the French king ; their lands went to form a principality for Peter Gaetani, the papal nephew. *Boniface quarrels with the Colonna*

Things in Sicily were not going any too well. There had been a Treaty in 1295 which was supposed to bring peace to the kingdom, but as the island itself had not been consulted it refused to accept the arrangements contemplated in it. James II was to marry Blanche, the daughter of Charles II of Naples, and to resign his claims to Sicily, receiving Sardinia and Corsica as a compensation, if he could drive out the Pisans and Genoese. The Sicilians offered the crown to Frederick, the brother of James, and after some vicissitudes he made good his position. But this was not to happen until the Treaty of Caltabellotta in Sept. 1302. By this time the Pope had much more serious troubles on his hands than the thwarting of his plans for Sicily. *Sicily defies the Pope*

The height of Boniface's power was the year 1300 when he proclaimed the first of the famous Jubilees.[75] It was a well-found device, for by it visits to the tombs of the Apostles at Rome [76] were to take the place of pilgrimages to the Holy Land which the collapse of the crusading movement had *The Jubilee Feb. 23*

[73] For Boniface's dealings with the Colonna see Ehrle *Die Denkschriften der Colonna gegen Bon. VIII etc.* in *Archiv* V. p. 521.

[74] It was, of course, the classical Praeneste destroyed by Sulla.

[75] By the Bull " Antiquorum " Register No. 3875 (ed. Digard, Faucon and Thomas). The Jubilee was really a revival of the Secular Games which in pagan Rome had marked the end of each century.

[76] Cf. Ricobaldo of Ferrara *Compilatio Chron.* in RIS. IX. col. 254 " ac si terram sanctam visitaret ".

5

rendered less attractive. The scheme caught the imagination of Christendom and in a frenzy of religious ardour crowds flocked to Rome. Some even came from Central Asia, and it was probably on this occasion that Giotto, who was present, saw the Mongolians whom he brought into some of his frescoes.[77] So great was the wealth offered by the pilgrims that at St Paul's two clerics stood day and night before the altar raking in the money.[78] The citizens, who charged what they liked for accommodation in face of the overwhelming demand, also gathered in much profit from the institution.

Boniface and the Empire

July 1298

With the Empire Boniface's relations were tolerably friendly, and he found that Albert of Austria, who followed Adolf of Nassau whom he had defeated and slain near Göllheim, was amenable to papal guidance since he needed papal recognition. In May 1300 the Pope insisted that Albert should give up Tuscany to the Papacy ; this caused a temporary deadlock. Later he asked for explanations of the death of Adolf within six months. Although the exact terms of the request were not carried out Albert proved submissive and in spite of an alliance with Philip of France proceeded to enter into friendly relations with Boniface who badly needed his help. By this act he succeeded at last in getting recognition as King of the Romans. Albert admitted the Pope's right to grant the imperial crown and the derivation of electoral rights from him.[79]

April 30, 1303

Affairs in Florence

In Central Italy the Pope was striving to gain control of Florence which at this time, the Ghibellines having been expelled, was divided into two hostile Guelf parties—the Neri and Bianchi. The latter, who were led by the Cerchi and numbered Dante among their supporters, at first proved more powerful than their rivals, like the equestrian order in ancient Rome they had the deeper purses ; but a certain timidity prevented them from pressing home their advantage and the Pope discarded them in favour of the wilder and more gallant Neri under the lead of the Donati.[80] In order to carry out his schemes Boniface brought in Charles of Valois

[77] With some of his successors, Altichiero in particular, the introduction of Tartars became almost an obsession.

[78] See Ventura *Chron. Astense* xxvi. in RIS. XI. col. 192 B.

[79] See his letters of July 17, 1303 in Theiner *Codex Diplom.* I. Nos. 569 sq.

[80] Dino Compagni says that the Pope declared his unwillingness to sacrifice the men for the old women—" Io non voglio perdere gli huomini per le femminelle " : see RIS. IX. col. 492 E.

who succeeded by his treachery in gaining Florence for the Neri—and incidentally exile for Dante. He left it in April 1802 to proceed on a futile expedition against Sicily.

The vital quarrel with Philip IV was by this time well advanced, in fact but for the defeat of the French by the Flemings at Courtrai it might well have been over, and Philip's will already enforced. The renewed outbreak was due really to Philip's high-handed way of ignoring the rights of the Pope and the French Church. The reaction in the mind of Boniface led of necessity to violent measures, and in December 1301 he issued another of his famous bulls *Ausculta fili*.[81] This threw France into an uproar and Philip replied by summoning the first meeting of the Estates General ; he wished to rally the nation behind him against alien inter-ference. The feelings of the Assembly were made more bitter by the production of a forged bull, *Deum Time* or *Scire te volumus*, in which Boniface was made to claim supreme temporal power in the kingdom.[82] The Pope had on his side called a synod to meet in Rome towards the end of 1302, and a few French prelates managed to get to it in spite of a royal ban ; but the bulk of them were behind the king and needed no excuse for absenting themselves. As a result of this synod a bull, the famous *Unam Sanctam* was issued, which represents the highest point reached by papal ambitions. It makes Communion with Rome the test of salvation [83] and claims that the State is in every way inferior to the Church. This was the final offence. Philip guided by the civil lawyers, who had taken the place of ecclesiastics as his most trusted advisers, despatched William Nogaret to arrest the Pope and bring him back to France for trial before a General Council. Nogaret hired a band of ruffians, joined forces with the Colonna who had their own score to settle, and on Sept. 7, 1303 seized Boniface at Anagni where he had taken refuge. The people of the neighbourhood and the lesser nobles who had been dispossessed of lands in favour of papal nephews were indif-ferent or hostile, and even the citizens of Anagni were probably privy to the plot. But more noble feelings soon asserted

Quarrel with Philip IV July 11, 1302

Novr. 18, 1302

The outrage at Anagni

---

[81] Register No. 4424 (ed. Digard, Faucon and Thomas III. pp. 328 sqq.).

[82] See Dupuy *Histoire du Differend* p. 44. ·

[83] Cf. the closing words : " subesse Romano pontifici . . . omnino esse de necessitate salutis ". The bull is printed in the Register No. 5382 (ed. cit. III. pp. 888 sqq.)

themselves, the outrage on an old man of 85 years and the Head of Christendom was felt to be intolerable.[84]   Nogaret and his allies fled ; it was impossible to drag their captive half across Italy and so he was left behind.   Boniface was now moved to the Vatican where he remained in the power or under the protection of the Orsini until his death on

Death of Boniface   Oct. 11.   Death after all was the only portion left for the proud spirit so utterly broken and confounded.   The whole story was a tragedy of temperament, and Boniface's pontificate was wrecked because he lacked a sense of proportion, a deficiency which has probably been the root of more tragedies than calculating villainy itself.

Loss of papal prestige   The raid on Anagni was only an incident, and the mishandling of the Pope nothing worse than Gregory VII had had to endure ; but it revealed the loss of papal prestige. Europe was only mildly shocked at the outrage, and perhaps at the bottom there were not a few who were pleased that mad ambition and overweening pride should thus have patently over-reached themselves.

Benedict XI   In the place of the dead Pope a Dominican, Cardinal Boccasini, was elected.   It was a good choice, for Boccasini had stood loyally by Boniface when the rest had fled from Anagni, and his upright and austere character was bound to win respect.   Moreover he was not one to pursue the path which had brought his predecessor to such a pitiful end.   If he was compelled to pardon the Colonna and to restore Palestrina, he was strong enough to except from the pardon those who had been personally responsible for the outrage at Anagni.   By a bull of May 12, 1304 the acts of Boniface were annulled, and a reconciliation effected with France. When living at Perugia, after having been compelled to desert Rome by civic strife, Benedict XI, for such was his style, shewed some signs of desiring to assert his powers more fully. It was perhaps fortunate that he was cut off by death at this juncture.   The defeated had to submit and any renewal of the struggle with France would only have led to a further loss of prestige.   The age of Gregory VII and the Innocents was over and all chance of a theocracy had gone for ever.

[84] Boniface met the crisis with commendable courage and dignity. After his attendants had deserted him he sat on his throne dressed in his robes.   On the approach of Nogaret he exclaimed " Ec le col, ec le cape " : see " Rishanger " *Ann. Regis Edward. I* p. 486 (RS.).

CHAPTER III

THE AGE OF FAITH

BEFORE proceeding on our way it will be well, at this The thirteenth century point, to desert the chronological sequence in order more thoroughly to explore what has been called the Age of Faith. This term has been applied to the thirteenth century, and although centuries are merely conventional divisions of time it is convenient to regard them as having a special character, even though such a character may not correspond exactly to the actual period involved. Certainly in the case of the thirteenth century the first half is the more important, at any rate for action ; though for thought the death of St Thomas Aquinas in 1274 marks the close of an epoch.

The thirteenth century was a brilliant period, if for no an age of great men other reason, on account of the great personalities which emerged during its course. There are periods in which the events seem to dwarf the actors—the Age of Faith was not one of them, for it was an epoch of great men rather than of striking incidents. Few centuries can shew a list of names worthy even of comparison ; Innocent III and Innocent IV among the Popes ; St Francis and St Dominic among founders of Orders ; St Albertus Magnus and St Thomas Aquinas among philosophers ; and Frederick II and Philip Augustus among rulers. It was indeed an age active and living, an age which exhibited a " perpetual blaze of dynamic force " such as was not again to be seen until the days of the Renaissance. Permanent memorials of its skill and devotion can be found in the great cathedrals as well as in the glorious parish churches. It was a time of growth in social things also. The manorial system was, indeed, decaying, but in its place there was growing up a new order ; the municipalities were developing rapidly ; new land was being brought under cultivation (the Cistercians and other orders played their part in this); and there were vast schemes of colonisation being carried out. So rapid was the development of the economic system that something of a revolution was taking place and a definite breach with the ancient world.[1] Whatever men's hands found them to do they did it with all their might. They pursued an object so earnestly that for the time they were blind to all else. This led to much inconsistency; for attempts were made to carry out the objects of Christ and His Church with little regard to His spirit.

**an age of
ideals**

To the better minds the actual was only tolerable as an embodiment of great principles. In Church and State alike men were constantly striving to realise an ideal, and even the individual was not without a vision for his own life. It is true that such ideals were seldom realised even in part. Like the pilgrim seeking God's hidden face beyond the West, they found that the golden gleam faded all too soon into darkness. But it was well that it had been seen at all, that even the rudest knight had some notion of chivalry to counter-act the barbarous elements of his nature. He might never be an Arthur or a Roland, but it was something to have the conception of the perfect knight before him.

But alongside the nobler seekers there were found many who, perhaps half unconsciously, allowed the cherishing of an ideal to become a substitute for effort to amend the real; who acquiesced in the actual and tried to make the best of it, often for selfish reasons. Thus it came about that an age of great conceptions, of affirmation and adventure in both religion and politics, ended in one of narrow ideals and continual compromises. To the saint and the warrior succeeded the banker and the mercenary. Even villany itself was to become less violent and more cunning—craft was to be substituted for force. The truth was that civilisation was advancing, and civilisation is often the enemy of ideals; for with increased security and prosperity men begin to love luxury and comfort, and the vision is lost.

Such a judgement may be a little hard on the fourteenth century; all generalisations are in their way unjust, and a period of quickened life and activity, in thought as well as

---

[1] See Cunningham *Western Civilisation in its Economic Aspects* (*Medieval and Modern*) II. pp. 9 and 74.

in action, is prone to make its neighbours look small and commonplace. Its shadow falls not only on the past which is gone, but on the ages yet to come.

Since belief in God often involves belief in the devil an age of faith is liable to be an age of torment. So it was in the thirteenth century, and the records of the spiritual experiences of the times reveal a vivid consciousness of the nearness of the divine, together with an unspeakable terror of the enemy of souls. The latter in practice if not in theory, such is man's natural pessimism, was often regarded as stronger in a given locality, than the former. It was only by the greatest watchfulness that his snares were to be avoided. To the monk in his cloister and to the priest at the very altar, in one shape or another the fiend would come : the whole world seemed a dense mass of evil spirits.[2] The native of Central Africa, or the devil-haunted Chinese, furnish a close parallel in the present day to the outlook of the medieval believer. The worst aspect of the situation was, however, that moral and ethical considerations seem hardly to have come in ; magic had to be met by magic. It was almost as if the ancient world of paganism had returned ; [3] for life was regarded, with little but a change of name, as it had been by the worshipper of Jove or Venus.[4] In this transformation the Blessed Virgin played a prominent part ; and to her were applied many of the attributes of Venus,[5] as well as the not dissimilar characteristics of the heroines of romantic poetry.[6]

[2] Cf. Caesar of Heisterbach *Dialogus Miraculorum* IV. 5 sqq., 33, 35, 38, and the late thirteenth century work *Liber Revelationum de insidiis et versutiis daemonorum adversus homines* in Pez *Thesaurus Anecdotorum novissimus* I. pt. ii. p. 22. One may perhaps be allowed to surmise that some of these visions, as in the case of the priests of Isis in Dryden's drama, were " Bred from the fumes of indigested feasts and holy luxuries ".

[3] Cf. Croce *Theory and History of Historiography* p. 201.

[4] " The life of the Middle Ages dissevered from its superstition would be as incomprehensible as the *Iliad* without its contending deities or *Paradise Lost* without its Satan " : Heywood *Hist. of Perugia* p. 15.

[5] One recalls the scorn of Erasmus in later days that one who had never taken a voyage in her life should be called " stella maris " : see the colloquy *Naufragium*.

[6] " La Vierge est la plus pure et la plus belle, la plus aimable des femmes : " Funck-Brentano *Le Moyen Age* p. 188. She could also be as jealous as a heathen goddess of an earthly rival ; see Coulton *Five Centuries of Religion* I. pp. 163 sq.

The Schoolmen

An age of faith may thus be an age of superstition; it may also be an age of intellectual stagnation. From such a reproach the thirteenth century was saved by the Schoolmen; a body of thinkers who were not so much advocates of a single system as exponents of a similar method. Scholasticism

Origins in Graeco-Roman Culture

as a movement grew naturally out of the medieval educational system, and indeed from the Graeco-Roman culture in which Christianity itself had arisen. With the fall of the Empire in the West that culture had largely vanished, for it was mainly the depressed classes who survived from the old civilisation, the cultivated classes had succumbed long ago to over-taxation, war and civic strife,—and the depressed classes had had but little share in its glories. Thus the too narrow foundation upon which the culture of the ancient world had been erected resulted in its partial disappearance. That it survived at all was in large measure due to the efforts of the Church. The Christian writers preserved the works of the Fathers; these in their turn had drunk not a little

Neglect of classics

from the well of classical culture. There were, of course, those who regarded classical learning as akin to paganism and frowned upon it; [8] but even after the fall of the Empire certain Latin authors were still studied in the schools, especially Ovid, Virgil, Cicero and Seneca.[9] Interest in the classics was, however, but meagre and the attempt to revive their study at Chartres in the twelfth century was not a success; [10] men found that Canon Law and theology, and, in particular the former, were much more profitable subjects for the enterprising cleric who desired promotion; and it was among this class that learning mostly flourished.

Learning in Ireland and England

The lamp of learning in the early middle ages had been preserved in Ireland which had escaped the barbarian invasions, and from it the flame spread to England,[11] and thence, as also from Ireland itself, to the continent. The continental

---

[8] On the dislike of classics see M. Roger *L'Enseignement des lettres classiques* pp. 195 sqq.

[9] Tertullian calls him "saepe noster" (*De Anim.* 20) and St Jerome speaks of "noster Seneca" (*Adv. Jovin.* I. 49); whilst in his native Spain he was, until recently, the subject of popular canonisation: see Lightfoot's Essay "St Paul and Seneca" in his *Philippians* pp. 270 sqq.

[10] See R. L. Poole *Illustrations of Med. Thought and Learning* pp. 101 sqq.

[11] Classical studies in England owed a great debt to the Greek, Theodore of Tarsus, Archbishop of Canterbury 669-690.

revival owed much to Charlemagne who as early as *c.* 787 recommended the foundation of monastic and cathedral schools in a capitulary to Baugulf, Abbot of Fulda. He it was also who brought over Alcuin from York.

During the period from the sixth to the ninth centuries monasteries were the seats of learning, and upheld a comparatively high standard in both religious and secular knowledge.[12] But the monasteries from their retired situations were not easily accessible to the student, and so more and more the cathedral schools took their place. The bishops tended to gather round them learned men and libraries of books; to them came those who desired orders, and their training in theology was naturally preceded by one in letters. In such instructions others would share who did not intend to proceed to ordination, and so the educational system was developed. It should be noticed that every school required the licence of a bishop, as later each university had to receive that of the Pope or Emperor. Cathedral schools flourished especially in the north of France, where Paris and Chartres were outstanding. In England Canterbury, which had a famous library, was a noted centre ; but the fact that so many of the English cathedrals were on a monastic basis made the system a little different. None of the English cathedral schools grew into universities. In Spain Toledo, after its recapture in 1085, became the source of a culture in which there was a large element derived from Moorish sources. In Germany and in Italy political unrest and the struggles between Pope and Emperor prevented the development of letters, and no university was established in the Empire before the middle of the fourteenth century. Rome itself was not eager to set forward higher education, it had enough unruly elements without the added burden of students, though Innocent IV established a school (*studium urbis*), and Charles of Anjou a university (*studium generale*). It was not, however, until Boniface VIII founded the Sapienza that a real start was made.

Margin note: Monasteries and Cathedral Schools

[12] See Laistner *Thought and Letters in Western Europe* pp. 107 sqq. and for later developments A. J. Macdonald *Authority and Reason* pp. 76 sqq. and L. Maitre *Les Écoles Epis. et Monast. à l'Occident.* It should be observed that the ' scholares ' who formed part of the court of the Merovingian kings were not students but young men learning the art of war and of politics.

The universities

The universities grew naturally out of the schools. In their inception the teacher was all-important, and not the place, and since they possessed no buildings migration was easy and not infrequent. The greatest of all the medieval universities was Paris [13], which was indeed the intellectual capital of Europe, as in later ages it was to be the social capital; *la ville lumière* of both epochs. As a centre of learning it first became prominent when crowds flocked to hear William of Champeaux lecturing on universals at the school of Notre Dame. He was publicly opposed by the famous Abailard, [14] who put him to silence and then stepped into his place. With Abailard the real greatness of Paris as an educational centre may be said to have begun. Fulk of Deuil, a contemporary, has left an interesting if somewhat rhetorical testimony to the width of his influence. [15] But it was not to last, for the zealous opposition of St Bernard, with his obscurantist point of view, drove him out to end his days an exile at Cluny. The university itself was not established until the reign of Philip Augustus at the beginning of the thirteenth century.

Abailard

Legal studies

The age which preceded the age of faith might well have been called the age of law, [16] for during the twelfth century there had been a great revival of legal studies in the West, following the development in the East of the previous century. [17] The law schools of Ravenna and Bologna helped in the evolution of the university. But a still more important result was also to follow, for it was not merely the Canon

---

[13] A list of its students and masters would include most of the great men of the middle ages from Innocent III to John Gerson. Cf. Budinszky *Die Universität Paris und die Fremden an derselben im Mittelalter.*

[14] See an excellent recent study by J. G. Sikes *Peter Abailard.*

[15] " Nulla terrarum spatia, nulla concava vallium, nulla via difficilis licet obsita periculo, et latrone, quominus ad te properarent retinebat. Anglorum turbam juvenem mare interjacens et undarum procella terribilis non terrebat : sed omni periculo contempto, audito tuo nomine, ad te confluebat. Remota Britannia (Britanny) sua animalia erudienda destinebat. Andegavenses (the Angevins) eorum edomita feritate tibi famulabantur in suis. Pictavi, Wascones, et Hiberi (Spaniards) : Normannia, Flandria, Teutonicus et Suevius tuum calere ingenium." *Epist.* XVI. in PL. CLXXVIII. coll. 371 sq.

[16] It must not be forgotten that the thirteenth century was also interested in legal matters for it saw not only Frederick II, St Louis, Edward I and other great lawgivers, but the compilation of popular codes such as the *Sachsenspiegel* (c. 1220) and the *Schwabenspiegel* (1275).

[17] Constantine Monomachus had founded a school of law at Constantinople in 1045, partly to train officials and administrators.

Law which was studied in them, but alongside it the old Roman or Civil Law, from which Western jurists were to derive their ideas of absolute monarchy and divine right. This study also provided a rival form of culture to that of the Church, and in the lawyer the Churchman soon found a rival and supplanter in offices of secular administration which he had almost come to regard as his own special prerogatives.

The atmosphere of the schools, moreover, was not entirely favourable to the Church since it fostered much intellectual conceit and a subtle materialism. Bologna in particular earned for itself no good reputation; [18] whilst in Paris the ribald poetry of the Goliardic school was notorious.[19] This literature, which was in part a re-action against puritanism,[20] was crushed out by the thirteenth century, which indeed produced very little Latin poetry of any kind in Paris.[21] There was thus a great need of a more orthodox element in the universities, this was to be supplied by the friars. Up to their coming there had been a serious lack of teachers; for this reason the decree of the Lateran Council of 1179, that divinity lectures should be set up, had to be repeated in 1215. It had been found impossible to observe it through the difficulty of obtaining qualified instructors.[22] *Materialism in the Schools*

It is quite impossible to say what proportion of the population made use of the universities; what is certain is that the numbers have been enormously exaggerated. It has, for instance, been stated that at Oxford in the fourteenth century there were between thirty and sixty thousand students in residence. But, as Workman has pointed out, ' gown ' never outnumbered ' town ' in the frequent riots, and as the population of Oxford, over the age of fourteen, in 1377 *Numbers in the universities*

---

[18] Bologna was attended by many clerics. Its state provoked the question of John of Salisbury (*Epist.* CLXVI.) " Can an archdeacon be saved ? "

[19] See Dobiache-Rojdestvensky *Les Poesies des Goliards* (Paris 1931).

[20] Much of it was produced by clerics and portrayed clerics as the leaders in amorous adventures :

" Quid Dione (i.e. Venus) valeat et amoris deus,
Primo novit clericus et instruxit meus,
Factus est per clericum miles Cythereus."
Carmina Burana p. 160.

[21] See Haskins *Medieval Culture* pp. 37 sq. The rise of vernacular poetry was also a cause of its disappearance.

[22] Denifle *Die Univ. des Mittelalters* I. p. 708.

was less than 2400,[23] the real figures were probably under a thousand.[24]   A similar exaggeration has taken place as to the number of German students who left Prague, after the famous quarrel with the Czechs in May 1409,[25] to found the university of Leipzig. The total entry of students in that year was only 369.[26]   But if numbers were thus exaggerated, the actual influence of the universities was very considerable, and the part which they played in the development of papal theory no small one.

Development of thought   Such then was the background against which Scholasticism grew up. We must now turn to the development of thought prior to its appearance as a definite system or method.

Lost authors   The position of thinkers in the early middle ages was very different from our own. We are in possession of practically all that has gone before us in the way of philosophical thought ; they were acutely conscious that much had been lost. Up to the middle of the twelfth century they had of Plato only the *Phaedo* and *Meno* and part of the *Timaeus* ; of Aristotle at first the *De Interpretatione* alone, then a little later the Categories, then the rest of the *Organon*.[27]   Many other great teachers were known as mere names, save for the fragments of their works which here and there had been preserved like fossils in extracts and quotations. Dr Clement Webb has compared them to " ship-wrecked children . . . haunted by the sense that they were ignorant of much that a past age had known." [28]

Influence of the Neo-Platonists   In the early middle ages the greatest influence was Plato ; but not in a pure form, for it was through the writings of the Neo-Platonists, especially through Plotinus and Porphyry, that it was exercised. To the original Platonic teaching these later thinkers had added a spirit of religious enthusiasm and an ardour for union with the divine which made a strong appeal to Christian philosophers, and not least to St Augustine.

[23] This is based on the poll-tax returns ; see Oman *Great Revolt* p. 164.
[24] Workman *John Wyclif* I. p. 89.
[25] See below p. 194.
[26] See G. Erler *Die Matrikel der Univ. Leipzig* in Codex Dep. Sax. Reg. xvi.
[27] Cf. Abailard's statement : " Aristotelis enim duos tantum, Praedicamentorum scilicet et Peri-Hermenias libros usus adhuc latinorum cognovit " : see *Dialectica* p. 228.
[28] *History of Philosophy* p. 117.

The later middle ages found Plato too discursive and preferred the logical mind of Aristotle.[29]   Yet the influence of Plato never died out entirely, and in the twelfth century the attempted classical revival at Chartres, to which reference has already been made, gave a prominent place to his teaching.[30]

Platonism, however, survived more through indirect than direct agencies, and in particular through the commanding influence of St Augustine.   The part played by this great father in shaping the mind of the West can hardly be exaggerated ; he handed on much of the teaching of the past that was to survive, and his very definiteness, although it provoked opposition in some quarters, was not the less serviceable.   Especially important was his doctrine that knowledge is a kind of intuition, that the mind is capable of receiving direct illumination from God.   This teaching was later on taken up and condemned by St Thomas Aquinas— it formed one of the great subjects of dispute between the Franciscans and Dominicans—as robbing reason of its proper function.   As a good Aristotelian he claimed that knowledge comes from the experience of our senses—*nihil est in intellectu quod non prius fuerit in sensu.* {St Augustine}

Space will not allow anything in the nature of a complete survey of the philosophical thinkers between St Augustine and the emergence of Scholasticism properly so called.   Mention must be made, however, of Boethius the inventor of much of its terminology and definitions,[31] and our English Bede who as a theologian exercised a great influence in the West.[32] Later came John Scotus Erigena, a brilliant but unorthodox thinker who stimulated the thought of his own and subsequent ages, but who cannot be regarded, as is done by some scholars, as in any sense the founder of Scholasticism. {Later influences 480-524 672-735 800-877}

[29] Aristotle has been called the ' father of text-books,' and a reputation for learning in the middle ages really depended on the ability to use text-books and to apply authorities ; a method which was the fruit of the legal mind which dominated them.

[30] The chief name connected with this attempt is Bernard of Chartres who was according to John of Salisbury " perfectissimus inter Platonicos seculi nostri " : see *Metalog.* IV. 35.

[31] See Grabmann *Die Geschichte der schol. Methode* I. pp. 157 sqq. Boethius also did good service by his translations of Aristotle.

[32] Erdmann *Hist. of Phil.* I. pp. 290 sq. (E.T.).   Bede's Commentaries were more important for the middle ages than the much better known Ecclesiastical History : see Laistner *Thought and Letters in Western Europe* p. 123.

Abailard
The real founder must be sought in Abailard to whom reference was made above. He it was who took up the method of the law students and applied it to philosophical questions. He it was who in the famous *Sic et Non* led the way to fuller and more detailed studies. This treatise has sometimes been regarded as an attempt deliberately to promote scepticism, since after stating the arguments for and against a proposition it leaves the reader faced by unreconciled difficulties. But if, as seems probable, it was meant to serve as a kind of basis for his lectures this objection will not stand.

The task of the Schoolmen
The task which the Schoolmen set themselves was nothing less than the reconciliation of philosophy and Christian dogma in a logical scheme which should include the whole of knowledge. It is a task which has constantly to be taken in hand anew and will continue to call forth the energies of Christian thinkers " as long as the human mind continues progressive and religion remains a vital force with it ".[33] This was a vast ambition, but a highly praiseworthy one, for so far as it was successful it gave a common end to education and a cultural tradition which could unite the whole of Western civilisation. Though the design seems to us, with our immensely wider survey of knowledge, to be impossible of attainment, it was a fit product of the architectural age in which it arose, the age which produced the great cathedrals and the *Divina Commedia* of Dante.[34] The new temple of truth was to be built up by a revival of that intellectual passion which had been characteristic of the Greeks and by the same tools, the trained and sharpened wits of men. To St Bernard, who had silenced Abailard, such an application of human reason to divine things would have been repellent if not blasphemous. It is probable that the methods of St Thomas Aquinas would have aroused in him equal alarm though he might have regarded his conclusions as less dangerous.

Medieval philosophy
It has been stated by an eminent authority, the late Hastings Rashdall, that fashions in philosophy change like any other fashions. We can therefore as little expect to

---

[33] Hastings Rashdall *The Universities of Europe in the Middle Ages* I. p. 367.
[34] Cf. Gregorovius *Roman Journal* p. 29 and M. C. D'Arcy *St Thomas Aquinas* p. 4.

appreciate medieval philosophy, without a real effort to understand its point of view, as to admire the pork-pie hats and mutton-chop whiskers of our grandparents. The conception of philosophy's function which then prevailed was vastly different from our own. Medieval thinkers, even in the West, were curiously content with the body of knowledge which had been handed down to them, and almost entirely unaware that whole fields of it might be beyond their ken. They seemed to assume that all the necessary factors were in their possession ; what remained to be done was to arrange them into a system. To ourselves the stock of knowledge increases so rapidly that philosophy has hardly time to grasp a new fact before fresh stores are poured in. Philosophy itself has caught the prevailing tone and desires to discover new truths, more even than to arrange the old. This then is one striking difference between our modes of thought and those of the Schoolmen. Another is the different place assigned to authority. The Schoolmen, depending as they *Foundation* did on logic and dialectic for building up their system, *of the system* had to postulate some solid basis from which to start. This *in revelation* they found in the double gift of God which came through *and reason* revelation and through reason. Revelation was contained in the Scriptures and in Church tradition ; reason was not so much that of the individual, active in themselves and their contemporaries, as the hoarded discoveries of great teachers of the past. Thus in practice the appeal to reason was but an appeal to authority in another guise, the method was entirely or almost entirely deductive.[35] To construct such a system an age was needed which took itself seriously, which tried to see life steadily and to see it whole ; it required an age when men had leisure for meditation, or made it ; an age which was free from the dreadful confusion of thought which arises from the modern notion that speed and progress are identical.

The middle years of the thirteenth century saw a great *The writings* advance in Christian philosophy ; this came about mainly *of Aristotle* from the discovery, through Arabic sources, of the meta-

---

[35] I make this distinction since no system can be purely deductive unless it is dead ; deduction and induction must go on side by side, the difference, considerable though it may be, is one of emphasis ; cf. W. Temple *Mens Creatrix* p. 15.

physical writings of Aristotle. The way for advance had already been prepared; in part by the dialectical training which Abailard and his followers had fostered; in part, by the work of Peter Lombard in mapping out knowledge in his *Liber Sententiarum*. But the acceptance of Aristotle was a necessary preliminary. This great philosopher, though known hitherto only as a logician, was already the supreme force in philosophy.[36] The discovery of the remainder of his writings, however, led to a conflict of opinions and to bitter disputings before finally they received the sanction of orthodox thought. As the opposition arose in the main on account of the immediate source through which his writings came to the West, the Arabic philosophers; it will be well before going further to consider, even if in bare outline only, the way in which it came about that Arabic philosophy should exercise this influence.

Arabic culture

d. 873

d. 950

In the first place it must be made clear that, although the Arabs gave their name to this philosophy, they themselves were not philosophers; the only native Arab whose name stands out is Al-Khindi the founder. After him those who wrote on philosophical subjects in the Arab tongue were not Arabs by race. While the West remained out of touch with the Greeks, Arabic culture was reaching its highest point of development. Probably the greatest of its exponents was Al-Farabi. His attitude towards Aristotle anticipated that of the Schoolmen, for he received him with reverence as a supplement to the revelation contained in the Qur'an and tried to shew that such differences as could be demonstrated were not incompatible with Moslem orthodoxy. This method became in the end dangerous, as it tended to act as a solvent of traditional beliefs, and when in the eleventh century the Turks gained control of the Moslem world, philosophy began to be suspected and so lost its influence just as it was prepared to play a great part in the West.

It is important to remember that the Arabic philosophers attributed to Aristotle, besides his genuine works, the so-called *Theology*; this was in reality Books IV to VI of the *Enneads* of Plotinus. The Neo-Platonic element which it

---

[36] Cf. John of Salisbury :

" Si quis Aristotelem primum non censet habendum
Non reddit meritis praemia digna suis."

Entheticus ll. 815 sq.

introduced into Arabic thought was a link with the Western world when the two cultures came into touch. This was not, of course, the only point of contact ; one might indeed say that Arabic philosophy directed Christian thought more or less unconsciously into new channels by presenting old material which actually underlay it in a new guise. Hence the ease with which it was assimilated.

The philosophers whose names are best known in the West 980-1036 were Avicenna (Ibn Sina) and Averroes (Ibn Rushd). They 1126-1198 both owed much to the teaching of Al-Farabi, and not a little of Neo-Platonism was contained in their writings. Avicenna and Maimonides (Ibn Maymun), the Jewish philosopher who wrote in Arabic, had done much to continue the work of 1135-1204 Al-Farabi by reducing Aristotle to Moslem orthodox standards. By so doing they had brought his teaching closer into line with Christian ideas. But Averroes refused to force Aristotle into a ready-made mould and even went out of his way, in order to redress the balance, to bring out points of difference. Hence in the eyes of orthodox Christians he came to be regarded as a potential source of evil; and it was largely because of this that the opposition to Aristotle was aroused and a definite campaign undertaken to reject him as a teacher of Western Christendom. In 1210 a Council at Siena forbade Attack on the use of his books on Natural Science ; five years later the the writings Statutes of the University of Paris banned the Physics and of Aristotle Metaphysics ; then in 1231 a commission was appointed to expurgate his writings and so fit them for orthodox readers. This last step was a sign that Aristotle was proving too strong for his opponents.[37] The commission never completed its work since the interpretations of St Albertus Magnus [38] and St Thomas rendered it unnecessary.[39] Their labours placed Aristotle in a position of security and authority, and by 1255 his writings were prescribed for the degree of Master of Arts at Paris itself.

But though Aristotle was restored to a somewhat doubtful The Averroists

[37] Jacques de Vitry records that even when he was forbidden men still read him in secret and so corrupted their faith : see Haureau *Phil. Scholastique* Pt. II. I. p. 108 n.

[38] Albertus Magnus was canonised on Decr. 16, 1931.

[39] Amongst other things they had new translations made without the Arabic glosses and free from any trace of the Arabic taint which had aroused the first opposition.

favour there was still to be considerable trouble with his
Arabic commentators.   Avicenna was comparatively un-
objectionable, but Averroes was a source of much unsettlement.   His chief advocate was Siger of Brabant who claimed
to hold his doctrines together with orthodox Christianity ;
as these included a belief in the eternity of matter and a single
intellect in all men (which involves the denial of personal
immortality) it is easy to understand the outcry which was
raised by his stand.   That he also advocated the theory of
two spheres of truth (i.e. that a thing may be true in theology
though not in philosophy [40]) did not help the situation.
Averroes, in spite of his unorthodoxy, exercised considerable
influence, and St Thomas himself seems to have owed a good
deal to him not only in philosophy but also in theology for
his method of treating doctrinal subjects is almost identical.[41]

The chief influence on St Thomas and his master St Albert
was Aristotle ; it is easy, however, to exaggerate its extent ;
certainly his authority was never regarded by them as un-
limited.[42]   St Thomas whilst accepting it wherever possible,
and indeed making his teaching the basis of his own, is never
enslaved by him.   Part of the excessive idea of his dependence is due to the scrupulosity with which any indebtedness
is acknowledged and any parallel adduced.

St Albertus
Magnus

Having come to these two great names something must
be said of their achievements and influence.   St Albertus
was a man of vast learning, part of which he had acquired in
Italy, and he had, what was not very common in the thirteenth
century, an interest in Natural Science.   His scientific researches led to his being popularly regarded as a magician.
In some quarters it has been the fashion to regard him as a
mere compiler and to see his chief service to learning in the
stimulus which he gave to his greater pupil.   But this was
by no means the case.   Albertus was an independent thinker

[40] This theory which was later to be adopted by more orthodox thinkers
is really an exceedingly old one and exists wherever there is a religion for the
people and a religion for philosophers side by side ; or, as Scaevola (Consul in
B.C. 95) put it, where you have a religion of the intellect and a religion of
tradition.

[41] See Fr Asin *El Averroismo de Santo Tomas de Aquino* (1904).

[42] " Qui credit Aristotelem fuisse Deum, ille debet credere quod numquam
erravit.   Si autem credit ipsum esse hominem, tunc procul dubio errare
potuit sicut et nos : " Albertus Magnus *Phys.* VIII. tract. I. cap. xiv.

and discoverer, and had he been less his influence would not
have persisted as it did right down into the fifteenth century.[43]

The supreme name, however, is that of St Thomas of St Thomas
the noble race, Lombard and Norman by origin, of the Counts Aquinas
of Aquino.[44]   In his person, in spite of his Teutonic lineage,
it is pleasant to see a revival of the philosophical traditions
of Magna Graecia ; later the same district was to see the rise
of Giordano Bruno and Campanella.

The industry of St Thomas was amazing, for during his
lifetime of only forty-eight years he produced thirty large
volumes of philosophy and theology, besides numerous
hymns.[45]   With his learning he combined a devout and even
mystical spirit.   It is often supposed that philosophy and
mysticism are naturally exclusive since the one demands an
intellectual, even a critical attitude towards life, the other a
receptive.   But in spite of this individual philosophers have
quite frequently been mystics.[46]   It is probable that this
combination of philosopher and saint gave to Aquinas his
deep insight into the problems which he set himself to solve ;
it certainly helps to explain his profound influence upon the
thought of the Catholic Church, which is exceeded, if exceeded
at all, only by that of St Augustine.[47]

In view of this it is almost startling to find that Opposition to
immediately after his death his teaching met with much his teaching
opposition.   No doubt the insistence on the function of
reason aroused a suspicion of rationalism.   There was also a
fear that he was unduly responsive to Arabic and pagan
influences; Aristotle, after all, was a dangerous master for

[43] M. Grabmann has recently been working on unpublished MSS and his
work shows Albertus in a more worthy light : see *Zeit. für Kath. Theol.* XXV.
pp. 153 sqq. and 313 sqq.

[44] It is curious to notice that Aquino was also the native town of Juvenal
and Pescennius Niger.   They form a strange trio; the satirist, the Roman
Emperor, and the medieval philosopher.

[45] Among them are " Pange lingua," " Tantum ergo," " Verbum supernum
prodiens," and " Adoro te devote, latens deitas."   The authorship, however,
is not always certain.

[46] Cf. Denifle's assertion that mysticism and scholasticism are not neces-
sarily antitheses ; see *Archiv.* II. p. 426.   It is significant that Mechthild of
Hackeborn, the thirteenth century German mystic, saw in a vision both
Albertus and Aquinas entering into Paradise.

[47] Acton, whilst recognising this, in one of his paradoxical statements once
observed that neither he, nor Aristotle, nor Cicero, nor St Augustine himself,
had produced so great an effect by his writings as Rousseau ;   see *Letters of
Lord Acton to Mary Gladstone* p. x.

a Christian philosopher. The writings of Aquinas were condemned at Paris in December 1270 and March 1277 ; [48] whilst at Oxford, where his influence never really took a firm hold, they experienced the same fate.[49] They were also denounced by Archbishop Peckham in 1284 ; [50] but as he was a Franciscan, the first to be Archbishop of Canterbury, party feeling may have prompted the action.[51] In 1323, however, St Thomas was canonised and from that time onwards he was safe from attack, as no unorthodox writer would have received such recognition.

The achievement of the Schoolmen We have seen the noble and ambitious ideal which the Schoolmen set before them, we have now to ask how far they were successful in realising it. If we make due allowance for the limitations under which they laboured it must be admitted that they succeeded ; they actually gave to the world of their day what we in the present so sorely lack—a unified outlook on life based on a systematic harmonising of the knowledge of the times. For generations the Schoolmen represented the central march of European thought ; others merely wandered in bye-ways. They might come of various races and disagree on many points of detail, but they held to one all-inclusive method and their thoughts were presented through the medium of one all-inclusive language. This last factor no doubt had much to do with the unity of their system and the extent of their harmony.[52] The method itself was an admirable training for the intellect, and in the ability to carry through an argument from agreed premises right to its conclusion the Schoolmen have never been excelled. This has been admitted by those who have no sympathy with their doctrines.[53]

[48] See Denifle and Chatelain *Chartularium Univ. Parisiensis* I. pp. 487, 543, sqq., and II. p. 280.

[49] See A. Wood *Hist. and Antiquities of the Univ. of Oxford* I. p. 306.

[50] *Reg. Peckham* III. pp. 852, 866 and 896 sqq.

[51] Archbishop Kilwardby, a Dominican, had already denounced parts of St Thomas' teaching.

[52] " When you read modern philosophy in English, French, German, and Italian, you may be struck by national and racial differences of thought : modern languages *tend* to separate abstract thought—mathematics is now the only universal language." T. S. Eliot *Dante* pp. 18 sq.

[53] Cf. Condorcet *Vie de Turgot* (quoted by J. S. Mill *System of Logic* p. 10). " Scholasticism, which in its logic, as in its ethics and in part in its metaphysics, engendered a subtilty and precision of ideas to which the ancient thinkers were unaccustomed, has contributed more than is believable to the progress of good philosophy."

In spite, however, of this high achievement Scholasticism, Loss of
as a system of philosophy, in the years that followed the death prestige and
of St Thomas, came gradually to lose prestige ; it experienced its causes
the fate of other systems and was enfeebled by the ravages
of time.   At last in the age of the Renaissance it was regarded
as so much intellectual rubbish, impressive merely by its
magnitude.   The reasons for this decay are fairly obvious.
They may be grouped under three heads ; the disunion of
the Schoolmen themselves ; defects in the method ; and,
perhaps most suggestive of all, defects in its application.

As to disagreements between Schoolmen.   We have Quarrels of
already noticed the struggle with Siger of Brabant and the the
Averroists, and that between the Franciscans—who held to Schoolmen
St Augustine and the possibility of divine illumination—and
the Dominicans, who, as followers of St Thomas, emphasised
the place of reason as a means of discovering truth.   Of the
former contest nothing more requires to be said ; of the latter
a great deal, for out of it grew a movement which was to
undermine confidence in the power of reason itself.   The
most noted names in this school, both be it noted Franciscans,
were Duns Scotus and William of Ockham.   The former by Duns Scotus
his criticisms really robbed the faith of all rational basis and d. 1308.
incidentally shook the validity of the whole scholastic position.   For him dogma was based on the authority of the
Church and could not be demonstrated by human reason.   It
was no accident that on the one hand he thought less of
Aristotle than previous Schoolmen, and on the other that
he exalted the place of tradition.   Though not actually a
nominalist himself, his writings prepared the way for the
triumph of the nominalists in the following century and
nominalism is always a disintegrating force.[54]   Ockham, who
held that thought can deal only with abstract terms and William of
that we have no knowledge of their relation to reality, was Ockham
still more agnostic in his outlook.   He applied the same d. 1347
principles to human society, and in consequence refused
to recognise in such institutions as the State and the
Church anything more than the aggregate of their members.
We shall come across Ockham again in the contest between

---

[54] He exercised great influence on the Ockhamist, Gabriel Biel, who in
turn influenced Luther.

Lewis of Bavaria and the Papacy. In spite of frequent condemnation by representative bodies [55] his teaching continued to spread and the realists lost ground steadily before it.[56]

Defects of the system

We come now to defects in Scholasticism as a system. In the first place there was, as Roger Bacon, another Franciscan, pointed out, too great a reliance on authority and too little place given to experiment.[57] The Schoolmen, whilst they accounted for moral and spiritual values, gave no adequate account of natural phenomena,[58] in fact they were strangely blind to physical nature as a whole, and the visible came almost to be regarded as the irrational, certainly as the insignificant. It is true that St Thomas has the promise of better things for he held that the scientific theories of his day were mere hypotheses which might at length be disproved ; it was never his business, however, to test them.[59] They were indifferent to natural instincts, except as the source of temptation. Art and beauty were outside their province and received but scant treatment ; even the aesthetics of St Thomas are very unsatisfactory when we consider that he was endeavouring to bring the whole of thought within his system.[60]

[55] As by the Faculty of Arts at Paris ; see Denifle and Chatelain *Chartularium* II. pp. 485, 505 etc.   Ockham was also summoned to Avignon to answer for statements made in his Oxford Lectures : see Pelzer " Les 51 art. de G. Occam censurés à Avignon " in *Rev. d'Hist. Eccl.* XVIII. (1922).

[56] Workman considers that " Hus was condemned as much for being a realist in philosophy as for being a heretic in theology " ; see *John Wyclif* I. p. 114.

[57] But cf. Hastings Rashdall in his edition of *Compendium Studii Theologiae* p. 3.   " Bacon was more the child of his age than he imagined himself to be. . . . There is a certain irony in the fact that the writer's argument in favour of independent thinking as against authority consists chiefly of a series of citations from Scripture, Cicero, Pliny and Seneca."

[58] There were exceptions such as Albertus.   It may be observed that present-day attempts to arrive at a philosophy err in the opposite direction.

[59] His remarks on the movements of the planets are a good instance : " Licet enim talibus suppositionibus factis apparentia salvarentur, non tamen oportet dicere has suppositiones esse veras, quia forte secumdum aliquem alium modum, nondum ab hominibus comprehensum, apparentia circa stellas salvantur."   Quoted by De Wulf *Scholasticism* p. 150.

[60] Father D'Arcy has commented on St Thomas' indifference to art and his failure to discuss the nature of beauty.   He regarded it, not as a supreme mode of being such as Truth and Goodness, but merely as part of the latter : see *St Thomas Aquinas* pp. 140 sq.   It is interesting to notice that St Augustine saw the highest manifestation of beauty, which he identified with symmetry, in Righteousness : *Epist.* CXX.

The result of this neglect of observation was that their Neglect of observation and criticism theories were spun out regardless of facts. The super-structure was raised upon a foundation which had never been examined, and as it rose higher and higher it took to itself very fantastic forms. When once the basis was attacked the whole system fell, because it contained so many unproved assumptions. As we have seen, the Schoolmen regarded the task of philosophy not as the search for new truth but as the arranging of what was already known. They had therefore an instinctive shrinking from what was likely to upset their scheme, of the very possibility of things outside it. In short they attempted to make a system before all the facts had been collected; a mistake into which man is ever falling, he desires to unify his experience, and is amazingly apt to be impatient of " the lingering processes of thought ".

The unwillingness of the Schoolmen to face new truth had Stereotyped also a practical side to it. Their whole mental outlook was legalistic, and the tendency of the legal mind is to become stereotyped. They would have echoed Cleon's paradox, and preferred bad laws that were stable to good ones which had lost their authority through constant change.[61] Thus change, even when it came in the form of improvement, was dreaded as the harbinger of confusion and uncertainty.

The very method of the Schoolmen had its dangers and Oversubtle tended to produce a race of thinkers who were oversubtle, and in the end sceptical. They forgot that truth is often to be recognised by its vagueness and that precision by no means denotes accuracy. Petrarch in 1823 had already begun to see the dangers of the method, and complained that philosophy was being prostituted, and had become a process of hair-splitting and vain words in which truth itself was allowed to slip out.[62] The desire for definition rather than truth ends in an exact system of theology and an entire absence of any trace of spiritual life.

The love of disputing for its own sake had been a mark of the early days of the movement. John of Salisbury was himself fired with ardour over such discussions. But time

---

[61] Thucydides III. 37.

[62] Roger Bacon bitterly attacked the older schoolmen, Alexander of Hales, Albertus and Aquinas as prolix and ignorant : *Opus Minus* pp. 325 sqq. (RS.).

brought disillusionment, and he has told how he returned to the scene of his former joyous debates, only to find the same old questions and the same old arguments still in vogue after the lapse of twelve years.   He concludes his description with the reflection ;   " thus experience taught me a manifest conclusion that whereas dialectic furthers other studies, so if it remains by itself it lies bloodless and barren, nor does it quicken the soul to yield fruit of philosophy, except the same conceive from elsewhere." [63]   Thus it had been in the first ages of Scholasticism and thus it came again to be after a period of more vigorous life in its period of decline.   The end of such a process is scepticism and disillusionment, the doctrine of the two truths became more and more the refuge of those who despaired of reconciling philosophy and religion. But even in its decay Scholasticism was preparing the way for fresh developments and the training which it gave had not been in vain.   The new constructive thought which grew out of the Renaissance was to be founded on a broader basis because of the critical work which the later Schoolmen had accomplished.   They had cleared the site for a new structure.

Effect on the Papacy   Scholasticism, in its growth as well as in its decay, had a profound effect on the development of the Papacy.   The method had reached its golden age at a time when the Popes had established their supremacy over the Church and seemed about to turn Europe into a theocracy.   A system of philosophy which was based on authority was obviously of untold value in giving a submissive tone to men's minds. Popes and Schoolmen alike aimed at unity based on authority. This service which the Schoolmen rendered was indirect. But there was also the direct bolstering up of the papal position ;   St Thomas was the first to include a chapter ' On the prerogatives of the pope ' as an essential part of a treatise on the Church.[64]

But the growth of Scholasticism was not all pure gain to the Papacy.   Aquinas himself had laid great stress on the test which Aristotle applied to an institution—was it fulfilling

---

[63] *Metal.* II. 10.   Quoted by R. L. Poole *Illustrations of Med. Thought and Learning* pp. 185 sq.   Cf. also the comparison by Alan of Lille of logic " to a pale maiden emaciated and exhausted by too protracted vigils " : see De Wulf *Scholasticism* p. 142.

[64] See Salmon *The Infallibility of the Church* pp. 451 sq.

its end ?   The time was soon to come when this test would be applied to the Papacy.   He had also insisted, again following Aristotle, that the State was a necessary element to a full and complete life, not a mere device, as some had taught, to counter-act the sin of Adam.   The spread of such teaching was bound to modify all theories of the relation of Church and State.[65]

So much then for the growth of Scholasticism.   Its decay also had an effect on the Papacy, for it brought with it a loss of prestige to its patron, the Church in which it had been the accepted philosophical creed.   In accepting fresh light from a novel philosophy religion tends to be re-stated in terms of that system ;   when the assimilation is carried too far and verges on identification danger arises.   The Church " has no more right to identify itself with any intellectual situation than it has to pin its fortunes to those of any political dynasty ".[66] Thus the decay of Scholasticism in itself was a blow to the Church and the Papacy.

Worse still was the critical and sceptical spirit which was engendered by the undue extension of the Scholastic method.   We have already noticed St Bernard's alarm at the idea of any discussion of the fundamentals of the faith ; the best of the Schoolmen had differed from him in this and they were, in the true sense of the word, rationalists.[67]   But the nominalists by reducing all things to a matter of opinion gave fresh life to that vague restlessness which had been secretly present for centuries and which ultimately was to lead to Protestantism.[68]   There was, of course, another side to the process, for the uncertainty which the nominalists aroused made the weaker spirits cling the more closely to the Church's authority.

One symptom of the extent to which the Papacy had lost the control of the educational and philosophical system was the change in the attitude of the universities.   In the thirteenth century they had furnished the chief defenders and advocates of the papal system ;   in the fourteenth they were

Growth of Sceptical Spirit

Changed attitude of the universities

[65] Acton used to say that " not the devil but St. Thomas Aquinas was the first Whig " ;   quoted by Figgis *From Gerson to Grotius* p. 9.

[66] H. Scott Holland in *Lux Mundi* (15th ed.) p. 27.

[67] The Schoolmen gave to reason a much higher place than did the Reformers.

[68] Cf. Inge *Christian Ethics etc.* pp. 228 sq.

to provide its chief critics and assailants ; " C'est Paris qui a fait Constance " [69]

The friars   We now turn to the other great movement which added distinction to the age of faith—the friars.   This movement was a development of monasticism, and in order to understand **Monasticism** it some space must be devoted to the earlier growth.   Monasticism arose first in the East, and has about it nothing distinctly Christian ; one might go even further and say that since its underlying principle seems to be dualistic, it is definitely sub-Christian.   It placed before men the ideal of complete renunciation of this present world.   Incidentally the earliest monks also renounced the secularised Church of their day, and cut themselves off from the sacramental system, for they were hermits living in isolation.   It should be noticed that the hermit *motif* continually crops up afresh in the history of what came to be known as ' religion '.[70]   The name most closely connected with this stage of Christian monasticism is St Antony.   The next stage is reached when a group of hermits collects round a common centre, and with this stage the name of St Pachomius, another Egyptian, will always be associated.[71]   Then there comes the need for a stricter organisation with a definite order and a common rule of life.

In the East   In the East monasticism remained out of touch with the world and even with the Church—save now and then when the monks intervened as a violently conservative force in theological disputes—the price of independence was, however, stagnation.   The monastic life was an end in itself ; the monk never went forth to succour humanity, as he did in the more practical West.   In silence he awaited the divine illumination. The West, indeed, found the new institution useful from the first ; Cassiodorus, for example, regarded the cloister as a

[69] In this connexion it is interesting to notice that one of the bases of conciliar action was the Aristotelian doctrine of ἐπιείκεια.   This was first brought out by Henry of Langenstein in his *Consilium Pacis :* " est quaedam virtus, quam Aristoteles V Ethic vocat epieikeian, quae est directiva justi legalis ".

[70] The parochial clergy were known as ' seculars '.   There is something a trifle arrogant in this distinction and Eugenius III (1145-1153), himself a monk, refused to recognise it : see John of Salisbury *Hist. Pont.* xlv.

[71] Egypt had many pre-Christian monastic establishments (see Dill *Roman Society in the Last Century of the Western Empire* p. 66) and some think Pachomius had been a monk of Serapis before becoming a Christian.

means of fostering learning and education, while Charlemagne valued it as a place for training learned men who as often as not were used as officials.[72]

Eastern monasticism was intense in its devotion to ascetic practices and anticipated the flaming fanaticism of Islam ; [73] Procopius wrote of the monastery of St Catherine under Mount Sinai, that life there was only a careful study of death.[74] The West, with a few striking exceptions, found that under harsher skies it had to be content with more moderate austerities ; but the connexion with the East, which had first grown up during the exile of St Athanasius, was never forgotten, and even in the days of St Bernard was remembered with pride.[75]

The first name in Western monasticism which deserves In the West mention is that of St Benedict. He began as a hermit, but about 528 founded the famous monastery of Monte Cassino. Probably he had no idea of starting a world-wide order and his rule was intended for single houses only. This independence of the Benedictine houses was to prove a source of weakness, for there was no check on unworthy abbots and monks, and no protection against the aggression of local bishops or nobles.

Decay soon fell on the order, for its members were drawn into secular business, the burden of administration came upon them, ideals grew dim and life relapsed to a worldly level. The monasteries suffered greatly from raids of heathen folk, Danes and others, and many were destroyed.[76] Then in the tenth century came a revival of monastic life,[77] in part Revival at as a reaction against the materialism which seemed every- Cluny where to have got the upper hand. The most famous centre of this revival was Cluny where Odo strove to restore ' re-

---

[72] See Hauck *Kirchengeschichte Deutschlands* II. pp. 578 sqq.

[73] Monasticism was no part of Islam originally, the practice was borrowed from other sources.

[74] Quoted *Camb. Med. Hist.* III p. 547.

[75] William of St Thierry on a visit to Clairvaux felt himself carried back to the ancient fathers of the desert—" quasi . . . me videre et antiquorum Aegyptiorum monacorum patrum nostrorum antiquas semitas ". See *Vita Prima S. Bernardi Abbatis* I. vii. (*Opera S. Bernardi* II. col. 1077 B.).

[76] So the Mediterranean pirates of the first century B.C. had plundered the rich temples along the coast of Greece and Asia Minor.

[77] There was also a revival in the East. It was in 961 that St. Laura on Mount Athos wa s founded.

ligion ', and was not unmindful of the part which the monk
might play in educating the young. Cluny was important
in other ways for it checked the tendency in Germany for
monasteries to become, like parish churches, the property of
families, and restored the Roman ideals of discipline and
uniformity.[78] One of the great means by which this was
carried out was the linking up of the whole order [79] under
the Abbot of Cluny who had jurisdiction over the daughter
houses.

The
Carthusians

At the end of the eleventh century came another experiment, the foundation by St Bruno of the Carthusians. They
were in a way a return to the Eastern ideal of the hermit,
since the monks were to live in separate cells or houses and to
join only in a certain number of common services and meals.
This order managed to avoid wealth and power more successfully than the rest and so was foremost in retaining its purity.

The
Cistercians

A little later came the Cistercians. The chief influence in
this order was Stephen Harding, the Englishman who although
he was not the actual founder gave to it its character by
the *Carta Caritatis*. Like the Cluniacs the Cistercians were
grouped under a single abbot, and their endeavour was to
avoid all ostentation and to live and worship in surroundings
of the greatest simplicity. They were, for example, to have
no rich vestments or decorated churches and even the books
in the library were not to be illuminated. The greatest name
among them was St Bernard of Clairvaux.

The achieve-
ments of
monasticism

If the services of the monks in preserving learning and
promoting education were not so great as has sometimes been
imagined they had much else to their credit. To them in
no small degree was due the extension of Christianity beyond
the limits of the Roman Empire, and the names of Columbanus,
Gall, Willibrord and Winfrith stand high in the list of
missionary heroes. In addition to this in their early days
they set a pattern of purity and self-denial ; they were pioneers
too in agriculture and in reclaiming waste and forest land.[80]
Perhaps one of their most important services was to preserve
in ruder times and people the distinction between laymen and

[78] See L. M. Smith *Early Cluny* pp. 2 sq.
[79] Although it is convenient to speak of the Cluniacs as an order, strictly
speaking they were a group of reformed Benedictines.
[80] See Cunningham *Western Civilisation etc.* II. pp. 85 sqq.

clerics, or at least to set before clerics the ideal of a life of Its decay separation.[81]

The first generations of monks were giants, " deep-chested and strong-lunged men, who held their heads high. They felled oaks and proclaimed new tidings." [82] But soon decay came upon them and the reasons for it lie close at hand : they are various and natural. It was, for example, necessary when the original members of the community grew infirm to relax the strict rule so as to preserve their lives.[83] The next generation of monks tended to start where these left off. Then again when an order was new and struggling it attracted only those who were in deadly earnest ; with fame there followed a rush of less worthy brethren.[84]

As wealth increased and property of one kind or another Increase of came into the possession of the monasteries the monks were wealth compelled to spend much of their time in secular affairs.[85] The papal favour had a similar effect as political missions were entrusted to monks. It was often enough only a small proportion who attended the chapel services with any regularity.[86] Even St Bernard's secretary complained that he was kept busy from morning to night whilst others had time for the contemplation of God. Some no doubt were glad to give themselves to administrative duties in order to fill the aching vacuity within.

The number of those who went into monasteries, after the Unworthy first flush of enthusiasm, from worthy motives was probably monks always small. They were safer within the walls and more comfortable than without, and they ' crept in out of the cold '. Life in a monastery was no harder than in a castle, much

[81] See Fisher *The Mediaeval Empire* II. pp. 81 sq. He points out that as late as the thirteenth century German councils had to order clerics to be tonsured.

[82] Anatole France *Life and Literature* I. p. 24.

[83] St Bernard himself was once found by the French king, much to his surprise, eating roast chicken. The saint explained that he did so by no wish of his own but in obedience to the order of his superior.

[84] Bede noticed already that many crowded into monasteries who had no vocation ; *Epist. ad Egbertum* § 11.

[85] The records of the times shew that the roads swarmed with monks riding about on secular business. The Abbey of St Edmundsbury had property in no less than 250 different townships.

[86] In the days immediately before the Reformation only a quarter of the monks attended the services at Peterborough ; the officials on great festivals only : see *Lincoln Records Society* XXIII. p. 273.

better than in a peasant's hut.   But it was not often that peasants were allowed to become monks save as lay brothers,[87] for the monasteries and convents were means of providing for the future of the younger members of noble families, and admission involved the payment of a premium.[88]   The monks were very like fellows of a College or even the country gentlemen of their day.[89]   It was to them only reasonable that those who desired to share their property should pay for the privilege or be such as would prove welcome companions.   It is true that the monasteries were supposed to dispense hospitality, and many did so ; but it was the great man with his train of servants who was the chief gainer, since he was able to enforce his rights, and to billet himself on the monastery.   The poor man had often a very cold reception.[90]

Much of the laxity, however, must be traced back to the almost superhuman standard set for the monk ; human nature was wound too high and reaction was bound to follow.   Even mirth was forbidden by some leaders.[91]   The height from which they fell meant often enough a plunge into the depths and any attempt at reform was liable to be resisted even with the dagger and the poisoned cup.[92]   The whole conception of the ascetic life as superior to that of the ordinary Christian was wrong, since it tended to make the monk despise those outside, and made asceticism an end in itself ; it brought its own punishment.[93]

[87] " To the coarse and common people the monastery remained as inaccessible as the castle " : Harnack *Monasticism* p. 95.   This was not so originally for St Augustine states that most monks in his day were " ex conditione servili " ; see *De Oper. Monach.* xxii.

[88] This practice was denounced by the Lateran Council of 1215.

[89] Such is Chaucer's idea of the monk in the Prologue to the Canterbury Tales.

[90] When St Francis was robbed near Gubbio he sought the nearest monastery.   He was sent into the kitchen, but nothing was done for him and in a few days he left in disgust.   When he had become famous the prior apologised ; but that did not make the case any better : see Celano *Leg. Prima* xvi.

[91] St Bernard considered that ' thoughtless mirth ' was the third degree of pride (*De Gradibus Humil. et Superbiae* xii in *Opera.* I col. 575) and his ideal Templar was to be free from *risus immoderatus* (*Ad Milites Templi* iv. in *Opera* I. col. 547 E).   Bede condemned a certain bishop for having about him men given to laughter and jesting ; *Epist. ad Egbertum* § 4.

[92] Attempts were made on the life of St Benedict ; whilst cases of abbots who were murdered or driven out because of their efforts to enforce discipline were distressingly frequent.

[93] Hastings Rashdall has remarked that " self-sacrifice for its own sake is always irrational and immoral.   It is the object for which the sacrifice is made that gives it its moral value : " see *Theory of Good and Evil* II. p. 70.

At the close of the twelfth century monasticism was at Importance the height of its power and influence; but its importance of monasticism came chiefly from the fact that the monasteries were great land-owners, and was political and economic rather than religious. There was evident need of a further revival. That revival came with the rise of the friars.

The original monks had thought to serve God by fleeing from the world; [94] the monastic settlements therefore had been generally placed in remote spots where quiet and retirement could be had most easily. The friars, on the other hand, The friars began as a species of religious tramp and chose for their settlements sites in the midst of the people whose burdens they desired to share. Many of the friaries were established in the newly developed suburbs. [95] Like the first monks the early friars were laymen [96] and like them again they were to support themselves by their labours although in case of necessity they were allowed to beg for food but not for money. [97] Brother Giles, even when staying with great people, always went out and worked to pay for his keep. [98]

Associations of lay people for spiritual purposes had been Lay a common feature of Christian life for some generations, associations especially in Lombardy; but their members had a tendency to run over into heresy and to take up a wandering life. The friars were at first to suffer for their likeness to these sectaries, and when Francis approached Innocent III in 1210 he had some difficulty in obtaining papal approval.

The two original orders of friars, the Franciscans and the The Franciscans and the Dominicans

[94] A favourite text, supposed to be Scripture (!), said that the monk who left his cloister would experience the fate of the fish that left the water.

[95] Strangely enough the early monasteries, such as were not built in lonely places, were founded in the suburbs of the old Roman towns which were very small and had no space for fresh buildings : Lot *The End of the Ancient World* p. 368.

[96] Francis himself began as a layman and never progressed beyond the diaconate. The Ministers General up to 1239 were also laymen, a source of some of the quarrels in the Order.

[97] The name mendicant friars and their later habits have obscured the original intention. Francis in his last instructions directed that friars were to be taught a trade. Cf. Burkhard *Chron.* MGH. SS. XXIII. p. 376 : " Pauperes Minores . . . neque pecuniam nec quicquam aliud praeter victum accipiebant et si quando vestem necessariam quisquam ipsis sponte conferebat, non enim quicquam petebant ab aliquo." Jacques de Vitry says of the Poor Clares : " Nihil accipiunt sed de labore manuum vivunt " : see Sabatier *Speculum Perfect.* p. 300.

[98] *Life* V. in *I Fioretti del . . . S. Francesco e de' suoi frati.*

Dominicans, arose at the same time, a sure indication to Dante of their providential origin.[99]   In their early stages they had some points of resemblance and some of difference ; later they tended to assimilate their methods and to become rivals.   This was good neither for them nor the Church. The Franciscans dealt with the poorer classes, the Dominicans with the more learned, until the death of Francis, who regarded learning with suspicion, released the former for this service also.   On the whole the Dominicans were the more conservative order and less extreme ;   the Franciscans the seed ground for various heretical beliefs.

The founders   Of the two founders St Dominic has never received that meed of attention which his merits and his achievements deserve.   He has not, of course, the winning grace of Francis, but he repays study.[100]   The interest in St Francis is worldwide ;   but it is well to remember that it is of comparatively recent growth and much of it dates from the magnificent biography by the Protestant, Sabatier.[101]

St Dominic was of noble birth,[102] and came to his mission when well advanced in his manhood ;   he was a crusader against heresy and unbelief ;   but a crusader who fought with the weapons of the mind.   St Francis arose from the wealthy merchant class which was then attaining to new importance with the growth of trade.   The one was a native of Spain, the other of that mystic hill country of Umbria which was also to see the visions of St Catherine of Siena and to live reflected for ever in the backgrounds of Perugino's masterpieces.

St Francis   St Francis was a supreme example of that order of souls who go through life scattering sweet influences around them, who when they are gone seem still to leave " a cometary wake of trailing music ".   The echo of his life comes to us across the ages like the faint tones of a melody heard in the stillness of the night.   He entered on his mission at a time when men had come to regard religion as a hard, unnatural

[99] *Paradiso* xi. 28 sqq.

[100] There is a good recent life of St Dominic by Fr Bede Jarrett.

[101] It is significant that when Goethe visited Assisi in October 1786 he tells us in his *Italienische Reise* that he passed by the Church of St Francis with disgust (mit Abneigung) to visit the Temple of Minerva.

[102] A. G. Little, however, questions his connexion with the house of Guzman ;   *Camb. Med. Hist.* VI. p. 737.

thing, and a saint as someone very different from common man. Francis shewed them that religion was very simple and natural ; it was not the life of the ascetic, full of morbid renunciations, but a life lived among men, the life of Jesus Himself. To the conventionally religious the outlook of Francis was a problem, and after his death his own order did its best to turn him into a conventional saint by the suppression of all evidence which did not fit in with such an ideal.[103] But though at times he did over-burden ' Brother Body ' Francis was no mere ascetic. We see that from the very human story of his death-bed when he longed for a visit from his devoted woman friend, Jacopa di Settesoli, and the marzipan cakes which she used to make for him. Jacopa was with him at the end, and when the saint was dead Brother Elias, a sympathetic act from that hard man, placed his body in her arms with the words ; " Hold even in death him whom you cherished when alive ".[104] All this was rather shocking to the later Franciscans, and they quietly set aside the story and Jacopa herself, leaving St Clare as almost the sole woman in his life.[105] Even his attitude to poverty has been mis-understood. He quite literally was in love with it, and re-garded the absence of the responsibilities of possessions as a welcome relief. " We are accustomed," as Dr A. G. Little has said, " to think of a poor man as one who lacks riches : St Francis thought of a rich man as one who lacked the in-estimable boon of poverty." [106]

The coming of the friars was followed by many and various Results of results. Their preaching, in particular that of the Franciscans, the coming of the friars

[103] When St Bonaventura had compiled the official life the Chapter of 1266 ordered all others to be destroyed. The order, however, could not be enforced and the two lives by Thomas of Celano fortunately survive. The *Fioretti* were not collected until the beginning of the fourteenth century.

[104] The visit is recorded by Thomas of Celano and confirmed from other sources ; see Sabatier *Vie de S. François d'Assise* p. 465 (1931 ed.).

[105] Mrs Strong says : " In the Franciscan legend Jacopa's place has been usurped by St Clare. Art, as well as the Fioretti, has made Clare the prom-inent, indeed the only woman knit in sympathy with St Francis " : see *Commemoration Essays* p. 297.

[106] The same idea underlies the poem of the later Franciscan poet, Jacopone da Todi, when he writes :

> " Poverty has nothing in her hand,
> Nothing craves in sea or land :
> Hath the universe at her command,
> Dwelling in the heart of liberty."

caused a wave of revival to sweep over the Church and influenced strongly the rising trading class. It was upon them also that the care of the ' suburban ' populations chiefly fell. By admitting to their order members of the middle and poorer classes they obtained a footing in the democracy which the older and more aristocrat orders could not have done. It is possible too that by elevating poverty into a virtue they staved off revolutionary outbreaks.[107] Their work for higher education also bore much fruit, and they supplied that deficiency in teachers which held up papal schemes for clerical education. In the universities they soon came to play a prominent if not altogether welcome part. As a kind of papal militia they were of immense service ; more mobile than the monks they penetrated everywhere and by public preaching and through the confessional they inculcated the ideas entrusted to them.[108] Their possibilities were first realised by Cardinal Ugolino, the future Gregory IX, though his desire to make bishops from their number was discouraged by both Francis and Dominic. But, as in the case of the monks, papal favour caused them more and more to plunge into worldly affairs and to lose their independence. In the thirteenth century the friars were violent opponents of the Indulgence system ; in the fifteenth and sixteenth active purveyors of pardons. This is a highly significant change.

The decay of the friars   The deterioration of the friars seems to have been peculiarly swift ; Matthew Paris says that they went further downhill in thirty years than the monks in four hundred ; [109] and even St Bonaventura can find a long list of causes for their decay.[110] Perhaps the chief of them was the quick growth of the orders, especially of the Franciscans. At first all seem to have been welcomed and there was no noviciate. How then was society to be protected from the sturdy beggar who took the name of Francis in vain ? Even the organisation of the orders when it came hampered the spirit and at

[107] So the Methodist Revival is said to have saved England from horrors similar to those of the Revolution in France.

[108] Lay politicians also made a similar use of them : see Workman *John Wyclif* I. p. 282 for the case of John of Gaunt.

[109] *Chron. Major* IV. p. 511 (RS.).

[110] *Opera* VII. pp. 336 sqq. (Mainz 1609). They have been summaised by Coulton *Life in the Middle Ages* IV. pp. 261 sqq.

length caused it to flee away.   There followed a general laxity
in many, with violent fanaticism in others who strove for the
literal observance of the rules.

As is well known the Franciscan Order was broken up Schism in
into rival camps on the question of the interpretation of the the Francis-
Testament of Francis with its command that the order was can Order
to hold no property.   Successively Popes tried vainly to cope
with the matter until at last the nominal vesting of the friars'
property in the Holy See salved the consciences of those who
could accept the device.   This quarrel within the Franciscan
Order was a grave disaster, as it not only weakened the whole
movement, but also engendered a spirit of bitterness on both
sides.   The ' Spirituals ' who clung to the literal rule became
more and more separated from the life of the Church.

Beyond this quarrel within the Franciscan Order there Rivalry of
was the perpetual feud with the Dominicans without.[111] the two
This was the more regrettable as the founders, if early accounts Orders
can be trusted, had a great love for one another ;   and in the
first days the orders exhibited mutual kindness.[112]   In 1255
the two Ministers, John of Parma and Humbert de Romans,
tried to check the growing jealousy by issuing a joint pastoral.

The spirit of rivalry extended still further, for the secular Religious
clergy were opposed to the religious, friars and monks alike. and Seculars
Much of the feeling against the friars arose from their habit
of ignoring the rights of the parish priests by preaching and
hearing confessions.[113]   Another cause of jealousy arose from
the presence of the friars in the universities, where they wished
to fill leading posts whilst remaining independent of academic
authority.   Paris in the middle of the thirteenth century saw
a bitter attack upon them by William of St Amour.   In
his *Contra Impugnantes* Aquinas made a vigorous reply and

---

[111] They even quarrelled over the privilege of persecuting heretics.   Dante,
with rare tact, tried to shame the two orders by making St Thomas Aquinas
praise the Franciscans, St Bonaventura the Dominicans ;   *Paradiso* xi. and
xii.

[112] When the first Franciscans arrived in London they lodged with the
Dominicans " as members of the family " :   see " Eccleston " *de Adventu
Fratrum Minorum in Angliam* II. xi. sq.

[113] This had been forbidden by St Francis : see *Speculum Perfectionis* pp.
10 and 50.   As in the case of a similar command by John Wesley upon his
Methodist Preachers the death of the founder caused his orders to be ignored.
The question lingered on until nearly the end of the seventeenth century,
when it was finally settled by Clement X.

as the friars were supported by the Pope and St Louis they naturally got their way.[114]

Exemptions   Some of the decline was due to the exemptions which the friars enjoyed from diocesan control; these exemptions were always resented by the bishops who as late as the Fifth Lateran Council endeavoured to get them modified. But the friars were too useful to the Papacy for them to contemplate any alteration; while the very fact that they had to rely upon the Pope made them all the more zealous in his service. But this reliance on the orders, though it may have helped the Papacy, was a bad thing for the Church as a whole since it tended to upset the ordinary machinery and to undermine the authority of the bishop in his own diocese.

Extent of abuses in the orders   In the case of the friars, as of the clergy in general, it is difficult to estimate the extent to which abuses prevailed; when men are conspicuous in the public eye the scandal which arises through a few notorious individuals quickly spreads over the whole order. The friars were more conspicuous than the monks, and seem to have drawn upon them a fuller stream of dislike and contempt. Their tricks and greed are a familiar theme in literature from the fourteenth century onwards, and Chaucer was not alone in regarding them as poor samples of the gospel, especially when put alongside the simple, hardworking parish priest.

Attempts at revival   From time to time efforts at reform were made and great preachers arose such as the Franciscan, St Bernardino, and the Dominican, Savonarola; but as a whole the friars never recovered their primitive zeal and purity. The decline was disadvantageous to the Papacy, as it took from their value as papal agents; to the Church at large it was disastrous as it lowered the standard of Christian life and brought it into contempt.

Independent attitude of friars   Though St Francis himself was entirely loyal to the Roman See,[115] some of his followers tended to become individualistic

[114] Hugh of Balsham, Bishop of Ely, tried to stop the rivalry by introducing seculars among the canons regular in the Hospice of St John at Cambridge in 1280. The plan did not work and the system of training regulars and seculars together was condemned by Benedict XII in 1335: see Leach *Educational Charters* p. 291.

[115] The Dominican Order shewed signs of independence at times. Hugo of Vancemain, Master General from 1333 to 1341, declared that no power, not the Pope nor God Himself, could compel the order to accept new rules against its will: see Mortier *Hist. des Maîtres Gen. des Frères Prêcheurs* III. pp. 118 and 136. We shall have a further illustration of this attitude over the Reuchlin quarrel.

in their outlook.   This was especially the case among the less orthodox who came under the influence of the writings of Joachim of Flora.   This twelfth century abbot held the Papacy at small value, and in the new epoch which he foretold there was to be no Pope ; the last of the line will perform the office of Symeon and hand over the Church to the new order of monks which is to be its ruler.[116]

When the Lateran Council met in 1215 it had seemed as if The Ebb of a new era was about to dawn in the Church's life ; [117] such was faith the vision of Innocent III.   But already in the days of this great Pontiff the signs of future decline were manifest, though not understood by his contemporaries.   The capture of Constantinople by the Crusaders, the beginning of the Albigensian persecutions, the growth of the temporal power, the emergence of ecclesiastical abuses, such as provisions, indulgences, and the elaborated penitential system ; these were all to bring discredit on the Papacy and to lessen its hold on the respect of Christendom.   They were all symptoms of a loss of spirituality and of the adoption of material standards.   It is significant of the decay of papal prestige that in the latter half of the century, Louis IX of France, a secular ruler, is the real leader of Christendom.[118]

The state of the clergy in this age of faith was deplorable. The state of Their importance had been greatly increased owing to the the clergy development of the Canon Law and their increased exemption from any kind of secular jurisdiction.   So too the parallel development of ritual had emphasised their special powers.   But morally they were, if one may take the judgement of a ' regular ' such as was St Bonaventura, in a very bad condition.[119]   It was their failure which led God to raise up the friars.   He accuses them of corrupting the laity, both in morals and doctrine ; and does not wonder that friars are

[116] See *Protocol of the Commission of Anagni* 94 sq. in *Archiv.* I. pp. 109 sqq.
[117] See *Innocent III* p. 168.
[118] This can be seen by the number of appeals that were made for his arbitration.   In 1246 the succession in Flanders was submitted to him jointly with Gregory IX ; in 1258 the Franks in Achaia appealed to him to settle a question of feudal law ; and in 1263 Henry III and the English barons laid their dispute over the meaning of the Provisions of Oxford before him.   Even the Canons of Lyons Cathedral asked him to decide a case in which they were engaged.
[119] In *Quare Fratres Minores praedicant* in *Opera* VII. pp. 341 sqq. (Mainz ed.).

preferred as confessors to people of such evil lives, men who keep concubines or visit harlots.[120]   The truth of the matter is that increased trade was bringing in increased wealth, and from prosperity luxurious habits of one kind and another were steadily growing ; pleasure and not duty was becoming the end of life.   Men might blame the influence of the court of Frederick II ; but that was but one out of many channels by which new ideas flowed into Christendom. From that court too there came the disruptive element of freedom of thought.

Free thought   Frederick might claim to be perfectly orthodox in his views, but he was accustomed to discuss matters of religion merely as problems ; seeking not to strengthen faith but to gratify curiosity.   Contact with other religions, moreover, led to the feeling that all might equally be true.[121]   Florence seems to have been especially notorious for its free thought; Villani complains of the Epicureans of his native city,[122] while Farinata degli Uberti held that Paradise was to be sought in this present life alone.[123]

The end of the Crusades   The close of the age of faith saw also the close of that splendid though mixed movement which for two centuries had added to the prestige of the Papacy—the Crusades.   Strictly speaking there was no European Crusade after 1229, for the enterprises of St Louis were almost entirely French.   The success of Frederick's diplomatic overtures was a great blow to the accepted method of obtaining possession of the Holy Land by force of arms.   But other causes contributed to the same end.   The transfer of similar privileges by the Papacy to efforts nearer home, such as the Albigensian Crusade, had something to do with the decline ; but still more the growing tolerance or carelessness, especially among the trading cities of Italy which like Venice were in close touch with the Turks.   It was probably for the good of Christendom that these expeditions should come to an end ; they were a means of lowering morals and bringing the name of Christ into disgrace in the East.   The despair and disgust with which St

[120] Many of the laity regarded the clergy as a danger to their women-folk *unless* they indulged in such habits, the confessional was otherwise unsafe : see examples in Lea *Clerical Celibacy* and Lecky *European Morals* pp. 331 sqq.
[121] This atmosphere is found in many of the *Novellino*.
[122] IV. xxix. (RIS. XIII. col. 122 D).   It should be noted that he is not speaking of his exact contemporaries.
[123] Benvenuto da Imola *Commentary* on *Inferno* x.

Francis turned his back on the camp of the crusaders before Damietta would have been aroused by almost any similar assembly. The ranks of the crusaders had included many whose ideals and whose lives were noble, but for the most part they were the scum of Christendom. St Bernard had not been far wrong when he commended the movement on the double ground that it might win back the Holy Land and it certainly rid Europe of large numbers of undesirables.[124] For the Papacy, however, the loss was severe as each fresh Crusade had been an opportunity for an impressive display of its powers. Moreover as advocate of the movement the Papacy had to bear a share of the loss which came from its failure, and that failure was final, as the Popes of the fifteenth century were to discover.

Thus the century of faith ended in bitterness and loss ; The end of the Crusades had had to admit final defeat, the Schoolmen were the age of becoming more and more sceptical, and the religious orders faith were quarrelling with one another and with the seculars. The Pope himself in spite of the glories of the Jubilee was shortly to fall beneath the heavy hand of a national king. Once again the harsh facts of life had proved too strong for man's desirings. Faith had not gone deep enough, had found no sufficient measure of good ground in which to fructify, and the crop was disappointment and vanity. The law of disenchantment is a law of nature and works wherever grace has not full scope for its beneficent activities. Imperfect humanity has to grasp the lesson both as a necessity and a duty. Over and over again the process of " unlearning the world's poetry and attaining to its prose " has to be repeated.

The ebb of faith had begun early in the thirteenth century,[125] and but for the efforts of the first friars in stemming it, even graver disasters might have ensued. The responsibility for the ultimate failure lies at the door of those who should have been the leaders of Christendom ; for they too, whatever excuses can be advanced by way of palliation, had thrown away the spiritual that they might seize the material.

[124] He stated that, with few exceptions, they were " scoundrels, vagabonds, thieves, murderers, perjurers and adulterers " : *Ad Milites Templi* V. (*Opera* I. col. 549 B). A similar testimony comes from Giraldus Cambrensis who records the surprise, and no doubt the relief, of the people of Usk when they saw " many of the most notorious murderers, thieves and robbers " taking the cross ; see *Itiner.* I. v.

[125] In 1237 Matthew Paris can write : " Temporibus illis ingruentibus igniculus fidei coepit nimis refrigescere " : see *Chron. Major* III. p. 389 (RS.).

CHAPTER IV

THE BABYLONISH CAPTIVITY

THE sojourn at Avignon was a strange interlude in a Papacy calling itself Roman, although a parallel can be found in the history of the Empire, for did not Constantine retain the name Roman although the seat of administration and authority had been moved to the Bosphorus. The saying of Herodian : " Where the Emperor is there is Rome " [1] received a new extension and *Ubi papa, ibi Roma* became almost a ' tag ' in the writings of papal defenders. But the Papacy found no Constantine, fortunately or otherwise, who should establish it permanently in a new home. Clement V was rather the Diocletian of the drama who abandoned Rome but founded no substitute. It must not be forgotten that he had no real intention of deserting Italy in perpetuity, for in the first years of his pontificate he expressed his purpose of returning thither, and even mentioned definite dates.[2] It was not until March 1309, nearly five years after his election, that he took up his residence in Avignon, and then only in temporary quarters in the Dominican convent. If we are to seek for a Constantine we must look either to John XXII, who began to build a permanent palace, or to Clement VI, who finally purchased the city from Joanna of Naples in 1348. Martin V will then be the new Charlemagne who restored the spiritual Empire to its original seat.

The residence of the Popes away from Rome and under French protection, was by no means so strange a thing to the fourteenth century as it seems to us. And this for two reasons. In the first place the Popes had, during several

---

[1] ὅπου ἂν ὁ βασιλεὺς ᾖ ἐκεῖ ἡ Ῥώμη.
[2] Cf. *Reg. Clem. V.* Nos. 3592 and 4302.

generations, been in the habit of spending the greater part of their time outside the city; some indeed never saw it after their coronation.[3]   Secondly, for an even longer period France—using the term geographically—had been the natural refuge of a Pope who found residence in Italy dangerous or distasteful.[4]

None the less the residence at Avignon was a disaster, for it checked the regular development of centuries, and when, after the long struggle with the Empire, quiet and stability were requisite, it plunged the Papacy into a fresh series of adventures.   The series ended only with the break-up of Western Christendom.[5] *Its evil effect on the Papacy*

Even when the Papacy had been moved back to Rome the fear of another upheaval was often present, and as late as 1464 each of the cardinals before entering the conclave on the death of Pius II, had to swear an oath that if elected he would not move the court beyond the Alps without the consent of the whole college.[6]

By the move to Avignon the Papacy passed into the sphere of French influence; this was perhaps the most notable feature of the change.   The city itself was not, of course, actually in French territory,[7] from which it was separated by the Rhone, nor was it French in speech, but Provençal. But the Popes at Avignon were surrounded by French cardinals,[8] their administration was largely in the hands of French officials, and individual Popes such as Clement V *French influence*

---

[3] See some interesting details of the papal movements during the latter half of the thirteenth century collected by Mollat *Les Papes d'Avignon* pp. xi. sqq.

[4] Some examples are Innocent II (1130-1143), Alexander III (1159-1181) and Innocent IV (1243-1254).

[5] Cf. Barry *The Papal Monarchy* p. 424 : " From Avignon to Constance, from Constance to Basle, from Basle to Luther at the Diet of Worms, we trace an ever-widening path, at the end of which appears the Reformation ".

[6] See Quirini *Vindic. Pauli II* p. xxiii.   The fear had also arisen on the election of the Catalan, Alfonso Borgia, as Calixtus III in 1455 : see *Instruction for Flor. Ambassadors in Venice* (Flor. State Archives Cl. X. dist. i. No. 44).

[7] The Popes had for some time been vassals of the French king for the neighbouring territory of the Venaissin given to them by Philip III in 1273.

[8] Out of 134 cardinals created during the period 113 were French : see Rivière *Le Problème de l'Église et de l'État* p. 345 n. 2.   Before the transfer Pierre Dubois had suggested the creation of large numbers of French cardinals as a means of controlling the Papacy : see *De recup. Terrae Sanctae* cxi. sqq. (ed. Langlois) pp. 101 sq.

and Benedict XII were, as we shall see, unduly French in their sympathies.

This has been exaggerated   The extent, however, to which French influence was allowed to affect papal policy has been greatly exaggerated, in particular by Italian and German chroniclers, who were naturally opposed to the setting up of the court away from Rome. But when all allowances have been made for prejudice, there is no doubt that the prestige of the Papacy was considerably lowered by the Babylonish Captivity, as some have been pleased to call it. That prestige depended largely on its catholic and universal outlook ; its independence, in theory at any rate, of any merely local and sectional influences. This universal outlook was compromised by the move to Avignon.

There had been periods during which the Papacy had been controlled by secular powers, by the Emperors, and in the depths of its degradation, by the petty nobles of Rome. But such control had had some kind of traditional justification ; control by a national monarch outside Italy was a complete innovation and the shock was great in proportion.   If, however, the Papacy was, at this juncture, to become dependent on any power, the French monarchy was the obvious claimant, for under St Louis the leadership of Europe had passed from the Empire to that kingdom.

France and the Papacy   The policy of the Papacy and that of France had many points in common, and the Popes, in weakening the Empire and striving to exclude its influence from Italy, were not ostensibly serving any but their own interests.   The same cannot be said of their attitude towards the two combatants in the Hundred Years War.   In this they came down quite heavily on the French side.   Not only did they advance enormous sums to the French kings,[9] but they allowed them to raise money by ecclesiastical taxation.   Furthermore they favoured French influences in Castile against those of England.

Scheme of this chapter   To give a detailed account of the Popes of this period is outside both the limits of space and the purpose of my volume.   I propose, therefore, after a brief outline of each

[9] In the five years between 1345 and 1350 592,000 gold florins were lent to Philip VI and no less than 3,517,000 gold florins to John II : see *Bib. de l'Ecole des Chartres* XL. pp. 570 sqq.

pontificate, to deal more fully with three aspects of their history which have a special bearing on the decline and fall ; the conflict with Lewis of Bavaria, the administration of the Papal States, and the episode of Cola di Rienzo. The last subject will give an opportunity for some general observations on the relations of the Romans and the Papacy during the middle ages.

Benedict XI died at Perugia in July 1304. The con- Election of clave which followed was sharply divided into two parties, Clement V each under the leadership of an Orsini, the Italians under Mattaio Rosso and the French led by Napoleone. The Italians were still deeply conscious of the disgrace of Anagni, while the French were determined to work for the restoration of the Colonna cardinals. After some delay Bertrand de Goth, Archbishop of Bordeaux, an English subject, but not unacceptable to the King of France, was elected. He took the name of Clement V. The new Pope was learned in both Civil and Canon law ; but weak as to character. This defect was no doubt due in part to the bad health from which he suffered. A chronic illness, possibly cancer, from time to time caused him to refuse to see all visitors.

The coronation took place at Lyons on Novr. 14, 1305 and the French king in person attended. The latter soon shewed his power by compelling the Pope to restore the Colonna and even to allow the rebuilding of Palestrina. Clement was no match for Philip and his first creation of cardinals, which consisted of nine Frenchmen and one Englishman, shewed the direction in which his policy was to move. Philip's real objective seems to have been to come to an understanding with Clement which would enable him to exploit the French Church for the benefit of the kingdom.[10]

The most notable event of this pontificate was the trial The trial of and condemnation of the Templars—a matter which has the Templars aroused fierce discussion in every subsequent age.[11] To dismiss it as a crafty scheme of the French king for obtaining the possessions of the Order is not satisfactory ; much more needs to be said on either side.

[10] Cf. Renan *Hist. litt. de la France* XXVII. p. 298 and Lizerand *Clément V et Philippe le Bel* p. 409.

[11] See E. J. Martin *The Trial of the Templars*, G. Mollat *Les Papes d'Avignon* pp. 229 sqq. A selection of documents has been made by Lizerand *Le Dossier de l'Affaire des Templiers*. He has also dealt with the matter in *Clément V et Philippe le Bel*.

The Templars had originally been founded, like their rivals the Knights of St John, for service in the Holy Land, but with the end of the Crusades and the capture of the last Latin stronghold in Syria in 1291, their work came to an end. The Hospitallers seized Rhodes and continued from that island to war against the Moslem ; but the Templars settled mainly in France, a body of trained soldiers with vast financial resources, and as such threatening to the kingdom.[12] Philip may have been inspired by covetousness, but his action, as distinct from his methods, was a piece of sound statesmanship.[13]

Charges against them

The many accusations which were brought against the Templars, had probably some basis in fact—there may have been cases of too close friendship with Moslems, cases too of heresy and also of immoral practices—but nothing to justify the condemnation of the order as a whole.[14] After some hesitation the Pope was persuaded to allow an enquiry into the charges and to his vacillation must be attributed, in part, the extreme steps which Philip found it necessary to take, that and the resistance of the order itself.[15] The final decision of the Church was delivered at the Council of Vienne,

The order suppressed

when the order was suppressed, although no definite condemnation was actually recorded. The presence of French troops in the neighbourhood, and the threat of raising afresh the question of the condemnation of Boniface VIII hurried the Council to a decision favourable to France.[16] But in any case the Templars had few friends and many rivals. By their extraordinary privileges and wealth they had been led into greed and insolence which rendered them objects of dislike to those who might have come forward to defend them.[17] The king got his way, though financially he made no great profit ; but probably this was to him not supremely

---

[12] In 1192 they had been offered Cyprus. If they had taken it their whole history would have been different. During the trial the Grand Master of the Teutonic Order significantly removed the Headquarters from Venice to Marienbad in East Prussia.

[13] So the massacre of the Janissaries in 1825 relieved the Turkish Empire of a dangerous force which had held power for centuries.

[14] Accusations of dangerous heresy were also made at this very time against the Moslem sect of the Nizaris or Hashishin, the notorious Assassins : see De Lacy O'Leary *Arabic Thought and its Place in History* pp. 162 sq.

[15] See Martin *op. cit.* p. 42.   [16] *Ibid.*, p. 56.

[17] See extracts from contemporary documents in Martin *op. cit.* pp. 20 sqq.

important, he had removed from his realm a dangerous element, and most significant of all, for our purposes, he had compelled an unwilling Pope to carry out his wishes. The shadow of Anagni hung over Clement. If Boniface had been outraged in his own territories how could he protect himself from the French king on the borders of France itself.[18]

The death of William Nogaret who had organised the suppression and that of Clement himself followed so swiftly upon the Council, that men in superstitious horror felt that they had been called before the divine tribunal to account for their share in the matter.

Clement died at Carpentras, the little town outside Avignon where at this time the youthful Petrarch was living. The conclave which assembled to elect his successor found it difficult to reconcile the Italian and Gascon points of view,[19] and when armed Gascon bands sought to terrify the Italian cardinals they took to flight. Two years of abortive negotiations followed, and it seemed that schism must inevitably arise. Meanwhile two kings of France, Philip and Louis X, had died, and it was not until June 1316 that the cardinals were again collected to a conclave in the Dominican convent at Lyons. They were told that they would not be set free until they had given a Pope to the Church. Finally they chose James of Cahors, Cardinal of Porto, who took the style of John XXII. *Abortive conclave at Carpentras*

The new Pope was a man of tremendous, even of brutal, energy, and in all directions it shewed itself. The lavish expenditure of Clement and the long vacancy had reduced the financial resources of the Papacy to a low ebb. John at once inaugurated a vast system for raising additional revenue by the exploitation to the full of various rights which his predecessors had exercised only to a moderate degree. These included provisions, annates, tenths and so forth. The Papacy, on its material side, owed much to the administrative ability of John, and although the stories which his contemporaries loved to repeat, of the wealth which *John XXII, 1316-1334*

---

[18] Ptolemy of Lucca says that Clement received 100,000 florins from the king, " quasi pro quadam recompensatione laborum circa dictam causam " : see RIS. XI. col. 1234 D.

[19] Dante urged the cardinals to keep out the Gascons and bring back the Papacy to Rome. His disgust is reflected in *Paradiso* xxvii. 58 sq.

he had amassed, are without foundation,[20] he certainly succeeded in rescuing the finances from bankruptcy and putting them on a new basis.

Secularisation of the Church

But there was another side to the picture. His measures encouraged that worldly spirit which had already gained too firm a hold on the Church. It is no wonder that he hated the Spiritual Franciscans with their doctrine of Apostolic Poverty, and that burnings and imprisonments became their lot.[21] By condemning the ideal of renunciation the Pope drove its advocates into rebellion, and they, in consequence, made their appeal from a secularised Church, whose development must have seemed to them one long apostasy, to the State which was at open warfare with it.

Missions to Central Asia

The pontificate of John XXII saw the development of that missionary enthusiasm which marked the Avignon period almost to its end. Perhaps the Popes recognised the need for restoring their prestige by the conquest of new lands, perhaps also they had a genuine care for the souls of the heathen. The movement had its rise in the impulse which led St Francis to go to Egypt, and was a recognition that the infidels were no longer to be won by force of arms, but by conversion.[22] In the middle of the thirteenth century the possibility of using the Mongols as allies against the Turks was seriously considered, and envoys were sent to the court of the Great Khan by both Innocent IV and Louis IX—the most famous of them were John of Plano Carpini and William of Rubruquis, both Franciscans.[23] But the great name on the roll of actual missionaries was John of Monte Corvino, the first archbishop of Pekin who laboured from 1294 to 1330.

In 1318 John XXII divided Asia into two distinct spheres of missionary influence—the northern was allocated to the

[20] Mollot shews that he left 750,000 gold florins only, a sum less than a million sterling : *Rev. Hist. Eccles.* V. (1904) pp. 530 sqq.

[21] Their doctrine, if pressed to its logical conclusion, would not merely have condemned luxury and wealth in the Papacy, but even the right to hold property : see Rocquain *La Cour de Rome et l'Esprit de Réforme* II. p. 387. The Spirituals relied on a Bull of Nicholas III *Exiit qui seminat ;* this was revoked by John after consultation with his advisers.

[22] This ideal was exemplified in the life of the famous Raymond Lull, missionary, mystic and philosopher, who met his death at the hands of the Moslems in 1315 after a long life of service.

[23] See C. R. Beazley *Texts and Versions of John de Plano Carpini and William de Rubruquis* (Hakluyt Society).

Franciscans, the southern to the Dominicans ; an anticipation of modern methods of procedure between different societies. The movement, however, did not survive the Black Death which ravaged the East as well as Europe. Moreover, the rise of the Ottomans and the conversion of the Mongols to Islam made access very difficult. Whilst it lasted it was a patch of heroism in an age which was too much given to calculation and selfishness, for the preachers of the gospel counted their lives at but little value in order to penetrate into distant lands ; many of them were murdered, not always without blame, for they found themselves unable to imitate the tolerant attitude of the Moslems and brought their fate on themselves by unwise demonstrations even in mosques.

Although John made strenuous efforts to stop pluralism,[24] and shewed a general desire to reform the Church, he was guilty of nepotism, and many posts were filled by relatives and fellow-countrymen. He had more excuse than most Popes for this weakness, as he was in dire need of trustworthy servants, and those whom he appointed were for the most part useful to the Church. *The Pope's Nepotism*

The Pope's restless energy caused him to stray into regions which he had better have left unexplored. He imagined that he was qualified to pronounce on theological questions, and the controversies over the Poverty of Christ and over the Beatific Vision aroused considerable trouble, and placed him in an undignified position. On the latter subject he had to make a retraction in the presence of the cardinals ; [25] whilst the former led him into the bitter struggles with the Spiritual Franciscans which we have already noticed.[26] *Theological controversies*

The next Pope was Benedict XII, a distinguished theologian. He had been born of poor parents in Saverdon in the County of Foix, and as Bishop of Pamiers had shewn admirable moderation in dealing with heretics. The same spirit distinguished his attitude towards the abuses which called for *Benedict XII 1334-1342*

[24] As in the Bull *Execrabilis* of Nov. 19, 1817.

[25] The retraction ended with the phrase : " Omnia submittimus determinationi Ecclesiae ac successorum nostrorum ". The text is printed in Mollat-Baluze *Vitae Paparum Avenionensium* I. pp. 180 sq.

[26] Robert of Naples, who had some sympathy with the Spirituals, tried to get the Pope to refrain from making any definite pronouncement on the Poverty question : see F. Tocco *La quistione della Povertà nel secolo XIV* (1910) pp. 284 sqq.

treatment during his pontificate ; but even so those who were concerned to defend them looked upon him as harsh and unsympathetic.   He certainly went far in his efforts to avoid any suspicion of nepotism for he refused to allow a niece to have a grand wedding ! [27]   It was he who built the palace at Avignon in which his namesake Benedict XIII was afterwards besieged.[28]

Clement VI,
1342-1352
Clement VI, who followed, was in striking contrast to the upright, almost puritanical, Benedict ; but his election was unanimous and seemed to contemporaries to have been inspired by God.[29] As Archbishop of Rouen he had won fame by his preaching.

His
generosity
The affability of the new Pope was notorious,—he prided himself on never refusing a request,—and it soon drew to Avignon swarms of suitors.   To satisfy their demands Clement made a scandalous use of papal powers.   So far did he go in ' providing ' for benefices, that the Bishop of Geneva complained that there was not a single benefice in his diocese which was not already filled by anticipation.   Such methods were not calculated to increase episcopal prestige and authority.

and luxury
As Clement was generous so was he fond of display, both ecclesiastical and secular.   A man of noble birth his court rivalled, for its luxury, that of any prince in Europe.   In addition he spent vast sums in building and, as we have already seen, it was he who finally bought the city of Avignon itself.[30] There could be but one result of such methods, and the sums, which the careful financial administration of Benedict had collected, were soon exhausted and a heavy burden of debt undertaken, an unwelcome legacy to his successors.   His efforts to raise money came at an unfortunate time, for France was ruined by the war with England, and the Black Death of 1348 had brought distress everywhere.

The Black
Death
This mysterious malady swept over Europe from the East and cut across the social and economic life of the times with grievous effect.   Since there was as yet no idea of contagion the plague seemed to be a direct visitation from God.   In

[27] *Register* (ed. Vidal) No. 7601.
[28] There is a recent study of this Pope by K. Jacob *Studien über Papst Ben. XII* (Berlin, 1910).
[29] See the letters of Annibal di Ceccano and Raymond de Farges to Edward III in Rymer *Foedera* II pt. ii. 1, p. 123.
[30] For an account of the transaction see RIS. II. pt. ii. col. 565.

some obscure way the Jews were held to be responsible and had to undergo terrible persecution. Clement very nobly took their part and threatened with excommunication those who attacked them.[31]   In their terror men turned to all kinds of fanatical practices to avert the wrath of God, and movements arose which caused no little anxiety to the authorities.[32]

The pontificate of Clement saw also the disastrous earth-quake in which much damage was done to the buildings of Rome including the unfortunate Lateran, as well as St Paul-without-the-Walls.   In some cases the churches mixed their ruins with those of the temples which formed their foundations.

In his anxiety to raise funds, and perhaps to divert men's Jubilee of thoughts from the disasters around them, Clement conceived 1350 the happy idea of holding a Jubilee in 1350.   The festival, as instituted by Boniface VIII, had had a pagan origin and was to be held at the end of each century ;   Clement now brought it into line with the Old Testament Jubilee and reduced the period to fifty years.[33]

The Pope had led a spacious and impressive life and even in the political sphere his influence had not been unfelt ; [34] but he had been a man of the world rather than an ecclesiastic, and when he came to die it was widely believed that the immediate cause was the dissoluteness of his life.   In actual fact he died through the breaking of an internal tumour which brought on hæmorrhage.[35]

After a conclave lasting only two days a Pope was chosen ; Innocent VI this was Stephen Aubert, a man advanced in years but famous 1352-1362 as a lawyer and the candidate favoured by the French king. Some had wished for the election of the saintly General of the Carthusians, but memories of Celestine V were against it.

Before the election the cardinals had sworn that whoever

---

[31] Raynaldus 1348 No. 33.

[32] The best known example is that of the Flagellants, a movement which arose in Swabia and spread rapidly in spite of papal condemnation ; Raynaldus 1349 Nos. 18-22.   See U. Berlière, " Trois Traités sur les Flag. de 1349 " in *Rev. Bened.* XXV. (1908) pp. 334 sqq.

[33] Leviticus xxv. 8-13.

[34] His chief enterprise was a league with Venice, Cyprus, and the Knights of St John to stamp out Turkish piracy in the eastern Mediterranean.

[35] See Mt. Villani III. xliii. in RIS. XIV. cols. 186 E-187 A, *Chron. de Melsa* III. p. 89 (RS.), and Matthias von Neuenburg (formerly cited as Albertus Argentinensis) in Böhmer *Fontes Rerum German,* IV. p. 227.

of them was elected should restrict the number of new creations and give to the sacred college certain additional rights and dignities ; there was evident among them a fear of the undue growth of the papal power. The new Pope, who took the name of Innocent VI, had been regarded as weak and complacent ; he soon shewed his independence by repudiating the agreement as contrary to the Canon Law.

His reforming zeal

Innocent VI was a reformer of the type of Benedict XII, but without his predecessor's determination. However he sent the train of suitors left by Clement about their business and did his best to encourage learning. He had some trouble with the religious orders, in particular with the Dominicans, whilst his treatment of the Fraticelli earned him, even after death, the reproaches of St Bridget of Sweden.[36] His reforms also extended to the finances of the Papacy which were in a desperate condition. To raise funds he sold some of the papal treasures.[37]

Trouble with mercenaries

The reign of Innocent was overcast by renewed threats from mercenaries who had been deprived of their employment by the truce of Bordeaux in March 1357. As France proper was already devastated, they were drawn by stories of vast papal treasures to attack Avignon.[38] In 1358 an indemnity was paid to Arnaud de Cervole, Archpriest of Velines, a notorious leader, who in consequence departed from the neighbourhood ; [39] but final relief came only with the departure of the bands into Italy.[40]

Urban V 1362-1370

The first election to fill the vacancy resulted in the choice of Hugh Roger, brother of Clement VI. To the relief of the cardinals as a whole he refused to accept the pontificate. They then proceeded to elect Guillaume de Grimwad, Abbot of St Victor. He took the name of Urban V.

---

[36] *Revelationes* IV. cxxxvi.

[37] See " Inventaire des obj. préc. vendus à Avignon en 1358 par le pape Inn. VI." in *Rev. Arch.* XLIII. (1882) pp. 217 sqq.

[38] For the efforts to put Avignon in a state of defence see R. Michel *La construction des Remparts d'Avignon* in Congres arch. de France LXXIII. vol. II. pp. 341 sqq.

[39] See H. Denifle *La Désolation des Églises etc.* II. pp. 188 sqq. and L. H. Labande " Bertrand du Guesclin et les États pontificaux de France " in *Mémoires de l'Acad. de Vaucluse* IV. pp. 43 sq. M. Labande has made good use of local archives and so supplements Denifle.

[40] The papal forces were very small. Urban V had only 160 men-at-arms and the same number of archers to defend the whole territory.

Even on the throne of Peter Urban lived the life, strenuous and holy, of a member of a religious order. All display and luxury were discouraged and his only extravagances took the form of ambitious building schemes and a too generous support of scholars and universities.[41] His real claim to notice lies in the determination, announced in September 1366, to the alarm of the French, of returning to Rome.[42]

At the end of April in the following year he carried out his resolve, after a deputation from the French king had done its best to make him abandon it. The cardinals, who feared Rome as the scene of outrage and anarchy, played a last card just before embarking at Marseilles by threatening to desert the Pope. Urban was undeterred and they meekly fell in with his wishes. Actually Rome, at the moment, was probably safer than Avignon, for the latter was in real danger from roving bands of mercenaries ; while Rome, thanks to the strong hand of Cardinal Albornoz, was comparatively orderly.

Temporary return to Rome

The Pope reached Rome early in October, and his first act was to visit the tombs of the Apostles. The Romans were overjoyed and began feverishly to repair the ruined churches and, a much more difficult task, to reform their own manners.[43] They had good reason for desiring to please the Pope, as the pilgrimage of Charles IV in October 1368 and the submission of the Greek Emperor, John Palaeologus, just a year later, were events to feed their pride ; it was long since Rome had had within her walls two Emperors within a year. But their innate love of civil strife could not be contained, and the Pope, disturbed by their tumults and even threatened by bands in the pay of the Visconti, turned his gaze fondly back to Avignon. In spite of the warnings of St Bridget he returned thither ; but only to die in the following December. His death seemed a divine judgement.

Sept. 27, 1370

The successor of Urban was chosen even more speedily

[41] Urban was a keen student himself and collected a considerable library. The universities of France were at a low ebb owing to the disturbed state of the country.

[42] Both John XXII and Benedict XII had considered the idea of moving the papal court to Bologna.

[43] If the Italians spoke of Avignon as Babylon, the French were able to retaliate by calling Rome Jericho, with a direct reference to Luke x. 30.

**Gregory XI
1370-1878**

than Innocent had been, and again a young man was elected, Peter Roger de Beaufort (Gregory XI). But if the new Pope was not advanced in years the state of his health promised no long pontificate. Gregory was of an upright and humble character and genuinely devout ; zealous in suppressing unorthodox views and ardent to reform the curia and the Church. Like his predecessor he had disputes with the religious orders. But the noteworthy thing about his reign was that it saw the return of the Papacy to Rome.

**Final return
to Rome**

In spite of the discouraging experiences of Urban V, Gregory made up his mind from the first to return to Italy as the only means of re-establishing the papal power there.[44] He announced his intention for the winter of 1374, but various causes, political and financial, prevented its being carried out before October 1376. The Pope and cardinals left Marseilles in a state of depression and a long and tempestuous voyage [45] did not serve to relieve it. Corneto was reached on Decr. 6 more than two months after the start and Rome on Jan. 17 of the following year. The doubts and discomforts of the voyage weakened the health of the Pope, and his powers were still further undermined by the change of climate. He lived in Rome for little more than a year, dying at the end of March 1378. None the less the move had been made, and Rome was again the headquarters of the Catholic Church. Avignon was thus shorn of its glories, for though during the Great Schism one line of Popes occupied it, its real importance was gone. The Popes had indeed done much for it in buildings and art, but their connexion, which seemed so permanent and so threatening to the true welfare of the Papacy, was only transient. Now Avignon, and the other cities of its neighbourhood, seem " to be perpetually dozing in the warm sun, like old men, dreaming of their historical and varied past ".[46]

**Evil reputation of
Avignon**

During the papal residence Avignon obtained a most unenviable reputation ; [47] but there are reasons for supposing that although this condemnatory opinion was justified, it was also exaggerated. There is always a tendency to seek

[44] It is said that he made a vow that he would do so if elected : see Mollat-Baluze *Vitae Paparum Aven.* I. p. 463.

[45] There is a poetical description of their sufferings by Peter Amiel in RIS. III. pt. ii. coll. 690 sqq.

[46] Lord Frederick Hamilton *The Days before Yesterday* p. 144.

[47] Cf. the phrase in Rot. Parl. II. p. 387 " la peccherouse cité d'Avenon ".

for a scapegoat and Avignon was an obvious sacrifice. As in the case of the supposed French influence allowance must be made for the Italian point of view, even in men like Dante and Petrarch. We are certainly justified in making a distinction between evils which originated in the period and those which were merely allowed to grow. Further we have to remember that luxurious habits were increasing all over Europe ; the development of commerce and improved means of transport were responsible for this, as well as that wider intercourse which spreads new fashions and creates new needs. That the papal court was luxurious cannot be denied, especially under a ruler like Clement VI.[48]

One of the chief evils of a luxurious court, apart from its corrupting influence, is that it needs large resources for its upkeep. The loss of Italy and jealousy of the French had in any case made a serious reduction in the revenues,[49] and to cover this and the increased expenditure devices were adopted which even a Roman Catholic historian has condemned as " most questionable ".[50] The Papacy seemed to forget that economic success may involve moral deterioration.[51]

Financial needs of the Papacy

The elaborate papal financial system involved the employment of numerous agents. These were usually Italians and with them it may well be said that we have the beginnings of international banking. Dues to other rulers were normally paid by personal service or in kind ; but to the Popes this form of payment would have been difficult to collect or to transport. Some of it, in the form of wool, was actually accepted by the Florentines, but for the most part papal revenue had to be turned into money and huge sums transferred from one country to another. Many of the papal agents, as other tax-collectors, were rapacious and harsh ;

[48] See description in Mollat *Les Papes d'Avignon* pp. 362 sqq.

[49] The German Church had also suffered during the period. In Sept. 1355 the clergy of Cologne and Trier protested against having to pay a tithe *contra Turcos* imposed by Innocent VI. The civil wars had impoverished them to such an extent that they had hardly enough to live on and there were buildings to be re-erected and so forth.

[50] Pastor *Hist. of the Popes* I. p. 72. On the following page he affirms that " The Avignon system of finance . . . contributed more than has been generally supposed to the undermining of Papal authority ".

[51] It might have learned a lesson from Tiberius Gracchus whose aims, according to Appian *Bell. Civ.* I. xi. 48 were οὐκ ἐς εὐποριαν ἀλλ᾽ ἐς εὐανδρίαν.

such men often caused scandal and brought the Papacy into loathing and contempt ; they were declared to be worse than the hated Jews. Wherever luxury is found in a court corruption is not far behind, and the veniality of the papal officials was notorious ; even so loyal a servant of the Papacy as Alvaro Pelayo protested against it.[52] Most people submitted to the exactions, but there was one at least who withstood them ; the English Bradwardine, after his consecration as Archbishop of Canterbury, caused much offence by refusing to pay fees which he considered excessive.[53]

But it must not be imagined that such funds were required merely to keep up papal luxuries. Far from it. The largest sums went to carry on the Italian wars,[54] much to meet the cost of the increasingly elaborate organisation which in this period was being introduced, much too in loans to the French kings.[55]

Nepotism

The subject of papal nepotism was too common to call for comment. Some of the best Popes struggled against it as we have seen, and one of them (Benedict XII) declared that a Pope should be like Melchisedec without any kin. But such sporadic efforts made only more glaring the abuses of the system.

Non-residents

Another evil arose from the swarm of suitors at the papal court seeking to gain notice or promotion. Petrarch compared them to sailors who have abandoned their proper tasks in the ship in order to crowd round the pilot and get in his way ; a sure prelude to disaster.[56] Much of the evil can be traced to the practice of provisions, for unless a cleric was actually at the papal court he could never tell whether a benefice to which he was presented had not already been ' provided ' for by the Pope. The case of Simon of Faversham deserves quoting in this connexion. In September 1305 he was appointed Archdeacon of Canterbury by the Archbishop.

---

[52] Cf. *De Statu et Planctu* II. xv. : " Nullus quasi pauper hodie ad papam intrare potest, clamat et non auditur, quia non habet quid solvat ".

[53] *Chron. John of Reading* (ed. Tait) p. 112.

[54] K. H. Schäfer *Die Ausgaben der Apost. Kammer. unter Johann XXII* pp. 8 sqq.

[55] In order to free the Papacy from this burden John de Rupescissa, a Spiritual Franciscan of the fourteenth century, proposed to discover the philosopher's stone by means of which to raise funds.

[56] *De rebus senilibus* VII. Ep. i.

This office and with it the living of Reculver he was compelled to give up to a papal nomine. His only chance of getting any remedy or compensation was to go in person to the papal court.[57]

    The reaction against all these abuses was at times intense. English In England this was natural in view of the suspicion that the opposition to Popes were helping the French. In Jan. 1307 the Parliament abuses of Carlisle voiced the opposition to payments made to foreign clerics,[58] that of 1343 took severe measures against papal exactions,[59] and in 1351 the Statute of Provisors was passed,[60] and that of Praemunire two years later.[61]   So too in Germany there was much opposition and numerous instances of the refusal of payments.[62]   As time went on this increased, and in 1372 the religious houses of Cologne made a league to resist the payment of a tithe, whilst the chapters of Mainz, Bonn, and Xanten, also took similar steps. There were also attacks on papal collectors [63] which were not unknown even in France.[64]

    Thus abuses grew in spite of all attempts to stop them on the part of well-meaning Popes and of opposition from those who were threatened by them. In previous centuries abuses had existed, but during the fourteenth and fifteenth they became firmly established. Moreover during this period there was a long step forward in centralising the government of the Church. The power of the bishops was lessened and the threads connecting the rest of Christendom with the papal court drawn tighter. Nothing was left but to wait for the final catastrophe of the sixteenth century.

    We turn now to events in the Empire. The interregnum Albert I had been ended, as we have seen, by the election of Rudolph

---

[57] See F. M. Powicke in *Mélanges offerts à Ferd. Lot* p. 653, and for the opposition to ' provisions ' in England Mollat *La collation des bénéfices eccles. etc.* (1305-1378), pp. 227-269.

[58] Rot. Parl. I. pp. 217 sqq.

[59] Rot. Parl. II. pp. 135 sqq., 172.   These enactments were never carried out.

[60] Rot. Parl. II. p. 232.   Edward III kept this measure in reserve as a weapon against papal exactions.   Clement VI ignored it.   So little use was made of the Statute that in the case of *Rex v. Chichele* in 1405 it was pleaded that it had never been enforced : Year Book 11 Hen. IV fo. 38.

[61] Rymer *Foedera* III. pt. i. p. 84.

[62] See *Chron. der Deutschen Städte* IV. p. 306, VII. p. 189, and IX. p. 583.

[63] See J. P. Kirsch *Die päpstlichen Kollektorien.*

[64] Mollat *La Fiscalité Pont.* pp. 95 sq.

of Habsburg in 1273 ; this event signalised the appearance prominently upon the stage of German politics of a great and famous house. The Habsburgs again held the imperial office, after the short reign of Adolf of Nassau, in the person of Albert I. For ten years Albert devoted himself to the task of recovering power in Germany, and in consequence he allowed Burgundy to come under the influence of Philip IV of France. Albert also favoured the growing municipalities and with their assistance and that of French auxiliaries he succeeded in defeating a hostile league. After this victory his policy towards France was modified by the need for gaining papal support. The murder of Albert by his own nephew left the succession a very open question. Philip tried to get his brother, Charles of Valois, elected, and urged Clement V to exert influence. But the electors were not anxious to have a French Emperor, and made their own choice, which Clement duly recognised. This time the Habsburgs were passed over, the Empire was not yet ready for hereditary succession, and Henry of Luxemburg was elected.

May 1308

Henry VII Henry VII, led away by dreams of Italian conquests, neglected Germany, and in order to leave himself free even reversed the policy of Albert, by withdrawing the concessions made to the towns and favouring the princes. The latter took full advantage of their opportunity to become increasingly independent of the central power.

Descends into Italy The journey of the Emperor-elect received the approval of Clement V, though only after some hesitation. From the Pope's standpoint a set-off against the predominant French influence in South Italy might be useful. But Italy itself was alarmed at his coming. Henry, however, had the highest ideals, and set out with no selfish or imperialist aims. He wished to do justice to Guelf and Ghibelline alike, but he had not been long in Italy before the impossibility of maintaining this attitude became evident. Six days after he had received the Lombard crown in Milan, the Guelf Della Torre were driven out in favour of the Ghibelline Visconti. This almost accidental circumstance was to have a profound effect on the future of Milan and of Italy.

Jan. 6, 1311

Coronation From Milan the Emperor moved down to Rome where the cardinals waited to give him the imperial crown. But St Peter's was held by the Neapolitans and at first the car-

dinals refused to crown him elsewhere. The threats of the
Roman people, however, compelled them to carry out the June 29, 1312
ceremony in St John Lateran then in a semi-ruined condition ;
no unfit symbol of both Empire and Papacy. The Romans
hoped that Henry would remain permanently in their city,
so that robbed of the spiritual head of Christendom they
might find compensation in becoming in actual fact the centre
of the Empire. But Henry had other plans, and soon moved
north again to make a gallant but abortive attack on Florence
with quite inadequate forces.

In the meantime the Pope was adopting a less friendly
attitude. He ordered Henry, in terms which the Emperor
resented, to make peace with Robert of Naples, and also to
take an oath of fidelity to himself.[65] The state of Clement's
health was making it increasingly difficult for him to hold
his own with the French.

Henry now determined to exert himself to the uttermost His death
against Robert and having collected a considerable army
he might well have been successful in his expedition against Aug. 24, 1313
Naples,[66] had not death suddenly cut him off. It was said
that he had been poisoned at Mass by his Dominican confessor. The dead Emperor was taken to Pisa, which in his
lifetime had been ever faithful to him, and there he was
buried.

The death of Henry gave the signal for the break-up of
the imperial army. The greater part returned to Germany
but a band of 1000 Brabançon and Flemish horse entered the
service of Pisa. They played their part in the rout of the
Florentines at Montecatani, and are interesting as one of
the first examples of the hiring of foreign bands which was
soon to be such a feature of Italian warfare.

The Habsburgs now made another attempt to gain the Schism in
Empire, and on October 19, 1314 Frederick, son of Albert I, the Empire
whose claims had been passed over in 1308, was elected
by a group of princes who met at Sachsenhausen. Next
day another group elected Lewis of Bavaria, a member of
the house of Wittelsbach. Both candidates were crowned
on the same day, and they divided between them the tradi- Nov. 25, 1314
tional place and person, for Frederick was crowned by the

[65] The documents are printed in MGH. Leges IV. ii. App. vii. No. 1248.
[66] Such was the opinion recorded by Villani, see RIS. XIII. col. 469 A.

right person—the Archbishop of Cologne—but at Bonn; Lewis in the right place—Aachen, but by the wrong person —the Archbishop of Mainz.[67] War then broke out and it Aug. 28, 1322 lasted until the victory of Mühldorf left Frederick in the hands of Lewis.[68]

The Popes and the schism   The schism in the Empire was not unwelcome to the Popes. Although the expedition of Henry VII into Italy had done little to advance imperial prestige it had shewn that in certain quarters the Emperor could still find support. With an absent Papacy this was a dangerous symptom. In 1313 Clement V, claiming to act as suzerain of the vacant Empire, appointed Robert of Naples imperial vicar. John XXII followed a similar policy, and his legate, Cardinal Bertrand du Pouget, actually proclaimed a crusade against the Visconti as imperial supporters. The situation created by the victory of Mühldorf was naturally unwelcome to the Pope, and he met it by reviving papal claims to settle disputed elections. Lewis was summoned to appear before him. The summons was ignored. Then he proceeded to excommunicate the Emperor, thus giving him the unforeseen distinction of being the last Emperor so to be treated.

Thus there was added a new chapter, or rather an appendix, to the struggle between Pope and Emperor. John, confident of French support, seemed deliberately to have provoked or extended the conflict; he resembled Boniface VIII, in that he lived habitually in the disappearing world of medieval imperialism and had little notion of the new world of national states that was about to emerge. Although the disaster of Anagni had been the work of the French king and not of an Emperor, none the less, to assert papal claims and to exalt papal privileges was a means of regaining something of the prestige lost by that event.

Lewis replies to John XXII   In May 1324 Lewis made his reply in the Appeal of Sachsenhausen. He levelled many charges against John, " the so-called Pope ", accusing him of deliberately stirring up trouble in both Germany and Italy ; of advancing fantastic claims to interfere in imperial elections and even to dispose

---

[67] There had been a time when Mainz had claimed the right : see Lambert of Hersfeld *Annales* sub 1073 (ed. Holder-Egger) p. 168.

[68] It is significant that the turning-point of the battle was a charge led by Frederick of Hohenzollern, Burgrave of Nuremberg.

of the Empire. The document has additional interest as exhibiting signs of the influence of Marsiglio of Padua, the political thinker who became so bitter an opponent of clerical pretensions.[69] For a time the Pope took no notice, but in 1327 he launched what is perhaps the most violent of all papal Bulls against an Emperor. In it he deprived Lewis of all his estates and dignities and at the same time condemned Marsiglio and his associate, John of Jandun, as heretics. In the meantime Lewis and Frederick had become reconciled and had entered upon a romantic friendship which probably did little to help either of them.

The quarrel over Apostolic Poverty to which reference has already been made, furnished Lewis with unexpected allies, for when John issued his Bull *Cum inter nonnullos* the more earnest Franciscans were driven into the Ghibelline ranks, which thus came to comprise " all that was most puritanical as well as all that was most licentious in medieval society ".[70] Among those who went over to Lewis was Michael of Cesena, the Minister-general, and William of Ockham. By their alliance with Lewis the Franciscans linked up their quarrel to larger political issues. Both sides gained substantially by the alliance, for the material resources of the Emperor seemed to offer a chance to the zealots of overthrowing the corrupt Papacy and replacing it by one more spiritual ; while the literary skill and theological knowledge of the friars found abundant scope in attacks on the theological ventures of John. Their adhesion, however, was not pure gain to Lewis for it stiffened the papal opposition and threw the Dominicans into the struggle with renewed ardour on the opposite side. *Is joined by some of the Franciscans*

Urged on by his new allies Lewis now determined to descend into Italy. The assembly which he held before starting out was attended by so many bishops and clerics that it seemed like a General Council. No delay was made and on the last day of May Lewis received the iron crown at Milan. By the following January he was crowned at *Lewis in Italy Feb. 1327*

---

[69] The Appeal as it has come down to us contains a long outburst on Apostolic Poverty but it is questionable if it formed part of the original document ; see K. Zeumer " Zur Kritik der Appellation Ludwigs des Baiern " in *Neues Archiv.* XXXVII (1912) pp. 221 sqq.

[70] Heywood *History of Perugia* p. 142.

Jan. 17, 1328 Rome itself, after the Romans, in public assembly, had declared their approval.[71] The religious ceremony was performed in St Peter's by two excommunicated bishops, whilst the crown itself was placed on his head by Sciarra Colonna in the name of the people.

Elects an anti-pope

May 12, 1328

1277-1280

Lewis next proceeded to declare John's election uncanonical and with the approval of the Romans he replaced him by Peter of Corbara, a Franciscan zealot who took the title of Nicholas V; doubtless because it was a Nicholas, the third of that name, who had declared in favour of Apostolic Poverty.[72] At Whitsuntide Peter and Lewis crowned one another.[73] But their mutual congratulations were short-lived, for the failure of the Emperor in an expedition against

August Robert of Naples compelled him to flee to Todi in Umbria. He remained in Italy until 1330 when, recognising the hopelessness of his position, he abandoned his anti-pope and returned to Germany. The unfortunate Peter, thus left to shift for himself, submitted to John, and was lodged in the Palace at Avignon as a constant memorial of the Pope's triumph.

Failure of Lewis

The failure of Lewis's descent into Italy, in spite of Franciscan support, revealed very notably the growth of national or racial feeling there. His presence on the soil of Italy induced Milan, Florence, and Naples to forget for the time their cherished rivalries in order to unite against the Teutonic invader. It was no accident which led contemporary Italian chroniclers to refer to Lewis almost invariably as *il Bavero*,

[71] Riezler suggests that Rienzo as a boy may well have been present at this recognition of the power of the Roman people : *Liter. Widersacher der Päpste* p. 50 n. 1. But as he was brought up ' among peasants,' he may have been living in the country. None the less the suggestion is an interesting one.

[72] See Eubel " Der Gegenpapst Nik. V und seine Hierarchie " in *Hist. Jahrbuch* 1891.

[73] Villani distinctly states that Lewis was crowned by Peter (X. lxxiv in RIS. XIII. col. 646 C). But, as the late Professor Waugh has pointed out, such a course, since it " suggested the dependence of the Emperor's authority on papal consent or countenance cut away the ground from under Lewis's feet ". He concluded that either Villani was mistaken or that Lewis " was guilty of gross folly " : see *Camb. Med. Hist.* VII. pp. 124 sq. In 1336 Lewis himself, desiring to gain John's favour, admitted the illegality of his coronation : " se unctionem in Roma perverse, male et iniuste et a potestatem non habente": see Riezler *Vatikanishe Akten* p. 641 No. 1841. This statement would apply to the first coronation, as well as to the second if the latter actually took place.

a custom which was even adopted by the Spanish theologian, Alvaro Pelayo.[74]

But Lewis was still strong in Germany where the con- Lewis in venient deaths of several Habsburg princes, including that Germany of his former rival, Frederick, had weakened the opposition against him. In Germany, too, racial feeling had been aroused, and the supposed identification of the Papacy with French interests carried much weight. Benedict XII, indeed, was so much impressed by the strength of German feeling that he tried to come to terms, but France and Naples would hear of no concessions. The opinions of the German princes July 16, 1838 found expression at the famous Diet of Rense [75] which declared that the King of the Romans received his office direct from God on being chosen by a majority of the electors, and that the coronation at Aachen gave him all the necessary powers without papal approval. In the following August at a Diet at Frankfurt this declaration was approved in the ordinance *Licet iuris* and even extended so as to make the elected actually Emperor without further process.[76] This was a bold position to take up and foreshadowed the separation which was to come about through the Golden Bull of Charles IV.

Lewis, however, threw away his advantages by breaking Mistakes of off the alliance into which he had entered with Edward III Lewis of England,[77] and going over to his adversary, Philip VI of France. He was inspired to do this by the hope that Philip would persuade the Pope to release him from excommunication. Yet further support was alienated by his grasping policy in Germany, where he even went so far as to usurp papal powers by declaring the marriage of Margaret Maultasch, the famous ' ugly duchess,' and John of Moravia, to be void

[74] E.g. " A persecutione et facie Bavari fugitivus " ; *De Statu* I. xxxvii. Strictly speaking Alvero was a Portuguese, as he was born at San Payo in Gallicia : but in the fourteenth century all natives of the peninsula were *hispani*.

[75] The assembly included representatives of " civitates et communitates ". Thus papal opposition, as in France, led to a wider franchise : see above p. 67.

[76] See the discussion in *Camb. Med. Hist.* VII. p. 181 where the actual words are quoted ; " Ex sola electione est verus rex et imperator Romanorum censendus et nominandus ".

[77] Lewis made him imperial vicar in 1838 and revoked the appointment in 1341.

since it had never been consummated.[78]   This left her free
to marry his own son, Lewis of Brandenburg.

Submits to Clement VI   In 1843 Lewis became desperate and submitted to
Clement VI signing a declaration of twenty-eight articles.
This did no harm to Germany, as the Diet refused to sanction
his concessions, but it lowered the personal prestige of the
June 11, 1346 Emperor and his continued foolish conduct led at last to
the election of a rival, Charles of Luxemburg, the son of John
of Bohemia who had supported Lewis against Frederick.
The position of Charles was not a strong one, and he made
it still weaker by joining his father in a chivalrous expedition
to help the French.   John fell at Crecy, but Charles escaped.
The whole position was, however, suddenly changed by the
Oct. 11, 1347 unexpected death of Lewis who was killed whilst hunting.

Weak character of Lewis   The causes of Lewis's failure are not far to seek.   He
was exceedingly well meaning and exceedingly weak.   When
he pursued a determined policy the reason was invariably
that he had behind him some councillor stronger than himself.
A good instance is the march on Rome, followed by the
coronation and the bold step of declaring John XXII deposed ; for this was due to the forceful inspiration of Castruccio
Castracani and the advice of Marsiglio and John of Jandun.
Castruccio died soon afterwards and the two philosophers
also passed from the scene. Lewis made John Bishop of
Ferrara, but he seems never to have occupied the see ; whilst
Marsiglio became Archbishop of Milan, though he too does
not appear to have ever functioned in that office.

His superstition   Lewis's hesitating policy, in the absence of the judgement
and determination of others, was largely due to his intensely
superstitious mind.   To be under papal ban was for him
a matter for real concern and had a material effect upon his
actions.   Another cause was his inability to read the lessons
of the past, and, in pursuit of obsolete pretensions, to involve
himself in the expenses and difficulties of an Italian campaign.
There are, however, those who consider that Italy was the
key to the situation.[79]   The choice was certainly a difficult
one, for Lewis had either to allow his rights to lapse, as

---

[78] This was done on the advice of William of Ockham.   Marsiglio of
Padua held that the emperor was entitled to dissolve an actual marriage : see
N. Valois in *Hist. Litt. de la France* XXXIII. pp. 617 sq.
[79] See Riezler *Die Literarischen Widersacher der Päpste* p. 16.

Rudolph of Habsburg had done, or else, with the help of the Ghibelline party, to attempt to enforce them.

Now his body lies in peace beneath its massive monument in the quiet of Munich's lofty cathedral—but the supporters, even as they watch around his tomb, seem half afraid that its weight will prove insufficient to hold down that restless spirit.

Before the death of Lewis the position of Charles had become parlous, for many of his supporters had grown luke-warm. This was due to the concessions which had been forced from him by Clement VI. Although these were secret the Pope openly boasted that the Empire was his to bestow on whom he would. The chief clause admitted the necessity of the papal coronation before the Emperor could be re-cognised as such. Charles had also promised to wait for the Pope's permission before going to Rome, and then only to remain within the city on the day of the coronation. This promise aroused the bitter scorn of Petrarch, who declared that the Pope would neither live in Rome himself nor allow the Emperor to do so.[80] The cities of Germany closed their gates against the *Pfaffen-kaiser*, as they called him, a title which recalls Otto IV's scorn of Frederick II. The op-position now sought a rival Emperor. After several dis-appointments, including Edward III, they settled on Günther of Schwartzburg, a distinguished soldier, though not of the highest rank of nobility. Unfortunately he died within a short time of his election, and so the stage was finally left clear for Charles.

The character and achievements of Charles IV have been very variously assessed according to the point of view from which they have been regarded. It is certain that he neg-lected Italy; but for that he ought perhaps to be praised rather than blamed; it must have been obvious to any wise statesman that the time had come for the Empire to ' cut its losses ' in that peninsula. His work for Germany was prob-ably sound, in spite of the taunt of Maximilian I, that he had been the father of Bohemia and the step-father of the Empire. He certainly did for Bohemia all that a ruler could; but his treatment of the Empire was by no means so blameworthy

Charles IV

His achievements

[80] *De Vita Solitaria* II. iv. 3.

as many have supposed. His policy seems to have been to make Prague its real centre. Two years before his election he had obtained from his old tutor, then Clement VI, its elevation into an archbishopric. He now took up his residence there, and proceeded to erect buildings, and also to found a university, the first within the Empire. These various schemes were carried out with all the business-like ability which characterised him, for he had none of the romantic notions of his father. But in the end the hatred of Slav and German rendered them abortive. The experiment, however, was worth the trying.

His coronation

April 1355

The coronation in Rome followed the lines of the agreement with Clement. Charles went to Italy definitely as the ally of the Papacy, and carefully abstained from taking any part in local politics. He was duly crowned in Rome where the Capitol, in Gibbon's graphic phrase, " was yet stained with the blood of Rienzi " ; and at once withdrew from the city when the ceremony was concluded.

The Golden Bull

The services of Charles in settling the electoral system of the Empire were considerable, and Bryce's epigram that " he legalised anarchy and called it a constitution " [81] is almost as inaccurate as it is brilliant. The Golden Bull was a constructive measure which did something to bring German politics into a more stable condition by the abolition of a number of uncertainties. Hitherto the rights of the electors had been by no means clear, and disputed elections were the ready prelude to disruption and disorder. The Golden Bull fixed the number and the qualifications of the electors. Three of them were to be ecclesiastics, the Archbishops of Mainz, Cologne, and Trier ; four to be laymen, the King of Bohemia (Charles very characteristically insisted on his precedence among the lay electors), the Count Palatine of the Rhine, the Duke of Saxony, and the Margrave of Brandenburg. The election was to be held at Frankfurt, and a bare majority was to suffice. The coronation was to be at Aachen and the first Diet at Nuremberg. In order to prevent disputes the territories which carried electoral rights were not to be divided, but the eldest son was in each case to succeed. An important point to be observed by the

[81] *Holy Roman Empire* p. 246.

student of the decline and fall of the Medieval Papacy is the entire ignoring of that institution. Thus the link binding Pope and Emperor was virtually severed, and in consequence the Empire became more purely German.[82] The renewed strife had left the Papacy weaker than ever in the Empire; though the apparently submissive attitude of several Emperors gave it a delusive sense of increased power.

A comparison of past struggles between Papacy and Empire is very suggestive. Perhaps the first point that emerges is the striking loss of stature on both sets of combatants. If Lewis is no Barbarossa or Frederick II, the Avignon Popes look small beside the giants of the old days. This is symbolical of the loss of power and prestige in both Empire and Papacy. Dante in *De Monarchia* might still look upon the Empire as the divine agent for civilising the world and bringing in peace and security; but when he wrote, the Empire was really a thing of the past and beyond revival; his treatise, as Bryce has well said, was " an epitaph and not a prophecy ".[83] What gave the struggle a further characteristic was the partial support received by Lewis from the two great movements which had come to maturity in the Age of Faith—the Friars and the Schoolmen. The attack on the Pope with the weapons of dogma and the accusation of heresy was a significant feature. The same can hardly be said of the election of the anti-pope. Nicholas V was but a feeble creature and during his brief enjoyment of power shewed himself as unworthy a follower of St Francis as the worst of the Conventuals. Pomp and luxury drew him as surely as they did a genuine Pope.

The theological literature called forth by the quarrel was vast, but by no means valuable; the political literature, almost equally vast, was of greater significance. It was not merely that new principles were advanced, but the admitted facts were given a new interpretation. Each side had its advocates and those on the papal side did perhaps more harm than good by their exaggerated claims. Even

Comparison with past struggles

Literature of the struggle

[82] It has been said by some authorities that Innocent VI made a protest which Charles ignored; but this has been denied, after searching examination, by Scheffler *Karl IV und Inn. VI* pp. 101 sqq.

[83] *Holy Roman Empire* p. 276. The *De Monarchia* was put on the index in 1554 because of its use by the Protestants, and not removed until the more liberal days of Leo XIII.

Pastor speaks of the "melancholy renown" achieved by Agostino Trionfo and Alvaro Pelayo, who exalted the Pope "into a kind of demi-god, with absolute authority over the whole world ".[84] This judgement is certainly more true of Agostino than Alvaro. The former, regarding the Pope as the representative of God upon earth, held that there could be no appeal from his judgements,[85] furthermore he could depose an Emperor,[86] and in certain cases replace him, and even alter the constitution of the Empire.[87] The latter gave to the Pope a double jurisdiction, corresponding to the two natures of the Son of God, a spiritual and a temporal.[88] He was the vicar of Christ, whilst the Emperor was the vicar of the Pope and his vassal.[89] But his powers are limited since he cannot, for example, alter the decrees of a General Council.[90]

The advocates of the Emperor were equally bold in their claims, and perhaps more dangerous, since the very discussion of the matter was bound to weaken papal prestige, especially as political and ecclesiastical ' heretics ' were joined together. The chief names on the imperial side were Marsiglio of Padua, John of Jandun, and William of Ockham.[91]

Marsiglio of Padua and his theories   Marsiglio is so important that a few words must be said of him and his theories. He became a supporter of Lewis for much the same reason as the Franciscans, because they had a common enemy. With Marsiglio the enemy was clerical privilege. To understand the steps by which he arrived at his position it will be necessary to glance at the state of contemporary Italy.

Perhaps because of its anarchy, both moral and social, and its numerous feuds, Italy, at this period was beginning to take a deep practical interest in political ideas and controversies. The Venetian Constitution, for example, comes from this epoch. In some cases the interest was more theoretical as

---

[84] *History of the Popes* I. p. 80.   [85] *De potestate Ecclesiae* Qn. VI.
[86] *Op. cit.* Qn. XL.   [87] *Op. cit.* Qn. XXXV.
[88] *De Statu et Planctu* I. xliv.
[89] *Op. cit.* I. lxviii. There is a good discussion of the views of Alvaro by N. Iung *Un Franciscain Théologien du Pouvoir Pontifical* (Paris 1931).
[90] *Op. cit.* I. xlvi. " Non posset tollere concilia generalia quae sunt sicut evangelia veneranda."
[91] Bryce has cited the different nationalities of these men, Italian, French, and English, as a good illustration of the unity of the intellectual life of Europe.

trade was looming larger than political liberty on the horizon.[92]
The pathetic failure of Henry VII had shewn that the imperial
idea had no future south of the Alps, and that the cities
were free to work out their own salvation. Few of them
realised what was to be the end of the process, and that an
age of heroism was to be followed by an age of despots.[93]

The Italian commune bore a close resemblance to the
Greek city state, and Italian thinkers on political subjects
were not slow to see the appropriateness of Aristotle's theories
to their own case. They longed for a *societas perfecta* in
which a good and strong government should ensure peace
and security. It was from this point that Marsiglio began
to work out his theories, which originally were concerned
with the government of the city only, later developments
led him to enlarge the scope of his enquiries and to apply
his principles on a larger scale.

These theories are expounded in the famous treatise *The
Defensor Pacis* [94] which he composed, in conjunction with *Defensor
Pacis*
John of Jandun, in 1324. What is surprising about his
thought is the manner, almost unique, in which he leaps
the centuries to a time far ahead of his own day. It was
this indeed which prevented the immediate spread of his
influence ; sound requires an atmosphere and the atmosphere
in which his voice could be heard was lacking. If the ideas
of Dante's *De Monarchia* belonged to an age that was dying,
those of Marsiglio belonged to a world which was yet unborn.

The basis of his theory of government is the belief in the
absolute sovereignty of the people ; they are the true ' fount
of legislation ' ; the ruler is merely an executive officer—
for this reason Marsiglio will not hear of an hereditary
monarchy—and may be deposed. Since the State is made
up of Christian men it is supreme on all questions, and the
highest authority in the Church is a General Council made up
of both lay and clerical members called together by the
State. The clergy are to be subject to the same laws as
other citizens, and are to confine themselves to the exercise

[92] The Lombard League was revived, for the last time, in 1252 (RIS.
VIII. col. 132) ; but only under pressure from Cardinal Octavian. It lasted
for a year and then fell to pieces.
[93] Cf. Jordan *Les origines de la domination Angevine en Italie* p. 53.
[94] The latest edition is by C. W. Previté-Orton : see also R. L. Poole
Illustrations of Medieval Thought pp. 231 sqq.

of spiritual functions. The real ownership of Church endowments is vested in the community, or in the patron as representing the original donor; thus the Church has the right of *usus* only, not of *dominium*. The claim of the Pope to represent St Peter is rejected, together with all privileges based on hierarchical pretensions. The clergy, in carrying out their duties, are to use no power of coercion, and excommunication is to be a weapon reserved for the use of General Councils. But even General Councils cannot decide on the truth of all things, errors of opinion lie beyond the cognisance of any merely human judicature; therefore in matters of religious belief, unless such beliefs are dangerous to society, there is to be toleration.

William of Ockham   Views similar to the above were, on certain points, put forward by William of Ockham, but with less freedom and power—Ockham was handicapped by his scholastic training—and with a spirit of scepticism which was absent from Marsiglio. Among other things Ockham condemned the Donation of Constantine, declared that a Pope is subject to the judgement of an Emperor and of a General Council, and affirmed that the coronation of the Emperor, since it has no political significance, can be performed by any bishop. His pessimism is shewn in the refusal to recognise any really trustworthy authority; all may err, Pope, Emperor, or even Marsiglio's General Council.

State of Italy   The absence of the Popes caused grievous harm to Italy; one old writer, indeed, stated that it was a blow more grievous than the barbarian invasions.[95] The extent of the neglect of Italy is, however, a matter upon which there are different opinions. Some authorities consider that the papal rule was merely nominal;[96] some that it was as complete as that of any other ruler;[97] some, taking a middle course, admit that there was neglect, but will not subscribe to the extreme views of the first school.[98]

[95] See Ughelli *Italia Sacra* (Venice 1717) I. p. 71.
[96] See Jordan *Les origines etc.* pp. 607 sq.
[97] See Theiner *Codex diplomaticus dominii temporalis Sanctae Sedis* I. p. ix. He goes so far as to say : " Jean XXII fut bien plus souverain dans ses états qu'aucun des princes temporals de son siècle."
[98] See De Boüard *Le régime politique et les institutions de Rome* p. 68 and Schäfer *Deutsche Ritter und Edelknechte in Italien* II. p. 71.

In the south things were different, for there the rule of Robert of Naples saved it from the misfortunes to which the Naples rest of Italy almost without exception was subject. Robert, like James I of England, may have been inclined to pedantry and to confuse statecraft and statesmanship ; yet his rule was effective, and his death without male heirs, in 1843, was a grave disaster for the kingdom and for the Guelf cause in all Italy.[99]

The names of Guelf and Ghibelline were still in use, but as so often happens to party labels, they had lost their meaning. Once they had stood for great principles and honourable loyalties ; they were now applied to the partisans in insignificant feuds and petty local strifes. The absence of the Popes weakened the Guelf cause, and the appointment of cardinals from among Ghibelline familes also tended in the same direction.

In all parts of Italy anarchy and civic strife quickly The shewed themselves, and tyrants sprang up, even in the Papal Campagna States, like weeds in an abandoned garden. The district round Rome was especially notorious for its turbulence. The nobles, from whom the senators had of old been chosen, ought to have had some notion of the first duty of a ruling class, to preserve order and to administer justice. But they were the chief disturbers of the peace, seizing the lands of the Church and, in spite of papal protests, taking possession of the palaces of the absent cardinals.[100] Even the spiritual leaders of the people shared in the common degradation. Many, including members of the religious orders, had lost their material resources, and wandered about, still wearing their habits, to commit all kinds of excesses even on the out-skirts of Rome itself. The Romans held it as one of their chief grievances that these renegade clerics were not put down by the papal officials.[101]

The papal officials themselves were actually a source of The Papal weakness as elsewhere. The Popes, instead of appointing officials native Italians to represent them, made a large use of French

[99] Petrarch dreamed that he would unite Italy.   On Robert see W. Goetz K. Robert von Neapel (1309-43) and Isidoro del Lungo Bianchi e Neri.
[100] See Antonelli in Archivo della Reale Soc. Rom. di Stor. Patr. XVII. p. 836 and Theiner Cod. Dipl. I. p. 506.
[101] See De Boüard Le régime polit. pp. 191 sqq.

and Provençal representatives.   These men naturally despised
the Italians and in return received their unconcealed hatred.
There are numerous instances of the ill-treatment of papal
agents,[102] and so bitter was the feeling against them that to
many the despots seemed like Italian patriots striving against
a foreign overlord.

Continuous wars   During the whole period the Popes, with hardly an interlude, were engaged in warfare in Italy.   From 1308 until
1313 they were disputing with Venice over the possession
of Ferrara.   The Venetians were eventually expelled after
suffering heavy losses ; but the dislike of the citizens for the
papal officials drove them into rebellion and the city passed
Aug. 1317   back again into the hands of its original owners, the D'Este
family.   During the next few years John XXII made a number
of reforms intended to check the unrest in the Papal States,
Bertrand du Pouget   and in North Italy, through his legate and nephew, Bertrand
du Pouget, he took a strong line.   It is probable that he contemplated forming a Lombard State in subjection to the
Papacy.[103]   His plans brought on a conflict with the Visconti,
then at the beginning of their surprising career.[104]   The papal
forces, on the whole, got the better of the struggle, and in
Feb. 1327 the important city of Bologna submitted to the
legate.   But in 1330 the intervention of John of Bohemia,
who was called in by Brescia against Verona, caused the formation of a league aimed at both Pope and king.   By the spring
of 1334 the ground gained had been lost, and even Bologna
was no longer in the power of the Pope.[105]   Benedict XII,
who followed, had a horror of all warlike measures and his
weak policy brought the Papal States to the brink of annihila-
tion.   On his death Clement VI renewed the vigorous policy

[102] See for examples Villani in RIS. XIII. col. 85 and Dino Compagni
RIS. III. col. 17.   One very bad instance comes from Perugia.   A lady, to
save her honour, tried to spring across a narrow street and, falling to the pave-
ment below, was killed.   Complaint was made to the governor, Gerard du Puy,
Abbot of Marmoutier, but the only satisfaction the relatives received was the
reply " Vos Italici credetis quod omnes Galli sunt eunuchi " : see *Chron. Reg.*
in RIS. XVIII. col. 85.

[103] This has been questioned by H. Otto *Zur Ital. Politik Joh. XXII.*

[104] Matthew Visconti was strangely amenable to papal admonitions, and
after the Bull of John XXII in 1317 he gave up the valued title of imperial
vicar, and eventually the lordship of Milan itself.   His son, Galeazzo, however,
took his place.

[105] See L. Ciaccio *Il Card. Legato Bertrando del Poggetto in Bologna* for
details of this campaign.

of John XXII, but the Visconti scored a great triumph when in October 1350 they purchased the lordship of Bologna. At the same time they secured many of the fortresses of Romagna from the papal mercenaries whose pay was in arrears.

Clement tried the use of spiritual weapons upon the Visconti. The Visconti At first they were ineffectual, but in April 1352 Bologna and the seized castles were handed back. Three months later Giovanni Visconti was appointed papal governor of Bologna. To the Guelfs this desertion, for so it seemed, was a heavy blow, following as it did the death of Robert of Naples.

This latter event had caused Clement no small embarrass- Joanna of ment owing to the youth and frivolity of Joanna, the grand- Naples daughter and successor of the Neapolitan monarch. In March 1348 she had been compelled to fly to Avignon and in order to return raised money by selling the city, with the consent of her overlord, Charles IV, to the Pope.

In 1353 the Peace of Sarzana left the Papacy free to devote Cardinal its energies to the reconquest of its own territories, and a Albornoz fitting instrument was to hand in Cardinal Albornoz, a Spaniard who had gained an immense reputation for his exploits against the Moors.[106] Albornoz was equally famous for his diplomacy, which was all to the good, for upon diplomacy even more than arms success in his new task would largely depend. In spite of the insufficient support which he received from Avignon, and in spite of the plots against him among the cardinals, he succeeded in restoring papal rule in the States of the Church, and but for the weakness of Urban V might have crushed the Visconti. On two occasions he was superseded by Androin de la Roche, Abbot of Cluny, who quickly revealed his incompetence. Albornoz died in August 1367, worn out by his strenuous labours, and by disappointment over his wasted efforts in North Italy. The Constitutions which he promulgated in 1357 for the States of the Church remained in operation, subject to necessary modifications, for nearly five hundred years.[107]

---

[106] See H. Wurm *Cardinal Albornoz, der zweite Begründer des Kirchenstaats* (Paderborn 1892). It is interesting to notice that the Cardinal's own name is presumably of Arabic origin for it must represent *al-burnusi*, the man in the burnous.

[107] So, too, the College which he founded at Bologna still functions.

The
mercenaries

One new factor in Italian warfare and politics which rendered the work of Albornoz especially difficult was the rise of the mercenaries.[108] We have seen the terror which they inspired in the papal court at Avignon before their departure for Italy. Until the Italian Company of St George was founded in 1379 they consisted of foreigners. Many of these had been men of simple life and habits before plunging into their new manner of life and the result was often appalling. The German soldier who had been infected with Italian habits became a proverb : *Tedesco italianizato diavolo incarnato.* As these bands were useful to kings and nobles and to the great cities, it was to no one's interest severely to check them.[109] They therefore came to regard themselves as above all law save that of their own commanders, and plundered a church or an abbey as readily as a castle or a village. Their ravages seriously disorganised the Church's system, and not a few of the non-residents at Avignon had been driven away from their cures by the ruin created by the mercenaries.

Florence stirs
up revolt

The defeat of the Visconti, although the fruits were lost, aroused the alarm of the Florentines, and taking advantage of the hatred aroused by the papal officials they succeeded in stirring up most of the cities in the Papal States in the winter of 1375. Rome alone, which was expecting the return of the Popes, remained loyal, although the government of Florence wrote at the beginning of 1376 urging its citizens to preserve their freedom and to resist any attempt by the Popes to re-establish their power over the city. So wide-spread was the outbreak that the end of papal rule seemed to be at hand.[110]

But is
compelled to
submit

Gregory XI, however, was equal to the situation. He saw clearly that the return of the Pope to Rome was necessary, and in the meantime, as his departure was delayed, he sent bands of Breton mercenaries into North Italy under the notorious Robert of Geneva, later to become Clement ' VII ' of the Avignon line. In addition he laid Florence under an

---

[108] The rise of these bands was a sign of the times and of the breakdown of the feudalism and the whole social system of the middle ages.

[109] Although Innocent VI and Urban V had issued Bulls against them Gregory XI found it necessary to employ the famous Englishman Acuto (Hawkwood) and Tournebarri (Thornbury) against the Visconti ; see *Papal Letters* IV. pp. 116, 121 and 124.

[110] " De mense Decembris Ecclesia Romana incoepit declinare," says *Chron. Estense* under the year MCCCLXXV in RIS. XV. col. 499 B.

interdict and ordered the goods of all her merchants, wherever they might be found, to be confiscated and the owners to be banished.[111] The Pope had some sharp arrows in his quiver—so long as men took them at his estimate. In the end the diplomatic skill of Gregory, and his advantage in the use of weapons, compelled Florence to sue for peace. The Feb. 3, 1377 fearful massacre at Cesena had helped to spread the terror of the Pope's mercenaries through Italy.

Gregory in his dealings with the cities of Italy had followed the policy of Urban V, by treating certain of them with special favour in the hope of preserving centres of loyalty. But this policy proved a failure, such towns were just as speedy in throwing off their allegiance as the rest, if they thought it to their advantage. However, the presence of the Pope in Italy induced most of the towns in the States of the Church to accept his rule ; the few who stood out were handed over to the tender mercies of the Bretons.

When compared with the thriving cities of North and Rome in the Central Italy Rome made but a poor showing. The eyes of middle ages her citizens were dimmed by the halo which surrounded her, and they wasted their energies in fitful revolts and impossible dreams of universal empire. Florence, Milan, Venice, and the rest, despising shadows, devoted themselves to the pursuit of definite and attainable objects. Hence they found their trade and wealth ever increasing and their influence daily becoming more considerable. But Rome had no trade, no crafts, no industries ; she produced nothing.[112] There was in consequence no middle class worth considering, to stand between the nobles and the people such as in other Italian cities formed the strength of the community and furnished it with able rulers.

Rome was too proud to labour, and like so many in that state of mind would stoop to any degradation to avoid the necessity of supporting herself. She depended on the numer-

---

[111] William Courtenay, when Bishop of London, excommunicated the Florentine merchants in that city at the request of the Pope. For doing so he received the censure of the Crown. See Workman *John Wyclif* I. pp. 285 sq.

[112] In this she was imitating her Republican ancestress of which Mommsen has written : " There has never perhaps existed a great city so thoroughly destitute of the means of support as Rome ; importation on the one hand, and domestic manufacture by slaves on the other, rendered any free industry from the outset impossible there " : *History of Rome* IV. p. 471.

ous pilgrims and suitors at the papal court for her living : and from them she neglected no opportunity of taking abundant spoil. Furthermore the revenues which the Popes exacted from all Europe enabled them to let off their own subjects with but light taxation.

In earlier days men had turned to Rome to recall the memory of a golden age, and her vast and mysterious ruins brought back byegone greatness. But the Romans themselves, in spite of their proud vaunting, had little appreciation of such remains, one proof out of many of their unworthiness to be the successors of the old Roman people. Even Rienzo had to declare that they had made the city more fit to be a den of robbers than the home of civilised men ; whilst Petrarch sadly declared that Rome was least known in Rome itself.[113] The remnants of the old buildings were chiefly used to provide materials for new habitations—the marble was even sold to be ground up—and from the abundant ruins the nobles carved out fortresses to supplement their strong towers.

Dependence on the Papacy The very position of Rome as the headquarters of a universal Church and the centre of a shadowy Empire cramped her development in every direction. Both economically and politically she was dependent on the favour of others, and the atmosphere in which perforce she lived made the flame of liberty burn but fitfully. Yet from time to time the Romans attempted to revive the past, to call up from their tombs the ghosts of consuls and tribunes. Such revivals were but superficial and transient, since the past was not only dead but uncomprehended. None the less loyalty to the city was the only approach to a generous emotion which the degenerate Romans ever knew.[114]

Pride in their past The chief characteristic of the Roman people was their pride ; little as they resembled their predecessors—one can hardly call them ancestors—they could never forget *Roma*

---

[113] " Qui enim hodie magis ignari rerum Romanarum sunt quam Romani cives " : *Epist. Fam.* II. 14.

[114] The Romans of the middle ages had but little of the old Roman blood in their veins. The Romans had indeed always been a mixed people. Caesar had declared that Rome drew to it " the beggars and idlers and scoundrels of all Italy " (*De Bell. Civ.* II. 120) and in the days of Seneca very few of the citizens were of native birth : see *Consolat. ad Helv.* vi.

caput mundi ; [115] even in the days of their greatest weakness they clung to this with pathetic intensity. Those who wished to gain their favour need look no further than an appeal to the city's past and an implied recognition of their identity with the old Romans. The Popes themselves were not above using this means of approach when it suited their purposes, and Innocent VI, in calling for their help against Giovanni di Vico, urged them to imitate the example of *vester Cato*.[116] Exalted by the contemplation of their greatness they despised the newly-formed republics of Lombardy. Some excuse can be found for their conceit in the general recognition, by the other cities of Italy, of the age-long primacy of Rome ; [117] but it was significant that the Jubilee of 1300 inspired Villani to write, not a history of the medieval Papacy, but the story of his own Florence.[118] He recognised that the one was rising the other decaying.

In spite of their exalted notions and the example of the universal spirit of the Papacy the Romans had but a narrow outlook and could see little beyond Tusculum. They were content, in practical politics, to ignore the world-wide Empire of the Caesars, and leaping the centuries, to repeat the squabbles with neighbouring towns which marked the early days of the republic.[119]

Unfortunately pride in the remote past led to an undervaluing of the privileges and benefits of the present, as also of things to come ; the love of their city gradually ousted the love of the *civitas Dei*. But at all times the Romans had been liable to turn back to their heathen past, and the character which Gelasius I gave them when an outbreak of 492-496 plague led to the demand for the revival of the licentious

[115] Others remembered it as well it is true. Cf. Gregory of Tours : " Urbs urbium et totius mundi caput " *Hist. Franc.* V. pref.

[116] Theiner *Cod. Dipl.* II. p. 254.

[117] When in 1208 Gualdo accepted Perugia as its suzerain both cities agreed to observe the terms " salvo in hijs (*sic*) omnibus honore et praecepto domini papae et domini senatoris almae urbis Romanae " : see Doc. vii. " Gualdo submissio " in *Bollettino della Soc. Umbra di Storia Patria* I. pp. 147 sq.

[118] " Firenze . . . a seguire grandi cose disposita, sicome Roma nel suo calare " : VIII. xxxvi. in RIS. XIII. col. 368 A.

[119] Gibbon, in commenting upon this, recalls the passage in which Florus (I. xi.) amused the Romans by the contrast between their vast campaigns and the infant wars against " nameless villages of the Sabines and Latins " VII. p. 236.

festival of the Lupercalia, was generally deserved ; they were neither pagan nor Christian and had neither faith nor morals.

Relations with the Papacy

The memory of the past, however, was not the only cause of the low level of the religious life of the Romans ; they saw too much of the ' seamy ' side of the Papacy ; the strife with the Emperor, the corruption of the curia, and the practical materialism of a great spiritual power. In later days Machiavelli was to account for the irreligion and low morals of Italy by the Church's example in her midst.[120]   In any case the fickle nature of the Romans [121] made it difficult for them long to remain constant to any opinion or loyal to any person.   They were enthusiastic and theatrical, fond of high-sounding protestations, fond too of welcoming among them some distinguished guest.   But they soon grew weary of him, and their welcome was as deceptive as an April day.   Perhaps if they had had a strong trading class its ballast might have overcome their general instability.

By the fourteenth century most of the cities which had originally had an ecclesiastic for their feudal lord had succeeded in throwing off his yoke.   But the position in Rome had no real parallel elsewhere.   The Popes clung to their rule over the city as the foundation of that temporal sway which they held to be necessary for the preservation of their power.[122]   Hence the struggles were more continuous, as perhaps they were more bitter, than elsewhere.   But the long fight could have but one conclusion, for the city was too dependent on the Pope, economically and politically, to stand alone.   Without him and his cardinals in her midst Rome was a body without head and eyes.[123]   The Avignon period revealed to the full what the absence of the Pope could mean ; Rome then lost her place in the drama of the world and sank slowly into insignificance.   The population

[120] *Discorsi* I. xii.

[121] Saba Malaspina compared them to a wanton woman " cuilibet venienti domino impudenter se exhibet " : RIS. VIII. col. 843 B.

[122] The action of that wise and farseeing statesman, Innocent III, in demanding the oath of allegiance from the prefect of the city as soon as he had been consecrated showed his estimate of the value to the Papacy of the possession of Rome.

[123] So St Bernard had concluded : " Nonne ille caput et illi oculi tui erant ? Quid ergo nunc Roma nisi sine capite truncum corpus ? "   Ep. ccxliii (*Opera* I. col. 241).

fell as low as 17,000 for men were quick to abandon the sinking ship.

The Romans learned their bitter lesson, but the dependence upon the Papacy became to them an occasion of shame. At one moment they were fawning upon the Pope; the next driving him from the city; then again, because they realised his commercial value, imploring him to return. So regular were these changes that they might, to an intent observer, have seemed to depend upon some system of equilibrium; as indeed they did. The Romans needed the Pope; they found his rule irksome, but not terrifying, and therefore they drove him out, rejoicing with shallow optimism over their feeble achievement.[124] When at the end of the fifteenth century the Pope's authority was finally established it was of real benefit to the city, for such instability of government was a source of constant weakness. To the Popes themselves their experiences were both annoying and absurd. That the Lords of Christendom should thus have been hunted about by the feeble citizens of a decayed metropolis was indeed a monstrous anomaly; its effect on papal policy and papal 'nerves' must not be ignored.[125]

Into the varying fortunes of the city during the middle ages we cannot enter in any detail.[126] It will suffice to refer to a few names beginning with that of Arnold of Brescia, Arnold of and the revolt of 1143 which restored the senate, gave a free Brescia burgher class to Rome, and began a struggle lasting, with but occasional interludes, for more than three centuries. Next comes Brancaleone, the first foreign podestà. He was Brancaleone a remarkable ruler and his death a grave disaster for the 1252-1258 Roman people. Seven years later the city received a more stable government than any it had yet experienced with Charles of Anjou as senator. The Pope tried to limit his

---

[124] One is reminded of the remark of Madame de Stael on the joy of the people of Paris over their frequent revolutions, that it was like the pleasurable sensations of a man falling from a high building : " C'est bel et bon tant que cela dure ".

[125] In the last days of the Republic the government of Rome without troops or even an effective police force was also " at the mercy of every gang of banditti " : Mommsen *Hist. of Rome* IV. p. 167.

[126] See Gregorovius *Geschichte der Stadt Rom im Mittelalter* (also an English translation), Gibbon *Decline and Fall* VII. pp. 209 sqq., L. Halphen *Étude sur l'administration de Rome au moyen âge*, Rodocanachi *Les institutions communales de Rome*, and De Boüard *Le régime polit. de Rome.*

office to five years,[127] but in spite of this, with a short interval, he held it for twelve. It came to an end when Nicholas III succeeded in excluding him and taking his place, not, be it remarked as Pope, *sed ratione suae personae.*[128]

From this time onwards the senators were chosen by the Popes from among the local nobles. After the expedition of Henry VII, however, Robert of Naples received the office ; his tenure was interrupted by the descent of Lewis of Bavaria, and the flattering display of Roman independence to which it gave rise. But in August 1328 a change of attitude drove him out, and the Romans sought reconciliation with their absent overlord, admitting their wrong-doing in the matter of the coronation of Lewis and the election of an anti-pope. John XXII, whose policy towards the Romans was milder than towards others, was easily appeased.

In 1337 the Romans elected Benedict XII as their senator and captain. But the state of the city was not improved by these various experiments ; the nobles were as unruly **Petrarch in** as ever, and life and property little respected. Petrarch **Rome** who paid his first visit to the city of his dreams in the spring of 1337 was amazed at the turbulence and anarchy which he **April 8, 1341** encountered. Four years later he came again to Rome to receive the poet's crown on the Capitol.[129]

Rienzo But a change was about to come, and from a most un-expected quarter ; unfortunately it was to prove as transient as it was unexpected. In January 1343 a deputation was sent to Clement VI by the city, and among its members was a young man of the lower orders known already for his eloquence and personal charm—this was Cola di Rienzo.[130] In him the aspirations of the Romans became for a moment incarnate, as two centuries later those of Germany were to become incarnate in a far different figure.

Birth and This remarkable man, if it could not be said of him as **early life** it was of Cleon, that he smelt of the tanyard, was born of humble parents, and until he was twenty lived, to use his

[127] Rodocanachi *op. cit.* pp. 55 sq.
[128] Guillaume de Nangis *Chron.* ad ann. 1278.
[129] See Gibbon VII. pp. 257 sq.
[130] For the detailed story of his life see Rodocanachi *Cola di Rienzo,* and for his letters Burdach *Briefwechsel des Cola di Rienzo.* The account in Gibbon VII. pp. 259 sqq. is based largely on secondary authorities and needs correction on a number of points. It is strange that no biography yet exists in English.

own phrase, "a peasant among peasants"; then by the exercise of perseverance, aided by a surprising memory, he gained a wide knowledge of the culture and antiquities of old Rome.[131] He was on this side of his varied nature an earlier Winckelmann. Inspired by the desire to restore the ancient glories of the city, and by a belief that he had a divine call to redress its present wrongs, Rienzo on his return from Avignon began to denounce the nobles and secretly to plot their overthrow. The Pope had appointed him to the post of notary in the civic camera, a post which carried with it a small emolument,[132] and, what was more important, the opportunity of exerting some influence in public affairs.

The revolution finally came to a head on Whitsunday 1347 during the absence of Stephen Colonna and other leading nobles from the city. Rienzo was escorted by a vast crowd to the Capitol, and after he had delivered the inevitable harangue he was entrusted with the government of Rome by popular acclamation. Nominally it was to be shared by the vicar apostolic, Raymond, Bishop of Orvieto; but as Gregorovius has said, he merely played the part of Lepidus to Rienzo's Octavius, and was almost entirely ignored by the latter. The laws which were to regulate the new community were proclaimed and accepted.[133] The nobles, taken completely by surprise, were overawed and slipped quietly away. Stephen Colonna on his return tried to take a high hand, but had quickly to fly for his life before the threats of the mob. *The revolution May 20*

An era of peace and justice ensued, and even the Pope came to look upon Rienzo with marked favour, especially after his successful attempt to deal with the troublesome Giovanni di Vico. Most of the nobles submitted and took the oath; but on November 20 the Colonna and some other disaffected nobles made an attack on the Porta San Lorenzo. They were easily driven out, and in the fighting almost a whole generation of the Colonna family was wiped out. *Its success July 1347*

---

[131] See Rodocanachi *op. cit.* p. 31 for an account of his studies. The statement in Gibbon that his parents "painfully bestowed" on him "a liberal education" is without foundation.

[132] The stipend was five gold florins monthly. Gibbon in giving this as the *daily* salary has been led astray, with many others, by the mistake of the Abbé de Sade in his biography of Petrarch.

[133] See Rodocanachi *op. cit.* pp. 63 sq.

Rienzo's ambitious conduct

Such speedy and apparently complete success was too much for the excitable temperament of the new tribune. Forgetting the traditional modesty which should have graced the office, he adopted almost regal state ; a taste for luxury and display revealed itself as well as a habit of favouring his relatives which was almost papal. To shew that he was an independent sovereign he now began to coin money [134] for which purpose he had to send to Florence for skilled craftsmen.[135] But an even greater ambition was cherished by Rienzo—that of uniting the whole of Italy under the rule

Aug. 1, 1847 of Rome. At an assembly of representatives of the Italian cities Rienzo, after bathing in the font of green basalt which legend connected with the supposed baptism of Constantine, assumed the armour of a knight. From the loggia of the Lateran, the scene of Boniface VIII's proclamation of the Jubilee of 1300, he declared Rome to be the mistress of the world, and called upon Lewis of Bavaria and Charles of Bohemia, as well as the German electors, some even say the Pope, to appear before him. The papal vicar made an ineffectual protest against these extravagances, but his voice was drowned by the blare of the trumpets which Rienzo ordered to be sounded.

The feeling that Rome was again to become the mistress of the world breathes through Dante's *De Monarchia* and is found also in Petrarch ; [136] even the idea that both Papacy and Empire were to fall and a third power based on Rome to take their place was current.[137] Rienzo himself does not seem to have contemplated a revival of the old republic but a renewal rather of the liberties of Rome and Italy on a

Quarrels with the Papacy

monarchic basis.[138] These wild proceedings alarmed the Pope and he sent his legate in Italy, Bertrand de Deux, to insist on the full recognition of the rights of the Church. The

[134] Sketches of his coins will be found in Rodocanachi *op. cit.* pp. 81 sq. Strangely enough the Popes ceased to mint in the twelfth century (not the tenth, as Rodocanachi states, for a coin of Paschal II is extant). Benedict XI resumed the practice : see P. Fabre *Le " Liber censuum " de l'Eglise romaine* p. 14 and Rodocanachi *Les inst. comm. de Rome* pp. 37 sq.

[135] Rome was often found lacking in skilled artisans ; another instance is the bell belonging to the clock in Sta Maria Aracoeli which at the beginning of the fifteenth century was cast by a Milanese and put in place by a Florentine : see RIS. XXIV. col. 1033.

[136] Cf. Piur *Petrachas Buch ohne Namen und die päpst. Kurie* pp. 226 sq.
[137] Burdach *Briefwechsel* pp. 32 sq.   [138] *Op. cit.* p. 89.

legate was received with insolent contempt, fled from Rome, and at once excommunicated Rienzo.

Rienzo's breach with the Papacy was a grave error of judgement. It was probably due to a growing nationalist feeling, for he declared that Pope and cardinals were scheming against Rome inspired by *odio nacionis*.[139] There was certainly much dislike of his proceedings at Avignon, especially among the French cardinals, but the reason for this was not national hatred, but the fear that if he pacified Rome they might be compelled to return there.

The people of Rome were already beginning to tire of Rienzo's despotic ambitions and the airs which he gave himself ; even the immature passion of his youthful eloquence had begun to lose its charm. This gave his enemies the opportunity for a counter-revolution. On Decr. 15 there was a sudden uproar in the city and shouts of " Death to the Tribune ". That was enough. Rienzo had no desire to share the fate of the Gracchi, and losing his head he sought safety in flight. The nobles speedily returned ; the legate quashed the acts of the Tribune : two senators, Luca Savelli and Bertoldo Orsini, were appointed : and things resumed their normal course. *Flight from Rome*

After his flight Rienzo made several futile attempts to return, but finally sought refuge in the Apennines with the Fraticelli. After two years one of the hermits had a vision in which he saw Rienzo, in conjunction with Charles IV to whom he was to play the part of John the Baptist, restore the world to peace. Rienzo took this seriously and made his way in the disguise of a Franciscan to Prague. In July 1350 he managed to obtain an audience with the Emperor ; but the outcome was not happy as Charles handed him over to the Pope. He was taken to Avignon and straitly confined, though allowed books,[140] until the accession of Innocent VI led to his release. *His wanderings*

In the meantime affairs in Rome had gone none too smoothly. At the end of 1351 there was a popular rising, which came to a sudden end when the leader was defeated by Giovanni di Vico. Both nobles and people now took up *Outbreaks in Rome*

---

[139] *Epist.* XLIII. *ll.* 66 sqq. in Burdach *op. cit.* p. 163.
[140] These included the Bible, Livy, and other historians : see Rodocanachi *Rienzo* p. 321.

arms and a fresh struggle began. The Pope's advisers thought that Rienzo might be a useful instrument for restoring order, and so in September 1353 he was sent back to Italy. As Rome was quiet by the time he got there Cardinal Albornoz ordered him to retire to Perugia.

Rienzo returns

In that city he came across the brothers of the famous condottieri leader, Fra Moreale, and with their help managed

Aug. 1, 1854

to re-enter Rome. He was received with tremendous rejoicing and men were reminded of the return of Scipio Africanus. But adversity had not taught Rienzo some needful lessons ; his character, moreover, had not improved during his wanderings and he had become intemperate and capricious. The memory of the previous failure must have been with him, for an institution which has once been decisively overthrown and then restored, seems to live under a shadow still. For this reason the exercise of its power is often marked by rancour and terror. Rienzo attempted to revive a despotic government and by putting to death his ally, Fra Moreale, aroused popular resentment. His resources were consumed in a prolonged and unsuccessful attempt to reduce Palestrina ; this compelled him to impose heavy taxation of Rome. Having captured a body of nobles he subjected them to outrageous treatment, and then weakly set them at liberty. The act may have been well meant, but history has no regard to motives and punishes an injudicious kindness as severely as any other mistake. Thus in every direction he lost support. At last on October 8, 1354 the Capitol, where he had his head-

His death

quarters, was attacked. After some delay Rienzo tried to escape in the disguise of a peasant ; he was recognised and for an hour he and the mob stood face to face. Then someone plunged a dagger into his breast and the rage of the people had free play. It was on the slopes of the Capitol that

133 B.C.

Tiberius Gracchus had been slain nearly fifteen centuries before.

The return of Rienzo to Rome thus proved fatal to himself, but for the Papacy it had been a serviceable interlude, for in the struggle the power of the nobles had been decidedly weakened, and Cardinal Albornoz had methods of dealing with the others.

The career of Rienzo

The career of Rienzo was a curious one and he himself was equally strange. At bottom he was, of course, a genius ;

but too wayward and fitful to be a successful statesman or leader. In him there was no real strength of character to support his vast schemes and fantastic ambitions. At times he could shew courage, especially when excited ; but he was apt to lose his nerve in the presence of danger and either to act with unwise ferocity or to lose heart ; both were equally fatal to the final success of his plans. Yet there was something in him that was admirable, for a man who in an age of violence is conscious of his physical cowardice and yet clings to ambition has surely some element of greatness about him. There is another side too, for Rienzo illustrates the saying of La Bruyère that all confidence is dangerous unless it is complete.

Byron may have called him the last of the Romans,[141] and his mind may have been full of dreams of the ancient glories of the eternal city and his hopes of reviving them ; but he was exceedingly ignorant of the past. Had he lived in the days of Cicero and Cato, as a private person the senate would not have allowed him a hearing. Perhaps he would have found a happier sphere in democratic Athens or some other Greek city state. But if he was ignorant of ancient Rome those whom he addressed were still more so, and his whole appeal was therefore based on principles which were only partially apprehended, and such an attempt invites the fate of the house built on the sand. Events quickly shewed the shallowness of his mind and the sterility of his ideas. What is surprising is that he was allowed a second attempt. But after all the Romans were fickle enough for anything. *Reasons for his failure*

Towards the Papacy Rienzo, when in power, had acted with a high hand. In his wanderings, perhaps influenced by the Fraticelli, he seems to have worked out new ideas of its place in his schemes. He wished for the reform of religion and for the return of the Popes to Rome ; but not as temporal rulers. He wished also to revive the electoral powers of the Roman people. But the Papacy used him as a tool, and when his usefulness was ended threw him aside, and perhaps even betrayed him. *Attitude to the Papacy*

[141] *Childe Harold* cxiv. l. 5.

CHAPTER V

THE GREAT SCHISM OF THE WEST

The Great
Schism

IT is easier to describe the Great Schism than to define it, and easier to define it, than to discover the secret springs form which it arose. What was it exactly? A drama certainly, and tragic at that. But there were times when it seemed in danger of becoming a melodrama—one thinks of Urban VI pacing to and fro reading his hours, whilst within earshot the wretched cardinals were being tortured, or of his dragging them over the Apennines under the hot midsummer sun to have them murdered at Genoa. At times it had almost the aspect of a comedy, when Christendom suddenly found itself with three Popes, or when Felix V was chosen for that high office.

Its causes

What were its causes? First of all it was not a schism, as that between East and West, based ostensibly on a doctrinal difference—though the schism between East and West really went down to something deeper than mere dogma—the division came about, and was perpetuated, by personal and political factors. The pious might see in it the punishment of the Church's sins,[1] the penalty for reforms too long delayed, and for abuses allowed to become inveterate. But though this may well be the ultimate cause, the historian must seek one more direct. He will be tempted to find it in the prevalence of party spirit and the growth of national jealousies. In every land in Europe at this epoch there was unrest and division; the year 1380 compares in this respect with 1848. Feudalism was making a last effort to preserve itself from the attacks of national kings above, and to crush the rising power of the people below. In the Empire there was the struggle between the nobles and the Swabian towns; the beginnings,

---

[1] So Nicholas of Clémanges, for example, *De Ruina Eccles.* I. pt. iii. pp. 6 sqq. Wyclif thought that it was due to the neglect of theology : see Workman *John Wyclif* II. p. 25.

too, of the Swiss Federation. In England the Lollards and
Wat Tyler's rising; a rising also in Flanders of the towns
against their overlords ; and in France the outbreaks in Paris.
These disturbances were more than merely isolated efforts;
there was a spirit of unrest behind them all, and though there
may have been no common policy, in different lands the same
effects were produced. It was no coincidence that the French
army which had reduced the Flemish towns, should on its
return suppress the democratic movement in Paris. That
Italy at this juncture was full of party strife had less significance for such a condition was endemic there.

Men were thus prepared to split into parties, the spirit
of schism was in the air. But the actual opportunity for
division lay in the rival attempts of the French and Italians
to control the Papacy. A Pope at Avignon meant that
French influence would be predominant, a Pope in Rome
meant the recovery of Italian supremacy. In that sense
the Schism was the sequel of the Babylonish Captivity.
Political rather than religious divisions were reflected in its
unhappy beginnings, and in its unnecessary prolongation ;
to these causes of division were added personal factors almost
as determined.

In order to grasp the full significance of the Schism as **Its extent**
a stage in the decline of the Medieval Papacy it is necessary
to realise its wide extent. For just as a disturbance in the
main stream sends ripples into every tiny inlet and creek,
so the greater Schism was reflected in many quarters, and its
evils carried into the smallest units of Christendom. Even
the beggar at the gates of the monastery knew of the division
in the Church.

Some of the most obvious and regrettable consequences **Its**
of the Schism were only temporary and came to an end with **consequences**
its healing—such were the minor divisions to which reference has just been made ; the cessation of public worship
in certain places ; [2] and the shock to individual devotion,
which lost the proud feeling of citizenship in a city at unity
within itself. It is not with these transitory effects that we
are now concerned, but with those, even more numerous and
deplorable, which wrought permanent damage, and speeded
a process of decline which had already set in. So serious

[2] Niem *De Schismate* I. p. 19.

were some of them that one cannot but feel that no merely human organisation could have survived them.

Delays reform   The first of these evil consequences was negative in character. The outbreak of the Schism had found the Church in urgent need of reform; the Avignon period had fostered the growth of many abuses, and brought others into existence; to deal with them in as drastic a manner as possible was the Church's most pressing duty. But a divided Church had neither the power nor the ambition to remedy such evils. Reform was indefinitely postponed. Meanwhile the abuses became more closely wrapped up in the life and system of the Church, until at last it was impossible to unwind them.

Lowers papal prestige   In previous generations the princes and nobles of Germany had laid the foundation of their own power and weakened that of the Empire by virtue of the concessions which, in time of schism, they had wrung out of rival claimants. A similar process, though on a considerably modified scale, now took place in the Church. The Popes, in return for the support of secular rulers, were compelled to make promises and concessions. This was a sad falling off from the position taken up by Innocent IV or Boniface VIII, and the prestige of the Papacy suffered accordingly. Kings and rulers were not likely to forget that the Popes had once exchanged their attitude as arbiters for that of suppliants. But if the rival Popes were dependent upon the great for political support, for financial resources they had to look to all and sundry, and the reckless and unscrupulous methods to which they were reduced in order to raise money, the feverish sale of benefices and dispensations, were a scandal to Christendom. The existence of two or more courts and organisations meant that taxation had to be spread over a much smaller area, and accordingly to become more burdensome to those who had perforce to bear it.

The spiritual weapons which the Papacy wielded had been used so frequently, and not always men saw in the cause of justice, that they had, even before the end of the fourteenth century, lost their edge.[3] Their use during the Schism still

---

[3] This was revealed in the treatment of Boniface VIII. The French chancellor, Peter Flote, is reported to have reminded him when he claimed the use of both arms, spiritual and temporal—" Utique, Domine, sed vestra est verbalis, nostra autem realis ": see Walsingham *Ypodigma Neustriae* pp. 217 sq. (RS.).

further blunted them, and the spectacle of two venerable
pontiffs hurling ineffective anathemas at the supporters
or even the persons of their rivals provoked the amazement
of Europe. Each side could console itself by the thought that
its opponent's weapons had no force behind them since they
came from a usurper and not a genuine successor of St
Peter. But when two or more Popes claimed, equally confidently, the homage of the West, who could have absolute
certainty that the one whom he had accepted was the actual
vicegerent of Christ upon earth ? The question was further
complicated for the individual by the habit of the various
rulers of settling or varying their own spiritual allegiance,
and that of their people, according to the requirements of
secular politics. After being in doubt between different
claimants men might be pardoned if they began to wonder
whether they would not be just as well off without any Pope
at all. The experiment of the French Church, which from
1398 to 1403 recognised no Pope, was a dangerous precedent.

The claims and counterclaims of the different parties led Scrutiny
scholars and thinkers not only to scrutinise the merits of of papal
the actual disputants, but to go farther back still and inquire claims
into the whole basis of the Papacy itself. Their fathers
had taken such matters for granted, but as much of the vast
structure rested on no firmer foundation than forgery and
aggression examination was the last thing which it could
endure. Moreover since the Schism affected, more or less
directly, the humblest member of the Christian society, the
discussion of such problems tended to spread from the lecture-
room into the pulpit and the market-place. As both sides
sought popular support it was to the advantage of neither to
curtail them, though the weakness of their opponent's position
would no doubt be freely exposed. Such exercises probably
played a considerable part in quickening the thought of
many minds, and thus had their share in preparing for the
Renaissance. But in this as in the general critical spirit which
they engendered they did no good to the medieval Papacy.

In all times of stress and struggle churchmen are tempted Growth of
to plunge into the excitement of the contest and to neglect heretical
the humbler duties of caring for the flock entrusted to their movements
care ; the lay-folk, conscious that their spiritual needs are
receiving no adequate attention from those whom they

have been taught to respect, in such circumstances often take the matter into their own hands. Thus it had been in the eleventh and twelfth centuries, and thus it was in the fourteenth. Everywhere lay conventicles began to establish themselves and heretical sects to abound. Such were the Beghards in Germany, and the Waldensians in Austria, the Rhine country, and Bohemia.

Appearance of "prophets" One curious feature of the period was the appearance of numerous prophetical teachers who claimed to be able to foretell the outcome of the Schism. Many of their productions were inspired by the ideas of Joachim of Flora [4] and the Spiritual Franciscans, especially in their emphasis on Apostolic Poverty.[5] They contained the inevitable mixture of politics and religion which marked the movement which called them forth. A certain Gamaleon, for example, prophesied the renewal of the Church by the conquest of Rome by the German Emperor and the removal of the Papacy to Germany.[6] On the other hand Telesophorus foretold the transfer of the Empire from the Germans to the French. This writer had a great following,[7] and very novel and exact ideas. He predicted that the Schism, which he regarded as a punishment for the sins of the clergy, would end in 1393 when the anti-pope (that is the Roman) would be killed at Perugia. The Church would then enter on a new period of life with the return of the clergy to the practice of poverty. He also foretold the recovery of the Holy Land and reunion with the Greeks. Much of his interest centres round a new Pope, *Papa Angelico*, who is to arise.[8] It is worth noticing that the multiplication of heresies through the Schism had been foretold as early as 1381 by Henry of Langenstein, a writer who did much to counteract unorthodox tendencies.[9]

Origin of the Schism When Gregory XI died at the end of March 1378 he left twenty-three cardinals, of whom all but seven were in Rome.

[4] On his ideas and importance see Bett *Joachim of Flora.*
[5] See Niem *De Schism.* III. 41 and 43.
[6] See Döllinger *Weissagungsglaube* p. 351.
[7] This is shewn by the large number of MSS found in different libraries : see Pastor *History of the Popes* I. pp. 152 sq.
[8] See Döllinger *op. cit.* pp. 317, 339 sqq.
[9] See Van der Hardt *Magnum oecumenicum Const. concilium* II. pt. i. col. 27.

To them fell the task of appointing his successor. The conclave, it may be pointed out, was the first to be held in Rome since the election of Benedict XI.

Oct. 1303

As eleven of the sixteen cardinals who assembled for the Conclave in Rome election were Frenchmen it seemed probable that another French Pope would be chosen. But among the Frenchmen themselves there were divisions and the matter was by no means so simple as it appeared to be. These circumstances suggested that the conclave might be a protracted one as the various interests bargained and schemed. But urgency came upon it from without.

The Roman people having got back the Papacy were determined not to be robbed of it again. In vast multitudes they swarmed in the great piazza of St Peter's expressing their wishes.[10] The fact that they had seized and plundered the papal cellars and drunk the wine no doubt added to the strength of their feeling, they were drunken rather than ferocious—*vinolentia non violentia*. The cardinals were not attacked and there was some protection, probably quite adequate, furnished by the municipal authorities. None the less it seemed dangerous to delay, dangerous certainly to elect a Frenchman.

In this situation the cardinals went outside the sacred Election of Urban VI college in order to chose a Pope and they hit upon Bartolomeo di Prignano, Archbishop of Bari, a Neapolitan by birth and so likely to commend himself to the Roman mob. As he had long been a resident at the court at Avignon he was also acceptable to the French. The election took place on April 8, 1378 and the new Pope styled himself Urban VI.

The Roman people, in the meantime, had heard that an election had been made, but as Prignano was not present he obviously could not appear before the people. In order to pacify them an aged Roman cardinal, Tebaldeschi, was decked in the papal insignia and, in spite of his feeble protests, received the greetings of the delighted Romans. The cardinals slipped away in the excitement. When the trick was discovered, however, no evil consequences followed as the

---

[10] " Dum Domini Cardinales vellent intrare Conclave pro Summo Pontifice eligendo, fere totus populus romanus armatus et congregatus in platea Sancti Petri vociferando et comminando : Romano lo volemo, o, almanco italiano " : St Vincent Ferrer *De Moderno Ecclesiae Schismate* fol. CCLXI.

people were so overjoyed at having escaped a French Pope
that they accepted a Neapolitan.

From this account it will be seen, that although there
was no direct interference with the liberty of the cardinals,
they were not really free, except at their own risk, to elect
whom they would.[11] They might have imitated the Italian
cardinals at Carpentras when threatened by Gascon Bands,
and abandoned the conclave to meet again in more secure
surroundings—but probably they were too well guarded and
too terrified even to attempt this.

His general recognition Once Urban was elected he was recognised by all the
cardinals without any sign of compulsion. Later they were
to declare that they did so from fear—it would perhaps be
more true to say that they did so, if not altogether willingly,
from a desire to have a share in the good things at the new
Pope's disposal. At any rate the recognition of Urban could
not have been more complete ; he was publicly acknowledged,
and at his coronation Cardinal Orsini, the only cardinal who
had not voted for him, placed the tiara on his head.[12] The
whole body of cardinals wrote to their brethren at Avignon
within a fortnight announcing that the election had been
made.[13] The latter then tendered their homage, and by
displaying the arms of Urban in the city gave full appro-
bation to his election. A collective letter was also sent to
the Emperor and to the princes of Christendom ; whilst
Robert of Geneva wrote personally to Charles V of France
and others. The other future Avignon Pope, Peter de Luna,
who had been a member of the conclave, wrote to his fellow
Spaniards accepting Urban and in celebrating mass inserted
his name as that of the reigning Pope. None of the cardinals
at this juncture made any protest or questioned the validity
of what had been done. There was really no reason why
they should have done so, for Urban represented no one party
and was familiar with Avignon. All parties no doubt hoped
that he would accept their standpoint or policy and perhaps
intended that he should be a mere figure-head, controlled
by the cardinals.

[11] Salembier puts it concisely : " Urbain a été élu dans la crainte, mais
non par la crainte " : see *Le grand Schisme* p. 43.
[12] Dietrich of Niem calls him John ; but Salembier *op. cit.* p. 36 corrects to
James,
[13] Text in Raynaldus 1378 No. 19.

The reputation of Urban and the unanimity with which he Character of was recognised seemed to promise well for the future of the Urban Church.[14]   In character the new Pope was temperate and simple, even ascetic, in his tastes and habits ; a zealous attender on his duties ; and not without learning, especially in the sacred Scriptures.   He had a complete knowledge of the routine of the curia.   At the same time he was resolutely opposed to worldliness and luxury among the clergy, as well as abuses such as simony and impurity.   Unfortunately his virtues were accompanied by grave weaknesses, weaknesses which perhaps it needed the sun of prosperity to bring to light.[15]   His desires after reform, sincere as they were, were not tempered by prudence nor pursued with tact.[16]   In his eagerness to stop the reputation for bribery and corruption, which rightly attached to the papal court, he forbade all gifts and pensions.   This was a drastic measure and from its undue severity likely to fail of its purpose, since no one would attempt to observe it.   It merely provoked annoyance.

But a worse fault was an arbitrary and violent temper. Quarrels Urban took an apparent delight in using his high position with the to inflict insults upon the cardinals, both in private intercourse cardinals and even in more public utterances.   There were in consequence constant quarrels, in which both sides forgot their dignity.   The Pope held over the sacred college the threat of creating a large number of Italian cardinals so as to gain entire control over it.   On grounds of statesmanship this very course had been commended to him by his self-appointed adviser, St Catherine of Siena.   Used as a threat, however, it aroused deep resentment ; the Cardinal of Geneva in particular shewed his anger by swift changes of colour,

[14] Pastor quotes from a letter which he discovered in the Gonzaga archives, written by the Mantuan representative in Rome to Lodovico Gonzaga, in which hopes are expressed for the rule of Urban, based largely on his Italian nationality and supposed lack of relatives.   The envoy ventured to forecast that such a shepherd had not been found among Popes for more than a century : see *History of the Popes* I. p. 379.

[15] Dietrich of Niem applies to him the judgement of Tacitus on Galba (*Hist.* I. 49)—" Capax imperii nisi imperasset ".   The same writer also records the opinion of the cardinals that his head had been turned by his unexpected elevation : *De Schism.* I. 7.

[16] He forgot Seneca's maxim that in converting others you must consider not only the truth but the ability of the hearer to receive it : *De Ira* III. xxxvi. 4.

though others also gave the same sign.[17]   Urban undoubtedly behaved in a quite unreasonable manner and it almost seems as if he sought a petty revenge for slights cast upon him in more obscure days.   St Catherine, strongly as she agreed with his aims, yet realised the lack of wisdom in his efforts to carry them out.   Like an earlier Portia she pleaded with him to temper justice with mercy and pointed out that it was much easier to destroy than to build up.   She went so far as to implore the Pope, by his crucified Lord, to exercise more control over his violent temper.

Before his death Gregory XI had left orders with the governor of St Angelo not to hand over the keys except by an order from the six cardinals left at Avignon.   These orders, although actually sent, had not been obeyed.   St Angelo therefore was a convenient centre for those who had become disaffected towards the new Pope.

In the following summer, the French cardinals, excusing themselves on the grounds of the severe heat in Rome, withdrew to Anagni as a healthier residence.   Their real reason was the desire to get away from the immediate presence of the Pope, whose absolute refusal to hear of any return to Avignon had permanently alienated them.   They wished to return thither, not merely because of its more congenial manner of life, but because it was within the sphere of French influence.

And with Joanna of Naples   In the meantime Urban had weakened his position by quarrelling with his natural sovereign, Joanna of Naples, as well as with Onorato Gaetani, Lord of Fondi.   From the latter the cardinals were to receive support and protection.   This alteration in the political situation and the assurance of French support,[18] emboldened the cardinals to carry out the extreme measure which they had in contemplation, nothing less than that of declaring Urban no true Pope.

The cardinals repudiate Urban VI   Their action in thus repudiating the Pope whom they had themselves elected was not taken lightly or hastily; time was given for Urban to open negotiations and even to

---

[17] " Immo vidit ipse Dominum Gebennensem . . . adeo mutasse colorem in facie, quod totus palluit, et ita alii " : Thomas de Acerno in RIS. III. pt. ii. col. 725 B.

[18] Charles V seems to have been told by Urban's own envoys that his election had been the result of duress, a piece of treachery unworthy of their calling.   The French king does not seem to have originated the revolt and up to the end of his life he was convinced that Clement was the genuine Pope.

offer, through the Italian cardinals, to call a General Council
to discuss the whole question.[19]   The Pope felt that he had
a strong position, as the opinion of leading lawyers whom he
had consulted agreed in declaring his election perfectly valid. And elect

At the end of August the cardinals moved to Fondi "VII" Clement
and there on Sept. 20 they chose a new Pope, by twelve
votes out of thirteen, in the person of Robert of Geneva.
He took the style of Clement VII, a title later to be held
by Giulio de' Medici.[20]

(1523-1534)

The choice of the French cardinals was, from their point Character of
of view, an excellent one.   Robert of Geneva was a man of Clement
noble birth, and his attractive manners were in strong contrast to the boorishness of Urban.   He was still young and
combined energy and wide experience.   The one stain on
his reputation was responsibility for the terrible massacre
of Cesena.   Before the election the three Italian cardinals
had gone to Fondi—it has been said that each hoped to
be the new Pope [21]—and although they took no part in the
election they afterwards gave their allegiance to Clement.
Urban seems to have lost heart for the time and to have been
weighed down by the course of events, he even gave way
to tears in private.[22]

Civil war for the possession of Rome and Italy now Civil war in
broke out between the two Popes.   Clement hired his old Italy
comrades in arms, the Breton mercenaries ; while Urban, for
his part, enlisted the newly recruited Italian Band, the Company of St George.   Under its leader, Alberigo da Barbiano,
the latter won its spurs in a fight near Marino, and to the April 29, 1879
delight of Italy defeated the Bretons.   Urban at once knighted
Alberigo and presented him with a banner bearing the significant motto *Italia liberata dai barbari*.   The struggle was

---

[19] See Raynaldus 1378 No. 43.

[20] Clement is called "l'Anti-papa di Fondi" by the *Cronica di Pisa* (RIS.
XV. col. 1076 B.) and "lo Papa di Fondi" by *Istoria Napolitanu* (RIS. XXIII.
col. 223 B.).   Giulio's action shewed that he did not recognise Robert as a
genuine Pope.   I cannot understand the argument of Salembier, who pleads
that this does not follow because certain anti-popes—Leo VIII, Boniface VII,
and Benedict X—retained their numbers (*op. cit.* p. 143).   The acts of all the
Popes during the Schism were accepted as valid by Martin V so as to avoid
a position of intolerable uncertainty : see Conrad Eubel *Die avignonesische
Obedienz der Mendikantenorden* p. vii.

[21] Dietrich of Niem *De Schismate* I. 9.

[22] *Op. cit.* I. 12, " Quandoque, me vidente, flevit amare."

becoming quite openly a national one, and Urban was well within his rights in appealing to Italian racial feeling. The battle was decisive. Clement gave up any further attempt to capture Rome and retired from Italy ; whilst the Castle of St Angelo surrendered at once. The Roman people in their fury tried to pull it down, but beyond stripping off some of its marble they did little damage.

The blame for the Schism   The blame for the schism must be divided between the cardinals and Urban. The Pope's policy, to free the Church from French influence, and to reform its manners and morals, was certainly the right one, and merited the support of all true lovers of religion ; but his tactless efforts to enforce his will were naturally provocative of opposition. The cardinals, on the other hand, had themselves elected Urban ; and even if their act had not been entirely free, the same could hardly be said of their subsequent recognition. One is tempted to feel that a schism was inevitable when once an Italian Pope had been elected, that political conditions demanded it. France was in no mood to allow her influence to be sacrificed.

St Catherine of Siena   St Catherine of Siena, as she had been outspoken in blaming Urban for his strange conduct, was equally outspoken in expressing her opinion of the cardinals ; for this reason her testimony is the more valuable. In her searching condemnation of these " devils in human form " she is moved to adopt strange figures, as when she tells them that they ought to have been " pillars to uphold the Vicar of Christ and his bark ".[23] More important is her opinion that the cardinals had no defence since they themselves had admitted that the election of Urban had been by the inspiration of the Holy Ghost, that they had taken part in his coronation, and had begged for and received favours from him.

Division of allegiance   As the schism was ultimately due to political causes so the division of allegiance among Catholic countries followed in the main political lines. Urban obtained the support of most of the countries of Europe. To him England, the greater part of Germany and of Flanders, as well as Italy, outside Naples, adhered. Lewis of Hungary, naturally took the side opposite to Naples ; whilst Scotland, just as naturally, sup-

[23] If this is pressed it suggests that the Ship of the Church had been dry-docked.

ported Clement, since England was numbered among Urban's supporters. The policy of England herself was, no doubt, dictated by hatred of France and the French Pope. In addition to France, Scotland, and Naples, Clement had the support of the Spanish kingdoms. The allegiance of these last was due largely to the efforts of Peter de Luna.

To the French Clement was to prove a financial burden and their supply was by no means unanimous ; the University of Paris hesitated for a time, and was only persuaded to fall into line by pressure from Charles V. The Bohemians in Paris at once left the University.[24] In Flanders and Germany allegiance was divided. In the former country the rulers were on the side of Clement, but the towns, which were dependent on English wool, adhered to Urban. The result was very bitter internal feeling especially as the Bishops of Cambrai, Thérouanne, Arras and Tournai, were on the side of Clement.[25] France in return for its financial support received not only the benefit of continued influence upon papal policy, but Clement made over to the crown the patronage of the chief benefices, and actually granted a great part of the Papal States, having no regard for the temporal power in Italy, to the Duke of Anjou. Among Clement's supporters in Germany was Leopold of Austria; he had received 120,000 florins as the price of his interest.[26]

Without French aid the schism would probably have died out ; but whatever may have been the benefits to France, which seemed to make the support of Clement a politic course, I think that Charles V acted according to the dictates of his conscience ; even on his deathbed he protested that he had followed the advice of the cardinals.[27]

---

[24] Urban arranged a marriage between Richard II of England and Anne of Bohemia in order to prevent the latter country from going over to France : see Walsingham *Historia Anglicana* I. p. 452 (RS.). This alliance led to increased intercourse between England and Bohemia, and among other things the teaching of Wyclif was taken from one to the other.

[25] See Meyer *Ann. Rerum Fland.* XIII. p. 210. A similar situation arose in Italy during the Social War at the beginning of the first century B.C. when isolated Italian communities remained loyal to Rome.

[26] For German support of Clement see Göller *Repertorium Germanicum* I. pp. 99 sqq.

[27] I am prepared to accept the judgement of Salembier *op. cit.* p. 105, who says : " Si le roi ne fut pas dans le bon chemin, tout au moins resta-t-il dans la bonne foi."

The saints divided

If the political support enjoyed by the two Popes was thus divided, the same may be said of their religious backing.[28] As we have seen, Urban had St Catherine of Siena on his side ; he had also Peter of Aragon, a Franciscan of royal blood,[29] and Gerard Groot, the famous preacher and reformer of the Low Countries. After the legal decision given in his favour, before the actual outbreak of the schism, he naturally enjoyed the support of the canonists. Clement for his part could boast that he was accepted by St Vincent Ferrer [30] and Cardinal Peter of Luxemburg. This division among men of saintly life was really more damaging than the division of kings and countries, for it extended right down to the lowliest ranks of the clergy. When the great part which they played in medieval life is remembered the seriousness of the situation will be better realised.

The split affected not merely the parish or the monastery, it extended into law, diplomacy, politics, even education.[30a] In many a diocese, to consider purely ecclesiastical aspects, there was a double choice of bishop, with the reproduction upon a smaller scale of the greater schism in the whole Church. Even the monastic orders were divided and the Franciscans actually had two rival Ministers-general.[31]

Warfare in Naples

In one case, at least, the schism led to warfare. The decision of Joanna of Naples to reject Urban led the Pope to declare her deposed and to offer the kingdom to Lewis of Hungary. Lewis himself did not intervene in person, but he supported Charles of Durazzo, who had some kind of a claim to the throne, with troops. Further supplies came from Urban who sold even the sacred vessels of some of the churches in order to hire mercenaries. Urban's support was not entirely inspired by the needs of the Papacy, or by resentment against his sovereign ; at the back of his policy

---

[28] On the division among spiritual leaders see Salembier *op. cit.* pp. 77 sqq.

[29] His influence in Spain was outweighed by that of Peter de Luna.

[30] This saint went over to the Roman Pope in 1416, being convinced that the obstinacy of Benedict was harmful to the Church.

[30a] " Non est regnum, non provincia, non dioesesis, non territorium, non capitulum, non collegium, vel conventus, imo nec vix domus, quin . . . inter se pertinaciter subdivisi." Bulaeus *Hist. Univ. Paris* V. pp. 4 sqq.

[31] See Wadding *Annales Minorum* IX. xvii. 23 and cf. an interesting article by Miss Rose Graham " The Great Schism and the Eng. Monasteries of the Cistercian Order " in *Eng. Hist. Rev.* XLIV. pp. 373 sqq.

lay the desire to found a principality for his worthless nephew, Francesco Prignano, known as Butillo.

Joanna thus threatened took the grave step of adopting Louis of Anjou as her heir; the house of Valois was thus once again dragged into Italian politics. For the time Louis could give but little help to his benefactress, as the death of Charles V kept him in France, and in spite of the skill and 1380 courage of Joanna's fourth husband, Otto of Brunswick, she was unable to resist the forces of Charles who was hailed as a national hero. Following on the capture of Otto she herself fell into the hands of Charles. The latter was ungenerous in his treatment, for failing to get from her the reversion of the kingdom, and fearing the approach of Louis, May 1882 he had her strangled.[32] The army of Louis was too strong to be met in the open field, but Charles had sure allies in the climate and the disease which soon broke out among the invaders. Fortune indeed favoured him as Louis himself died in the autumn of 1384.

Meanwhile Urban was growing impatient over the slow Urban and development of his plans. He entered the territory of Charles Charles of to urge him to more active measures, and to his surprise Durazzo found himself besieged in Nocera by his former protégé, Alberigo, now in the service of Charles. The cardinals who were with Urban, hating their surroundings and their master, consulted a famous canonist, Bartolino of Piacenza, as to the legality of putting the Papacy into commission, on the grounds of the Pope's unfitness for his office. The plot, for such it was, came to the knowledge of Urban, and he did not scruple to employ torture to extort from the cardinals the full extent of their guilt.

Nocera did not hold out for long against the mercenary leader, but the citadel, in which Urban had established himself, resisted all attacks. Day by day, and several times a day, the Pope excommunicated the besiegers. This brandishing of the spiritual weapon served only to arouse the derision of the godless mercenaries, and Alberigo, on his side, set a price on the Pope's head. The position of Urban was be-

---

[32] *Istoria Napolitana* which is not very reliable in its chronology places this event in the previous year : " Regina Giovanna . . . fu strangolata alla Castiello de San Fele per lo detto Re Carlo, e fu portata a Santa Chiara di Napoli a sepilire."   RIS. XXIII. col. 223 C.

coming desperate, when a sudden move by a daring band of his supporters, perhaps with the connivance of Charles, who might have found Urban an embarrassing captive, succeeded in rescuing him. The Pope, accompanied by the reluctant cardinals, made his way across the Apennines in the heat of midsummer, careless of the sufferings of his companions, and reached the galleys sent by the friendly Genoese. At Genoa itself he landed safely on Sept. 23, 1385.

Flight of Urban

Genoa, however, had no wish for any prolongation of the Pope's visit and bluntly told him so. There was much difficulty in finding another city of refuge ; but at last Lucca consented to receive the fugitive, and thither he set out at the end of 1386. Before leaving Genoa Urban committed a monstrous and amazing crime, he had four, if not more, of his cardinals murdered, and according to one account left their corpses in a stable.[33]

Death of Charles and of Urban

Charles of Durazzo, having got rid of Urban, was free to cross over into Hungary; only to meet his death by treachery in February 1386. Troubles at once broke out in Naples, and the Pope thought that he saw a fresh chance of providing for his nephew.[34] But a term had been set to his strange career and he was rapidly nearing it. In October 1389 in that same Vatican Palace, which had been the scene of his stormy election, he breathed his last, and all his ambitious plans were left to the mercy of his successor. Thus ended a pontificate which a great historian has described as " one of the most disastrous in the whole history of the papacy ".[35]

Boniface IX

The death of Urban furnished an opportunity for bringing the schism to an end. But the natural reluctance of the Italian cardinals to submit to an Avignon Pope rendered it abortive. They made their own choice, and it lighted on another Neapolitan, Piero Tomacelli. The new Pope was in all things, except race, a contrast to his predecessor. He was only thirty-three years of age, and, if lacking in learn-

[33] There is no doubt of the fact of the murder though the details in some accounts are untrustworthy : this applies especially to the record of Andrea Gatarus *Istoria Padovana* in RIS. XVII. col. 460 A.

[34] As a means of raising funds for a possible expedition he ordered 1390, and not 1400, to be kept as the year of Jubilee.

[35] Creighton *History of the Papacy* I. p. 104.

ing and experience of administration, made up for it by his singular tact. He took the style of Boniface IX.

Boniface at once recognised the youthful Ladislas as King of Naples. In spite, however, of papal support Ladislas made but slow progress, and it was not until 1393 that he was secure in his kingdom. For the Pope friendship with Ladislas was valuable as a check on the Romans. *Ladislas of Naples*

For the first few months of his pontificate Boniface and the Romans were on good terms ; the approach of the Jubilee was regarded by the citizens in much the same spirit as the farmer regards the harvest. To quarrel with the Pope at such a juncture would be disastrous. No doubt the schism was a great draw-back as it cut off half Christendom from Rome, but in spite of it vast multitudes made their way thither.[36] But when the Jubilee was over relations became strained, and in September 1392 Boniface fled to Perugia from which he moved, in the following summer, to Assisi. By this time the Romans, with characteristic fickleness, were anxious to have him back again. Boniface seized the opportunity to enforce harsh terms ; among other things he insisted that clergy and members of the papal court should be exempt from the jurisdiction of the municipality and from taxation. No sooner was the Pope back than fresh disputes arose ; but this time Ladislas intervened and the citizens were frightened into submission. By 1398 the papal power was firmly imposed, never again to be broken.[37] *Boniface and the Romans*

If Boniface was subject to annoyance from those of his own obedience, his rival, Clement, was in no better case. France was torn between the warring factions of Burgundians and Armagnacs ; this in itself was a source of weakness, but since both could obviously not support the same Pope, the number of his adherents was greatly reduced. The French of his allegiance, however, made great efforts and the expedition against the rebel citizens of Ghent had the nature of a religious enterprise. The Flemings, led by the ill-fated Philip van Artevelde, found fresh fuel for their hatred of the *Civil war in France*

[36] In order to extend the benefits to a wider circle Boniface allowed certain cities in Germany to be counted as substitutes for Rome. Unfortunately scandals arose as unauthorised persons began hawking indulgences.

[37] One sign of his triumph, which the Romans bitterly resented, was the rebuilding of the Palace of the Senator burnt down in the days of Rienzo.

French in the belief that the latter were responsible for the schism.[40]   But the success of the French armies did not bring Flanders to the obedience of Clement.

The University of Paris and the schism

In spite of this expedition all was not going too well for Clement, even among his professed adherents in France. The methods of his agents disgusted the people ; above all, the University of Paris, whose adhesion had never been ardent, now became increasingly critical, and in January 1394 arranged a ballot for arriving at the best means for ending the schism.   The voting favoured the abdication of both Popes.[41]   When this result was reported to the king by Nicholas of Clémanges it met with a favourable notice ; but nothing practical was done, and the University, in order to move the court to action, decided to suspend its lectures.[42]   Clement himself was deeply affected by this drastic action, and shortly before his death endeavoured to recover the support of the University by sending for D'Ailly and other leaders.

Benedict "XIII"

It was now the opportunity of the French cardinals to shew that they placed the welfare of the whole Church above their personal predilections.   But they followed, instead, the disastrous example of the Italians and, after an unsuccessful attempt by the University to get a royal veto, elected the energetic Peter de Luna as Benedict " XIII ".[43]   Peter had openly declared his willingness to resign when called upon to do so.   His subsequent course of action was to reveal him as the most obstinate of all the Popes of the period.   The cardinals seem to have wished to restore peace to the Church, but the desire to save their faces and not to cast doubt on their own positions led them to make a new election.[44]   All the cardinals, save three, signed a declaration promising to abdicate if requested to do so by the majority of the college.

[40] Meyer *Ann. Rerum Fland.* XIII. p. 189.

[41] It was exactly a century after the abdication of Celestine V and to Peter D'Ailly it seemed a hopeful precedent.

[42] See *Chron. Karoli* by a monk of St Denys XV. iv.

[43] On Benedict see S. Puig y Puig *Pedro de Luna, ultimo Papa de Aviñon.* The same title was taken later by Pietro Francesco Orsini (1724-1730).

[44] His name Luna offered scope for punning attacks ; e.g. " Petrus ille de Luna, homo nunquam non lunaticus, turbavit omnia " : *Ann. Rerum Fland.* XIII. p. 225.   Another was led into inaccuracy by his use of the figure : " Luna instabilis est, mutabilis est, crescit, decrescit, in eodem sistere nescit " : Theodore Vrie in Van der Hardt I. pt. i. p. 187.   Whatever else might be said of Benedict he could not be accused of instability.

Benedict was a man of upright character, deeply learned His character
in the Canon Law—as his opponents were to find to their
cost—and experienced in affairs; but he was too much
addicted to intrigue and verbal fencing; above all he was
determined to have his own way in all things. The election
seems to have wrought a change in him as deplorable as that
in Urban VI, or perhaps it would be more accurate in the case
of each of them to suppose that it revealed the character
in a new light and gave occasion for fresh traits to manifest
themselves.

Relations between Benedict and the University of Paris Quarrel with
now became more strained. The efforts of the University the Univer-
to end the schism were offensive to the Pope in theory as well sity
as in practice. He was annoyed, not merely as Pope but as
canonist, by the attempt to exercise compulsion. Though
the feelings of the University as a whole were becoming increasingly hostile and strong measures were contemplated
by them, some of the more moderate members were approaching the papal side. Nicholas of Clémanges went over in 1394
and was appointed secretary to Benedict, he was followed
by Peter D'Ailly who became Bishop of Cambrai.

In February 1395 an influential meeting of the French
clergy was held in Paris. It decided that the method of
cession was the wisest, and even went so far as to talk of the
use of force against Benedict if he proved obstinate. Things
had come to a strange pass when a French Pope was threatened
with violence by his own supporters. An embassy was sent
to Benedict in May by the king and University jointly; he
met it by suggesting that the two Popes and their adherents
should hold a combined conference. It was soon evident that
the skill of Benedict was too much for the French.

Things drifted on for some time longer and then the grave Sept. 25,
disaster of Nicopolis made the restoration of the unity of 1396
Western Christendom in the face of the Turkish advance a
matter of extreme urgency. The French king approached
the other monarchs of Europe in order to secure their co-
operation in ending the schism. Amongst other things he
held a conference with Wenzel of Bohemia who was Emperor Rheims
at this juncture. The healing of the wounds of the Church Mar. 23, 1398
could hardly have been entrusted to stranger physicians—
a madman and a drunkard. Eventually Charles promised

to get his Pope to abdicate by every possible means, whilst Wenzel, for his part, was to take steps to overcome the resistance of Boniface IX.

Withdrawal of French obedience

Charles really carried out his side of the agreement. A synod was held in Paris on May 22, 1398, presided over by Simon Cramaud, Patriarch of Alexandria; it decided by 247 votes out of 300 that allegiance should be withdrawn from Benedict.[45]   The edict giving effect to this decision was published on July 28.   Obedience was not restored until May 1403 when Louis, Duke of Orleans, who favoured Benedict, succeeded in getting power into his hands.   During the intervening five years the king, acting through the bishops, was the real ruler of the French Church.   This was an important innovation and shewed the possibility of a national church being carried on without a Pope—an example which the English people was to copy after the lapse of more than a century. At the same time it would be quite unjust to attribute to Charles any idea of adopting a policy of aggression towards the Roman Church; he was moved solely by the needs of his kingdom and the desire for the restoration of unity.

Wenzel deposed

Sept. 1398

Wenzel was neither so energetic nor so fortunate in his measures against Boniface.   Indeed it was the Emperor and not the Pope who eventually lost his throne.   The latter, alarmed by the activities of Charles VI against his rival, tried to gain the favour of the Emperor-elect by offering to crown him.[46] Wenzel, however, took no steps to end the schism, and in August 1400 the electors, disgusted by his inactivity, decided to depose him.[47]   The failure to end the schism was only one reason for their action; others were perhaps more damaging, especially his policy, if such it can be called, in Italy, where the recognition of Gian Galeazzo Visconti as Duke of Milan was a sacrifice of imperial rights and required the sanction of the electors.

Election of Rupert, Count Palatine

In the place of Wenzel the choice of the electors fell on Rupert, the Count Palatine, a well-meaning ruler, but with

[45] Such are the figures given by the authorities.   But as the voting papers are still extant it has been possible to check them.   The real figure of those who voted in favour of the withdrawal was only 123 and 80 were against it : see Waugh *History of Europe 1378-1494* pp. 137 sq.

[46] See Lindner *Gesch. des deutschen Reichs unter K. Wenzel* II. p. 365.

[47] The action of the electors was partly inspired by Florence, which was alarmed, and not without reason, by the growth of the Visconti power.

resources utterly inadequate to the task which confronted
him.   This was made abundantly clear when in 1401 he descended into Italy to take action against Milan.   The power of
the Visconti was much more considerable than that of the
Emperor, and indeed Gian Galeazzo, but for his sudden death, Sept. 1402
might well have conquered the whole of Central Italy and
founded a North Italian Kingdom.   The election of Rupert
began a sehism in the Empire parallel to that in the Papacy.

Wenzel's weak handling of Boniface had probably had Benedict's
much to do with the stubborn refusal of Benedict to make firm
attitude
any concession to the French king ; he saw that there was
a real danger that if he went so far as to abdicate there was
little prospect of his rival doing the same.   Benedict had
indeed great need of stubbornness to maintain himself in face
of the action of the French king in withdrawing the obedience
of the nation, for it was followed by the desertion of all save
seven of his cardinals [48] and even of the people of Avignon.
Nothing daunted the Pope fortified himself in his palace
and withstood a siege, more or less serious, which lasted for
two months before a truce was agreed upon.[49]   The use of
arms against the Pope was a shock to moderate opinion, whilst
the courage and determination with which Benedict defended
himself could not fail to arouse admiration.   In March 1403
he succeeded in making his ecape in disguise and during the
next four years and more Avignon, or at least the palace, was
left in a state of blockade.

Secure in his freedom Benedict shewed himself magnani- Recovers
mous, even to those who had deserted him.   To the king he French
obedience
was ironical, and to the University of Paris ; the former was
so far affected that he agreed to submit to the Pope once
again if the latter would recognise measures taken during
the withdrawal of obedience.   Things were thus more or less
where they had been, except that the Pope was finding fresh
support in the other universities of France, who were jealous of

[48] Ehrle *Archiv* V. p. 424.
[49] This was in the autumn of 1398.   The mercenaries who carried out the
operations were under the command of Geoffrey Boucicaut, the younger
brother of the famous marshal.   Froissart XVI. p. 127 says it was the
marshal himself, but this is a mistake.   Another mistake concerning the
marshal is that of Gibbon who kills him at Agincourt (VII. p. 36).   He was
actually taken prisoner and died in England without recovering his liberty :
see *Notice sur Boucicaut* (Collection Michaud and Poujoulat) II. p. 212.

the too great preponderance of Paris ; Toulouse, Orleans and Montpellier now openly took his side.

The way of cession had thus failed, as fail it was bound to do, since it was improbable that either Pope would consider the interests of the Church before his own ; or rather each Pope was bound to identify these interests. Not a little blame attaches to the French for the tactless and provocative manner in which they tried to coerce Benedict ; such tactics could have succeeded only with a weak Pope, and he was the last person to submit to browbeating, whilst as a controversialist he was superior to his opponents.

Avarice of Boniface It might have been thought that the French would have transferred to Boniface the obedience which they withdrew from Benedict ; but Boniface was too purely Italian in outlook and policy, and his shameless avarice shocked his own supporters. Simony had become rampant in the court of the Roman Pope and everything had its price. Even when the price had been paid the purchaser was by no means sure that he would get what he had paid for. One source of papal income was the selling to monks of the privilege of changing their order, and to friars the right to hear confessions or to preach in parish churches, even against the wish of the incumbent. Both these practices caused much discontent.[50] Avarice was about the only blot on the character of Boniface. It was a real difficulty for the reformers that Popes of austere personal life should adopt such practices, urgent as their need of resources might be.

Innocent VII On the death of Boniface in the autumn of 1404 the cardinals of his obedience, after agreeing that whichever of them should be elected would do all in his power to end the schism even by abdication if necessary, chose in his place Cosimo dei Migliorati, another Neapolitan. This Pope, who took the style of Innocent VII, was of blameless life, gentle and accommodating in temperament. He had considerable legal knowledge and was well acquainted with the business of the curia. Unfortunately his accommodating temperament made him weak and indolent, whilst he lacked all proper

---

[50] Gobelin Person, the papal secretary, naively expresses his amazement that ' religious ', who were supposed to have no private possessions, could yet find the considerable sums demanded for these privileges : *Cosmodromion* VI. p. 84.

sense of responsibility. This weakness allowed his relatives to gain complete control over him.[51] Through them he came into conflict with the Romans and had to flee to Viterbo, which gave an opportunity to Ladislas of Naples to attack the city;[52] but it proved unsuccessful and in the end the Pope returned in March 1406.

Some futile attempts to negotiate between Benedict and Innocent were now undertaken, but the chief result was to stiffen both sides. Benedict, on the whole, was making some progress, as French influence was now on his side once more and this brought over Genoa and Pisa.

Innocent died, after a pontificate of only two years, from apoplexy. His life and death made little difference to the situation. Innocent's real interests were probably in literature and art—he anticipated the Popes of the next generation—and in spite of the unsettled state of Rome for the greater part of his reign, he succeeded in reviving the University which Boniface VIII had founded, and in promoting in it the study of Greek. His action, if it was not merely the expression of his personal tastes, shews the growing realisation of the power of humanism and of the wisdom of controlling and using it. *Character of Innocent*

Gregory XII, the next Pope, was advanced in years and made the most elaborate protestations of his willingness to end the schism. He even wrote to the French king offering to abdicate if Benedict could be persuaded to do the same. This action was so far effective that it moved the French to exert fresh pressure on their Pope, and a council was held in Paris. In calling it together the king was careful to define its objects; it was not an attempt to deal with questions of faith or discipline—its sole task was to seek for a method by which the schism could be ended. A leading part in the deliberations was taken by the University of Paris which supplied six representatives, a similar number represented Benedict. As the dispute continued the University grew more and more critical of the Pope and more aggressive towards the bishops. At times it went too far, and by trumping *Gregory XII* *Nov. 18, 1406*

[51] They even went so far as to stable their horses in St Paul's which was turned into a barracks : *Diarium Antonii Petri* RIS. XXIV. col. 979 D.
[52] Leonardo Bruni expounds the policy of Ladislas : see RIS. XIX. col. 921 E. " ipse vero mentem erexit ad Urbem Romam capiendam ".

up charges against the personal character of Benedict stiffened the opposition. The University at last came round to the method of holding a General Council. The adherents of Benedict thereupon took shelter behind the Canon Law, a very strong position. The practical outcome of the Council was a partial withdrawal of obedience ; but in order to encourage moderating efforts and to give Benedict an opportunity for abdication, its decrees were not immediately put Nov. 23, 1407 into effect ; in fact it was not until after the murder of the Jan. 12, 1408 Duke of Orleans, Benedict's chief supporter, that they were finally published.

Negotiations between the rivals   In the meantime Benedict, who professed to be just as anxious to resign as Gregory, had entered into direct negotiations with his rival. The latter appointed as one of his envoys his nephew, Antonio Correr, an unfortunate choice as the nephew had every reason for prolonging his uncle's pontificate. The influence which his relatives had acquired over the weak old man was a decisive factor for the moment.

The delegates of the two Popes agreed at length that Savona would be the most convenient place for an interview. But such a meeting and the possibility of ending the schism which lay in it, was not to the taste of Ladislas. Accordingly he did all in his power to prevent it. To this end he stirred up strife in Rome, and forced Gregory to take refuge in St Angelo; but as Paolo Orsini, the commander of the papal troops, promptly crushed the outbreak it had no lasting effect on papal policy.

Benedict arrived at Savona on Sept. 29, 1407. Gregory got as far as Lucca, and then suggested, under pressure from Venice and Florence, the substitution of Pisa as a meeting place. Benedict thereupon raised difficulties, and it seemed as if it was not possible to get the two pontiffs together ; Leonardo Bruni even surmised that one must be a land animal, the other a denizen of the water, so that a meeting could hardly be expected.[53] More serious minds began to harbour the suspicion that the two apparent rivals were really playing into one another's hands, and whilst making the most solemn protestations had their tongues in their cheeks.

[53] *Epist. ad Petrilio* in RIS. XIX. col. 926 C.

Then Gregory took a new line. Throwing off all profes- Gregory becomes defiant
sion of belief in the way of cession, which he denounced as
mala et injusta et diabolica, he declared his intention of resisting French influence. His policy was probably inspired
by Ladislas of Naples who in April 1408 had seized Rome
and the bulk of the Papal States. One result of Gregory's
action, however, was the desertion of all his cardinals who
by May 11 assembled at Pisa.

The withdrawal of revenue from Benedict which had fol- And also Benedict
lowed the Council of 1406 had seemed only to make him more
defiant ; and in reply he issued a Bull of excommunication May 11, 1408
which did not even spare the king. To this the University
of Paris made their response, which was hardly worthy of
so dignified a body. They denounced Benedict as a worthless
person, not fit to be recognised as a cardinal, much less a
Pope. His Bull was publicly cut in pieces by the Rector
in person. The government now began to persecute the supporters of Benedict, and the Pope, to avoid possible arrest,
fled to Perpignan.

Suddenly all parties turned to the way of a General Council The way of a General Council
as offering the best solution of their difficulties. Both Popes
convoked assemblies ; Benedict for Perpignan on Nov. 1,
1408, Gregory for the following Whitsuntide at some place
near Ravenna which would be specified later. The cardinals
of the two parties had a meeting at Leghorn in which each
obedience was represented by four delegates. They, too,
agreed to call a council and to press for the resignation of
both Popes.

When Gregory protested against this proposal he was
informed that he had power to summon only those of his
own obedience, and was urged to abandon his council, and
attend that to be summoned by the cardinals. Benedict,
when the cardinals of his obedience made similar approaches,
replied that his council was already assembling and that he
hoped soon to end the schism. After expressing surprise
at their proposed action he professed to be willing to recognise
their council if they could justify it according to Canon
Law, which of course they could not do.

Benedict's council actually met on the appointed day and Council of Perpignan
more than a hundred prelates attended it. But the numbers
gradually decreased as the bishops slipped away one by one.

A commission was appointed, however, to suggest a means of ending the schism, and eventually reported in favour of Benedict's resignation and the sending of envoys to the Council of Pisa.   At last Benedict agreed to this course, but unfortunately his envoys were seized by the French and imprisoned at Nismes.   The Pope was not unnaturally annoyed at this treatment and once more took up a position of obstinate refusal to make concessions.   He even went to the length of excommunicating the cardinals and those who held to them.

Sept. 1408
Council of Cividale
June 6, 1409

Gregory, who had found refuge under the protection of Carlo Malatesta, then took the step of creating ten cardinals, the nucleus of a new college.   His council duly met at Cividale,[54] though not until the Council of Pisa was already in session.   It was brought to a speedy end when Venice declared for Alexander V and refused to allow it to continue. It had never, however, attracted more than a meagre attendance.

Difficulties of the two Popes

Our impatience with the two pontiffs must not blind us to the difficulties of their situation.   Both deplored the schism for selfish reasons if for nothing higher ; but neither was willing to make a move which would give his opponent an advantage and suggest doubts of his own position. Gregory, moreover, was in the hands of relatives whose interests demanded his continuance in office ; whilst Benedict clung to his rights, as he conceived them, with all the vigour of his nature and the skill which his academic training had given him.   His resistance was made the more determined by the high-handed proceedings of the University of Paris and fear of undue control by the French government.

---

[54] Fresh light has been thrown on this assembly by the researches of Finke : see *Hist. Jahrbuch* XIV. pp. 320 sqq.

CHAPTER VI

THE CONCILIAR MOVEMENT

T HE situation which arose in consequence of the con- *The schism* tinuance of the schism had had no parallel in the *demands new methods* history of the Church, and the ordinary apparatus seemed incapable of meeting it. In their need Churchmen now began to consider the adoption of unusual methods. The device most favoured was that of the calling of a General Council by someone other than a Pope, and the deposition of one or more Popes for a cause other than that of heresy. By the Canon Law each of these acts was illegal. But it could be argued, as indeed it was argued, that the Canon Law had never contemplated a continued schism in the Papacy,[1] and that it had grown up in a period anterior to the rise of national feeling. To keep the letter of the law might involve the negation of its spirit.[2]

As no one person was universally recognised as the vicar of *The* Christ, and the unity of the Church was broken, the duty of *responsi- bility of the* restoring it fell to the cardinals. Fortunately the two bodies *cardinals* of cardinals were, as we saw above, willing to act together. This was an important point, as it gave, or should have given, more complete authority to them in the course upon which they now entered. Moreover they had behind them the opinion of the leading universities such as Paris, Bologna, and Oxford.

I stated above that the new situation demanded unusual *Precedents* methods. But the principle of applying them was not itself *for unusual methods* new, and, if we can accept the authority of Liudprand of Cremona, it had already been invoked by the clergy of Rome

---

[1] See *Appellatio interposita per Leodienses a Papa* in Martène and Durand *Thesaurus Anec.* II. p. 1255 where the situation is described as one not covered by Canon Law " ubi verba ipsius legis cessant ".

[2] Cf. Henry of Langenstein *Consilium Pacis* printed in Gerson's *Opera* (ed. Du Pin) II. p. 881 : " Contra intentionem eorum qui canones constitue- runt ".

when in 965 they called upon Otto I to depose John XII.[3]
Moreover the series of great reforming councils of the eleventh
century provided a *modus operandi*.[4]   In this period the right
of the Emperor to summon a General Council seemed to go
unchallenged, and the case of Otto I and John XII was actually
cited in support of this contention during the dispute on the
Great Schism.[5]   Barbarossa had even claimed that God had
appointed the Emperor for the very purpose of ending schisms.[6]

Appeals to a General Council   That an Emperor, or any other who felt himself aggrieved
by the Pope, should appeal to a General Council was only to
be expected ; obvious examples in the period before the
schism can be found in the contests of Frederick II with
various Popes, and that of the Colonna with Boniface VIII ;
but most significant was the proposal by Urban VI, that his
dispute with the cardinals should be referred to a General
Council.   Thus a Pope himself recognised the usefulness and
validity of the method.   In the same way his rival, Clement
' VII ', wrote in 1387 to the Florentines, who were at odds
with Urban, suggesting that they should call a council to
end the schism.   He received the judicious reply that to
convoke a General Council was the office of Emperors and
kings not of a simple republic.

Underlying principles   Before narrating the steps actually taken to apply the
method as a means of ending the schism, it will be useful to
go a little more fully into the principles upon which such
action was based.   In doing so we shall also need to consider
the criticisms of those who disapproved of it.

Method illegal by Canon Law   The advocates of the method were faced by one great
difficulty, they were going against what was perhaps the
strongest political theory of the middle ages, the supremacy
of law.   Underneath the most confident statements in favour
of conciliar action it is, here and there, possible to discover

---

[3] See above p. 22.
[4] Dr. A. J. Macdonald has recently drawn attention to the importance of
the councils at Rome from Leo IX onwards as setting an example of conciliar
activity which was to be followed in the Norman reformation of the Church
in England : see *Lanfranc* pp. 95 sq.   The first council, so far as I know, to
take drastic action against a bishop was that held over the case of Paul of
Samosata in 267.   Its decision to depose him could only be carried out by an
appeal to the state in the person of the Emperor Aurelian : see Eusebius
Hist. Eccles. VII. xxx.
[5] Niem *De Schismate* III. 9-12.
[6] Carlyle *Med. Pol. Theory* IV. pp. 321 sq.

a certain uneasiness inspired by this knowledge.[7] The extent to which, quite apart from any legal theories, the Church had become dependent upon the Papacy, particularly as a centre of unity, made more urgent the task of restoring it ; at the same time it made the adoption of any single plan all the more difficult.

Although the first practical attempt to apply the method, at the Council of Pisa, did not arise until 1409, the method itself had been frequently discussed from as early as 1380. Further, it will be remembered that Peter D'Ailly, in the following year, had advocated the conciliar method as one possible means of ending the schism. But many of the principles underlying the ideas of D'Ailly and those who thought with him, had been put forward at the beginning of the century by John of Paris (Quidort) in his tract *De Potestate Regia et Papali*. He suggested, for example, that the form of government which was best for a secular state—that is the combination of the aristocratic, democratic, and monarchic elements—was also the best for the Church.[8] This is really an anticipation of the conciliar theory, and it may be noticed in passing that the democratic element in the movement tended to become more and more powerful until in the later stages of the Council of Basle it became supreme.[9] He considered further that a General Council had greater authority in matters of doctrine than a Pope,[10] and, most important of all, that a Pope might be deposed by a council.[11] It is possible that Marsiglio of Padua was influenced by the ideas of John,[12]

Theories of John of Paris

[7] The University of Bologna, for example, in arguing in favour of taking proceedings against a Pope is careful to guard itself against violating the traditions of the Church and declares its willingness to withdraw any statement which so offends (" ex omni parte revocamus ").

[8] *Op. cit.* xx. This form is, of course, that advocated by Aristotle, and commended by Polybius as giving to the Roman state its strength ; the three elements of the latter were consuls, senate and popular assemblies : cf. also Cicero *De Repub.* I. xlv.

[9] Cf. Salembier *Le grand Schisme* p. 121 n. 1 : " A la 33e session, qui prit des décisions graves, on ne compte que 20 prélats, tant évêques qu'abbés, et 400 autres ecclésiastiques ". I cannot entirely agree with Ranke's judgement that at Basle the conciliar movement became an attempt to apply to the Church " das aristokratisch-republikanische Wesen, welches in den Staaten eine so grosse Rolle spielte " : *Deutsche Gesch. im Zeit. der Refn.* I. p. 81 (E.T. p. 22).

[10] *Op. cit.* xxi. " concilium maius est papa solo ".

[11] *Op. cit.* xxiv.

[12] So R. Lane Poole suggests : *Illustrations of Med. Thought* p. 231 n. 12.

and the political doctrines of Marsiglio certainly prepared the way for the acceptance of the conciliar theory.

Grounds for deposing a Pope   The claim that a Pope might be deposed by a council was of great importance, since it enabled those who advocated the policy to make their appeal to another great political principle of the middle ages, that namely by which all political power was regarded as a trust, and its holders as responsible to the community for its exercise. It is, of course, true that the attempt to apply this principle to the Papacy failed; none the less it gave force to the arguments of those who desired to see the schism ended by a General Council. At the same time, in order to give a more legal complexion to the attempt, pathetic efforts were made to shew that the Popes under judgement were really guilty of heresy, the one offence for which, according to Canon Law, they could be deposed.[13] The University of Bologna, accepting the general principle that schism long continued becomes heresy, applied it to the actual circumstances of the controversy, and declared that a Pope who has taken an oath to end the schism is guilty of heresy unless he makes genuine efforts to carry out its terms.

Theories of Conrad of Gelnhausen,   We now come to Conrad of Gelnhausen whose tract *De congregando Concilio tempore Schismatis* written in 1380 was the first real attempt at a comprehensive and scientific treatment of the subject.[14]   In this treatise he endeavours to shew that the conciliar method is both possible and necessary. The Pope, after all, is but the head of the Church in a secondary sense, since the real head is Christ; and since Christ is in the Church it can never be headless—*acephale esse non potest*. In the sacraments unity is still preserved. Since a Council may be called without the authority of the Pope he begs the King of France [15] to end the schism. In his view, a democratic one, the council should include not only the cardinals and bishops, but representatives of the lower orders of the clergy and even of the laity in their various " ranks, orders and sexes ".

[13] Heresy it will be remembered was used in the middle ages in a very wide sense and was extended to cover opposition to the Papacy, when there was no question of unorthodox opinions.

[14] In Martène and Durand *Thesaurus Anecd.* II. pp. 1200 sqq.   [Professor Potter considers that this tract is later than that of Henry of Langenstein.]

[15] Charles V, to whom the treatise was dedicated.

Similar ideas may be found in a writer exactly contem- of Henry of
porary with Conrad, Henry of Langenstein, who in his Langenstein,
Consilium Pacis (1381) discussed the office and function of
a General Council, not merely as a means of ending the
schism, but of effecting reforms of various evils in the Church
at large.   His point of view, like that of Conrad, was democratic, and he regarded a General Council as the only infallible
authority, since it alone represents the whole Church.   Again,
like Conrad, he is more concerned with the powers of the
council than with the manner of convoking it ; though he
insists that to do so is the right and responsibility of the
secular power.   One interesting and significant suggestion
is that a council can take from the cardinals the right of
electing a Pope and make its own choice.   This treatise
has been well described by a recent writer as " a call to action
rather than a plan of campaign.   It is the warning of a Prophet
rather than the mature scheme of a statesman." [16]

Later writers and thinkers followed much the same line of D'Ailly,
of argument with slight modifications and supplements.   The
most prominent of them were D'Ailly and Gerson.   D'Ailly
works out the general principles of the conciliar theory and
applies them to the necessities of the situation.   He affirms that
the real unity of the Church is in Christ who is its true Head,
and not the Pope.   Turning to the question of councils he
points out that they were held in the early Church, but that
at the Council of Jerusalem it was James who presided and
not Peter.   Whilst admitting that the right of calling a
council was vested in the Pope, he claimed that this was only
for the sake of order, and that power to do so was still inherent in the Church itself.   At the same time he admitted
that this was not the ruling of the Canon Law.   The Church
must recover and preserve its unity by means of a council
even if this is irregular, for the example of nature shews
that a body must do all it can to preserve itself from division
or destruction.   The present emergency requires a General
Council, and it is the duty of the cardinals to summon it ;
if they fail, then other Christian men must take their place.
To this council the rival Popes will be answerable and must
resign if required so to do ; otherwise they may be deposed.

[16] Jordan *The Inner History of the Great Schism* p. 68.   This small book
contains a number of useful extracts from relevant documents.

12

If a new election is required it should if possible be unanimous, for otherwise fresh trouble may break forth.[17]

of Gerson,   Gerson's chief anxiety is to shew that both divine and natural law sanction the attempt to go behind Canon Law in the crisis. He agrees with D'Ailly on the expediency of an unanimous election, and, like Henry of Langenstein, he is concerned over the state of the Church, which he regards as being responsible for the schism itself. He feels strongly that reformation must be taken in hand lest worse befall.[18]

and of Dietrich of Niem   One of the most important and comprehensive of all the tracts produced by the struggle is that entitled *De Modis Uniendi et Reformandi Ecclesiam* by Dietrich of Niem.[19] It begins by making a distinction between the Catholic Church and the Apostolic—the former consists of all believers, and since Christ is for ever its Head, it cannot err nor be divided.[20] The latter of which the Pope and cardinals are the heads, can err and be divided, as it is in the writer's own day. Since the ' end ' of every society is the common good, the Pope has no rights against the well-being of the whole body. The notion that he is above all judgement is contradicted both by reason and Scripture ; his very primacy is due to guile, fraud, and aggression. After all the Pope is human, and as such liable to sin.[21] He must be ready, if the good of the whole requires it, to resign or even to die. Two or more of the contemporary Popes must resign in order to restore unity. By striving after their own interests the Popes have committed mortal sin, and have thus forfeited the allegiance of Christendom. The writer then goes on to consider the status and functions of a General Council. He regards it as representing the whole Church, and since the Pope cannot call it together at the present juncture, some secular power ought to do so. When it has assembled the Pope is bound to obey its decrees. He attributes wide powers to a council ;

[17] D'Ailly's theories are set out in *De Materia Concilii Generalis* most of which is printed in Gerson's *Opera* (ed. Du Pin) II. coll. 867 sqq.

[18] The opinions of Gerson will be found in various tracts and sermons collected in Du Pin *Opera* II. pp. 1 sqq.

[19] The text is printed in Van der Hardt I. pt. v. On the authorship see Jordan *The Inner History of the Great Schism* pp. 200 sqq.

[20] Alvaro Pelayo had made the same claim for " Romana Ecclesia " : see *De Statu et Planctu* I. xix.

[21] This was granted by so good a papal apologist as Alvaro at the beginning of the fourteenth century : see Iung *Alvaro Pelayo* p. 228.

it can abrogate the laws of the Church and make new ones; its duty is to reform the Church by the abolition of abuses and it ought to curb the power of the Pope and restore the full rights of the bishops.   At the present crisis a council should be called to carry out these suggestions, and in addition to elect one undoubted Pope and to provide against the recurrence of a schism.

I have given the arguments of those who advocated the conciliar theory at some length and in some detail because it is important to realise the kind of ideas which were circulating in the minds of men at this epoch.   Even if they were not widely accepted they had to be reckoned with.

The literature on the other side was by comparison *The papal* meagre.   This was to be expected as their opponents in the *apologists* main recognised the correctness, in theory, of their position ; they tried to avoid its implications on the plea of necessity. There was thus no need to produce fresh arguments in favour of papal rights as against a General Council ; all that was necessary was to appeal to the accepted law and to repeat the arguments of earlier apologists.   But since the appeal was to necessity or expediency, the papal defenders concentrated their efforts on proving that the conciliar method was impracticable and that any council which might be convoked would be abortive.

The practical difficulties, apart from the question of *Practical* any real precedent, were mainly three : the general state of *difficulties in* warfare and unrest would prevent a really representative *the way of a* gathering ; the difficulty of deciding who should summon *Council* the council, one or both Popes, the cardinals, the Emperor or some other secular ruler ; and finally the immense numerical preponderance of the Italian bishops.   This last difficulty was a real one and was finally overcome by the system of voting by nations.

We return now to the course of events and the Council of *The Council* Pisa.   The cardinals had summoned the council to meet in *of Pisa* this noble city, now fallen from its former wealth and splendour and no longer independent.   But the actual holding of the council required certain precautions of a military nature if its members were not to suffer the fate of the cardinals who

defied Frederick II. The new Frederick was Ladislas of
Naples.

Threats of
Ladislas

Ladislas had just acquired the Papal States from Gregory
XII by purchase ; [22] but as the consideration had been merely
nominal, he was not at all willing to see Gregory replaced
by a Pope who might seek to cancel the arrangement. Thus
Ladislas, who was actually living in the Vatican, had every
reason for preventing the meeting of a council or, if it met,

met by
Cardinal
Cossa

of rendering it ineffective. But on the side of the Church
a ready champion was found in Cardinal Cossa, the legate
in Bologna ; a cleric whose habit was but a poor covering for
the activities and mentality of a *condottiere*. The cardinal,
afterwards John XXIII, formed a league with Siena and
Florence ; this step compelled Ladislas, who had already got
as far as Siena, to think better of his design, a decision which
was hastened by the death of Alberigo da Barbiano who was
then in his service.

Opening of
the Council
Mar. 25, 1409

Thus the members of the council could attend the opening
ceremony in the cathedral without fears for their personal
safety. The assembly was a representative one ; for if
neither of the rival Popes was present either in person or by
proxy, their respective cardinals were there in great force.
Benedict XIII had, as we have seen, sent envoys, but their
capture made them arrive late ; when they actually arrived
they were refused a hearing. As full powers seem to have
been given them, even to the extent of committing Benedict
to resignation, this double harsh treatment was decidedly
unfortunate. [23]

Its
recognition

The council was recognised by the majority of the secular
powers, though Spain remained true to Benedict, and Gregory
retained the allegiance of Ladislas and Carlo Malatesta of
Rimini. The support of the former was primarily a matter of
self-interest ; that of the latter, a man of outstanding virtues,
was really inspired by high motives. The schism in the
Empire was inevitably reflected in the attitude of the two

[22] For the details see RIS. XVI. col. 1193 E. and XXI. col. 100 B.

[23] Boniface Ferrer, the brother of St Vincent, claims that they had
" plenissimam potestatem pro exequendo et complendo effectualiter quid-
quid esset necessarium pro vera unitate ecclesiae " : see *Pro Defensione Ben.
XIII.* in Martène and Durand II. p. 1146. Niem, however, was very sceptical,
and put them down as spies. He points out that Benedict, far from wishing
to end the schism, had just made twelve new cardinals : *De Schismate* III. xlv.

claimants. As Wenzel, under French influence, had written as early as Novr. 24, 1408 promising to send envoys in return for his own recognition as King of the Romans, Rupert and his supporters were naturally in opposition. Soon after the council opened they definitely challenged it ; the Bishop of Worms, who acted as spokesman, raised no fewer than twenty-four objections.[24] The two most powerful contem- April 15, 1409 porary monarchs, however, were united in support of the council, and the arrival of French and English delegations under the leadership of Simon Cramaud, Patriarch of Alexandria, and Robert Hallam, Bishop of Salisbury, re-spectively, added greatly to its prestige. Cramaud was elected president.

The first act of the assembly, after the necessary arrange- Proceedings ments for transacting business had been made, was to unite of the the two bodies of cardinals. The rival Popes were then Council summoned aloud from the steps of the cathedral, and on their failing to appear were declared contumacious and deposed. June 5, 1409

In the eighth session a slight difficulty arose, as it was pointed out that the two sets of cardinals were not in exactly the same position ; those of Gregory had definitely withdrawn their allegiance, while those of Benedict, except by implication, had not. After some delay a formal withdrawal was made by both colleges.

The council, having disposed of the two Popes to its satis-faction, had the obvious duty of finding a successor. This was not quite so easy an undertaking, for the cardinals were anxious to preserve the right of election in their own hands. The fact that they had needed a General Council to remove the rival Popes was an awkward recognition of its superior powers and they had no wish to go further in that direction. On the other hand some of those present hinted that the cardinals' own titles were doubtful, now that the Popes from whom they had received them had been deposed. In the end a conclave was formed in which were fourteen of Gregory's cardinals and ten of Benedict's. Fortunately their decision, when they made it, was unanimous and thus no suggestion that the new

[24] So Hefele VI. pp. 997 sq., and Weisäcker *Reichstagsakten* VI. pp. 334 and 497. Creighton, who makes the Bishop of Verdun the spokesman, gives the number of objections as twenty-two (*Hist. of the Papacy* I. p. 242), whilst Salembier (*op. cit.* p. 255) gives one more.

Pope had been elected by schismatic cardinals could be maintained, since one set of cardinals must obviously have been appointed by a legitimate Pope.

Election of Alexander V   Their choice fell on Peter Philarghi, a man advanced in years. He was a native of Crete, and had the double distinction of being the last Greek [25] to become Pope, as well as the only member of the University of Oxford to hold that office.[26]   Alexander V, for such was his title, was a Franciscan, learned and of a kindly and generous disposition; but he was weak and lacking in positive qualities. During his short pontificate he was entirely under the influence of the cardinals, and in particular, of the forceful Cossa. After his election he remained at Pisa, and though Ladislas was speedily driven from Rome, the Pope did not live to enter his capital, dying at Bologna on May 3, 1410. His only act was to issue a Bull *Regnans in Excelsis* supporting the Franciscans against the University of Paris. But even this proved abortive as the French government persuaded his successor to withdraw it.

Reforms postponed   As at Constance later, the election of a Pope seemed to exhaust the energies of the council, and no effort was made to carry out the reforms which were urgently needed to restore the Church's life and health. The subject was postponed to a further council to be held in three years' time; a method of procedure which was again and again to prove effective in stultifying councils.

The council thus failed to correct the abuses that were crippling the Church. It was equally unsuccessful in its attempt to heal the schism. The rival Popes might have been deposed and a successor appointed by the unanimous vote of the cardinals; but the only result was that the Body of Christ found itself with three earthly heads instead of two.

Reasons for the failure of the council   The question at once arises as to why such absolute failure attended the efforts of a council so influential and so necessary. I think that the answer is to be found in the fact that its supporters, and the cardinals in particular, were not really certain of themselves or their position. This led them to act feverishly and tactlessly. When calmness and confident

---

[25] The previous Greek had been John VII in 705.

[26] He took the degree of B.D. in 1370. Cambridge, in a forged charter of the fifteenth century, claimed that she had been the " Alma mater " of Honorius I (625-638).

strength were required, they exhibited haste and an unwise desire to demonstrate their power.[27] Had a spirit of conciliation been shewn towards Benedict and Gregory it is probable that some final solution might have been found. Instead they were treated like malefactors and, with the crude humour of the times, were publicly referred to as Benefictus and Errorius.[28] The acceptance of the resignation of Gregory XII by the Council of Constance was a definite condemnation, by those who themselves accepted the conciliar principle, of what had been enacted at Pisa, a confession that the older council had exceeded its proper functions.

The Council of Pisa was thus an acknowledged failure. None the less it was a blow to the papal autocracy, and in forging the weapon the cardinals themselves were preparing the way for those who would attack with greater violence, not only the Papacy, but the whole hierarchical system.

The successor of Alexander was Baldassare Cossa. It has been said of his election that it was the most miserable of all the consequences of the " disastrous Synod of Pisa." [29] But as he obviously deserved well of the Church, and the actual power was in his hands, the cardinals had little choice. Carlo Malatesta, working as usual in the interests of the whole of Christendom,[30] vainly endeavoured to postpone an election in the hope of finding some means of ending the schism. *John XXIII*

John XXIII, to give the new Pope his title, if not the monster depicted by his enemies,[31] was about as little fitted *His character*

---

[27] This is admitted even by those who were favourable to the conciliar theory : cf. the statement in *De Modis Uniendi et Reformandi Ecclesiam* (in Van der Hardt I. pt. v. col. 114) : " Secundum opinionem multorum, omnia fierunt quasi primis motibus facta et agitata, spiritu vehementi, et non matura deliberatione, ut etiam concilium decebat, ordinata, nec completa ".

[28] The two Popes were drawn together by their common ungracious treatment : see Finke *Acta Concilii Constantiensis* I. pp. 44 sqq.

[29] Pastor *History of the Popes* I. p. 191.

[30] Creighton pays him the well-deserved tribute of being " the only Italian who awakens our admiration by his honesty and integrity of purpose in endeavouring to end the Schism ", *History of the Papacy* I. p. 280. For these efforts see Finke *Acta* I. pp. 4 sqq.

[31] The fact that he retained the friendship of Carlo Malatesta is in his favour.   There are also distinct testimonies to good points in his character : e.g. *Vita di Bart. Valori* in Archiv. Storico Ital. IV. p. 261, and the monk of St Denys who calls him " virum utique nobilem et expertum in agendis " (*Chron. Karoli* XXXI. vii.).   I owe these instances to Hefele VII. p. 11.   He points out that they are not inconsistent with a licentious life for " towards the end of the middle ages chastity was unfortunately as rare among the clergy as conjugal fidelity among the laity ".

for his high office as the worst of his predecessors.   There was nothing clerical about him except his orders ; his real vocation was that of the *condottiere*.   But even when judged as a soldier he cannot be considered a worthy type ; some of his exploits could hardly be condoned by the licence of the camp. Accustomed to the easy ways prevailing among mercenaries he soon found his new office, and the manner of life which it demanded, a grave embarrassment, and his new associates a poor exchange for his lawless comrades.[32]   But even had his private character been blameless, John was not the kind of Pope which the situation required ; he might be a vigorous soldier and mercenary leader, but he was lacking in the gifts of the statesman, and it was by statesmanship rather than by force that a permanent settlement was to be found for the Church in its distress.

Confusion in the Empire Oct. 1410   In the Empire there was almost as great confusion as in the Church.   The death of Rupert led to a double election ; one party chose Sigismund, the brother of Wenzel, and another their cousin, Jobst of Moravia.   As Wenzel still refused to recognise the legality of his deposition there were actually three claimants for the dignity of King of the Romans as well as for that of Pope.   But no one took Wenzel seriously, and the death of Jobst, within a short time of his election, left Sigismund virtually without a rival.   His recognition of John as Pope added considerably to the prestige of the latter.

War in Italy   It will be remembered that before his election Cossa was carrying on warfare against Ladislas of Naples who, for reasons of his own, was supporting the cause of Gregory XII.   He and Carlo Malatesta now made common cause in the hope of compelling John to abdicate by force of arms.   To oppose them the Pope seems to have sought help from Venice,[33] but with no success ; he managed, however, to get the four leading *condottieri* [34] of the day to enter the service of his ally Louis of Anjou who claimed the kingdom of Naples.   With their

---

[32] " Plus . . . delectabant hominem scuta et cristae quam pallia et apices " says a monastic chronicler of Milan : RIS. XIX. col. 41 D.

[33] See the instructions of Jan. 15, 1411 sent to the Venetian ambassador Michalete de Cagnolis : *State Archives Delib. del Senato* IV. fol. 148 printed in Finke *Acta* I. p. 24.

[34] They were Braccio, Sforza, Paolo Orsini, and Gentile da Monterno. " Capitanei migliori del mondo " the writer of *Giornali Napolitani* calls them : RIS. XXI. col. 1073 D.

help Louis gained a decisive victory over his rival at Rocca May 19, 1411
Secca. If Louis had followed up his victory Rocca Secca
might have ranked with Benevento or Tagliacozzo, but he
allowed the chance to slip, his ill-paid mercenaries accepted
ransom for their prisoners, and Ladislas was as strong as ever.
Louis soon afterwards left Italy and Sforza went over to
Ladislas. John was thus in a very awkward situation, but
he soon came to terms with Ladislas, who realised that the
new Pope might serve his purpose more effectively than
Gregory. By their agreement both parties treacherously
abandoned their former allies. Gregory was completely
helpless and had no course left but flight to Carlo Malatesta
at Rimini.

The Pope held a Council in Rome in the spring of 1413 The Council
about which surprisingly little is known.[35] The summons of Rome
to the council had been sent out as early as April 29, 1411,[36] 1413
but the actual assembly did not take place until Feb. 10, 1413.
Its only real piece of business seems to have been to condemn
the works of Wyclif,[37] and as the numbers were very small
John quickly dissolved it after less than a month's sitting.
He then sent out invitations for a council to be held on
Decr. 1 of the same year.[38] But his plans were upset by the
further treachery of Ladislas whose troops suddenly seized June
Rome. John fled in panic to Florence. The wily and
unprincipled Neapolitan was aiming at the sovereignty of all
Italy and the Papal States hindered his northward advance.
As it happened Ladislas gained little by his treachery; the
consequences for the Pope, however, were much more serious,
in fact it set in motion a series of events which ended only with
his degradation. Incidentally it brought prominently upon
the stage the figure of the newly elected King of the Romans.

Sigismund had a passion for appearing in exalted posi- Sigismund,
tions; but unfortunately a grave and dignified bearing was King of the
his chief qualification for such responsibilities. In conse- Romans
quence he rushed madly from one grandiose scheme to an-

[35] See Antonius Petri in RIS. XXIV. cols. 1029 E, 1030 A-C, and 1033
C-E, also *Vita Johannis XXIII* in RIS. III. pt. ii. col. 846 B, C. In the latter
the well-known incident is recorded of the owl which hovered over the Pope's
head : " Hoc est malum signum " he observed.

[36] Raynaldus 1411 No. 7. Also in Finke *Acta* I. pp. 127 sqq.

[37] Raynaldus 1413 No. 1, Finke *op. cit.* I. pp. 162 sq.

[38] Finke *op. cit.* I. pp. 165 sqq.

other, regarding anybody's business as his own if only it gave him the chance of " keeping in the limelight ". In the present instance, however, his intervention was no mere impertinence, as he was called in by John himself, and after all the safety of the Pope did concern the Emperor-elect. In return for promises of help against Ladislas, Sigismund insisted on the summoning of a General Council. To this John reluctantly agreed and sent envoys to arrange the place of meeting. Leonardo Bruni, the Pope's secretary, has recorded his doubts and vacillation beforehand. He drew up a careful list of instructions for his representatives and then tore it up, relying on their good sense and care for his interests.[39] Unfortunately they were persuaded to agree on Constance,

Dec. 9, 1413 an imperial city. John was unable to draw back and a Bull was issued fixing Novr. 1, 1414 for the opening of the council. In the interval the whole situation was changed by the death

Aug. 6 1414, of Ladislas ; but it was too late for John to recover himself, he was definitely committed to a council.

The Emperor-elect had secured a great triumph, as a successful council under his auspices would revive imperial prestige and add enormously to his own reputation.[40] No doubt he regarded himself already as another Henry III and Constance as his Sutri. On wider grounds the success of his policy was significant, for it transferred the leadership of the reforming movement from French hands, and made the University of Paris a little less prominent.[41]

The Council of Constance To most people the Council of Constance is known for its condemnation of Hus. But although this action was one which carried the approval of practically all parties, the highest significance of Constance must be sought elsewhere ; it was, as Bryce has put it, both " the last occasion on which the whole of Latin Christendom met to deliberate as a single commonwealth, (and) also the last on which that commonwealth's lawful temporal head appeared in the exercise of his inter-

---

[39] RIS. XIX. col. 928 D.

[40] Sigismund worked exceedingly hard on behalf of the council : see the numerous epistles printed from various folios of Cod. Pal. 701 in the Vatican Library by Finke *Acta* I. pp. 358-391.

[41] The university had drawn up plans for reform intended perhaps for presentation to the Council of Rome. Finke has printed them from a MS. in the Vienna Hof und Staatsbibliothek (Cod. 5097 fol. 29-85) see *op. cit.* I. pp. 131 sqq.

national functions." [42]   Neither Basle nor Florence, it must be remembered, was recognised by the whole of the West, and Trent came after the Reformation had split it into two antagonistic sections; Constance thus takes a foremost place among the assemblies of the Church.

As at other councils the members were slow to arrive; but the numbers eventually were large. The presence of twenty-nine cardinals, nearly two hundred prelates, one hundred abbots and nearly two thousand priests, shewed the importance attached to it by the clergy; whilst of the laity there were a hundred nobles of high rank and more than two thousand knights. [43]

Above the lake upon which Constance stands the Rhine is divided into two streams which converge at Reichenau; below it a single great river flows on its way to Basle. In like manner those who came to the council could be divided into two distinct parties; it would have been well for the future of Christendom if they too could have left it as a united whole. But it was not so to be and their progress, also towards Basle the scene of the next council, was marked by further divisions. These two parties may conveniently be termed the Conservatives and the Reformers. The former, of whose standpoint the University of Paris were good representatives, regarded the schism as an obvious inconvenience, not only to the Church, but to themselves, and a council as rather a necessary evil than a regular part of the Church's machinery. Their sympathy with reforming projects was but tepid at the best, and they were liable to have their fears aroused if serious attempts were made to discover remedies for evils in a system under which they enjoyed special privileges. *Parties at the Council* *The Conservatives*

Among the Reformers there was a general desire to remove abuses, which in the extremists reached the avowed intention of restoring the Church to its primitive condition, by the abolition of papal and other privileges and usurpations. *The Reformers*

[42] *Holy Roman Empire* p. 349.
[43] Ulrich von Richental *Chronik des Const. Concils* (ed. Buck) pp. 154-215. This writer has left vivid details of the city during the meeting of the council. He records among other things the presence of more than 30,000 horses. One wonders where they were all put to; but as Workman has said " the medieval horse had learned to stow himself away ": *John Wyclif* I. p. 57.

The Reformers were for the most part Germans, and the best representative of their views is perhaps the monk Dietrich of Niem to whom reference has already been made.[44] The current of thought in Germany is revealed as definitely moving in the direction of the Reformation of the sixteenth century. The council thus seems like a meeting place of the medieval and the modern world ; but the efforts of the Reformers, for good or ill, were to be thwarted, and the old system to have another century of life.

John at Constance

To Constance came John XXIII in due course. He came with very bad grace, and seems to have felt that he was being borne along by a stream of fate too strong to be resisted.[45] Accordingly he was full of suspicions and anxieties. When he arrived the very appearance of the city reinforced his fears, it looked like a trap ; [46] and trapped indeed he was.

At first he was well received, but he soon found that there was no intention on the part of the assembly to regard him as the sole legitimate Pope, a reasonable expectation on his part, as both his rivals had been deposed at Pisa.[47] That his position was on a par with theirs was made quite plain when the council agreed to recognise the status of the cardinals sent by Gregory and Benedict as their envoys. Before the

Order of proceedings

arrival of Sigismund there was some manœuvring, and in this too the Pope was worsted. He and his supporters wished to make the case of the Bohemian heretic, John Hus, the first business of the council. All parties were agreed in their opposition to Hus and his teaching ; but the bulk of the members of the council regarded the ending of the schism with its threefold Papacy—" an impious mockery of the Trinity "— as its most pressing task. Hus could well wait.

But John's most serious defeat was on the question of the proceedings of the council. If matters were pressed too

[44] See above pp. 178 sq. Also Creighton *History of the Papacy* I. pp. 304 sqq. and Pastor *History of the Popes* I. pp. 192 sq.

[45] *Vita di Bart. Valori* in Arch. Stor. Ital. (first series) IV. pt. i. p. 262.

[46] Ulrich von Richental records that when the Pope came in sight of the lake surrounded by its hills he exclaimed " sic capiuntur vulpes " : *op. cit.* p. 25.

[47] Constance was supposed to be a continuation of Pisa and it is noteworthy that Cardinal Fillastre begins his journal with the statement : " Origo generalis Concilii Constanciencis ex Pisano concilio cepit " : Finke *Acta* II. p. 13.

far he had relied on the number of the Italian bishops who had swarmed to the council—it is even said that the Pope had created fifty new ones in order to swell his following. The overwhelming numbers of the Italians were neutralised, however, by the successful proposal of Robert Hallam that the council should be divided up, as were the universities, into nations, and that each nation should have a single vote.[48]

John tried to make the best of the situation, and, in order to prevent measures to depose him, offered to abdicate Mar. 1, 1415 if his rivals could be persuaded to do the same. He gained little by this, for his refusal to name proctors only provoked enmity. He seems to have hoped to gain time by setting the French and English against one another ; in this he had a partial success, and Sigismund rather unwisely tried to bring pressure to bear on some of the French delegates who were imperial subjects.

The next step was a dramatic one. Whilst the attention Flight of of the members was diverted by a tournament outside the John walls of the city the Pope, disguised as a groom, fled from Constance and took refuge in the Castle of Schaffhausen under the protection of Frederick of Habsburg.[49] John Mar. 20, 1415 hoped that his withdrawal would throw everything into such confusion that the delegates would melt away and the council come to a sudden end. His anticipations came within measurable distance of fulfilment, for the Italian and Austrian bishops began at once to prepare to depart, and the mob seeing a chance of plunder hastened to seize it. In this emergency the vigour and decision of Sigismund saved the situation, and he quickly took all the necessary steps to secure the continuance of the council and the arrest of the fugitive. The spirits of the conciliar party were further revived by a sermon preached by John Gerson on March 23, in which he

---

[48] The matter seems to have been settled by agreement between the English, German and French nations ; no decree of the council has been found accepting the method. Fillastre states the fact only : " Interim nationes, videlicet Gallie, Germanie, et Anglie et ita postea Ytalie, per se ipsas se congregaverunt et deciderunt de facto questionem, utrum per nationes vel per capita singula procederetur " : Finke *Acta* II. p. 19. The Italians wrote a letter of protest to Sigismund, to which Cardinal Fillastre replied : see Finke *op. cit.* III. pp. 102 sqq.

[49] Such is the account accepted by Creighton *Hist. of the Papacy* I. p. 327, and it seems a likely one, though almost all the authorities state that he fled in the darkness of the following night.

claimed that as a General Council represented the Church it was guided by the Holy Spirit, and that even the Pope must obey it.[50]

Difficult position of the cardinals

The supporters of John, and in particular the cardinals, found themselves in a position of great delicacy. But the Pope shewed them no consideration, and any attempts to wait on the course of events were prevented by an order, under threat of excommunication, to join him forthwith. Seven cardinals and the majority of the officials at once obeyed. The cardinals, indeed, were in the position of an aristocracy which, having allied itself with the people to check the power of a monarch, finds itself in danger of being swept away with him. Both Pope and council regarded them with suspicion, and the latter began to favour very drastic schemes. The only cardinals who at this juncture acted with dignity were D'Ailly and Zabarella.[51] Without abandoning the council they openly declared that they must remain loyal to John so long as he was Pope and stood by his promises. But though John still professed to be willing to resign his office it was difficult for anyone except the cardinals to believe him. His subsequent conduct justified all such doubts.

Mar. 29

Fearing that Schaffhausen was too near the council to be safe John suddenly fled again, taking refuge in the fortress of Lauffenburg about thirty miles farther down the Rhine.[52] This time he threw off the mask completely, and declared that any promises of abdication which he might have made had been under duress. The wretched cardinals who had joined him were left in ignorance of his second flight, and nothing remained for them to do but to slink back to Constance where they were received with polite contempt.

Mar. 30 Decrees of the Council

The council now proceeded, in the famous Fourth Session, to profess its beliefs in the principles set forth by Gerson, and to affirm that a General Council was superior to a Pope. A further resolution declaring its ability to undertake the reformation of the Church met with resolute opposition from the cardinals who felt that their powers and privileges were

**April 6
April 17**

seriously endangered. But the decrees were re-affirmed in the Fifth Session, and at a later session still, the proposal

---

[50] *Opera* II. p. 201, Van der Hardt II. col. 265, Mansi XXVIII. p. 535.
[51] The famous canonist referred to by commentators as " the cardinal ".
[52] Creighton *op. cit.* I. p. 333 by a slip says " higher up ".

was actually made that the cardinals should be excluded from participation in the council. This step was too drastic for the majority, and in the end the cardinals were allowed to count as a separate nation. Their help was needed in deposing the Pope. May 25

Before this, however, the luckless John, and his still more pitiable protector, had fallen into the hands of their enemies. Sigismund, after the Pope's flight, had at once put Frederick of Austria under the ban of the Empire. As a consequence his territories were immediately over-run by jealous and grasping neighbours, and even the Swiss were persuaded to break their treaty with him in order to join in the general rush. Disaster followed disaster until Frederick's spirit was completely broken. On May 5 he made a public confession of his misdoings to the man whom he hated, and Sigismund enjoyed another success.[53] One of the chief agents in the fall of the Habsburg had been his namesake of the house of Hohenzollern ; thus the final triumph of 1866 was anticipated. The fortunes of the future rulers of Prussia were firmly laid by the services of the latter, for he received as his reward the Electorate of Brandenburg. Frederick of Austria submits
April 7

It was next to be the turn of John, who was then at Freiburg, to suffer humiliation. The council cited him to appear before it, and, rejecting his suggestion of proctors, it insisted on his answering in person. An amazingly long list of his crimes was prepared, together with confirmatory attestations of each item.[54] Meanwhile the ever useful Frederick had brought him to Rudolfszell, and thither a deputation was sent on May 20, announcing that he was suspended from his office and demanding the surrender of the papal insignia. John, whose one anxiety was now to be spared personal humiliation, submitted unconditionally, and even went so far as to recognise the infallibility of the council.[55] Such seemly behaviour on the part of the ex-condottiere moderated the fierceness of his enemies, and the terms of his final deposition were much milder than the list of his outrages might have warranted. But perhaps the list was not taken altogether seriously. As does John himself

[53] Frederick's conduct had been inspired largely by jealousy of Sigismund and the desire to wreck his plans.

[54] This is now printed by Finke *Acta* III. pp. 157-209 and IV. pp. 758-891.

[55] Van der Hardt IV. p. 275 : " Concilium . . . scio errare non posse ".

Reasons for his fall   Thus ended the career of one of the most remarkable men who have occupied the throne of St Peter. His fall was due to his own foolishness and moral worthlessness ; at the same time he was, as Creighton has well said, " a victim to the zeal for the union of the distracted Church ".[56] The council was still suspicious of its victim, however ; and Cossa, as he was again called, had to endure a tedious imprisonment in the Castle of Heidelberg, where his warders were ignorant of Italian and could hold no converse with him.   Eventually he was set free and ended his days under the protection of **Decr. 1419** Cosimo dei Medici at Florence.[57] We are told that he preserved his dignity to the end, and grew rather corpulent.[58] His tomb in the Baptistery with its simple inscription : " Here lies the body of Baldassare Cossa, once Pope John XXIII " [59] is very effective.

The council and heresy   The council had thus dealt with the subject of unity, and in doing so had degraded the Pope elected by its predecessor at Pisa. It now turned aside to consider the question of heresy ; leaving the third matter which demanded its attention, that of reform, to the last. It must be confessed that the fathers assembled at Constance shewed much greater zeal in their attempt to suppress heresy—in pursuance of which they burnt an upright and godfearing teacher and alienated the larger part of a nation—than in their efforts to set the Church in order by the removal of admitted abuses and corruptions. We must remember that the Council flushed with its victory over John XXIII, was anxious to shew that it could act quite well without a Pope at its head. In the second place it wished to place its own orthodoxy beyond question ; to have delayed longer the trial of Hus might have compromised this. Its members were reformers, and

[56] *Op. cit.* I. p. 346.

[57] It was rumoured at his death that he left vast sums to his benefactor ; but Amminiato *Stor. Fior.* II. p. 1047 says, with greater probability, that he died penniless. No doubt the contemporaries of Cosimo could not imagine that he would care for a broken old man unless he was going to get something out of it.

[58] See a letter of June 1419 to Alfonso V, now in the Crown Archives at Barcelona : printed in Finke *Acta* III. pp. 295 sq.

[59] Gregorovius observes that John was the last Pope to have his tomb away from Rome, and that in consequence this monument, which is of high artistic worth, is a fitting symbol of the end of the schism : *Grabdenkmäler* p. 84.

not revolutionaries ; the condemnation of Hus would make this abundantly clear.

Religious unrest in Bohemia was no new thing; it can be traced back at least as far as the days of Charles IV. This Emperor in his zeal to make Bohemia a model kingdom nurtured plans, not only for the growth of culture, but also for the purification of religion. As these plans were worked out they led to an attack on the wealth and arrogance of the higher clergy and of the monks. The most powerful of the advocates of reform was the famous preacher, Milicz of Kremsier, who was accused of heresy before both Urban V and Gregory XI. He ended his career at Avignon in 1374. Religious unrest in Bohemia

Thus, before the days of Hus,[60] there was a widespread, if rather vague, feeling after spiritual revival in Bohemia, and a number of reforming preachers. By his position as Rector of the University of Prague Hus gave form and cohesion to the movement, and made men feel that the reformers had to be taken seriously.[61] For its theology the movement had gone largely to the teaching of John Wyclif, and the writings of Hus himself are many of them little more than translations or adaptations of those of the famous Englishman.[62]

But behind the desire for reform of the Church there lay a deeper aspiration, that for Bohemian independence from foreign influences. More and more it is coming to be recognised that the Hussite movement, especially in its later developments, was a racial rather than a religious enterprise ; that religious differences, genuine though they were, were cherished as a distinguishing mark from other peoples. Czech aspirations

The university which Charles IV had founded in 1848 had been intended to be the centre of the cultural life of the Empire, and quite a number of its students were German by

---

[60] The latest life of Hus is that in two volumes (1919-1921) by V. Novotny.

[61] A similar effect followed Pusey's adhesion to the Oxford Movement : see Newman *Apologia pro Vita Sua* pp. 67 sq.

[62] See Loserth *Wiclif und Hus* for the relations of the two reformers. Undue credit was for long given to Hus for originality as his works were printed whole those of Wyclif " slumbered undisturbed in Continental libraries " (Workman *John Wyclif* I. p. 8). Hus seldom acknowledged the source of his borrowings. It must, however, be remembered that he may have made use of a common tradition and whatever he used was touched by his own genius : cf. Waugh *History of Europe 1378-1494* p. 215.

13

race. Between them and the Czechs there was continual
friction ; this came to a head in 1408 when Wyclif's doctrines
were condemned, mainly owing to the action of the German
masters. Five years later Wenzel found that his own ecclesiastical policy had the support of the Bohemian masters, whilst
the Germans favoured the archbishop. The Bohemians
seized the opportunity to obtain from the king a decree recti-
fying certain anomalies in the constitution of the university
which gave a preponderance of votes to the Germans. This
victory of the Czechs was so bitterly resented by their
opponents that, adopting a course which was not uncommon
in the middle ages, they left in a body ; many of them took
part in founding a new university at Leipzig. The bitterness
against Bohemia which this migration fostered in Germany
probably made it easier in years to come to raise ' crusades '
for the invasion of the stricken land. Hus was thus a national
as well as a religious leader, a point which cannot be too
clearly brought out, if we are to understand the wars which
broke out after his death.

The question
of indul-
gences
During the years 1410 and 1411 the ill-feeling between the
reformers and the clergy did not diminish, and the public
burning of the works of Wyclif only added to it. But a
more serious cause of difference was to arise in the following
year, a cause which anticipated the Lutheran movement of
a century later. In order to raise funds for his campaign
against Ladislas of Naples John XXIII offered indulgences
to all who should support him, not merely by personal service,
but also by contributions to his war-chest. Hus protested
against this ungodly traffic, and was upheld by the students.
Unhappily the latter, perhaps having in mind the fate of
Wyclif's works, burnt the papal Bull, to the accompaniment
of unseemly jesting. Feeling became so fierce that civil
war seemed imminent, and in order to restore quiet Wenzel
persuaded Hus, who in the meantime had been excommunicated, to retire to the country. Here he remained
until he was summoned by Sigismund, under promise of a
safe-conduct, to appear before the Council of Constance.

Hus goes to
Constance
In going to the council Hus realised that he was taking a
step which might lead him into danger ; but he was anxious
to uphold his beliefs and to defend them publicly. He relied,
Novr. 3, 1414 moreover, on the honour of Sigismund. On his arrival he

found himself among enemies,[63] and the Pope, perhaps hoping to embroil Sigismund and the council, haled him before the cardinals. Hus complied, though under protest. At the meeting he was treated as a criminal on trial, and after the accusations against him had been duly formulated he was interned in the Dominican convent which was situated on a small island in the lake.[64]

Sigismund was enraged at this treatment of one who was under his protection,[65] and when he arrived at Constance he threatened to abandon the council; he was pacified by Frederick of Hohenzollern. The council declared that no promise was binding which was against the interests of the Catholic faith,[66] and Ferdinand of Aragon actually wrote to Sigismund to express his surprise that there should be any question of keeping faith with a heretic who had not kept faith with God.[67]

Hus was thus left at the mercy of the council, and although the consideration of his case was postponed, as we have seen, the outcome was certain. In the actual trial he made three appearances before the council, and then on July 6, 1415 he was condemned, degraded from the priesthood, taken outside the walls of Constance and there burnt. In order to

[margin notes:]
Novr. 28
Sigismund arrives Decr. 25

Hus abandoned by Sigismund June 5, 7 and 8, 1415

---

[63] For Hus at Constance see the account of Peter of Mladonovic (in Palacky *Documenta* pp. 237-324 and new edition by Novotny in *Fontes Rerum Boh.* VII. pp. 25-120).

[64] At first he was lodged in the house of one of the canons, later he was moved from the convent to the Castle of Gottlieben belonging to the Bishop of Constance. Here he had the deposed Cossa as a fellow-prisoner. During the trial he was moved back to the city and lodged in the Franciscan convent.

[65] On the question of the safe-conduct see Bartos in *Zeit. für Kirch. Geschichte* XXXIV. pp. 414 sqq. Salembier avers that it was merely a passport and applied only to the journey (*Le grand Schisme* p. 333 n. 1). If this was so it is hard to account for Sigismund's anger and Ferdinand's letter. Hus took it in no such manner, but as covering the return journey if he failed to satisfy the council; see Palacky *Documenta* p. 114. According to Mladonovic its terms were : " Transire, stare, morari, et redire libere permittatis " (Palacky *Documenta* p. 238). Salembier cannot have read the actual document and does not seem to have realised that Hus did not receive the safe-conduct until two days after his arrival at Constance.

[66] The actual words are : " nec aliqua sibi fides aut promissio de iure naturali, divino vel humano, fuerit in praeiudicium catholicae fidei observanda " in Van der Hardt IV. col. 521.

[67] The reply of Sigismund has been printed by Finke *Acta* IV. pp. 513 sqq. from a MS. in the Vatican Library Cod. Lat. 701 fo. 240 v.

prevent the preservation of relics his ashes were collected in a barrow and tipped into the Rhine.[68]

Procedure in dealing with Hus   The case of Hus is important, not so much for the views which were condemned in his person,[69] as for the method of procedure adopted against him. The fear of being involved in defence of a heretic made a man of honour, as Sigismund was in most matters, break his word ; persecution and death were brought to bear upon a reformer by a council which claimed itself to be reforming. Worst of all there seems to have been no sincere desire to understand Hus's exact position, views were attributed to him which he did not apparently hold [70], and the main anxiety seems to have been to secure a conviction. Hus was difficult it must be admitted, and not at all averse to martyrdom ; but he might have been willing, with sympathetic treatment, to modify the statement of his teaching in such a way as to make it appear orthodox ; he himself always claimed that it was entirely so. The council was too fearful for its own reputation to allow it to be merciful, except on terms of absolute submission and complete abjuration. By its rigidity it made understanding impossible, and so Hus chose death. He " deliberately asserted the rights of the individual conscience against ecclesiastical authority, and sealed his assertion by his own life-blood ".[71]

May 30, 1416   Less than a year later Jerome of Prague met a similar death, after making a similar stand. But Bohemia was not to be browbeaten ; the nation rose in defence of religious and national liberty, and much bloodshed and much disgrace to the Catholic cause was the consequence.

---

[68] A similar precaution was taken in the case of Arnold of Brescia and later of Savonarola. Wyclif's body, after being taken from the grave, was burnt and its ashes likewise scattered. It is interesting to notice that the ashes of the martyrs of the early Church were scattered in order to rob them of the hope of Resurrection : see Eusebius *Hist. Eccles.* V. i., VIII. vii.

[69] I have not given a detailed account of Hus's views. The most important of them from a practical point of view (though he himself did not attach great weight to it) was the right to take communion in both kinds—hence the name Utraquists given to the Bohemians. His teaching that the Church consists of the predestined only, his denial of papal claims, and the declaration of the right of private judgement based on the Scriptures were inconvenient to Catholics.

[70] Such as the denial of transubstantiation.

[71] Creighton *History of the Papacy* II. p. 51. Louis Blanc saw in Hus the champion of Liberty, Equality, and Fraternity : see Salembier *Le grand Schisme* pp. 324 sq.

Two days before the burning of Hus a long step towards ^{July 4, 1415} the ending of the schism had been taken—nothing less than ^{Abdication of} the abdication of Gregory XII. Gregory, it will be remem- ^{Gregory XII} bered, had been deposed at Pisa ; the council now went behind that decision, and by allowing the Pope to issue a Bull summoning it afresh recognised his status and secured its own.[72] The way to a fresh election was now open. But two years were to elapse before it actually took place, and by that time Gregory was· no more.[73]

The resignation of Gregory, following upon the deposition ^{Sigismund at} of John XXIII, left Benedict as the sole claimant to the ^{Perpignan} Papacy. On July 18, 1415 Sigismund left Constance to secure his resignation, and thus get an entirely clean start for a new Pope. His visit to Perpignan, however, proved fruitless, and Benedict, driven into hopeless opposition, retired to the strong castle of Peniscola, still defiant. Sigismund's efforts were more successful in another direction, for he managed to obtain ^{Decr. 18} the withdrawal from Benedict of the Spanish allegiance.[74]

The condemnation of Hus marked a definite stage in the ^{Inertia of} council, and during the absence of Sigismund very little busi- ^{the council} ness was transacted. It might have been expected that the reforms demanded by the admittedly corrupt state of the Church would speedily have been embarked upon ; actually the council shewed an inertia in dealing with them which amounted almost to indifference. It is true that a commission was appointed in July 1415, and that it was supplied with an enormous amount of evidence ; but most of the necessary reforms would have involved the sacrifice of revenue and that in particular on the part of those who formed the commission. A report was presented on October 8, 1416. This document was colourless and unimpressive ; nevertheless it was handed over to yet another commission for further consideration.[75]

The question which aroused the greatest feeling at this ^{The question} ^{of tyranni-}

[72] The Bull is printed in Van der Hardt IV. pt. iii. pp. 370 sqq. and Mansi ^{cide} XXVII. pp. 733 sqq. If the decree of Pisa was ignored Gregory had the best title to the supreme pontificate. He had previously referred to the assembly at Constance as a ' conciliabulum ' : see Finke *Acta* I. p. 269.

[73] He died at Recanati, near Ancona, on Oct. 18, 1417, less than a month before the election of Martin V.

[74] The terms are contained in the Articles of Narbonne for which see Mansi XXVII. p. 811 and XXVIII. p. 224.

[75] For the findings of these commissions see Finke *Acta* II. pp. 549-565 and 606-700.

period, apart from the trial and condemnation of Jerome of Prague to which reference has already been made, was the lawfulness of tyrannicide.[76]   The dispute arose over the case

Novr. 1407
Mar. 1408
of the murder of the Duke of Orleans, which Jean Petit, a famous theologian, had justified on the ground that traitors, and those who usurp the power of the king, ought to be slain. This opinion had been condemned by the Bishop of Paris in 1414, but the Duke of Burgundy had appealed to John XXIII against the sentence.   The matter now came before the council, *sede vacante*.   Gerson, who had been instrumental in obtaining the original condemnation, was anxious that the council should take a strong line, and that doctrines so subversive of society should be opposed to the uttermost.   But the council was content with a condemnation in general terms, and made no mention of Jean Petit or the specific case.   Gerson was bitterly aggrieved, and losing all sense of proportion, pressed the matter in season and out until the patience of everybody was exhausted.   There is little doubt that the action of the council was influenced by political considerations. The realisation of this damaged its prestige, and led in turn to further political complications and the emergence of discord between the nations.

The return of
Sigismund
Sigismund returned to Constance in January 1417 after an absence of eighteen months.   The objects of his protracted tour had been but imperfectly achieved ; in fact all that he had done was to bring the Spanish kingdoms into line with the rest of Europe.   In his political aims, which were centred round the restoration of peace between England and France as a step towards a new crusade, he had had no success whatever.   France had been placed at the feet of Henry V

Oct. 25, 1415
of England by the defeat of Agincourt, but party spirit was as rife there as ever.   Sigismund's visit in the spring of 1416 was quite abortive ; even the pleasure-loving Frenchmen were scandalised by his loose manners, whilst he himself is reported to have said that he might have relatives in France,

---

[76] Additional documents relating to this debate will be found in Finke *op. cit.* IV. pp. 237 sqq.   It will be remembered that the doctrine of tyrannicide had been approved by John of Salisbury " Tyrannum occidere non modo licitum est sed aequum et justum " ; *Policraticus* III. xv.   This doctrine was condemned by St Thomas Aquinas *De Reg. Principum* I. [Professor Potter drew my attention to A. Coville *Jean Petit. La question du tyrannicide au commencement du XVe siècle* (Paris 1932).]

but his friends were in England. In this country he met
with more encouragement, and abandoning his efforts at
reconciliation he concluded an alliance with Henry at Canter- Aug. 15, 1416
bury. This was a surprising change of policy ; for friendship
with France had been traditional in the House of Luxemburg
and Sigismund's grandfather, John of Bohemia, had sealed
it by dying on the field of Crecy. But Sigismund seems to have
come to regard the French as the chief obstacle to unity in
the Church, and to peace in Europe.[77]

The return of Sigismund, in spite of his lack of complete
success, was hailed by the council with every outward rejoicing. But his authority had really suffered diminution.
The Treaty of Canterbury raised against him the enmity of
the French, and he, for his part, did nothing to conciliate
them, but shewed marked favour to his new allies.

Just before the return of the Emperor-elect the council Deposition of
had cited Benedict to appear before it. The mandate was Benedict
delivered by two Benedictine monks, and as they approached
in their black habits the Pope murmured " Here come the
crows ". " Yes," someone muttered in reply, " crows flock
round a dead body." Benedict refused to accept the citation
and was deposed. For nearly six years he lingered on defiant July 26, 1417
to the last, and consoling himself with the thought that just
as the few souls with Noah in the ark were all humanity,
so his scanty following on the rock of Peniscola was all that
remained of the true Church. Before his death he created
four cardinals. Three of them elected a new Pope, who took
the title of Clement ' VIII '. The fourth cardinal elected
still another, Benedict ' XIV '. Clement ' VIII ' at first received the support of Alfonso V, but through the influence
of one of his counsellors, Alfonso Borgia, he went over to
Martin V. The anti-pope submitted in 1429 and was given
the Bishopric of Majorca. Benedict ' XIV ' survived three
years longer, when he was handed over to Martin by the
Count of Armagnac. Thus the schism petered out, an almost
absurd ending to a grave and serious threat to Roman prestige.
Its end was perhaps hardly worth tracing out save for one
notable feature ; it was the occasion of the introduction of
the Borgia family to the Papal court.

[77] Rymer *Foedera* IX. pp. 377 sqq.

Quarrel of France and England

Since Spain had agreed to recognise the council room had to be made for an additional nation. This gave the French an opportunity for shewing their hatred of the English, for they now proposed that the latter should be absorbed in the German nation.[78] It is probable that they did not expect that their suggestion would receive the approval of the council, but it was too good a means for annoying their rivals to be ignored.[79] The English made a long defence and produced some amazing arguments for their rights. In the end the number of nations in the council was increased to five.

Election of a new Pope

The question which had now to be faced was the relative importance of reform and the election of a new Pope, as the next matter to be dealt with. Sigismund wished at once to proceed with the urgent task of removing abuses from the Church and curia ; in this he had the support of the German and English nations. The Italians wished to postpone the consideration of such matters until the Church had a head ; the Spaniards took the same line,[80] and the French naturally chose the side opposed to the English. Even the latter, in the end, acting on instructions from Henry V, went over to the curial party. Henry probably felt that there was a chance of getting a Pope favourable to his interests and did not wish to miss it. Sigismund saw at last that he could not get his own way and on Oct. 2 agreed to the holding of an election.[81]

Small reforming measures approved

Before, however, the actual order of proceedings was decided, a slight concession was made to those who had wished for reform as the immediate step. On Oct. 9 a number of reforming decrees were passed. Most of these dealt with small practical abuses in the administration of the Church's

---

[78] At Paris the Germans had originally been included in the English nation, but the diminution of the number of English masters led to a reversal of the name, and the nation was called German.

[79] But Ulrich von Richental seemed unable to get over the fact that the English had been recognised as a separate nation ; he refers to it repeatedly : see *Chronicle* pp. 14, 50 sq., 154. John XXIII had complained that the English with only three bishops ranked as equal with the Italians and French who had each 200 : see Hefele VII. p. 95. But in 1416 additional English delegates were commissioned : see Rymer *Foedera* IX. p. 370.

[80] On the Spanish nation see Fromme *Die spanische Nation und das Konstanzer Konzil.*

[81] New documents bearing on the matter will be found in Finke *Acta* III. pp. 618 sqq.

system which fell hardly upon the clergy, such as the seizure of the possessions of a dead cleric and the compulsory translation of bishops. The most important of the decrees, however, was that known as *Frequens*.[82] By its provisions the holding of a General Council became a part of the regular machinery of the Church, and not simply a means of meeting an emergency. The next council was to assemble in seven years' time ; thereafter, at intervals of five years. This seemed a very considerable victory for the conciliar method ; but history ·was to shew how little it really represented the mind of the Church, how easy it would be to evade its provisions and finally to render them void.

The way was now clear for the assembling of a conclave. The conclave Among the articles agreed upon in drawing up the arrangements was one which provided for the reform of the Church by the future Pope along ·the lines suggested by the Reform Commission. By another it was decided that the conclave should consist, not of cardinals only, but of an additional thirty members, six from each nation. As the number of cardinals was twenty-three they were in a minority ; but as a two-thirds majority was declared to be necessary in each section of the electors their rights were safe-guarded.[83] As there had been a fear in the sacred college that they might be excluded altogether from the election, they had reason to congratulate themselves on these terms.

The first scrutiny, when voting began on Novr. 10, gave Election of no decisive result. On the following morning, however, Martin V four of the candidates drew ahead of the rest ; they were the cardinals of Ostia and Venice, with Saluzzo and Colonna.[84] The last became favourite for he had already received all the English votes, as well as the necessary majority in the Italian nation and, unlike his rivals, votes from all the rest. But the cardinals were not agreeable. At last among them too the necessary majority was secured, and, as Martin V, Colonna duly ascended the papal throne.

[82] In Van der Hardt IV. col. 1435.

[83] That is in each of the nations separately as well as among the cardinals. It was important to get a Pope who would be universally acceptable.

[84] Other candidates were said to be D'Ailly, and the famous English statesman, Henry Beaufort, later to be made a cardinal by his successful rival. It is said that Beaufort prevented the election of D'Ailly : see Gascoigne *Loci e libro veritatum* (ed. Thorold Rogers) p. 155.

His determined conduct

The choice was about as good a one as could have been made, for Colonna was pledged to no particular party, and owed his election neither to curial nor to French influence. He was a man of simple tastes, and hitherto had taken no leading part in affairs.[85] But if the reforming party placed hopes in his compliance with their views, they were soon to be disappointed. Immediately after his election he confirmed the rules of the Papal Chancery in which many abuses were enshrined. This was perhaps a necessary step to enable business to be carried on, but it provided a forecast of his permanent attitude. Martin was determined to raise papal prestige as high as ever, and to discourage any perpetuation of the conciliar method, and even any reforms which might strike at the root of the absolute monarchy of the Pope. Before the council was dissolved on April 22, 1418 the Pope, by making a number of small concessions to the several nations, managed to have the general question of reform postponed until another council should be called.[86] This was a wise move in the circumstances as the members were wearied by the long continuance of the assembly ; but by dealing with the nations individually Martin had established a precedent dangerous to the Papacy, as he might seem to have sanctioned the existence of separate national churches.

Failure of reform

As a reforming council Constance must be pronounced a failure. Its failure was the more regrettable as there was, in not a few quarters, a genuine desire for reform among its members ; but this was neutralised by the clash of separate interests, and, as so often happens in reforming m⁓ ⁓ements, each was anxious to reform his neighbour, but very loath to take any step which might injure himself. It is possible that if the council, after deposing John XXIII, had immediately tackled the question of reform something more might have been done. But during the long absence of Sigismund it sank down into inertia, quickened only by the emergence of national jealousies. It was by playing upon these that the curial party succeeded in defeating the ardent reformers and in stultifying their efforts.

[85] Cf. the opinion of Leonardo Bruni : " Vir antea nequaquam sagax existimatus, sed benignus ".   RIS. XIX. col. 930 B.

[86] He also confirmed the decrees of the Council so far as they were concerned with matters of faith and had been passed " conciliariter," and not " nationaliter " (i.e. merely by the nations in their separate sessions) : see Hefele VII. p. 369.

CHAPTER VII

THE PAPAL TRIUMPH : NATIONALITY

A GREATER burden of responsibility was placed upon The task of Martin V than upon almost any other Pope. It was Martin V for him to lay down the lines upon which the revived Papacy was to develop. For more than a century the Church had been torn by dissension, and the Papacy itself had seemed to be on its death-bed ; now the unity of the Church had been restored and power had again come to the Popes. What use would Martin V make of his opportunity ? In particular how would he solve the two grave problems which called for immediate settlement—the seat of the Papacy, and the urgent matter of reform ?

It was the wish of Sigismund that the Papacy should be transferred to a German city. Some wild scheme of another Avignon in which he and his successors were to play the part of the French kings of the fourteenth century had perhaps entered that over-fertile brain. But Martin V was a Roman and a Colonna ; and although Rome for the moment was not safe for a Pope, it was towards Rome that he set his face—a very momentous decision.

The Pope left Constance in the middle of May 1418 and He returns to made a leisurely progress into Central Italy. He seems, Italy quite wisely, to have desired to exhibit himself as much as possible, and by making the Papacy visible to exalt or restore its prestige. In this he was reverting to the methods of Leo IX in the eleventh century.[1] After a stay in Geneva, and the consecration of a new altar at Milan, he spent the autumn and winter in Mantua, and then went on to Florence where for two years he quietly waited until Rome was ready to receive him. At last the way was clear, and at the end of September 1420 he made his entry.

[1] See above, p. 17.

Condition of
Rome

But if Rome now enjoyed the blessings of quiet, its condition in other ways was deplorable.[2] Six years earlier it
had been noted that the people were so poor that even the
great festivals were but meanly observed ; [3] now poverty and
misery were so evident that the streets were filled with
rubbish and the city was so insanitary as to be actually unhealthy. Many of the churches were in ruins, and the few
houses which were still sound seemed to stand out among
the rest almost in isolation.

The work of
restoration

A century or more had elapsed since a Pope acknowledged
by all the West had been permanently resident in the eternal
city, and it called for a brave and resolute spirit to undertake
the task of healing the ravages wrought during this disastrous
interval.[4] Martin's first efforts were devoted to the restoration of the churches. He himself advanced huge sums for
this purpose, and he urged the cardinals to undertake the care
of the churches from which they took their titles. The mother
church of the West, St John Lateran, had been one of the
chief sufferers during the absence of the Popes, and more than
once outbreaks of fire had occurred in it. Much care was now
lavished in its adornment, and among the painters who were
engaged in its decoration was Masaccio.[5] When this work
was well in hand Martin turned his attention to the state of
the walls and gates of the city, and then to the bridges and
houses. He also built for his own use a palace on the Quiri-
nal and a castle at Genazzano, near the Colonna fortress of
Palestrina. Progress in all these vast undertakings was of
necessity slow, but before his death a definite start had been
made.

The
Campagna

These good offices of the sovereign pontiff increased his
favour with the Romans who gladly accepted his rule for the
time. He further benefited them by suppressing the robbers
and brigands which still haunted the city and the neighbouring Campagna.[6] Further afield he managed to obtain
recognition from the various tyrants and nobles in the Papal

---

[2] *Vita Martini V* in RIS. III. pt. ii. col. 864 D.

[3] Antonius Petri *Diarium* in RIS. XXIV. col. 1043.

[4] Urban V and Gregory XI in their day had made some attempts to
repair the city.

[5] The fires which so frequently broke out in the Lateran have destroyed
these and other paintings.

[6] Infessura *Diarium* in RIS. III. pt. ii. col. 1122 ; cf. col. 866.

States. The deaths of two famous condottieri, Sforza and Braccio, early in 1424 made for quiet and helped on the papal plans. It must be confessed, however, that in carrying them out Martin was not always scrupulous or entirely careful of the needs of the rest of Italy. The disturbances in Naples were used and even fostered by him for the furthering of his schemes.

Martin's successes in Rome and its immediate neighbourhood were made easier by his powerful family connexions, and he seems to have thought that the temporal power of the restored Papacy could best be supported on the ' pillars ' of his own Colonna. It is impossible to acquit him of nepotism ; but he had more excuse for this indulgence than most Popes, and his family, if they reaped their reward, had done much to deserve it.

In Europe in general Martin was a strong upholder of the rights and liberties of the Church. This attitude brought him into conflict with several states, including Portugal, Poland and Scotland, and in Italy with Florence and Venice.[7] In France, however, the ancient rights of the Papacy were restored by Charles VII in February 1425. *Martin and Europe*

The question of reform also occupied Martin in the earlier years of his pontificate, and he made some efforts to regulate the lives of the secular clergy, as well as to restore the discipline of the religious. But his political schemes seem more and more to have absorbed the Pope's attention, and reform was gradually forgotten. His failure was something of a calamity, and the difficulties by which he was faced, although they explain it in part, do not altogether excuse it.[8]

Before the breaking up of the Council of Constance it had been decreed that a further council should be held in seven years' time. Martin, although he had no love for such assemblies, held a council at Pavia in April 1423, before the lapse of the required interval. The assembly was, however, so poorly attended that after its transference, owing to the plague, to Siena the Pope was able to dissolve it. Before it dispersed, however, Basle had been fixed as the meeting-place of its successor.[9] *Council of Pavia* *Mar. 7, 1424*

[7] See Pastor *History of the Popes* I. p. 237 for details.
[8] This is admitted by Pastor *op. cit.* I. pp. 210 and 240. A Bull of reform was issued in May 1425 but it was superficial and ineffective.
[9] Basle had been suggested as an alternative for Constance : see Finke *Acta Concil. Constant.* I. p. 243.

Seven years were to pass before the new council met, and in them important developments were to occur, providing matter for the deep consideration of the assembly. They concerned more particularly events in Bohemia and the East.

Civil war in Bohemia

Sigismund had left Constance with lowered prestige, but the worst consequences of his broken safe-conduct had not then been revealed. Bohemia burst into a flame of civil and religious warfare. Army after army of German crusaders vainly tried to reduce the rebels to submission ; disgrace and shame for the invaders was the invariable result. A witty contemporary declared that the Germans had such a horror of heretics that they fled at the very sight of them.[10] The only hope of restoring peace was in a General Council.

Death of Martin V

The members of the Council began to assemble on the appointed day, March 4, 1431, but by this time the Pope, who however reluctantly had called them together, was no more.[11] Martin V died on Feb. 20 after having nominated Cardinal Cesarini as president of the Council. He was succeeded on the throne of St Peter by Eugenius IV, a capable administrator, but not a man of much intellectual ability or training.

Eugenius IV

The conclave which elected Eugenius is noteworthy on account of the attempt made by the cardinals to provide for their rights against papal aggression and tyranny. The capitulation then signed was accepted by the new Pope, and its articles incorporated into a Bull. They were sufficiently drastic and included the allocation of half the revenues of the Roman Church to the Sacred College, to which all officials were to take an oath. The Pope was not to transfer the Court from place to place without the consent of the cardinals and he was pledged to hold a General Council for the reform of the Church.

The Council of Basle

Eugenius as a cardinal had favoured the summoning of the Council of Basle, but after his election he shewed as great reluctance as his predecessor to encourage it. Many of its members had obviously set before them the trans-

---

[10] France might mock the Hussite wars by calling the abortive rebellion of 1440 a Praguerie, but to Germany they were a real danger.

[11] The Pope had been warned that if he did not summon a council the secular powers would do so and that he might suffer the fate of John XXIII.

formation of the organisation of the Church from a monarchy into a republic. In its own organisation the Council went far in a democratic direction. Voting by nations was abolished, and in its place four committees (*deputationes*) were set up, one each to deal with the subjects of the Restoration of Peace in Christendom, Matters of Faith and Doctrine, the Reform of the Church, and finally General Business (*pro communibus*). The bishops were overwhelmed by the large number of the inferior clergy who shared with them the right of voting.

At first the attendance was meagre. Cesarini himself was still in Bohemia where a final resort to arms was being tried. It proved as disastrous as former efforts and shewed clearly that Bohemia was not to be coerced. Cesarini arrived at Basle in September and the work of the council then began.

On the advice of Cesarini, the Bohemians, although they were under sentence of excommunication and heretics in the eyes of the Church, were invited to send delegates to the council. This step added to the alarm of the new Pope, and in December 1431 he issued a Bull dissolving it, and appointing another to meet at Bologna in the summer of 1433. This action on the part of Eugenius was very ill-advised, and the council, which had not realised that he would be offended by their taking what seemed the obvious course of summoning Bohemian representatives, refused to admit his power to dissolve them. Their attitude was supported by the Emperor as well as by Cesarini himself, who wrote a very outspoken letter to the Pope.[12] For a time it looked as though there would be another schism, as Eugenius and the cardinals who supported him would not give way, whilst the council actually cited them to appear before it within three months.[13] But the Pope was fighting a losing battle, and came out of the struggle with little credit, in spite of three Bulls issued against the council,[14] he was at length compelled to submit when in December it threatened to

Eugenius tries to dissolve the Council

April 29, 1432

---

[12] Printed in Aeneas Sylvius *Opera* pp. 64 sqq.

[13] This revolutionary action was defended by Nicholas of Cusa in his tract *De Concordantia Catholica* : see Bett *Nicholas of Cusa* pp. 16 sqq.

[14] The genuineness of the Bull of Sept. 13, 1433 which went to great extremes was later denied by Eugenius ; but his repudiation has not found universal acceptance.

suspend him, and by the Bull *Dudum sacrum*—the second of that title—solemnly to recognise Basle as a lawful assembly and to confirm its decrees as so far issued. The council graciously accepted his withdrawal and from Feb. 1434 peace reigned between them.

Eugenius was forced to give way because public opinion was against him, and his original action had been precipitate and unwise. But there was an additional motive. For the sake of his dear Venetians he had quarrelled with Milan, and had in consequence been driven into a position of no small difficulty and danger.[15] Thus enemies were gathering on every side, and it was a prudent move to reduce their number by submitting to the council for the moment and so gaining freedom of action in the future.

Bohemians at Basle

The papal disapproval had not led to the dropping of negotiations with the Bohemians; his recognition of the council made the hopes of settlement much greater. Their representatives had arrived at Basle at the end of 1432, and as a concession to their puritan prejudices the streets had been cleared of prostitutes. The subsequent discussions centred round four main points, those contained in the so-called Four Articles which had been drawn up at Prague as long ago as 1420.[16] They constituted the minimum demands of the Bohemian nation and included (*a*) Liberty of preaching; (*b*) Communion in both kinds; (*c*) The non-interference of the clergy in secular matters and the refusal to allow them to hold private property; (*d*) the subjection of the clergy to the law of the land for criminal offences. For three months the debates were continued, Cesarini, as chairman, handling the disputants with great tact and preserving order and good feeling. The leader of the Bohemians was Prokop, who had already distinguished himself as a military commander of genius; he now earned fresh laurels on another field of battle. As the Bohemian envoys had not received powers to enter into an agreement—in fact their object seems almost to have been to 'convert' the

---

[15] In spite of his concessions to the council a revolution in Rome in the following May drove the Pope to seek refuge in Florence.

[16] Lützow *Life and Times of Master John Hus* pp. 343 sq. thinks that a draft was prepared as early as 1417. In 1421 " to the surprise and horror of all Christendom " they were accepted by the Archbishop of Prague.

members of the council—the debates, although they cleared up a number of misunderstandings, produced no final settlement. This, however, was to follow, for delegates from the council proceeded to Prague, and there a compromise, the *Compactata*, was agreed upon. By its terms the chief demands of the Bohemians were conceded, but with certain qualifications. These terms unfortunately did not prove acceptable to the extremists, and civil war broke out in Bohemia. In the end the moderate party gained the upper hand and in the battle of Lipan most of the malcontents met their death.[17] May 30, 1434 The *Compactata* were finally signed at Iglau in July 1436.

It is probable that neither party to this agreement was acting in entire good faith. Both were anxious for a settlement, and as the terms were taken in different senses by the two sides, each could claim that it had got its way. Disputed points in the documents were left undecided and qualifications and conditions deliberately ignored.[18]

In 1434 the prestige of the council stood at its highest. Diminishing It had to its credit a striking victory over the Pope, and in prestige of addition the Bohemian dispute seemed well on the way to a the council settlement. But the question of reform, and the continuance of the Bohemian negotiations, brought out the essential weakness of the council's position. As it lost power it tended to act from mere spite, as if trying to shew that it could still hurt its enemies. This seems the only explanation of the abolition of annates in June 1435, and of other extreme measures of reform. The death of Sigismund in December 1437 removed one who might have played a mediating part, though by this time he had passed over to the papal side.[19] Gradually the more moderate members lost their influence as the extremists gained control, until at last they were compelled to abandon the council altogether. Even Cesarini

[17] The situation was not unlike that during the Commonwealth in England, though the result was different since the army did not in Bohemia succeed in imposing its will on the country.

[18] See Voigt in Sybel's *Hist. Zeitschrift* V. p. 413.

[19] Sigismund, in spite of his imposing appearance as exhibited, for example, in the magnificent statue in Berlin—where he figures by virtue of his Electorate of Brandenburg—is a pathetic figure. He was a conservative at heart, one who loved the good old days, yet realised that they were passing away. This comes out in his speech at the Diet of Vienna in 1425 : quoted by Molitor *Die Reichsreformbestrebungen* p. 28.

himself took this course and left the leadership in the hands of Louis d'Allemand, Cardinal of Arles.

It was over the negotiations with the Eastern Church [20] that the breach between the council and the Pope became complete, and it was there that the council sustained its decisive defeat.   The Greeks in their desire for help against the advancing Turk applied to both Pope and council; all they wanted was to obtain the best terms they could.   Both tried hard to obtain their confidence, and the matter was indeed of supreme importance, for if they had decided to join the council it would have had some claim to be considered Oecumenical.   A new stage in the Church's life might thus have begun, with the Pope left out, or in which he would have played but a minor part.[21]   It is not surprising that papalists love to compare Basle and the Robber Council of Ephesus of 449.

The council in order to induce the Greeks to journey to Basle offered to pay all the expenses of the delegates—one imagines this would have been a necessity in any case—and to raise funds for this purpose it issued indulgences, a strange act for a body of men who claimed to be anxious for reform, and moreover a distinct breach of papal privilege.   Eugenius replied by denouncing the assembly at Basle and promising to call a genuine council to which the Greeks could come.

In dealing with the Greeks the council had one serious disadvantage—Basle was obviously an unsuitable place to which to invite them.   The papal legates proposed that the council should be moved to an Italian city so as to be more convenient.   The reformers suggested Avignon as the only possible alternative.   There were angry quarrels and the papal legates were suspected of having tampered with the records of the assembly.   Then came the news that the Greeks had finally decided to place their hopes in Eugenius.   This aroused very bitter feelings, and in July 1437 the council ordered the Pope and cardinals to appear at Basle within sixty days to meet various charges against them.   On October 1 Eugenius was declared to be contumacious.   But already he had played his trump card, for on Sept. 18 he had

---

[20] See further, pp. 241 sqq. below.
[21] Cf. Norden Das Papsttum und Byzanz p. 722.

issued a Bull dissolving the council at Basle, and fixing Ferrara as the site of his own promised assembly.

The council duly met at Ferrara in January 1438 and Eugenius presided in person. A year later it was transferred to Florence owing to an outbreak of plague. The Greeks attended as they had agreed to do, but the debates between them and the Latins were long and wearisome. At last through sheer weakness they had to give way—*filioque* clause, leavened bread, and even the papal supremacy, were all accepted in their need. The Pope appeared to have scored a great triumph, and so far as the Council of Basle was concerned he had ; but anyone with real knowledge of the feelings of the Eastern Church must have known that the decree of Union so proudly proclaimed on July 6, 1439 would never be accepted in Constantinople. So it proved. But in the meantime Florence had drawn to it the best of those who had formed the strength of the assembly at Basle. If it had brought but a hollow agreement with the Greeks it had been a politic move against the extremists at Basle. Their assertions of the rights of General Councils over Popes were definitely rejected in a decree passed after the Greeks had left Florence.

The Council of Florence

After this set-back Basle could only hope for success if it received adequate support from the secular powers. But the latter had their own ends to serve, and these could best be attained by exacting concessions from the Papacy under threat of giving such support. So the Pragmatic Sanction of Bourges in 1438 and the similar agreement at Mainz in the following year registered the triumph of the rulers of France and Germany respectively over the Church.

Sept. 4, 1439
The secular powers and the Papacy

On June 25, 1439 the reformers had taken the extreme step of creating another schism in the West. They declared Eugenius IV to be heretical and the Papacy to be vacant. This anticipated by less than two weeks the issue of the decree of Union. To elect a new Pope was the natural sequel and although only one cardinal—Louis d'Allemand—was to be found among them they recked little of that, and appointed a body of thirty-two electors to make a suitable choice. But this was no easy matter, for the new Pope would find himself with a very dubious title, and in addition the necessity of supporting himself from his own resources, by no means

Election of an anti-Pope

a desirable situation.   However at last Amadeus, the eccentric Duke of Savoy, who was living as a quasi-hermit on the shores of the Lake of Geneva, was chosen and consecrated as Felix V.[22]

German Neutrality   The extreme measures taken by the council robbed it of much sympathy, but if it could have gained the allegiance of the new Emperor-elect, Frederick III, it might yet have raised its head.   In the Diet of Frankfurt in 1438 the German Electors had declared for neutrality between Pope and council, and for nine years Frederick maintained this attitude, in spite of strenuous efforts on the part of the adherents of either party to gain him over.   On the side of the Pope the most effective advocate at the beginning of the period was Nicholas of Cusa ; [23] later, Aeneas Sylvius, the future Pius II, by a timely transfer of his allegiance was to be a deciding force in the contest.[24]   For many years, by voice and pen, he worked on behalf of the council, becoming secretary to Felix V in 1439.   Three years later he accepted a similar post with Frederick III.   From this time forward the Emperor gradually drew nearer to the side of Eugenius, until in 1446 they came to a definite agreement, which was followed on Feb. 7, 1447 by the submission of the German people.

Germany decides for the Pope   This result, so happy for Eugenius, was not obtained without much striving and, it must be confessed, in spite of papal blundering.   In return for his support, the Pope had promised Frederick to hand over a considerable part of the ecclesiastical revenues of Germany, as well as the presentation to a number of bishoprics and livings.   The agreement was a secret, but the German princes suspected that it had been made, and the Archbishops of Cologne and Trier in protest went over to Felix.   Angered by this Eugenius made a false move.   He branded the archbishops as heretics and traitors and deprived them of their sees.   But Aeneas stepped in and persuaded the Pope to withdraw his condemnation, and then, by a series of complicated intrigues, he succeeded in getting Eugenius, now on his death-bed, to conclude the

[22] As Duke of Savoy he had brought in new statutes for his duchy : see L. Cibrario *Degli statuti d'Amadeo VIII* in *Operetti e frammenti storici* pp. 273 sqq.   The council can hardly have regarded its choice as another Celestine V.

[23] " Hercules . . . omnium Eugenianorum " Aeneas Sylvius had called him : *Opera* p. 3.   See further Bett *Nicholas of Cusa* pp. 33 sqq.

[24] For his career see Creighton *History of the Papacy* III. pp. 51 sqq. and C. M. Ady *Pius II.*

agreement which made possible the return of Germany to the papal fold.[25]

The next Pope was Thomas of Sarzana, who took the title of Nicholas V. As the policy of Eugenius was continued by him he received the recognition of Germany, the ever-useful Aeneas again acting as intermediary. All matters in dispute were finally settled by the Concordat of Vienna in 1448.   *Election of Nicholas V*

Meanwhile the council at Basle was still sitting, although its own Pope had left it in disgust in 1444. It was, however, little more than a ghost with hardly enough vitality to make a decent end; but Nicholas smoothed the way, and at last it was allowed to dissolve itself, and so to retain some remnants of dignity. Felix received a cardinal's hat and a pension,[26] whilst Louis d'Allemand returned to Arles where his devoted labours gained him, in the following century, a place in the canon of the Roman Church: a strange fate for a revolutionary leader.[27]   *The end of the council*

So the great Conciliar Movement came to an end. Basle, although it had been so long drawn out, was a decisive struggle. Its end had about it no elements of grandeur, hardly of pathos. There are movements known to history which, after long battling with opposing forces, at length find shipwreck and go down beneath the force of wind and waves. The Conciliar Movement had had its storms and struggles, but its conclusion was that of an abandoned hulk rotting away in some deserted backwater.

The failure of the Conciliar Movement is usually attributed to the clash of interests represented by the various nations, and the skill with which the curia made use of them. Behind national jealousies, however, there were other causes even more profound. It seems probable that those who pressed for reform were, for the most part, not entirely sincere; they had some axe to grind, some secret purpose to serve; the Popes played upon this and brought numbers of them over by the offer of promotion. Some of the greatest and most sincere, as for example Gerson, allowed themselves to be " side-tracked " and their influence to be rendered innocuous. In   *Final failure of the Conciliar Movement*

[25] See Creighton *op. cit.* III. pp. 74 sqq. and Ady *op. cit.* pp. 82 sqq.
[26] Felix made his submission at Lausanne in a house called La Grotte. By a strange coincidence it became the home of Gibbon and there he finished his great work. It has recently been pulled down.
[27] See further G. Pérouse *Le Cardinal Louis Aleman etc.*

the later stages of the movement its adherents were painfully conscious that things were going wrong, and were yet quite incapable of coping with them.

Its reasons   The tactics of the conciliar party were not well chosen. At first they were too academic and paltry. The academic mind has obvious virtues, but it has equally patent defects, and among them are pedantry and timidity in practical affairs. The movement had for its chief inspiration a University, and it was pervaded by the speculative, rather than the practical, spirit. Petty and irritating changes are much more liable to arouse opposition and resentment than sweeping measures of reform. There is about the latter something irresistible. But when more vigorous measures were attempted, in particular at Basle, the council acted in so un-conciliatory a manner that it alienated many who had been its friends, it seemed bent on weakening the Papacy rather than on reforming the Church. Often enough those who were keenest on reform were those who stood to gain by it. In any case the councils were largely self-constituted bodies, and in so far as they were representative they transformed the movement into a rising of the organised Church against the Papacy. Furthermore the leaders were deficient in political skill and experience,[28] not an uncommon phenomenon under a despotic government.[29]

At Pisa the method was too new and too conscious of its own lack of standing to be really effective ; but at Constance it proved its worth, and at least put an end to the Schism. Perhaps this was the limit of its powers, for the reformers allowed themselves to be out-manœuvred into electing a Pope, although with safeguards, before the work of reform had seriously been tackled. This left them in a very weak position tactically, for the Pope had a very definite objective, whilst the reformers were not agreed among themselves as to the abuses they wished to see remedied, much less as to the best method of dealing with them.

Although they did not realise it the conciliar party were

[28] This has been well brought out by Figgis *From Gerson to Grotius* p. 261 : " The Council, ignorant of the distinction between control and administration, attempted without training, knowledge or cohesion to grasp the whole governing activity of the Church, judicial, executive and legislative ".

[29] Rousseau and the French revolutionaries of the eighteenth century are a striking instance of this.

more out of touch with reality than their opponents. They were working on medieval lines; the curia towards the modern Papacy. The Papacy was quick to recognise the existence of national divisions, and to make use of them; [30] the councils would have liked to ignore them. The time was not yet ripe for the emergence of this problem into full light.[31] The action of Martin V was based on no principle, was a mere piece of expediency, and a dangerous one at that. But for the moment it served his end.

The Conciliar Movement was a real challenge to the Papacy, and had it succeeded the centre of gravity of the whole Church would have been shifted; the Pope would have been reduced to the position of a limited monarch ruled by the College of Cardinals or by the meetings of the council. It was a life and death struggle, and the Papacy, during its whole course, never lacked skilful and devoted protagonists who saw this quite clearly.[32] The papal triumph probably saved the Church from a break-up, as its unity depended, not on a creed or a collective spirit—the council shewed that such a spirit was entirely absent—but on an absolute monarchy. This triumph was due largely to the mistakes of the reformers and to the patience and persistency with which the Popes held their ground. Future ages were to shew that if complete, the triumph was largely illusory; it gave the Papacy a chance of setting its house in order, for Christendom was not yet ripe for its abolition; but instead of using the opportunity the Popes allowed abuses to multiply and scandals to increase. Thus the failure of the Conciliar Movement involved as a consequence the failure of attempts at constitutional reform. For this the Papacy was itself to suffer, as Cesarini in his daring letter to Eugenius IV had foretold. The next serious effort at reform would take the shape of a revolution. Other consequences, more remote, were to follow the papal triumph; for its logical sequence was undoubtedly infallibility and,

Significance of the contest

[30] Cf. G. Pérouse *Le Cardinal Louis Aleman* p. 499.

[31] Cf. Croce *Theory and Hist. of Historiography* p. 192 : " In every historical period exist problems theoretically formulated and for that very reason solved, while others have not yet arrived at complete theoretical maturity, but are seen, intuited, though not yet adequately thought ".

[32] It is remarkable that those who were responsible, in the main, for the papal victory had been themselves advocates of the conciliar theory ; e.g. Cesarini, Nicholas of Cusa, and Aeneas Sylvius.

in the secular state, absolutism.[33]   It was for the time a complete defeat of the democratic spirit and a fit opening to a century which saw the decline of all representative institutions.

Later attempts at conciliar action

Published Jan. 18, 1460

Although the conciliar theory seemed quite suppressed and in spite of the condemnation by Pius II in the Bull *Execrabilis* it never quite died out.   Within a generation of the death of Pius its use was urged by Savonarola and others as a weapon against Alexander VI.[34]   This attempt to revive the conciliar method was probably a sincere one ; but it was often invoked merely as a means of frightening a Pope into a desired course of action ; in fact the appeal to a General Council became a recognised move on the political chessboard.   The French monarchy, in particular, seemed unable to give up the idea, and as late as 1682, during the dispute with Innocent XI, it was contained in the famous Four Articles drafted by Bossuet on behalf of Louis XIV.

Sequel to the papal triumph

In the introductory chapter I traced the growth of the papal power both within the Church and over against the Empire ; its final successful struggle with the latter was described in Chapter II.   The Conciliar Movement may be looked upon as an attempt by the Church, after centuries of acquiescence, to free itself from the growing papal despotism.   Over this attempt also the Papacy was triumphant as we have seen. But each of these triumphs had a similar and alarming sequel. The fall of the Empire left the Papacy face to face with the national spirit as exhibited in the French king ; the failure of the Conciliar Movement was also to bring the Papacy face to face with Nationalism—but this time on an even more portentous scale.   The rôle which it played in the decline and fall of the Medieval Papacy was so potent that we must now turn aside to consider its growth and development so far as space will permit.

Definition of Nation and Nationality

It will be necessary, first of all, to arrive at some kind of definition of a nation, as well as of the term nationalism.   The

---

[33] Figgis rightly speaks of Eugenius IV as " the forerunner of Louis XIV " (*From Gerson to Grotius* p. 41), and of the papal victory as the " Beginning of the triumph of centralised bureaucracy throughout the civilised world " (*op. cit.* p. 43).

[34] Another Dominican, St Antonino, the beloved and learned Archbishop of Florence, clearly recognised that in matters concerning the faith a council was above the Pope, and that even a private person might arrive at a more accurate result if " moved by better reasons and the authorities of the New and Old Testaments " (*Sum. Theol.* III. xxiii. 2).

former is often confused with words of cognate meaning, such as race, people, country, and even culture.[35] Each of these may supply elements to a nation ; its strength lies in the extent to which they are combined within it.   A nation one might say is a human group generally with a common speech, a common country, common blood, and common traditions especially in religion.   This is, of course, an ideal nation to which actual nations only approximate.   Perhaps the best short definition is " a sovereign society " ; [36] whilst of nationalism a useful definition is that it is " the complete and consistent theory that the state and the nation must be co-extensive ".[37]

Nationalism, viewed from within, thus involves the sub- *Demands of* ordination of all sectional interests to the good of the whole ; *Nationalism* in practice, however, unassimilated groups are nearly always found within nations, the root of much bitterness and of many insoluble problems.[38]   Nationalism also tends to be suspicious of a universal society, such as the Catholic Church, which may threaten to divide the allegiance of the members of the political group.[39]   Its real danger is thus to become self-sufficient and self-seeking.

The defects of Nationalism to the world outside are *Nationalism* similar.   Just as it tends to extirpate all groups within *and the* its borders, so it strives to overcome its neighbours or to isolate *world* itself from them.   Creighton points out that England was the first to develop a national character, and it did so by tending " to withdraw cautiously from the general system of Europe, and go its own way ".[40]

[35] Race and culture are often confused ; it is for example correct to speak of Latin culture, hardly of Latin races.   I notice that Pittard, after exposing this confusion (*Les races et l'histoire* p. 55) goes on to speak of ' races latines ' (*op. cit.* p. 60) which shews that the term, if not strictly accurate, is very convenient.

[36] W. Temple *Mens Creatrix* p. 245.   The archbishop continues :   " The state is the organ of the nation for the purpose of collective action, whether in control of the nation's own constituent members, or in dealing with other states ".

[37] Lord Acton *Letters to Mary Gladstone* p. xxvi.

[38] The position of the Jews is such a problem.   Acute national feeling, as in Germany to-day, recognises them as an alien element and seeks to exclude them.

[39] Pagan Rome had shewn that men might combine its citizenship with a continued membership of their own state, without damage to the smaller group :   a valuable contribution to political life.

[40] *Historical Lectures and Addresses* p. 218.

In the ancient Western world the city was the unit and not the nation ; this is true in particular of the city-states of Greece. To the later Romans national feeling was always a potential source of trouble, and as such to be suppressed. They feared it as a disintegrating force, for to their orderly and legal minds, difference of race or nationality were obstacles to the unity of the Empire, and liable to break the uniformity at which they aimed.[41] The nation thus leads us towards modern times, for if the city-state was the ancient ideal, so was the Empire the ideal in the middle ages.[42] But the growth of a nation really involved the birth not only of a new political unit but of a new economic unit in addition. As nations arose they adopted their own economic policies with national rivalries as a consequence.[43]

Rise of national feeling

It is difficult to say when national feeling first shewed itself in the middle ages. Tout suggests that we have an instance of it in the election of Hugh Capet to the throne of France in 987.[44] But it was not till long after this date that it became widespread ; though perhaps one may see in the quarrels of the crusading armies in the Holy Land the foreshadowing of later national divisions. The ideas and the institutions of the times were against the nation. It had to struggle with the Church, the Empire, and the feudal system for its existence. Of the two opposed and antagonistic tendencies which form part of man's heritage ; the instinct to combine into social groups and the instinct of self-assertion or separation ; the former prevailed in the middle ages ; the spirit of the age favoured universal, and not separatist tendencies. None the less the conflict between the Empire and the Papacy gave opportunity for the growth of nationalism, and it was during the later phases of this conflict that we can observe the first signs of its rise. Such it seems to me is the significance of the lack of response to

[41] This attitude was perpetuated by the Civil Law which Stubbs once described as " one of the greatest obstacles to national development in Europe " : see *Letters of W. Stubbs* p. 159.

[42] But cities remained the chief economic units to the close of the middle ages in many parts of Europe.

[43] See Cunningham *Western Civilisation* II. pp. 158 sqq. As England was the first country in which the national spirit shewed itself so was it the first to organise itself on a national basis, not only politically, but economically ; see Cunningham and McArthur *Outlines of English Industrial History* p. 24.

[44] *The Empire and the Papacy* pp. 78 sq.

Frederick II's appeal to the rulers of Europe against the Pope's activities. They refused to accept his argument that they too were threatened ; already it was realised that the position of a national king was very different from that of an Emperor.

But if national feeling was emerging—the expulsion of the Jews at the end of the thirteenth century from both France and England is perhaps a sign of it—long years were to pass before it became fully manifest. This comes out in the wars of the period ; for even in the fourteenth century warfare was still a dynastic rather than a national undertaking, and the king merely a greater feudatory leading forth his vassals. Examples of national wars were not unknown, such undoubtedly were the Hussite Wars in Bohemia.[45] It was not, however, until improved means of transport and commissariat had enabled warfare to be conducted on a larger scale that nation could rise against nation, and not merely one feudal sovereign against another. But this stage was hardly reached before the French Revolution and the wars which followed it.[46] *Nationality and warfare*

The breaking up of the ideal unity of the Empire is definitely acknowledged in the Golden Bull of Charles IV in 1356, and from that point onward the consciousness of national distinctions becomes more and more prominent. The Great Schism was largely caused by the struggle of the Italians and French to make the Papacy subservient to national interests, whilst the Conciliar Movement failed because of the same spirit. *Break-up of the Empire*

The failure of Europe, after the Fall of Constantinople in 1453, to unite against the Turk, in spite of the efforts of Calixtus III and Pius II, clearly revealed the presence of separate policies in the different nations and their carelessness as to the fate of others. If Constance was the last occasion on which the Emperor played an international part, *Nationalism in the fifteenth century*

---

[45] The Battle of Tannenberg in 1410 when the Poles defeated the Teutonic Order, was another result of the Slav reaction against the German " Drang nach Osten ".

[46] In other departments of life, such as finance and justice, the idea of tenure was gradually being superseded ; the king, from being overlord, was becoming a sovereign with subjects. In this matter Frederick II was far in advance of his age and Sicily in the thirteenth century had a highly organised system of government, even in military matters the feudal system was giving way : see Cohn *Das Zeitalter der Hohenstaufen in Sizilien.*

1459

the Congress of Mantua was the first assembly of national powers. From the same period comes another interesting example of the strength of national feeling. When in 1457 Ladislas Posthumus, King of both Bohemia and Hungary, died, the separate nations, ignoring entirely all dynastic considerations, elected separate rulers, Matthias Corvinus to the throne of Hungary, and George Podiebrad to that of Bohemia.

By the end of the fifteenth century in all the leading countries of Europe, except Italy and Germany, an absolute monarchy had been established and the king had become the centre of the unity of the nation and the symbol of its separate life and interests. The steps which led up to this demand more detailed study.

Nationalism in England,

England, as we have seen, was the first country to realise its national character, and indeed the task of moulding it into a separate whole was begun by the Normans ; though it was not until Normandy itself had been lost that the process was much advanced.[47] The wars in France during the fourteenth century quickened this development still further, for not a few of the great nobles had finally to decide whether they would side with the French or English.[48]

The policy of these great nobles was different in the two countries. In France they sought to gain their independence from the central power, in England to control it. Thus instead of weakening the government the English feudatories strengthened it. But the Wars of the Roses saw the end of them. They destroyed one another, and, as Workman has put it, " Laid liberty at the feet of a triumphant crown ".[49] For the nation this was all to the good for a strong king was a centre round which national feeling could be developed.

One great factor in fostering national feeling in England had been its separate legal system. In 1234 Henry III had forbidden the teaching of the Civil Law in order to preserve this separation, and two years later the Council of Merton refused to bring the English law of bastardy into line with that of other nations almost entirely for the same reason—*Nolumus*

---

[47] The abolition of ' nations ' in the University of Oxford in 1274 is a sign of the realisation of national unity.

[48] John de Montfort, Duke of Brittany, is a good example. He decided to adhere to the French cause and his fief of Richmond was accordingly forfeited.

[49] *John Wyclif* I. p. 217.

leges angliae mutare was the only real argument against the change.   What really preserved English law, especially in the age of the Renaissance, when there might well have been a ' reception ' of the Roman Law similar to that in Germany, was the existence of the Inns of Court, unique schools of national law, and the Year Books which they issued.[50]

The growth of nationalism in France has special impor- in France tance and interest ; partly because it was the first to challenge the Papacy ; partly because its reactions were seen not only against the Papacy, but also against the Empire.[51]   At the beginning of the thirteenth century the power of France had become so considerable that it might well feel that it stood on an equality with the Empire, especially after the victory 1214 of Bouvines ; by the end of that century the claim was openly advocated in the treatise *Disputatio inter clericum et militem.* In this treatise it is argued that the King of France has just as great authority as the Emperor himself.[52]   A contemporary writer, James of Révigny, speaks of him as *magistratus principis ;*[53] but the most significant statement was the famous phrase devised by Bartolus of Sassoferrato *Rex est imperator in regno suo.*[54]   Less importance must be attached to the wild schemes of Pierre Dubois in his *De Recuperatione Terrae Sanctae* (1305-1307), in which he actually proposes that the Pope should surrender his temporal power to the French king, and that the latter should become Senator of Rome.   The Pope is thereupon to settle in France and to confine himself to purely spiritual functions.   If these ideas had any widespread existence in France, and the Avignon period in part fulfilled some of them, the Hundred Years' War crushed them for a time, together with any ambitions which may have been cherished for the extension of French influence in Italy.

The struggle with the Papacy was an affair of much greater France and
the Papacy

[50] See Maitland *English Law and the Renaissance* pp. 23 sqq.

[51] English national feeling was also afraid of imperial claims ; but the threat was not so serious owing to England's geographical position and earlier history.

[52] " Imperio portio, pari divisione ab eo discreta et aequali dignitate et auctoritate . . . insignita " : see Carlyle *Hist. of Med. Pol. Theory* V. p. 381.

[53] See Tourtoulon *Les oeuvres de Jacques de Révigny* p. 48.

[54] For a discussion of this phrase see Fr. Ercole *L'origine francese di una nota formola Bartoliana* in Arch. Stor. Ital. (1915) LXXIII. pp. 241-294.

importance, because it was concerned with a more practical matter than claims to equality with the shadowy Empire. Even in the early middle ages France, or at least the French Church, had shewn a very independent attitude towards the Papacy ; Gallicanism goes back well into the tenth century. An instance may be cited in the Synod of Rheims (995), famous on account of its attempt to depose Archbishop Arnulf and to elect Gerbert (the future Sylvester II) in his place. At this synod abuses in the Papacy were denounced, and the threat actually put forth that France might imitate the Eastern Church and become independent.

During the dispute between Innocent III and Philip Augustus at the beginning of the thirteenth century, a breach between the Papacy and the kingdom was only narrowly averted.[55] A century later the breach actually came, or rather a struggle in which the Papacy, in the person of Boniface VIII, was worsted and dishonoured. Papal arrogance was as galling to national pride as it was to the king himself,[56] and another Philip found a united people behind him, or so he claimed in resisting aggression.[57] Philippe le Bel himself, in the last year of his reign (1814), was to find both nobles and people united against him to resist the infliction of an unjust tax. Their opposition was successful ; but sectional interests soon broke up the alliance, and the monarchy continued to develop, as the real interests of the nation as a whole undoubtedly demanded that it should. National feeling, as distinct from feudal, was at the beginning of the fourteenth century only rudimentary ; for it is easy to confuse administrative centralisation with national unity. The experiences of the Hundred Years' War were needed to demonstrate the evils of division and jealousy, and in the end to unite the nation to undertake the task of expelling the foreigners. Those experiences were to teach another lesson and to make dread of the presence of an invader on his native soil almost an obsession to the Frenchman.

[55] Cf. my *Innocent III* pp. 90 and 194 sq.

[56] By a strange coincidence France, which at the beginning of the fourteenth century heralded the break-up of the old system and the rise of nations, was at the end of the eighteenth to reverse the process ; for the French Revolution, as Disraeli once wrote, " introduced the cosmopolitan principle into human affairs instead of the national " : *Endymion* p. 105.

[57] Philip's policy was ostensibly based on an appeal from the Pope to the people.

The power exercised by the French monarchy, and by the University of Paris, during the Schism did not make it easier for the nation to respect the Papacy. At the Council of Paris in 1406 Simon Cramaud, although he professed to observe the rights and privileges of the Roman Church, asked why French causes should not be settled in the country itself instead of being transferred to Italy.[58] When such matters were publicly discussed, and the suggestion made that France, and other countries as well, should have each its own Pope, all was ready for the Pragmatic Sanction of 1438.[59]

A few words may well be written on the development of nationalism in Spain. In 1266 the Moors had been driven back on Granada. This left Castile alone in touch with them and tended to weaken the bond of national feeling which the Moorish threat had kept alive.[60] But from 1339 onwards a fresh offensive, by Moslems from Africa, again knit the Spanish nations together. The final conquest of Granada lies beyond the scope of this chapter; it was carried out in 1492 by Castile and Aragon in partnership.[61] *Nationalism in Spain,*

In Germany national feeling was developed during the struggle between the Empire and the Papacy; but it was retarded by the peculiar position of the Emperors, which made them act as a distintegrating force, the very reverse of the monarchs of other states. The first instance of combined action on the part of the German people, according to Ranke, was the resistance offered to the attempt of the ecclesiastics in the ninth century to dethrone Lewis the Pious.[62] There was a different alignment two centuries later when the German bishops defied the Emperor and the Pope together, because there had been a recognition of the national and ecclesiastical independence of Hungary and Poland.[63] But from the first *in Germany,*

[58] See Bourgeois du Chastenet *Nouvelle Hist. du Concile de Constance* p. 120.

[59] For the theories underlying Gallicanism, as it is called, see Imbart de la Tour *Les origines de la Réforme* II. pp. 80 sqq.

[60] Patriotism in Spain was largely provincial.

[61] Even after the union Castile and Aragon were not actually merged; each retained its own institutions and its own life, although both were ruled by the same monarch. The tariff barriers between them were, however, thrown down. The lack of unity between the two great Spanish nations was probably an important factor in the rapid decay of Spain after its brief summer of power.

[62] *Deutsche Geschichte im Zeitalter der Reformation* I. p. 9.

[63] Tout *The Empire and the Papacy* pp. 45 sq.

the development of nationalism was hindered by the fact that Germany was not really a single nation, but a collection of four at least ; there was always a tendency to split up.   In the latter period the needs of the emperors compelled them to make numerous concessions to the nobles and cities of Germany, and thus to set up and strengthen a large number of small centres of authority.   This state of affairs lasted, with varying fortunes and many permutations, right into the nineteenth century.

The interregnum which followed the fall of the Hohenstaufen exposed the weakness of German feeling, for both candidates for the Empire, Richard of Cornwall and Alfonso of Castile were foreigners.   In the next century, however, the opposition to Lewis of Bavaria did something to revive it, especially as the Pope was suspected of acting under French influence.   Lewis lost his opportunity, through his own weakness and superstitious dread of the papal power, and by following the traditional course of descending into Italy. But the electors knew their duty and the Diet of Rense in 1338 put a check to papal interference in the Empire ; the Golden Bull, eighteen years later, brought about its final exclusion.

The growing weakness of the Empire, however, prevented it from cultivating German national aspirations ; by the middle of the fifteenth century the legs of iron, as Aeneas Sylvius did not fail to note,[64] had become feet of clay. Germany, more and more, was a little world to itself, within which each ruler was striving to make himself independent, and since he held of the Emperor he regarded himself as the equal of a national king.

and in Italy   In Italy a similar state of things prevailed, for there too the tradition of the Empire still lingered on, and made men despise merely national dominions ;   there too the petty despot regarded himself as the equal of kings.   But I am sure that Italian national feeling was more common and more widespread than is often supposed.   One continually comes across expressions which reveal its wounded pride.[65]   But

[64] *Hist. Frid. III*. pp. 288 sq.
[65] Passages in Dante (e.g. *Purg.* vi. 78 sqq.) find parallels in earlier times. I chanced to notice two from the times of Barbarossa.   In the *De Obsidone Anconae* (in RIS. VI. col. 925 sqq.) the use of " Italia " is significant

it was usually transitory, and such expressions of unity as
the cities in their leagues were intended to serve purely selfish
aims.   Innocent III might appeal to hatred of the Teuton in
his efforts to restore the temporal power of the Papacy,[66]
but the response was spasmodic and partial.   " The Germans
clung like limpets to their crags or lived prosperously in the
towns sheltered by the sunny indifference of the Italian middle
class to all things papal and national." [67]   So they remained
until finally absorbed in the following century.   Differences
of race, especially the marked distinction between the northern
and southern Italian, may have been a further cause of weakness, as the geographical situation, with its great length and
the dividing Apennines, most certainly was.[68]

The slowness of Italy to develop any real national feeling
was due above all to that narrow outlook on life which made
the city the unit and not the whole land.   When St Francis,
on his last journey, blessed Assisi his action was typical of
the Italian people, at least in the north and central areas.
As in the second century B.C. the land was " poor in national
aspirations . . . rich in short-sighted political ambitions ".[69]
It had intense patriotism, but only a limited area over which
it worked.   Elsewhere, save in Germany, the cities gave their
strength and energy to feed the life of the nation and acted
as unifying forces ; they were, as Dean Church has happily
put it, " knots in the political network ".[70]   But in Italy, by
their mutual jealousies, they postponed any possibility of
national union.   Their attitude was exactly that of the ancient
Greeks to whom the inhabitants of every strange city were,
if not barbarians, at least foreigners.   Time has avenged
itself on the Italian cities, for their influence most unexpectedly
failed to outlive the middle ages.

It was owing to these rivalries within the peninsula that

Reasons for slow growth of National- ism in Italy

and the protest " Non est Provincia sed Domina Provinciarum ".   Romuald
of Salerno records that in the negotiations between the Pope and the Lombards
at Ferrara in 1177 the cities claimed that they had rejected the offers of the
Emperor in order to preserve " the honour and liberty of Italy and the dignity
of the Roman Church " : MGH. SS. XIX. p. 445.

[66] See my *Innocent III* p. 16.

[67] Fisher *The Mediaeval Empire* II. p. 243.

[68] It is often forgotten that London is approximately the same distance,
as the crow flies, from Milan as Reggio.

[69] *Camb. Anct. Hist.* VIII. p. 592.

[70] *Dante and other Essays* (Eversley Edition) p. 10.

15

Italy became for centuries the battlefield of foreigners. To call in the French to redress an unfavourable balance of power was such an easy device, though it seldom proved entirely satisfactory to those who adopted it. But it was a symptom of a defective national spirit and the cause of still further disunion. The policy went back, of course, to distant centuries, to the summoning of the Franks by the Papacy for help against the Lombards ; it was revived by Innocent III,[71] and became an important element in the papal policy during the struggle with the Empire in its later stages. But not to the Popes alone must the blame for this action be assigned, but to the whole Guelf party.[72]

The Papacy and Italian unity The Papacy has been accused, by competent scholars, of being the chief cause of the disunion of Italy, it was as Burckhardt has said, " strong enough to hinder national unity . . . not strong enough to bring it about ".[73] That was the trouble ; no state was sufficiently strong to overcome the rest ; the balance of power was so exact that things remained in perpetual suspension. Florence had tried in 1376 to form a league of cities to expel the foreigner and preserve Italy for the Italians, but the Papacy stood out, and the Romans also realised that their interests were bound up in the return of the Popes to their city, and they too refused to take part.[74]

Two other lines of papal policy also hindered the realisation of Italian unity—the necessity, in the thirteenth century, of keeping Sicily and the Empire in separate hands so as to preserve the Papal States from being surrounded—and the change in attitude towards the communes when once the fall of the Empire had rendered their aid unnecessary. The municipalities were moreover often seed plots of heresy and shewed no willingness to accept papal rule.[75] Thus the Papacy soon came to occupy the place which the Empire had held as the opponent of the republican spirit.

For a time during the Great Schism the Roman Pope stood out as an Italian and the centre of Italian feeling. It was no

---

[71] See my *Innocent III* pp. 39 sq.

[72] Gregorovius *Geschichte der Stadt Rom.* II. p. 10.

[73] *Die Cultur der Renaissance in Italien* p. 4.

[74] Cf. Rodocanachi *Hist. de Rome* p. 62.

[75] Even in the days of Innocent III they were not eager to accept papal rule, and in more than one instance elected a heretic to the chief magistracy : see *Innocent III* pp. 24 sqq. and 116 sq.

mere coincidence that the first Italian mercenary band won its spurs fighting for Urban VI against the Bretons of his rival.

There was one possible bond of union which the Italians The Italian most unaccountably neglected for a time—that was their language language. During the thirteenth century French influence was decaying in Italy, and poetry especially was being written in the vulgar tongue.[76] At the end of that century the poet arose who was to lay the foundations of Italy's real greatness as a literary people, and do that " which bound him for ever to his fellows : which made all Italians henceforth brethren ".[77] But this beginning of Italian literature was followed by a long neglect, even by deliberate discouragement.[78] Petrarch, although he was to write immortal verse in his native language, was ashamed of it, and trusted to his Latin composition for abiding fame ; a strange misjudgement. But such mis-judgements are common in literature, for contemporaries seem utterly incapable of recognising that an epoch or an influence is declining, just as they are prone to hail as the founder of a new age one whose works are but the last sudden flaring-up of the old.[79]

If the growth of the vernacular exercised but little in- Growth of fluence on the development of national feeling in Italy, vernaculars elsewhere it proved an exceedingly important factor. For centuries Latin had been accepted as the only perfect and permanent medium of expression for the higher kinds of thought and literature. But the growth of the vernaculars, and above all the achievement of Dante, shewed that such themes were possible for them. The effect of this was immense; for ultimately it involved a fatal breach in the unity of the middle ages, that unity which was based on a single language, a single culture, a single philosophy, as well as one Church and

---

[76] Perhaps the influence of Arabic poetry coming in from Sicily helped to foster the growth of the vernacular : cf. Amari *Storia dei Musulmani di Sicilia* III. pp. 738 and 889.

[77] Church *Dante and other Essays* p. 248.

[78] One of the strongest opponents of the spread of Italian was Del Virgilio, the youthful poet of Bologna, whom Dante met towards the close of his own life ; see Wicksteed and Gardner *Dante and Giovanni Del Virgilio*. Italian was only revived in the days of Lorenzo dei Medici.

[79] Cf. Swinburne, who to the Victorians seemed the inaugurator of a " new age of lyric gold ". The more sober judgement of posterity will, with greater insight, doubtless regard him as ending an epoch.

Empire.   Separate languages were bound to lead to the development of separate ideas, and these would not be confined to the secular sphere.   The German Bible and the German Reformation existed in embryo within the earliest attempts to write and to popularise German literature.[80]

Effect of Nationalism on the Papacy

It is probable that nationalism had a more profound effect upon the Church and the Papacy than the scandal aroused by continually deferred reforms and tolerated abuses.[81] If this was so it is surprising that the Church delayed so long to take account of it.   The reason was doubtless that nationalism was so novel a phenomenon as not to be recognised. The spirit of nationalism grows almost without observation ; just as the individual nation is only in part aware of its own generation.   As George Saville observed at the end of the eighteenth century :   " A Nation is a great while before they can see, and generally they must feel before their sight is quite cleared ".

Nationalism novel

The original gospel had been preached to a world from which national, as distinct from racial differences, had wellnigh disappeared.   The heavy hand of Rome had abolished boundaries and effaced frontiers and by deliberate policy had divided up peoples.   So the rising Catholic Church made its way in a political system which was a single unit.   Nationality came in as a new idea, a new factor in the situation and few had the insight to recognise its significance.   The Papacy is not unduly to be blamed if it failed to realise the greatness of the force which was to be generated by national aspirations ; or that so often the craving for political freedom would go hand in hand with the desire for ecclesiastical change, as in the early example of the religious wars in Bohemia.[82]

[80] It is significant that German was substituted for Latin in the chancery of Lewis of Bavaria : see Burdach *Vom Mittelalter zur Reformation* II. pt. i. p. 12.   Henry VII employed French, but Charles IV finally restored the use of German : see Jacob *Quellenkunde der deutschen Geschichte* I. pp. 20 sq.

[81] The failure to make reforms was due in part to national jealousies as Constance shews.   Cardinal Gasquet finds an even earlier instance of national distrust thwarting attempts at reform in the failure to cleanse the papal court after the Fourth Lateran Council : see *Henry III and the Church* p. v.

[82] In failing to estimate the force of nationality the Papacy was repeating the mistake of the Republic, for the troubles which arose in Macedonia in 149 B.C. were due to such a miscalculation : see *Camb. Anct. Hist.* VIII. p. 276.

The heaviest accusation which Pastor lodges against It breaks up
Nationalism is that of breaking up the political unity of the political
middle ages and introducing the selfish spirit of modern unity of the middle ages
times.[83]   With certain qualifications both halves of the charge
can be maintained with justice, for the unity was certainly
ruined and the national spirit is very often an exceedingly
selfish one.   I think it would be generally admitted that
the work of the Church in the middle ages could not have
been accomplished save by a single organisation.   This has
been recognised by Ranke who held that the naturalisation of
Christianity in the West depended on the recognition, by
the separate peoples of Europe, of a common membership
in one political and ecclesiastical society—*einer einzigen welt-
lichgeistlichen Staat.*[84]   The point need not be laboured,
though perhaps one reason at least may be given—a universal Church is able to give its own impress to a civilisation
which is developing around it ; a national Church is much
more likely to receive impressions than to make them.   It
is not in literature alone that provincialism is the besetting
note of nations.   At the same time we must guard against
the error of imagining that even in the middle ages Christendom ever possessed " the social and cultural homogeneity
of the great oriental civilisations, such as China.   It incorporated and overlaid a number of distinct and earlier cultural
traditions." [85]   At length these traditions reached a state of
maturity in which they were bound to reassert themselves.
The effect was to break up the single society, and to recon-
struct Christendom along national or racial lines.

A word must be said here on the subject of National National
Churches.   National feeling, from its very nature, is concerned Churches
to sustain restricted aims—a Catholic Church is ever striving
after the universal.[86]   In one sense the development of religion along national lines seems like a reversion to that
tribal religion which Jesus came to fulfil and to abolish.[87]
But in point of fact the Roman Church by the fifteenth

[83] *History of the Popes* I. p. 87.   [84] *Die römischen Päpste* I. p. 23.
[85] Christopher Dawson *Progress and Religion* p. 177.
[86] See Ranke *Deutsche Geschichte im Zeit. der Reformation* I. p. 3 " strebt
ewig die allgemeine zu sein ".
[87] This was used by the Italians at Constance as an argument against the
council voting by nations : see their protest to Sigismund in Finke *Acta* III.
pp. 104 sq.

century was ceasing to be Catholic and becoming more and
more the property of Italy and the papal curia. This loss
of its universal character was a grave disaster for the Roman
Church and one of the causes of its forfeiting the allegiance
of the North.

Effect of Nationality on the Papacy The vigorous new life within the nations found itself re-
strained by the traditional unity of the Church, especially when
the Papacy began to act as a rival nation itself and to pursue
an antagonistic secular policy. In any case the nation was
a new centre round which loyalty and enthusiasm could
group themselves. There was bound to be a consequent
loss of these commodities to the Church. In the ardent
effort to realise themselves the nations tended to forget that
they were, as an eighteenth century writer has put it, but
provinces in the universal kingdom of humanity.[88] In face
of the actual state of the Church in the fifteenth and sixteenth
centuries a breach was probably inevitable in order that the
powers and gifts of the nations should gain adequate opportunity for development and manifestation. But national
ideals and achievements become narrow and cramping unless
a wider ideal is retained. Nations like individuals can pay
too dearly for self-expression.

The task of the Empire and of the Church had been to fuse
the " undisciplined Teuton force and enterprise into the
civilised and ordered mould of a Latin Church and a Latin
Empire ".[89] They did their work so well that one of them
was to become entirely superfluous, and the other to be robbed
of half its subjects.[90] This falling away from medieval institutions was after all natural; in the eyes of the developing
modern world they were little better than abstractions;
whilst the nation with its geographical boundaries and its
strong central government was something very definite. Men
had become tired of theories, and desired, not necessarily for
their own good, to be practical. By the end of the fifteenth
century the rulers of every country in Europe had become
very independent in their attitude to the Papacy, even in

[88] Cf. De la Rivière *Ordre Nat. des soc. pol.* p. 526.
[89] Fisher *Mediaeval Empire* II. p. 137.
[90] Cf. Bryce *Holy Roman Empire* p. 436; " The work of the mediaeval
Empire was self-destructive; and it fostered, while seeming to oppose, the
nationalities that were destined to replace it."

Spain and Italy.[91]   The Popes were well aware of this, and had often to accept promises which they knew would never be kept.[92]

But we must look still earlier for the beginnings of this *Early* attitude, and I think that we shall find the first serious mani- *opposition* festation of it in the reign of Innocent IV.   The records of that Pontificate include many letters from kings and even nobles, as well as from bishops and abbots, in which the view is clearly expressed that the papal supremacy is in serious danger from the excessive taxation which the Pope is endeavouring to impose, and that persistence in this course of action will lead to a breach.   St Louis made his protest on behalf of France ; whilst in England opposition to papal greed, even if we allow that Matthew Paris has exaggerated it, fostered national feeling.[93]

This attitude of practical opposition began soon to find theoretical support.   In the first half of the fourteenth century William of Ockham put forward the thesis that a single earthly Head of the Church was by no means essential.   Christ Himself is the chief shepherd of the Church, and just as kingdoms have their own rulers in secular matters, so different territories may have their own primates who will be responsible to Him alone.[94]   The same tendency for the separate nations to take their own line in religious matters was shewn in the Pragmatic Sanction of Bourges in 1438 and the Diet of Mainz of the following year.   National feeling and the realisation that the interests of the different nations were not identical was everywhere growing at this epoch ; the Pope and the Emperor were of little importance in comparison.[95]   By the time of Machiavelli the service of the State, as in the ancient world, had be-

---

[91] For instances see Ranke *Die römischen Päpste* I. pp. 22 sq.

[92] Cf. the comment of Antonius Gallus on the policy of Lorenzo dei Medici : " Iam vero Regum maiorumque Principum contumacem licentiam adversus Romanam Ecclesiam sequebatur, de iuribus Pontificis nisi quod ei videretur nihil permittens " : RIS. XXIII. col. 282 B.

[93] For this last point see A. L. Smith *Church and State in the Middle Ages* p. 178.

[94] *Dialogus* in Goldast *Monarchia* pp. 818 sq.

[95] " The Pope and the Emperor are considered as merely proud titles and splendid figure-heads.   Each state has its own prince and each prince his own particular interests. . . . What mortal could reconcile the English and the French, the Genoese with the men of Aragon ? " : Aeneas Sylvius *Epist.* CXXVII.

come the supreme duty. It was " felt as something divine, to which even the salvation of the soul must be sacrificed— that is to say, as the institution in which the true salvation of the soul is to be found ".[96]   Sooner or later national development in spiritual matters was bound to clash with the dogmas of the universal church—it had already done so in the case of Bohemia. The sources of the conflict might be political, or intellectual, or even fiscal ; but the conflict would extend beyond these spheres.

[96] Croce *Theory and History of Historiography* pp. 231 sq.

CHAPTER VIII

THE FALL OF THE EASTERN CHURCH

UNTIL recent years both the tasks and the achievements The Byzantine achievement of the Byzantines were quite inadequately understood in Western Europe. For this Gibbon himself must take a large measure of blame. No reader of his great work would imagine that during the greater part of the period of the Decline and Fall of the Roman Empire the East was far superior to the West in civilisation, government, and military arts.[1] But for the efficiency of the Eastern Empire, the West would never have been permitted to develop its manifold life.

The Eastern Empire had stood guardian of the gates, not only in the eighth century, when the defence of Constantinople by Leo the Isaurian in 717 [2] was probably just as decisive as the victory of Charles Martel fifteen years later in holding up the advance of Islam into Europe, but later when it stemmed the Turkish flood. Behind its shelter the young nations of the West could grow to maturity and the Roman Church extend its sway over Western Europe.

But in one thing the Byzantines were behind the West; they never got from their barbarian invaders, such as the Slavs, the new life which came to it from the Teutons. They gave to them their culture and their religion, but received little in return. Lack of life and vigour was indeed the besetting weakness of the Eastern Empire. Hence its influence did not spread far beyond its own borders; whilst within them it seemed content for the most part to live on the hoarded

---

[1] English-speaking people owe a debt to historians such as Finlay and Bury for having brought to their knowledge a truer picture. There is a noble vindication of the East in Church's *Gifts of Civilisation* pp. 222 and 246 sq.

[2] The fall of the Umayyads in 750 and the removal of the capital from Damascus to Baghdad freed Constantinople from further Moslem aggression for several centuries.

treasures of the past, and to remain impervious to other cultures.

Inertia of the East   There had, it is true, been a period when vivid interest was taken in theological controversies ; but after the sixth century Orthodoxy became the distinguishing mark of the Eastern Church as Catholicity was that of her sister in the West. With the passing of great issues came stagnation ; pedantry was valued above originality, and after the death of John of Damascus no great names are found among her scholars.[3] Constantine had desiderated unity of belief in the Church which was to be the means, as he hoped, of unifying the Empire : his successors, in the city which he had founded, saw to it that the Church was fitted to serve this purpose.[4] Some of them, unfortunately, by their intervention in theological disputes were to bring upon them disaster rather than the agreement which they sought.[5]

Power of the monks   More even than the West the Byzantine Church had been the home of monasticism. The immense power and influence which passed into the hands of the monks, and the extent to which it deprived the state of those who might have been its officials and soldiers, naturally aroused the alarm of wise rulers. The Iconoclastic Controversy of the eighth century was, in large measure, directed against the growth of monastic power and of the steady passing of lands and wealth into the dead hand of the monks. Certainly the dispute saw the secularising of many monasteries, and not a few monks were put to death during its course. In Egypt in particular the blazing fanaticism of the monks was ever a potential source of

---

[3] There was, however, Maximus who introduced the Pseudo-Dionysius into the Greek Church—his works form vols. XC. and XCI. in PG.—and a number of good historians, of whom Psellus is the best known : see further Sandys *Hist. of Class. Scholarship* chh. XXII. and XXIII.

[4] It must not be forgotten that many of the heretical opinions which arose in the East and were displayed in the Greek language had an oriental origin and were thrown up by national and racial partialities. Syria and Egypt were their homes and not Constantinople. If Byzantine Christianity was not quite so orthodox as it claimed to be it was much less given to speculation than the West chose to think.

[5] Political needs were often at the root of such interventions, though Justinian was more famed among his contemporaries as a theologian than a legislator. Examples of these vain efforts to find formulae of reconciliation are the " Henoticon " of Zeno (482), intended to win back the Monophysites, and the " Ekthesis " of Sergius, put out in the reign of Heraclius (638) and signed by that Emperor.

danger, and even the armed forces of the state had at times
to give way before the fierce sons of the desert brought in to
champion some theological formula.   Islam itself was anticipated and perhaps surpassed.

What, however, gave to the Eastern Church its special Church and
importance for the student of ecclesiastical politics, was the State
fact that it constituted what Bury has called " the longest
and most considerable experiment of a State-Church that
Christendom has ever seen." [6]   The Church was practically
a department of the State.   The East was thus saved from
continued conflicts such as were waged in the West between
the Empire and the Papacy.   There is one important exception to this statement, and, as it is not without significance
for the relation of the East and the Papacy, we must for a
moment turn aside to consider it.

During the second phase of the Iconoclastic Controversy 815-842
Theodore of Studium and his followers, who were opposed
to the Imperial policy, saw in union with Rome a possible
way of escape from undue state control.   They therefore
agreed to recognise the spiritual authority of the Pope, calling
him " first of pastors and our apostolic head." [7]   Such opposition of the Church, or a section of it, to the State was
very unusual in the Eastern Empire.   The real understanding
which normally existed between them was immensely helpful
to the secular power ; though the Church probably suffered, not
merely by its lack of independence, but from the absence of
that intellectual and political activity which was called forth
by the struggle in the West.   But the Eastern Empire needed
the help of the Church as a unifying power ; for no civil
power in the West had to face tasks so urgent and to undertake burdens so overwhelming.   It was indeed the Church
which gave it courage and its only basis of unity, since neither
race nor language was found in common among the motley
collection of Byzantine subjects.   The Empire was always
on a war-footing ; always, as it had been in the East for
centuries, on the defensive. [8]   At the same time the union
of Church and State pointed to a higher ideal for the latter,

[6] See *Camb. Med. Hist.* IV. p. xiv.
[7] See letters in PG. XCIX. coll. 141, 1017, 1020, 1022, 1332.
[8] The Eastern Empire was often fighting on two fronts, for the threat
from the Balkans was almost as persistent as that from Asia Minor.

a fact which was apt to be overlooked in the West, for it meant that the State too had a religious character. In the West, in spite of much talk about the spiritual nature of the State, it became in practice subordinate to the Church, as the Church to the Empire in the East in secular matters. In neither was there found the ideal combination of full and free partnership.

Different races in the Eastern Empire

The variety of race and tongue among the subjects of the Eastern Empire, although it might seem to have been overcome by the power of the Church, continued to exist beneath the surface ; the religious differences which from time to time emerged, not without violence, were symptoms of a deeper divergence of interest and ambition. In Syria and Egypt in particular there were strains of ancient culture which resented the domination of Church and Empire alike, and saw in it the tyranny of Graeco-Roman culture. The welcome extended to the Moslem invaders in the seventh century was the measure and the result of this resentment, which was at the bottom not so much doctrinal as racial. To the same cause the great Schism between the East and the West itself was ultimately due.

Rome and Constantinople

From the foundation of Constantinople in 330 there was an ever growing jealousy between the New Rome and the Old.[9] As the seat of the secular government and the home of the Emperor it naturally tended to draw power to itself. Constantinople, moreover, had been " born and educated in the bosom of the faith," it had never been " polluted by idols ".[10]

Gibbon saw " the first symptoms of discord between the Greek and Latin Churches, which were separated by the accidental difference of faith and the permanent distinction of language "[11] as early as the Council of Sardica in 343. With the advance of Islam in the seventh century differences were further emphasised owing to restricted opportunities of intercourse, and when Charlemagne was crowned in 800 political separation also came in further to accentuate them.[12]

---

[9] Renan declared that Constantine was the true author of the Schism of East and West : *Hibbert Lectures* pp. 198 sq.

[10] Gibbon II. p. 384.   [11] II. p. 369.

[12] The custom of dating papal documents by the regnal years of the Eastern Emperor, which had been made compulsory by Justinian (*Nov.* xlvii), had already been dropped by Adrian I in 781. It is significant that this action followed the visit of Charlemagne to Rome in the same year.

In the same century, the bitter quarrel between Nicholas I 863-867 and Photius led to a temporary schism. This ended in 898 ; but a fresh quarrel broke out when Sisinnius became Patriarch in 996 ; and again in 1009. It is remarkable that the Roman Church never imitated the Roman Republic in its almost sentimental toleration of the Greeks.[13] The Popes were ever trying to thwart the ambitions of the Eastern Patriarch and even to humiliate the Eastern Emperors.[14]

It must be remembered that Constantinople did not claim a right of absolute rule over the whole Eastern Church,[15] such as Rome possessed in the West, and in earlier days it had found it necessary to struggle even to establish its primacy.[16] So in regard to the Papacy, all that Constantinople demanded was a recognition of its independence, and the right to rule within its own territory. The title of Oecumenical Patriarch, which the Bishop of Constantinople adopted, meant nothing more than this ; although Gregory the Great regarded it as a presumptuous claim for any bishop to make. He little imagined that his own successors at Rome would advance similar claims, and with the real intention of making the Pope *sacerdos universalis*, a title which suggested to Gregory that pride which makes men forerunners of Anti-Christ. The East set much store by the title and Basil II vainly tried, by bribes, to get Pope John XIX to recognise it. His efforts provoked considerable alarm in the West, and

[13] This was accompanied by contempt for their moral instability and inferiority ; a fact which was acknowledged by Polybius who wrote in the second century B.C. just before Rome began to lose its own moral fervour and honesty.

[14] An instance of this may be found in the refusal, towards the close of the tenth century, to call the Eastern Emperors, Roman. The Popes justified this on the ground that the Eastern Empire had given up the Latin language and Roman manners of life. Cf. Liudprand of Cremona *Legatio* li. in MGH. SS. III. p. 359. The Easterns had always despised Latin. On the election of Valens, who knew no other tongue, the orator Themistius said with insolent flattery that at last he wished that he had learnt it, since it was the dialect of his sovereign. Justinian, who had little Greek, declared that Latin was the ' national ' language, though as Greek was the ' common ' speech many *Novels* were written in it (*Nov.* vii). Latin remained the legal language until the publication of the revised code in Greek (the Basilica) in the middle of the tenth century.

[15] When Basil II conquered Bulgaria he promised that the Church should remain autonomous.

[16] In the later half of the fifth century Basilicus tried to gain the primacy for Ephesus : see Zacharias of Mytelene V pp. 3 sqq.

the Pope received an outspoken letter from William, Abbot
of St Benignus, Dijon, condemning the presumption of the
Greeks.[19]

The Schism   Responsibility for the final breach must rest with the
Patriarch, Michael Cerularius.[20]   His ambition seems to have
been to found an Eastern Papacy with rule over both Church
and State.   He succeeded in dethroning Michael VI, and
putting Isaac Comnenus in his place.   But when the Patriarch
appeared in public wearing the purple buskins, which were
the mark of imperial power, he found that he had over-
reached himself.   He was deposed and banished to a monastery.   With the Pope, who happened to be the strong Leo IX,
he seems deliberately to have provoked a quarrel ;   perhaps
regarding a breach with Rome as a step to independence
and power at home.   His final action in closing the Latin
churches in Constantinople was a declaration that peace was
impossible between the East and the West during his patri-
archate.[21]

About this time a letter of a much more conciliatory tone
was apparently written by Michael to the Pope ;   if this is
a genuine letter (we know it only from extracts in Leo's reply
and allusions elsewhere), it must have been produced under
pressure from the Emperor who needed papal aid against the
Normans in South Italy.[22]

Leo, for his part, if not so aggressive, was equally determined that peace should only come on his own terms, and he
did not hesitate to use extreme language, warning the Patriarch
that every church which was not in communion with Rome
was " a synagogue of Satan ".[23]   Finally on July 15, 1054
two papal envoys laid a Bull of Excommunication on the altar
of St Sophia.   From that day until this, with brief intervals,
the schism between Eastern and Western Christendom has
been maintained ;   a schism as disastrous and fundamental
as that of the Reformation.   It was the end of the undivided
Catholic Church.

[19] See MGH. SS. VII. p. 66.
[20] For details of the relations between the two churches and the events
leading up to the Schism see *Camb. Med. Hist.* IV. pp. 246-273.
[21] He was opposed by a Roman party having its headquarters, as in the
ninth century, in the monastery of Studion.
[22] L. Bréhier *Le Schisme Oriental* pp. 97 sqq.
[23] See Gay *L'Italie méridionale* p. 494.

During the period between 1054 and 1453, the date of the Attempts at re-union fall of Constantinople, some thirty or more attempts were made to end the schism.[24] One is guilty of no misrepresentation in avowing that in none of them were the Greeks sincere. They were moved by politicial necessity, the approach of the Turks ; and not by spiritual compunction, the realisation of their share in the guilt of schism.[25] Newman, in discussing the relations of the church of his baptism and the great Mother Church of Western Christendom, laid down the principle which explains the failure of all negotiations ; " No good can come ", he writes, " of a change which is not a development of feelings springing up freely and calmly within the bosom of the body itself. . . . Political reconciliations are but outward and hollow." [26]

It must be confessed, however, that the actions of the West Widening of the breach did not make it easier for the Greeks to desire any restoration of communion. From the definite breach until the closing disaster of 1453 events served only to widen it. In the later part of the eleventh century the Normans continued to threaten the Byzantine possessions in South Italy until Bari, the last of them, fell in 1071. They then attempted, more than once, to establish themselves across the Adriatic. Although they actually invaded Macedonia and Thessaly,—the Bulgarians were at this time imperial subjects,—they had over-reached themselves and were compelled to withdraw.

In the very year in which the Byzantine dominion came to an end in Italy the disastrous defeat of Manzikert laid 1071 open the Eastern Empire to the Turks.[27] Michael VII thereupon made overtures to Gregory VII. On March 1, 1074 the Pope published a letter in which he called upon the

[24] For fuller details see W. Norden *Das Papsttum und Byzanz* and *Camb. Med. Hist.* IV. pp. 594-626. The relevant documents from 1124 onwards may be found in Theiner and Miklosich *Monumenta Spectanta ad unionem Ecclesiarum Graecae et Romanae.*

[25] The difference of attitude comes out well at the Council of Lyons 1274. The Papacy exhibited what may be called a universal outlook and shewed a real desire for unity—it may be of course that this was to enhance its own power and prestige—the Greeks, apparently, were only interested in unity so far as it would serve national ends : see Norden *op. cit.* p. 898.

[26] *Apologia pro Vita Sua* (Pocket Edition) p. 168.

[27] This first Turkish wave consisted of the Seljuks. It has been suggested that before embracing Islam they had been for a short time Christian : see L. Cahun *Turcs et Mongols* p. 170.

West to arm in defence of the East.[28] Twenty years later Alexius Comnenus made a similar appeal to Urban II, with results far beyond anything that he could have anticipated ; for from it came the great series of enterprises named the Crusades.

The Crusades

Urban hoped that the crusading movement would lead to a new understanding between East and West. The effect of the movement was exactly opposite. The rude manners and ineffective discipline of the Western hosts on the one side, and the retaliatory measures of the Greeks on the other, increased bad feeling to such a pitch that a Patriarch of Constantinople could proclaim the murder of a crusader a Christian act.[29] In 1182 the bitterness was enormously increased by a massacre of Latins in Constantinople. One result was a renewal of the Norman attempts to seize Macedonia,[30] and possibly the diversion of the Fourth Crusade.[31]

The Latin Empire

The Latin Empire, which followed this last achievement, lasted from 1204 to 1261 and helped to make more impossible any understanding between Catholic and Orthodox. It was at best an exotic growth, and after the death of the Emperor Henry of Flanders in 1216, it gradually shrivelled up. The prolongation of its existence for another half-century was mainly owing to the strength of the walls of Constantinople and the protection of the Venetian fleet. New energy came to the Byzantines with the accession of Michael Palaeologus to the throne of Nicea in 1259, and within two years he had surprised the capital during the absence of the Venetians. This happened a fortnight before the election of Urban IV, and the Venetian ambassadors sent to congratulate him were the first to announce the end of the Latin Empire in the East ; [32] the Pope's consternation was almost as great, though for different reasons, as that of Innocent III on hearing of its inauguration.

The capture of Constantinople in 1204 was really the

[28] *Register* I. 49. See further A. J. Macdonald *Hildebrand* pp. 125 sq.

[29] This is a sad falling off from the days of Nicephorus Phocas (963-969) who was told by the Patriarch of his day that it was unchristian to slay even an infidel. In the early eleventh century pilgrims received considerate treatment in the East : see Bréhier *Le Schisme Oriental* pp. 18 sqq.

[30] Ralph de Diceto II p. 37 (RS.).

[31] See my *Innocent III* pp. 145 sqq.

[32] Dandolo *Chronicon* in RIS. XII. col. 369.

death-blow of the Eastern Empire, for even after 1261 much
of its territory remained in the hands of the Franks. But
the ghost lingered on, haunting the strong city which
Constantine had chosen so wisely, and his successors had
fortified so skilfully.[33]

For the next few years the papal policy towards the East
was complicated by the desires of Manfred to revive Latin
rule at Constantinople.[34] Urban obviously could not act
with him, whilst rival attempts to achieve the same object
would be mutually destructive. Manfred's threat, however,
drew Urban and Michael into insincere negotiations. When
Manfred was slain Charles of Anjou took his place, at first
with papal support.[35] By 1271 his elaborate preparations
had alarmed not only Michael but the new Pope, Gregory X,
as well. This led to negotiations at the Council of Lyons
1274 and a temporary union. Eleven years later Charles, 1282
in alliance with the Venetians and once more assured of papal
support, seemed about to succeed in his enterprise,[36] when the
Sicilian Vespers put a sudden end to his plans. Michael,
who had himself tried to cultivate friendly relations with the
Turks, even allowing them to restore their mosque at Constantinople,[37] died in the same year.

During the Avignon period a number of approaches were Attempts at
made by the Eastern Emperors to the Popes ; but they seldom re-union in
got beyond the bare appeal for aid, the religious question century
remained in abeyance. Anne of Savoy, as regent for her son,
John V, was genuinely eager for re-union, but nothing came
of her efforts, nor of those of John himself, although he made
a secret treaty with Innocent VI in 1356 offering submission
in return for help. The treaty, however, in the words of Gibbon,
" was neither executed nor published. The Roman galleys
were as vain and imaginary as the submission of the Greeks." [38]

<hr />

[33] For the story of the fortifying of Constantinople see Van Millingen *The
Walls of Constantinople*. Much was done in the reign of Theodosius II by the
regent Anthemius, the namesake of the architect of St Sophia.

[34] Canale *Cron. des Veniciens* in Arch. Stor. Ital. (Ser. I) VIII. p. 501.

[35] Clement IV withdrew his support from fear of the growing power of
Charles ; see Norden *Das Papsttum und Byzanz* p. 395.

[36] Charles was the more dangerous as he had an understanding with the
Egyptians. It was supposed that it was his influence which had diverted the
last crusade of St Louis from Egypt. For his embassy to Beybars see S.
Lane-Poole *Hist. of Egypt* p. 266.

[37] S. Lane-Poole *op. cit.* p. 266.   [38] *Op. cit.* VII. p. 88.

16

John made a further attempt, equally futile, in the reign of Urban V when on a visit to Rome.

Dec. 1899-
June 1408

Manuel II came to the West during the schism, but naturally his efforts were vain. He even visited Henry IV of England. Constantinople, however, was saved when on the brink of destruction by the swift advance of the Tartars. Gibbon states that during the next fifteen years Manuel was at peace with the Turks, and so had no need to open further negotiations with the West.[39] Both halves of this statement are incorrect, for Constantinople was actually besieged by the Turks in 1411, and Manuel attempted to gain the support of both Alexander V and John XXIII.

And in early
fifteenth

The election of Alexander, who was a Greek,[40] in 1409 was an obvious call to make fresh approaches. Accordingly the Emperor sent a letter of congratulation on Christmas Day 1409.[41] But the Pope lived too short a time to act; his successor, however, the luckless John XXIII, took an interest in re-union, and promised that although nothing could be done at his Council of Rome the matter should come up at the next council.[42] Sigismund also shewed his interest in the question, doubtless with memories of the disaster of Nicopolis.[43] Bréhier mentions an embassy which Manuel sent to Constance in 1417; but there are reasons for believing that an earlier one had already appeared. Ulrich von Richental mentions an embassy which seems clearly to belong to January 1415 [44] and to have consisted of laymen. Representatives of the Greek Church remained some time at Constance, for Cardinal Fillastre mentions a sermon preached

[39] *Op. cit.* VII. p. 96. Bréhier in *Camb. Med. Hist.* IV. p. 619 practically repeats the same statement.

[40] The election inspired Gerson to hopes of re-union; see his sermon in Du Pin II. p. 144.

[41] Printed by Simonsfeld *Abhandlungen der Kgl. Bayr. Akad.* Cl. III. vol. XX. pp. 45 sq.; also in Finke *Acta Concilii Constanc.* I. p. 234.

[42] See his replies to the questions of the University of Paris: Simonsfeld *op. cit.* pp. 47 sqq. and Finke *op. cit.* I. p. 156.

[43] Letter of May or June 1411 in Vatican Library Cod. Pal. 701 fo. 270v-272 printed by Finke *op. cit.* I. p. 391.

[44] The following are the appropriate passages from his *Chronicle :* " Es komen och zwen hertzogen von Tropi, uss Kriechenland, in bottschaft des kaysers von Constantinopel " (p. 47). He refers to these envoys later and gives their names—" Philipp von Troppouw uss Kriechen " and " Michael von Troppouw, sin sun " (p. 191 and also p. 206). The later embassy is referred to in Palacky *Documenta* p. 623.

by Gregory, Archbishop of Kiew, before Martin V on Feb. 25, 1418 for which he received the papal thanks.[45]   At the council the Greeks were treated with courtesy and allowed to use their own ritual; but they saw the dis-union of the West, and this may have been a factor in deciding them twenty years later to chose the Pope instead of the Council of Basle.

Manuel later entered into negotiations with Martin V, but he was only using him as a threat to the Turks; he finally agreed upon a Treaty with the latter in 1425.[46]   In spite of these insincere efforts to approach the West there was growing up a party in the Eastern Church which definitely favoured re-union; chief among it were Isidore and Bessarion who were later to play an important part at Florence, and as individuals to be reconciled to the Papacy.

The agreement reached at the Council of Florence has already been dealt with; the papal supremacy was swallowed by the reluctant Greeks, and a Decree of Union [47] read aloud in the new Duomo by Cesarini and Bessarion.   But on their return to the East the Greek delegates had to face the consequences of their weakness.   Many of the bishops excused themselves by telling the truth; but the Emperor still adhered to his policy of submission.   One bishop had been true to his convictions at Florence, and Mark of Ephesus now came forward as the opponent of any submission to the Latins, and even when committed to prison still opposed the work of union. *The Council of Florence*

The West, in the meantime, was shewing unusual activity, and a crusade was launched under Cardinal Cesarini to reinforce Hunyardi.   A great victory was gained over Murad II at Nish and the way to Constantinople seemed to be open. In the following July Cesarini, as papal legate, dispensed Hunyardi from a treaty into which he had meanwhile entered with the Sultan.   But this piece of trickery brought only disaster.   The Sultan suddenly reappeared and on the field of Varna punished the perjurers.[48]   It was fitting that *The West and the Turks 1443*

---

[45] See Finke op. cit. II. pp. 164 and 526.

[46] Cf. Gibbon VII. p. 97.

[47] Text in Hefele VII. pt. ii. pp. 742 sqq.

[48] There is a legend that the violated treaty was carried on a lance before the Turkish army : see Edwin Pears *Camb. Med. Hist.* IV. p. 692.   Zinkeisen *Gesch. des Osmanischen Reichs* I. p. 702 rejects it as late.

Cesarini, " the lying prophet " as Church called him,[49] should have been among the slain.

John VIII died in 1448 and efforts to denounce the union continued with new vigour. In 1450 the Patriarch Gregory who supported it was driven into exile.[50] But the Turks now encircled Constantinople, and, whatever the people might think, their leaders were prepared to go to any lengths to obtain Western help. On December 12, 1452 the union was proclaimed in St Sophia itself. But the Greeks regarded this as an act of profanation and refused to enter the cathedral until the great service on the eve of the fall of the city.

Differences of East and West   Thus all attempts at reunion failed, as they were bound to fail, for the schism rested on deep, underlying causes which were left unregarded by those who endeavoured to heal the breach. The differences between East and West were not only racial and political, they were intellectual and temperamental as well. What Gwatkin has written of the Early Church applies all through—the East " is philosophical and speculative, seeking after knowledge, and tending to resolve revelation into philosophy " ; the West " is legal and practical, holding to the faith once received, and tending to convert the revelation into law ".[51] The East was much less active than the West, or perhaps it might be more accurate to say that its activities were within rather than without the soul.[52] It was more interested, especially among the monks, in the eternal background of man's thoughts and feelings than in the events of the passing moment.

Theologically the mind of the West had been dominated by St Augustine who was no Greek scholar and was unsympathetic to the Greek point of view. Moreover, the political hostility which began so early led to much ignorance and to a separate development of Byzantine and Roman Christianity. The West forgot Greek, the East despised

---

[49] *Misc. Essays* p. 417.

[50] The supposed synod of 1450 is unhistoric and its acts spurious ; there was no definite repudiation of the union when Gregory was driven out : see Bury's note in Gibbon VII. p. 136.

[51] *Early Church History* II. p. 213.

[52] Cf. Eucken *The Life of the Spirit* p. 117 for the distinction.

Latin [53] and hardly knew the works of the Schoolmen.[54] In the actual dispute over *filioque*, which loomed so large, there can be no question that technically the West was in the wrong, since it had made an addition to the creed without the consent of an Oecumenical Council.[55] As to lesser matters, such as the state of those in Purgatory, the use of leavened bread, the exact rights in the matter of images and icons, all these were of minor importance. Thus a difference of outlook went to reinforce the division which race and politics had made.

The original division of the Empire into East and West was to be followed by the later Schism with slight variations. If the power of the Emperor had survived effectively in the West after 476, Christendom might have continued to be a single community ; but its head would have been inevitably the Bishop of Constantinople. The Council of Chalcedon was obviously moving in that direction, when it gave such exalted rank to the Patriarch in spite of the protests of the papal legates, and later of Leo himself.[56] In after years it was only natural that the Byzantines should refuse to recognise the Bishop of Rome as superior to their own Patriarch.

Before the Schism broke out there had been much ill-feeling over questions of jurisdiction; there was for example the matter of Bulgaria in the days of Nicholas I,[57] and of South Italy and Sicily.[58] In the case of the Slavs of Bohemia

Quarrels over jurisdiction

[53] It is rare to find translations of Latin works into Greek. There was, of course, Maximus Planudes (1260-1310) who translated Caesar, parts of Ovid, and Boethius *De Consolatione* among other writings.

[54] The works of the Schoolmen were not so entirely unknown as is often supposed. There were a few definite followers such as Gregory Acyndinus, Demetrius Kydonis and Nicephorus Gregoras, the historian.

[55] Leo I held the doctrine (*Epist.* XV *ad Turibium* in PL. LIV. p. 680). The first creedal statement in which it appears is a Spanish version of the Nicene Creed of 589. Charlemagne unsuccessfully pressed the Pope to adopt it in 787.

[56] In *Epist. ad Marcianum Augustum* in PL. LIV. pp. 993 sqq.

[57] Bulgaria had been converted, from Constantinople, in the early ninth century ; but Tsar Boris tried to get Roman protection. The Roman priests sent by Nicholas were expelled through Greek action in 869. When Bulgaria regained its independence in 1197 Kalojan was crowned by a papal legate. But it was always dangerous for a Balkan ruler to toy with Rome ; his subjects were incurably orthodox.

[58] In 733 the Emperor Leo III had taken South Italy, as well as Greece and the Balkans, from the jurisdiction of Gregory III. This act " went far to decide the medieval history of Southern Italy " wrote Bury *Hist. of the*

and Moravia, although they had been converted by Constantine (Cyril) and Methodius,[59] who were Easterns, the rise of the Magyars in 906 cut them off completely from Constantinople and threw them into the arms of the West. In the middle of the thirteenth century there was an attempt made by the Teutonic Order to bring Russia, which had been cut off from Constantinople by the advance of the Cumans in 1061, under papal jurisdiction. It was, however, defeated by Alexander Nevsky in the battle of Lake Peipus in 1242. At the same epoch the attempts of the Latin missionaries to convert the Tartars were regarded with a good deal of suspicion by the Byzantine Church. Unfortunately they did not stir them to a similar activity.

Western arrogance   The Greeks were under an intolerable disadvantage, for all their approaches to the West were made from necessity, and they had perforce to adopt the attitude of suppliants. The Romans, for their part, were not always careful or even anxious to conceal the superiority which they undoubtedly felt. The *vexatio* of the Turkish advance might bring the Greeks to a better mind and make them more ready to submit.[60] The negotiations at Ferrara and Florence saw Western arrogance at its highest because Eastern need was then at its greatest.

The Turkish advance   The capture of Constantinople by Mohammed II in 1453 was a culminating stage in a movement which began as long ago as the second century B.C., when the Parthians shewed that the East was reviving, and that the tide, which under Alexander the Great had carried Western influence far into Asia, was about to recede. The ebb had been gradual, with frequent checks ; the most important of which had been the crusades, but their work was over by the fourteenth century when the final advance, under the Ottomans,[61] was preparing.

Later Empire II. p. 446. At the beginning of the following century there was much indignation in the West because Nicephorus I altered the ecclesiastical divisions of South Italy without consulting the Pope : see Liudprand *Legatio* in MGH. SS. III. pp. 361 sqq.

[59] Gibbon very strangely ignores this mission.

[60] See the instructions of John XXII to the Dominican agents sent to Constantinople in Raynaldus 1333 No. 19. The same Pope suggested to Robert of Naples in Decr. 1328 the formation of a League against " Greci scismatici, Bulgari, Alani, Turchi, aliique infideles " (*Reg. Vat. MS.* vol. CXV. fo. 144). Urban IV had written in similar terms of the *vexatio* of the Latin occupation of Constantinople (Raynaldus 1263 No. 35).

[61] Earlier authorities on the Ottomans are superseded by N. Jorga *Geschichte des osmanischen Reiches* (Gotha 1908-1913).

At this period the Byzantines were frittering away their resources by internal strife, just as if they had been Italians living in comparative safety, and not faced by inflexible foemen.   The real strength of Eastern Europe lay in the Balkans, and had Stephen Dushan, the Serbian king,[62] moved down and captured Constantinople, he might have made it the centre of a permanent power able to resist the Turk at the gates of Europe and to save Byzantine civilisation from extinction.   But he died in 1355 and his Empire fell to pieces.[63]

In the previous year Suleiman, the son of Orkhan, had crossed the Bosphorus and surprised Gallipoli,[64] thus bringing the Turks definitely into Europe.   Thenceforward it was only a question of time before Constantinople became their possession.   With real statesmanship they left it for the moment, and concentrated their efforts on clearing the Balkans. In the first battle of Kossovo the allied Balkan nations were **1389** decisively defeated by Murad I, and, though he was murdered, the Turks advanced to the Danube.   Europe now became alarmed and a new crusade, " a posthumous offspring of dead ideals," [65] was launched.   But the crowd of feudal warriors collected by Sigismund was no match for a trained army, and Western chivalry was cut to pieces under the walls **1396** of Nicopolis.

The fall of Constantinople now seemed imminent and the **Checked by** Sultan advanced confidently against it.   But in his rear a new **the Tartar invasion** enemy suddenly arose, and on the field of Angora the slaughter of Nicopolis was avenged by the invincible Tartars.   The **1402** Tartars, however, soon withdrew, and by 1413 the Greeks were again subject to Turkish rule, and their little plot of independent soil held only by Turkish permission.   There was another unsuccessful attack on Constantinople in 1422, when revolts

[62] Gibbon failed to realise the importance of Stephen Dushan, another of his lapses over Eastern affairs.

[63] Freeman, whose interest in the Near East was well known, used to speculate upon the changes which might have been wrought in history if Constantinople had been held by a Balkan power, or even if it had fallen into the hands of Russia in the ninth century when " a Varangian Emperor might have proved the Theodoric or the Charlemagne of the East " : see W. R. W. Stephens *Life and Letters of E. A. Freeman* I. pp. 160, 269, 271.

[64] A crusade under Amadeus VI of Savoy recaptured it in 1367, but the relief was only temporary.

[65] Previté-Orton *Outlines of Medieval History* p. 488.

in Asia saved it ; but if the Greeks were deluded into a false sense of the inviolability of their sacred city by such escapes they were speedily to be disillusioned. Constantinople had looked many and various enemies in the face, and seen them turn away ; but now the conqueror was about to appear.

Fall of the Eastern Empire

The disaster of Varna in 1444, to which reference has already been made, and a second defeat on the fatal field of Kossovo reduced the Balkan peoples to carrying on guerilla warfare in the mountains ; their efforts might annoy the Turks, they could do nothing to thwart their plans against Constantinople. These began to be developed with grim determination on the accession of Mohammed II in 1451. The story of the city's last agony has been told with inimitable skill by Gibbon,[66] and need not detain us here. The last of the Byzantine Emperors died a death worthy of the highest traditions of the past, and the young Sultan rode into the city which for nearly five centuries was to be the capital of a new Ottoman Empire.

The West did not rise to meet the challenge to Christendom contained in the capture of Constantinople. The Venetians and the Genoese and others on the spot were much more concerned to preserve their trading rights than to stir up fresh strife with the infidel. Mohammed pursued his victorious career, although checked beneath the walls of Belgrade, and within rather more than ten years he had reduced Bosnia, Serbia, and Wallachia to Turkish provinces. His death in 1481 brought relief to the West, for the Turkish forces, which in the previous year had landed on the sacred soil of Italy and occupied Otranto, were then withdrawn.

1456

In attempting to assess the effect of the fall of the Eastern Empire and Church two things have to be kept distinct—the effect of the fall itself, and the effect of the Schism which was its ultimate cause.

Effects of the Schism

The Schism was not all pure loss to the West for it allowed, as we have seen, a time for unfettered development, but it had consequences which were serious both for the Roman and for the Byzantine Church. The separation was a standing testimony to the failure of two great bodies of Christians to carry out the wish of their founder that His followers might

---

[66] VII. pp. 170 sqq. See also E. Pears *The Destruction of the Greek Empire* which makes use of sources unknown to Gibbon.

be one. Consciously or otherwise weakness must have come to them both from this failure, which Wyclif regarded as sharing responsibility with the Donation of Constantine for the loss of the Church's early purity.[67] Moreover each half of Christendom had talents in which the other was lacking, to have shared them would have more than doubled their efficiency and spiritual power. The separation made for suspicion and even the gifts of the Greeks were suspect.[68] In the East there had been no break with the ancient culture; had friendly relations existed with the West the latter would have been irrigated by the full stream of Greek learning, instead of having to depend for centuries on the trickle which came in, mainly through Spain, from Jewish and Arabic sources.

It is not possible to estimate the damage that was done Ill-feeling by the ill-feeling generated by the Schism.[69] Both sides were between alike guilty of provocative conduct, and neither was free from East and indulging in sly thrusts at the other.[70] It must have been West especially galling to the Papacy that its claim to be the Head of Christendom could be made to look foolish by the spectacle of so considerable a portion of Christ's followers, and those in the region from which His religion had come, refusing to acknowledge its jurisdiction. Every group in the West which was critical of papal claims could turn to the East for support,[71] or regard the Orthodox, mistakenly or not, as having preserved the primitive faith which the Papacy had corrupted. This was one accusation brought against the Spiritual Franciscans, and, at a later date, Wyclif declared his conviction that the faith of Christ had been more perfectly preserved in

[67] *De Ecclesia* pp. 274 and 288.

[68] Nicholas I looked unfavourably on Erigena's translation of Dionysius because it was the work of a Greek ; though the views of the translator may have been in part responsible.

[69] An example may be found in the Bull *Unam Sanctam* of 18 Novr. 1302 which included the following passage : " Sive ergo Graeci sivi alii, se dicant Petro, eisque successoribus, non esse commissos, fateantur necesse est se de ovibus Christi non esse " : *Reg. Bon. VIII* No. 5382 (ed. Digard, Faucon et Thomas III. p. 888).

[70] Innocent IV actually tried to persuade the Mongols to attack the Eastern Empire in 1248. He was informed that they did not wish to foster the mutual hate of the Christians. Mt. Paris *Hist. Min.* III. 38 sq., *Hist. Maj.* V. 38.

[71] It is interesting to notice that Jerome of Prague had some vague scheme for the union of the Bohemians with the Eastern Church : see Creighton *History of the Papacy* II. p. 86.

the East.[72]   Those who felt that the pure faith must somewhere have survived looked for it in the unknown East—
ignorance made judgement charitable—for obviously it had
not been preserved in the West.[73]

Weakened   From the military point of view the Schism was disas-
Christendom trous.   Had it never occurred there can be but little doubt
that the advance of the Turks would have been stayed long
before it could have reached the Bosphorus, might never
indeed have gained a footing in Asia Minor.   The Crusaders,
backed by the power of the Byzantines, and with safe lines of
communication behind them by land as well as by sea, would
have been capable of holding their own ; instead of which East
weakened West, and West weakened East.   It is, of course,
easy to judge after the event, but the West repeated, in the
case of the Byzantine Empire, the mistake which the Romans
made when they destroyed the Seleucids who were the natural
champions of Greek culture and the obvious defenders, if
properly supported, of the Western world on its eastern front.[74]

Failure of   When the end was drawing near the West was but tepid
West to   in its efforts to aid in the defence of Constantinople.   It was
support   felt that the treasures which the Greeks were supposed to
East   have hoarded might have well been used in hiring mercenaries
instead of being left for the Turks to capture.   Many regarded
Hungary rather than Constantinople as the bulwark of the
West.   Among those who actually gave support the Venetians
were exceedingly anxious to avoid warfare with the Turk,
and Jacopo Loredano who commanded the fleet sent to defend Constantinople—it arrived too late—had received instructions not to provoke hostilities.[75]   The presence in the
city of a few thousand additional troops of good quality would
have preserved it ; whilst a really determined and well led
effort would have cut off the Turkish forces in the Balkans
and compelled them to withdraw from Europe.   But so great

[72] *Trial* p. 446 : cf. also his *Ninth Conclusion.*
[73] As early as the twelfth century Gerhoh of Reichersberg in *De Inventione Anti-christi* could lay the blame for the Schism on the avarice of the West.
[74] The Byzantines had themselves made a similar mistake in warring against the Armenians whose weakness ultimately let in the Moslems.
[75] The exact terms of his instructions are worthy of quotation : " licet hanc classem pro honore dei et conservatione civitatis Constantinopl. para-verimus, attamen si possible fuerit ad aliquam novitatem vel guerram cum Teucro devenire nollemus " : State Archives Secreta Senatus XIX. 194.

were theological bitterness and racial hate, that the West
was not altogether sorry to look on at the *vexatio* of the East ;
whilst the East itself, even in its agony, could prefer the
Sultan to the Pope.[76]

It now remains to consider the effect of the fall of the Effects of
Eastern Church and Empire especially as it concerned the the fall
position and future prospects of the Papacy.

In the East itself one result was to bring Russia to the front Rise of
as the leading secular power in the Orthodox communion. Russia
The very year of the fall saw the consolidation of that country
by the success of Moscow in gathering supreme power to itself.
The Russian Church was very independent in its attitude
to the Papacy, as Isidore of Kiew, who had accepted papal
supremacy, had been dethroned in 1448, and a new Archbishop
elected.   This latter, who took the title of Metropolitan, was
not subject to Constantinople.[77]

Some of the Greeks fled to the West and several ecclesiastics Greeks
received office in the Roman Church.   This was not the first accept
occasion when this had happened, for when the Moslems in- Turkish rule
vaded the Eastern Empire in the seventh century Sergius,
the Metropolitan of Damascus, had taken refuge in Rome and
founded the abbey of St Boniface there.[78]   But the majority
of the Greeks preferred to remain where they were and to
accept their new masters.   There were two reasons for this,
apart from man's natural instinct to remain by his home
and native-land, the considerate treatment received from the
Turks and hatred of the Roman Church.

Mohammed treated the conquered Greeks with kindness, Good treat-
such indeed had ever been the Turkish way from the beginning ment by
of the fourteenth century, when some of the inhabitants of Turks
Asia Minor had definitely preferred the rule of the Sultan.[79]
This helped to separate them from their fellow-Christians of
the West and explains why some of them were, as Cristobulus

[76] The same conclusion had been reached by the Oriental and Greek
Christians when Jerusalem fell before Saladin in 1187 : see Gibbon VI. p. 345.

[77] The title of Patriarch was not assumed by the Head of the Russian
Church until near the end of the sixteenth century and then with the full
consent and assistance of the Patriarch of Constantinople, Jeremiah II.

[78] See Gregorovius *Geschichte der Stadt Rom* I. p. 782.

[79] Orkhan (1326-1359) actually formed a regiment of Christians, the forerunners of the famous Janissaries.   There was an exception to the favourable
treatment of Christians in Murad I (1359-1389).

testifies, but languid defenders of their city when its fortunes were finally put to the test. The Ottoman treatment was especially effective in districts, such as Bosnia, where there was a large peasant population; Bosnia, moreover, had suffered much persecution from the Roman Church owing to the prevalence of the Bogomile heresy, the Turk was an effective protector against its renewal.[80]

Converts to Islam

Not only did the Eastern Christians turn to the Moslems for protection; a number of individuals actually adopted that form of religion. These included Manuel, son of Thomas, Despot of Morea; all the children of Catherine, Queen-Mother of Bosnia (she left her kingdom to the Papacy unless they returned) and George Crnojevic, Prince of Montenegro, who thus hoped to regain his dominions.[81]

Hatred of Rome

There is ample evidence that the Eastern Christians had a deep hatred of Rome and were willing to help the Turk rather than submit to its rule. It was not only at the time of the fall of Constantinople, but even afterwards that the " turban" was preferred to the " tiara ". The Greeks in Lemnos betrayed the papal troops to the Turks ;[82] whilst a number of Serbian cities opened their gates rather than be " rescued " by the Hungarians, who were Catholics.

Effect on Papacy

The Roman Church might regard the downfall of its sister in the East as a manifest judgement on the sin of schism, but the West suffered by the fall, and the advance of the Turks raised a good deal of alarm.[83] In fact apprehension for themselves rather than pity for the Greeks was the predominant feeling. The Popes it is true made some efforts to recover Constantinople, and drive back the Turks ; but the failure of their efforts was the measure of their lost prestige. But even apart from this the Papacy was bound to suffer, just as it suffered from the fall of the Empire in the West. In each

[80] " Bosnia . . . presents us with a curious phenomenon of an aristocratic caste, Slav by race, yet Muslim by religion " : *Camb. Med. Hist.* IV. p. 582.

[81] Quite a number of the best Turkish leaders had been soldiers under the Byzantines and on being captured had gone over to the Moslems. An interesting instance of an early apostasy is John, the elder brother of Andronicus II, who became a Moslem in 1140, married the Sultan's daughter, and begat an offspring, from whom Mohammed II claimed descent.

[82] Christobulus in Müller *Frag. Hist. Graecorum* V. pp. 128 sq.

[83] Innocent VIII was seriously troubled : see Secret Archives of the Vatican Instr. IV. vol. 55 Doc. 283.

case an institution supported by age-long traditions had perished, and the Papacy which depended for its power so largely on traditional acceptance was shaken. " The capture of Constantinople and the extinction of the Eastern Empire had dealt a fatal blow to the prestige of tradition and an immortal name." [84]

[84] Bryce *Holy Roman Empire* p. 359.

CHAPTER IX

THE RENAISSANCE

Introduction

AT this juncture it will be well again to desert the strict chronological sequence in order to examine as a whole the movement known as the Renaissance; a movement which had a profound part to play in the decline and fall of the Medieval Papacy. It is from this point of view alone that it will be studied in the following pages.

At the outset I must attempt to answer two questions. What were the causes of the Renaissance and when did it begin ? A few generations ago the replies would have come glibly enough—the Renaissance was due to a revival of Greek culture and it began when the Fall of Constantinople in 1453 drove fugitives to the West. Neither of these statements can now be accepted, though the second is still repeated sometimes by those who ought to know better ; for Greek was by no means the chief influence in the Renaissance, and the Fall of Constantinople far from increasing that influence, diminished and almost ended it.

Gradual rise

The movement came so gradually that to give even an approximate date for its beginning is difficult. It spread slowly as the light of the dawn spreads before the sun itself appears. Tout used to say that one could never be sure that there was a Renaissance at all, since it seemed to be there all the time. Certainly if a date is to be hazarded it must be at least a century earlier than 1453. For the Renaissance is falsely so-called ; it was nothing so sudden, or so definite as a re-birth ; it was rather the attainment of maturity, the culmination of a period of observable preparation, the gradual blossoming of the Italian genius. This latter was the supreme cause of the movement rather than Greek influence, the growth was native to the soil from which it sprang.

It seems probable that but for the Renaissance Italy as Effects in a cultural force might have gone the way of Greece and Italy Byzantium. The revival gave her a new lease of life and a new importance. Its first rising coincided with a brief period of Italian liberty ; the Emperor was no longer to be feared, and the French and the Spaniard had not yet established themselves. For the time the patriotic Italian might find consolation for the political degradation and feebleness of his country in the knowledge that its oppressors were his fellow-countrymen, and that in the Empire of the mind Italy was without a rival.[1]   Both these sources of consolation would soon be snatched from him ; for alien powers stepped in to quench the last of the Italian despots, and the crown of learning fled across the Alps.

For centuries Italy had been striving to assimilate the Revival of various races which had made their home within her borders ; Latin culture Lombards, Normans, Germans,[2] not to speak of the Greeks and Saracens of the South, and even the descendants of the numerous slaves from Asia Minor planted in Sicily in the second century B.C.   By the fourteenth century this process of absorption had well nigh been completed ; moreover by that century the Empire was little more than a name, and the twin institutions of feudalism and chivalry which it had brought into Italy had decayed with its passing.   The old primitive things began to revive, and the ancient stock of Latin civilisation to send forth new shoots.

Thus the Renaissance, in its earlier stages, was a revival New of the native culture, Latin, and I also believe, Etruscan.[3] elements The influence of Greek culture came later and was never so intense a force.[4]   On the cultural side this double revival gave significance to the movement.   But in addition new elements were to be introduced and new methods to be acquired.   The Renaissance, viewed in its totality, was to prove revolutionary and disturbing, not because of the old,

---

[1] Cf. Marco Vida *Poemata Selecta* p. 245.

> " Artibus emineat semper, studiisque Minervae,
> Italia, et gentes doceat pulcherrima Roma ;
> Quandoquidem armorum penitus fortuna recessit."

[2] The Italian nobles, as their names shew, were mainly of Teutonic origin.
[3] This was especially true of art : see below, p. 271.   In any case early Roman civilisation owed an immense debt to this mysterious people.
[4] See below, pp. 266 sq.

but because of the new; not because it brought the ancient classics to light again, nor even because it gave a new æsthetic value to life; but because it released a new spirit and coincided with discoveries of incalculable import. The notebooks of Leonardo da Vinci are typical of one side of the movement, the voyages of Columbus and Vasco da Gama of another.

Geographical discoveries   The geographical discoveries had their repercussions in the intellectual sphere; in fact it may be said that they revolutionised the imaginations of mankind. Men had become used to a Catholic Church which did not include the East; but the discovery of a new hemisphere with new races of men was a severe blow to their ideas. St Augustine had taught that all men came of one stock, and the Inquisition had enforced this as the orthodox view; now, in spite of a papal decree, the belief that the Indians were not descended from Adam began to make way.[5] In another direction the Pope's authority was also to be flouted. The newly discovered territories in both the Indies were divided between Spain and Portugal by papal decree;[6] but nobody except those who benefited by the division respected it. In the New World the Pope's writ had no currency.

Characteristics of the Renaissance —Vitality   We come now to consider the characteristics of the Renaissance. The most striking of them was perhaps, especially in the earlier phases, an abounding vitality. The spirit of man seemed to rise from the stagnation of the previous age (though this has been exaggerated) as the lark rises from the marsh. In every direction new knowledge and new experiences were being sought. This curiosity was so unbounded, that it would have been excessive, had it not been modified by a sincere and refined appreciation of beauty in all its varied manifestations. Later this intensity of life was to become somewhat artificial, as disillusionment descended, and to take on an aspect that was almost feverish; as that of a man who hoped by hard running to rid himself of a haunting shadow. And the Renaissance had indeed

[5] See Pittard *Les races et l'histoire* p. 39.
[6] By the bull *Inter caetera* published in 1493 but modified in the following year by the Treaty of Tordesillas.

its haunting shadow — the fear of *ennui* and that quiet which provokes reflection.

To those who lived this life of passionate ardour the thought that it might be extended beyond the grave, and that an account might one day have to be given of its use, was far from welcome. Had they been challenged on the point no doubt they would have pleaded that man should at least have the option of breaking the entail. It was no accident that a later writer who shared the Renaissance spirit, though living in a situation of greater security—did he not boast that he had no guard nor sentinel but the watching stars—should have adopted Cicero's aphorism that philosophy is to teach men how to die.[7]

Next to this abounding, almost feverish, vitality, the characteristic which attracts the attention is the contradictory nature of the age as seen in the men in whom its spirit appears to have been incarnate. Two figures may be taken in illustration—Cesare Borgia and Pietro Aretino, a man of action and a man of letters. The former had many fine feelings, and in his manners was courteous exceedingly ; but he would quite indifferently perform a kind action or order the commission of a revolting crime. The latter could also be extraordinarily generous, he was moreover loyal and candid ; but this did not prevent him from being brutal and sensual, and so childishly vain that, with no thought for his mother's reputation, he gave out that he was the bastard of a great noble. Contradictory age

The combination of barbarous cruelty with childishness is a common feature of this refined and over-cultivated age. Another example was the delight of the conspirators who assassinated Galeazzo Sforza in anticipating their vengeance by insulting and stabbing a lay figure made in his likeness. On almost every page of contemporary records acts of horrible cruelty are inscribed. Even the dead were not safe from insult, and men were found who did not consider that they had slaked their enmity until they had outraged the corpses of their foes. Some even went so far as to tear the flesh with their teeth, some actually ate it.[8]

[7] Montaigne *Essays* I. xix.
[8] *Chron. of Matarazzo* in Arch. Stor. Ital. (2nd series) XVI. p. 118 mentions the case of a man who died of a surfeit of human flesh.

17

Self-centred   Men were frivolous, selfish, vain ; dazzled not a little by the amazing gifts which had been showered upon them ; yet sufficiently practical to know their own minds, and to press such gifts into the service of their desires ; a characteristic of devotees of pleasure in all ages.   Meanwhile the source of the gifts was forgotten, and man displaced God as the centre of the universe ; [9] little realising that he himself would soon be deposed by the revolutionary discoveries of natural science.

Individual-istic   During the earlier middle ages the individual had undoubtedly been sacrificed to the community.   But by the time of Dante there were signs that he would some day be restored to a place of fresh importance.   Dante's choice of figures in the *Divina Commedia* reveals a conviction " that wonderful histories are latent in the inconspicuous paths of life, in the fugitive incidents of the hour, among persons whose faces we have seen." [10]   The revival of humanism, that is the recognition of the inherent dignity and significance of individual human beings, is seen by the place given in art to actual living men and women, and in letters by the reappearance of personal memoirs, a type of literature which " had been driven underground, its course checked and hidden beneath the fallen masonry of the Roman Empire ".[11]

Self-expres-sive   Each man, as he was touched by the spirit of the times, felt a passionate necessity to express himself through some medium or other ; sometimes this expression took strange forms, though I cannot recall anyone who chose ' gastronomic verse ' as his special line, as did a certain Archestratus of Gela in the second century B.C.   This desire for self-expression carried with it the craving for distinction.   Men " could not be contented to sail quietly down the stream of reputation without longing to taste the froth from every stroke of the oar ".[12]   To such lengths did this craving for notoriety go that Gabrino Fondolo, Lord of Cremona, finding himself at the top of a high tower in company with the Emperor Sigismund and Pope John XXIII, was minded to gain for himself perpetual fame, by flinging them both from its summit.

---

[9] There is much significance in the fact that this era saw the production of Pico della Mirandola's *Dignity of Man.*
[10] Church *Dante etc.* p. 75.   [11] P. S. Allen *The Age of Erasmus* p. 8.
[12] This was Dr Johnson's criticism of Samuel Richardson.

To the end of his days Gabrino regretted that he had not killed them, and also Filippo Maria Visconti, Duke of Milan, who was in Cremona at the time.[13]

This excessive desire for fame, and its immediate enjoyment, was probably responsible for the violent quarrels which were continually breaking out between the scholars of the epoch. Lytton Strachey once expressed the opinion that in no other place and at no other epoch have people ever squabbled so much as in eighteenth century France : [14] but Italy in the days of the Renaissance would have just as good a claim to this distinction.   Seekers after truth and beauty are very like other travellers, they are more concerned to reach their destination than to shew consideration for their fellows.

This intensely individualistic outlook was natural in an age of pioneers, and as a reaction against the repressions of that which had gone before ; natural too in an age of transition when the repudiation of acknowledged authorities had left men to follow their own devices.   But sooner or later it was bound to be modified, for as men are truly human only in the society of their fellows, so a genuine humanism must transcend the mere individual.   From the first, however, checks were imposed on the individual, in so far as the movement was a definite attempt to revive the ideas and standards of classical antiquity.   He might repudiate more hallowed sanctions, he dare not go against the prevailing fashion of the times.   In philosophy there was greater freedom, as the fact that no single predominant school arose to replace the discredited Scholasticism testifies.   The Renaissance might be Italy's Reformation, as Gregorovius has said,[15] freeing learning from the bonds of dogma ; but it surpassed the Reformation in that it forged no new fetters.   Freed from illusions, or what they held to be illusions, men were content, for the time, to allow the temple of thought to remain swept and garnished.   New objects of devotion would doubtless claim it in their season.

Men were obsessed by the visible and the tangible, and it was to beauty that they assigned the fairest lodging in the habitation of their minds.   They followed it eagerly

Opposed to tradition in general,

not to classical

Love of beauty

---

[13] *Chronicon Eugubinum* in RIS. XXI. col. 956 B.
[14] " The Rousseau Affair " in *Books and Characters* p. 165.
[15] *Geschichte der Stadt Rom* etc. II. pp. 579 and 874.

as the golden clue between the twilight of dawn, and the twilight, ever hastening, which heralded the darkness of night.   It flamed up before them ardent and gleaming ; but the wind of life blew so strong that it soon burnt itself out, leaving only dead ashes behind.   But while it remained men found themselves in a state of enthralment ; asking no questions, seeking no future, content with the exquisite rapture of the moment.

Just as in the whole movement there was something not quite healthy, so was it with this fierce pursuit of beauty.   It comes out, not only in the works of art of the period, but also in the writings, such as those of the circle round Lorenzo the Magnificent, and not least in his own poems.   At their best, they are graceful compositions, the poetry of souls " tuned to Arcadian repose " ; at their worst, a curious illustration of the type of beauty which appealed to an over-refined age.[16]

Love of nature   Perhaps the most wholesome sign was an increased love of nature ; fostered, no doubt, by the influence of Virgil and other pastoral poets, and seen in glimpses in the poems of Lorenzo, as well as in the gardens which men began to cultivate with increasing ardour and good taste.[17]

Ruskin has condemned this excessive craving for beauty, on the ground that it subordinated truth, and so led to the loss of spiritual power ; especially when it involved the substitution of " bodily beauty for spiritual life." [18]   In the reproduction of " bodily beauty " the painters of Florence had no rivals and even improved upon the sculptors of the ancient world.[19]   This was all to the good ; but the price paid was too exacting, if the highest beauty was lost sight of ; for it is only when the soul of beauty is also the soul of enduring life, that it truly diffuses composure and ennobling harmony.[20]

Lowering of moral standards   Because of their blindness men saw no inconsistency in the juxtaposition of beauty and defiance of the moral law. Bernardino Corio, writing at the end of the fifteenth century,

---

[16] What it " treasured in women was not a wholesome and robust, but a suffering beauty of ethereal pallor, with deadly sick enchanting eyes—the beauty of consumption from which Simonetta died " : Muther *Hist. of Painting* I. p. 150.

[17] See Julia Cartwright *Italian Gardens of the Renaissance.*

[18] *Modern Painters* III. pp. 66 sq.

[19] Holmes *Introd. to Ital. Painting* pp. 51 sq.

[20] Cf. Wordsworth *The Prelude* VII. *ll.* 769 sqq.

describes the " magnificent Courts of the Princes ; the rivalry between the schools of Minerva and Venus, as he calls them ; [21] the unblushing, cynical immorality which was reputed *stupendissima cosa*, contrasting with the gathering of poets and scholars, painters and sculptors, musicians, and of everything that made life externally beautiful and gorgeous ".[22]

What is the explanation of this strange combination of artistic achievement and moral obtuseness ? It can, I think, be found in the fact that the artistic sense had for the time entirely obscured the ethical. So long as life was handled in a grand or a graceful manner the generality of mankind was content to regard the virtues as of merely academic interest. Every activity of life was treated as the opportunity for artistic excellence—not only sculpture and painting, but war,[23] and even crime.[24] The logical goal of all this was the " superman " of Nietzsche, and indeed the Renaissance was not lacking in supermen, to whom morality was but a relative term, and the lives of their fellows simply raw material for the use of the great artist. About them there was a strange fascination, for they sinned by the eager and unquestioned following of their instincts and their passions ; full-blooded animals such as abound in every active age. But there were others more repulsive, who seemed to sin calmly and coldly ; perverted idealists inspired by nothing that could be termed generous or even human, moved only by the notion that vice could give the occasion for the exhibition of elegance. It was these latter, rather than the former, who proclaimed the degradation of the times.

That same degradation was manifest in the drama of the time. It is true that drama is precluded by its conventions from exactly reflecting contemporary society ; it is none the less a reliable index of its tastes and preferences, The drama

---

[21] The same idea occurs in the writings of Rudolf Agricola, who in 1474 wrote that Ferrara was the home of the muses—and of Venus ; quoted by Allen *The Age of Erasmus* pp. 16 sq.

[22] Gardner *The King of Court Poets—Ariosto* p. 16.

[23] War was a game of chess in which manœuvres took the place of fighting. The result was much the same, and lives were saved—a matter of importance to the professional soldier who had no loyalties save to his kind.

[24] Cesare Borgia's treacherous massacre at Sinigaglia is called " un bellissimo inganno " by Paulus Jovius ; and a notorious bandit, Arrighetto of San Paolo, is described by Matteo Villani as making " grandi e belli furti di bestiame " (RIS. XIV. col. 132 A.).

for if the plays produced in any given period do not reveal the minds of the common people, at least they expose the mentality of those who patronise the stage. By this test the patrons of the Renaissance drama were over-refined, cultivated men of the world, asking only that by some novelty their boredom might be stayed. The high esteem in which antiquity was held gave ample licence for the introduction of that coarseness which is present in all men, though the veneer of manners may conceal it.

Art and immorality   It is a widely held opinion that persons of artistic gifts are less moral than others ; this opinion is hardly justified, for such evidence as can be produced merely goes to shew that they are less careful to keep up appearances. Equally unjustified is the related opinion that great art can only be found in company with moral excellence. Art is often the expression of the highest mind of a painter, his conduct of the lowest. One would naturally wish that the painter of religious subjects should himself be a religious man. History does not satisfy such desires, and some of the greatest artists of the Renaissance were the most notorious for their moral laxity. The case of Fra Lippo Lippi, so well known through Browning's poem, is but one example. What gives it special interest and value, is the revelation which incidentally it furnishes of the attitude of the Church, as seen in its representatives, towards the question of art and morals. Amongst other crimes committed by this cleric were forgery and the abduction of a nun from the convent of which he was chaplain ; yet so great was the pride of the times in artistic achievement that after his death the following note was placed in the register of his old monastery, the Carmine at Florence : " He had been guilty of many crimes and follies, but the Church forgave him for the sake of the grace and excellence of his art ".[25]   Could anything be more enlightening than this naïve admission ?

One is almost tempted to doubt the usefulness of applying any kind of moral standard to the age, for moral standards were so openly set aside. We can well understand why Machiavelli arrived at the conclusion that " human nature was essentially bad and that the art of government like that of navigation should be considered apart from morals ".

[25] Julia Cartwright *The Painters of Florence* p. 156.

None the less there were those who stood for higher things,
and endeavoured to maintain a standard which was repudiated
by their contemporaries.[26]

It seems strange that an age of increasing dissolution Antiquarian
in the political and moral sphere was an age in which art interest
and literature blossomed in new splendour.[27] But history
furnishes many parallels, one thinks of the eleventh and twelfth
centuries of the Byzantine Empire ; and, furthermore, an
age which is interested in antiquity is often an age of moral
degradation.   Such were the first centuries of the Christian
era when " the disintegration of the old Roman life was
accompanied by the rise of antiquarianism ".[28]

There is in man a nostalgic element which compels him thus Reaction
to turn back with eagerness to the ideals and even the insti- against
tutions of his fathers. So now amid all the chances and changes medieval
of the world around them—and they were many and alarming
—men were groping, half unconsciously, after a serener,
more stable world, the shadowy world of their own past,
But the past which they sought was not the immediate
past ; for in their ignorance of its true nature they despised
the middle ages in favour of something more remote.   From
the days of Petrarch the reaction against medieval ways of
thought had become a principle ; his followers turned deliberately to the ancient world. But they were not unopposed,
and those who feared the new spirit saw in the movement,
as Aristophanes had seen a similar development in his day,
the dethroning of Jupiter and the coronation of the whirl-
wind.[29]

We turn now to a brief examination of the form which the The new
movement took as a revival of learning. For such a revival learning
it would seem that two things are necessary : a new awakening
of the human mind, and a new equipment,—either by way

[26] The low standard of morals can be seen, not in the attitude of the
corrupt, but of the godly. Even so great a man as Sir Thomas More did not
lead a blameless life, and what is most significant, had apparently no objection
to its being publicly known. In his appreciation of More in 1519 Erasmus
" stated the fact in quite explicit, though graceful, language . . . More took
no exception to the statement, which was repeated in edition after edition " :
Allen *The Age of Erasmus* p. 205.

[27] Villari *Hist. of Florence* p. viii.

[28] Glover *The Conflict of Religions in the Early Roman Empire* p. 8.

[29] The Renaissance, in spite of its interest in the past had not the true
historic spirit : cf. Figgis *From Gerson to Grotius* pp. 277 sq.

of new methods, or new material.   In the thirteenth century
the possession of additional works by Aristotle had enabled
Scholasticism to make great strides ; but here was a movement more active than Scholasticism, and with newer materials
at its command.   Not only had the men of the Renaissance
the opportunity of using newly discovered classical writings ;
they had also a whole new world gradually coming within
their ken.   Athens and Rome could give them the message of
the past, the Americas demanded an entirely new orientation
of the mind.   The ancient world had been dominated by the
lands round the Mediterranean.   So had it been in the middle
ages.   The discovery of vaster oceans, and the continents
beyond them, brought a fresh centre of gravity and ushered
in the end of the Mediterranean era of Western civilisation.
It coincided with the end of the middle ages themselves.

Not chiefly the product of the universities   The new learning, as Professor Adamson has pointed out,
owed less to the routine education of the schools and univer-
sities, than to the less formal education of those who were
not clerks or men of letters, but knights and dames and
even merchants.   It was through the latter channel that
" the humanism of the classical revival became effective ".[30]
During the middle ages literature, and poetry in particular,
had been cultivated by the nobles ; the majority of the poets
of Provence, Germany, France, and England, were men of
gentle birth.[31]   In Florence, on the other hand, poets and
writers had been drawn from the merchant classes.   The
two were to combine in bringing to birth the literature of the
Renaissance.

Influence of Petrarch   Those who in Italy revealed the first signs of the revival
of letters were connected, either as friends or as pupils, with
Petrarch.   There was that strange figure Cola di Rienzo, whose
letters [32] shew a deep enthusiasm for the past, and to whom
the revival of archæology must be credited ; there was
Boccaccio, the populariser of the novel as well as the student
of Greek.   Others, not so well known, there were in plenty who
looked back to the same source of inspiration ; amongst

[30] In *The Legacy of the Middle Ages* p. 282.
[31] On the other hand, the standard of education in the narrower sense of
the word was much lower among the western nobles than among the Byzantines.
[32] See the recent edition of his correspondence by Burdach and Piur in
Vom Mittelalter zur Reformation II. pts. iii and iv.

whom mention may be made of his pupil and secretary, Giovanni of Ravenna, the type of the wandering teacher who became so common ; and Luigi Marsigli, who in the Convent of San Spirito at Florence held the first literary circle and linked the age with that of Poggio. But perhaps the most interesting example of this influence is contained in a story told by Leonardo Bruni. Bruni as a boy was confined, during an outbreak in his native Arezzo, in a small chamber in which there hung a picture of Petrarch. On that picture, he tells us, he would daily gaze with increasing desire to become a scholar and man of letters such as Petrarch had been.[33]

The business of supplying the new material was quickly undertaken by a variety of collectors, whose tastes or ambitions had been aroused by the knowledge that MSS and works of art were to be discovered by the ardent searcher. Most of them were inspired by a real love of beauty and of truth, but mingled with it often enough the mere lust for possession or the desire for notoriety. The example had been set as long ago as the first half of the thirteenth century, for Frederick II was a collector. The theological disputes of the fifteenth century incidentally furthered the cause of classical studies, for men in search of new MSS of the Fathers found also new MSS of still older writers. Among the most successful was Poggio Bracciolini ;[34] one of whose most important discoveries was a MS containing the greater part of Ammianus Marcellinus, a work which had been lost for centuries. Another collector was Cardinal Giordano Orsini, who acquired a collection of twelve comedies of Plautus, which had not been known before, from a famous German dealer, Nicholas of Trier. The cardinal was no mere collector, however, and made an attempt to restore the text which in places was corrupt. Shortly before his death he presented his collection to the Library at St Peter's. Cardinal Bessarion had a very large library ; he too did not wait for death before disposing of it but gave it to Venice, as an ancient link between East and West. Thither the library of Petrarch had already gone.[35]

The collectors of MSS

[33] " Erat in ipso cubiculo picta Francisci Petrarchae imago, quam ego quotidie aspiciens, incredibili ardore studiorum eius incendebar " : RIS. XIX. col. 917 D.

[34] See Walser *Poggius Florentinus' Leben und Werke.*

[35] Mention should also be made of the libraries of Niccolo Niccoli, and Galeazzo Visconti at Pavia.

The patrons　　By these collections men made reputations for themselves, for all now felt that learning and art were the things that really mattered.　In a similar way, and for similar reasons, others became patrons of scholars and artists.　Even a city was not above realising that by the patronage of culture it glorified itself.　The elder Sforza, who came of peasant stock and to the last had rustic manners, would give large sums for the translation of Greek and Latin historians and expressed his regret that he had never learnt to hold a sword and a book in the same hand.

Teachers of the new learning　　In addition to collectors to supply him with MS and patrons to support him, the scholar needed teachers to instruct him. The roll of Renaissance teachers is a full one, and in it must be included the names of a number of wandering Greeks—some of whom knew little beyond the elements of the language. The names of many of these teachers are known by a mere accident—such was Gregorio da Spoleto, the master of Ariosto [36]—but many, because they were not sufficiently fortunate to have an Ariosto among their pupils, having done their work passed from the memory of man.

Extent of Greek influence　　Whilst it is true that wandering Greek scholars had their share in quickening men's minds their influence must not be exaggerated ; the Renaissance was predominatly a revival of the native culture, Latin rather than Greek.[37]　When Ariosto reached manhood in the Court at Ferrara we are told that all men loved and hated, and even dreamed, in Latin.[38] The poet himself was so proud of the great literary past of his country that he expressly says that Latin must not be neglected in order to learn Greek.[39]　Pomponius Laetus went even further and refused to have anything to do with the

[36]　　"Fortuna molto mi fu allhora amica
　　　　Che mi offerse Gregorio da Spoleti,
　　　　Che ragion vuol ch'io sempre benedica.
　　　Tenea d'ambe le lingue i bei secreti
　　　　E potea giudicar se meglior tuba
　　　　Hebbe il figliuol di Venere o di Teti."
　　　　　　　　　　　　　—Ariosto *Satire* VI. *ll.* 166-172.

[37] See my *Erasmus the Reformer* pp. 4 sq.
[38] Carducci *La Gioventù di Ludovico Ariosto* p. 37.
[39]　　　　"Chè'l saper ne la lingua de gli Achei
　　　　　Non mi reputo honor, s'io non intendo
　　　　　Prima il parlar de li latini miei."
　　　　　　　　　　　　　Satire VI. *ll.* 178-180.

latter language in order to preserve the purity of his style. The wiser minds, however, recognised that a knowledge of Greek was necessary for a true understanding of Latin culture.[40]

It is possible that Greek as a spoken tongue never entirely died out in Italy, especially in the south, where it is still possible to find Greek-speaking communities.[41] But the extent to which Greek was known by scholars was not nearly so great as has sometimes been supposed, for the ability to write the characters was enough, in the general ignorance, to give a man the reputation for Greek learning. That the need for Greek learning was recognised, however, is shewn by the petition of the University of Paris in 1300 asking the Pope to grant leave for a college to teach that language, alongside Arabic and Tartar. The combination suggests that the purpose was not literary, but controversial. The Council of Vienne a few years later recommended the establishment of Greek lectureships in the Universities of Paris, Bologna, Oxford and Salamanca. These efforts proved abortive, most probably because Greek was the language of the schismatic East.[42] By the end of the century, however, a real beginning was made, when the magnates of Florence brought over Emmanuel Chrysoloras to teach in their city. The advance of the Turks drove many Greeks to the West; the actual fall of Constantinople was only an incident, for by that time copies of all MSS had been safely transferred, and the best of the teachers had already migrated to securer climes.

Those who wished to become scholars had to undertake immense labours, but their reward was equally great. Men felt that their writings could bring immortality and establish fame.[43] Was not Cobelli, the Chronicler of Forli, admitted to the Secret Council because he wrote history ?[44] The pen was indeed mightier than the sword, and not a few

The reward of the scholar

[40] So Battista da Verona in *De ordine docendi et studiendi* (1459).

[41] There was a large influx of Greeks during the seventh century owing to the Moslem advance. On the survival in the present day see G. Rohlfs *Griechen und Romanen in Unteritalien* (Geneva, 1924).

[42] Pastor thinks that had the humanists derived their culture " directly from Greek sources rather than from the degenerate Roman civilization, the whole later development of the movement would have been different " : *Hist. of the Popes* II. p. 201.

[43] The career of Pietro Aretino (1492-1556) illustrates the growing power of the " press " : see his life by E. Hutton.

[44] Pasolini *Catherine Sforza* (E.T.) p. 91.

warriors were willing to admit it. Even the Papacy, alongside its mercenary soldiers, had to employ pagan or semi-
pagan scholars to compose its documents, and argue with its
assailants. In the choice of papal secretaries there seems
to have been no regard paid to either belief or conduct ;
all that was demanded was a good Latin style ; but, as
Pastor says, " The improvement in the Latinity of the Papal
documents was too dearly purchased ".[45]

Printing The invention of printing finally gave to the man of letters
his supremacy, for it not only multiplied the copies of his
writings and sent them to the ends of the earth, but for the
first time made him independent of patrons.[46] Incidentally
some disservice was done, by the invention, to the highest
type of scholarship, for the possibilities of error in printed
matter were not fully realised, and when once a MS. had
been set up the original was felt no longer to be of value.[47]

Debt to the past, yet scorn for Schoolmen The humanists regarded it as their function to call men
forth from the lampless depths of ignorance and superstition,
in which for so long they had been content to dwell, that they
might enjoy the " warm precincts of the cheerful day ". But
in their condemnation of the old learning they forgot how
great was their own debt to it. Scholasticism, it cannot be
denied, had drifted into unanticipated situations, and ad-
justment to its new environment seemed beyond its powers ;
thus the process of evolution was stopped and torpidity came
upon it. Its votaries could only offer cold and lifeless abstractions which compared but sadly with the vivid realities
of the world which was throbbing around them. None the
less as a method of training, if nothing else, Scholasticism had
done its work.

and for legal studies The scornful attitude of the scholars of the Renaissance
towards the old philosophical system is, of course, notorious ;
equally scornful, though not equally well known was their
attitude towards legal studies.[48] Here too they had some
justification, for the methods of the Commentators were anti-
quated. Their aim, surely a praiseworthy one, was to restore

[45] *Op. cit.* I. p. 259 (cf. p. 305). The college of Apostolic Secretaries was
not finally suppressed until the days of Innocent XI (1676-1689).
[46] Cf. *Erasmus the Reformer* p. 7.
[47] Allen *The Age of Erasmus* pp. 159 sq.
[48] See Voigt *Die Wiederbelebung des class. Altertums* II. pp. 477 sqq.

the classical jurists, who had been mutilated by the medieval lawyers, and, as far as possible, to " establish legal science on the broad foundation of history and philosophy ".[49]   But the Law is naturally conservative in its methods and in its procedure and progress was slow ; as late as 1520 Zasius could write to Alciatus : " All sciences have put off their dirty linen : only jurisprudence remains in her rags ".[50]

The scholars of the Renaissance might be scornful of others ; but their own methods, judged by modern standards, were exceedingly defective.   They were much more set on the acquisition of copies of old authors than on creating new works of their own.   It is notable that such works as they did produce had no abiding worth and, with few exceptions, are now known only to specialists.   The test of success or failure in such compositions was the extent to which they had succeeded in imitating those who had gone before.   The crowning folly was reached in the efforts of the Ciceronians whom Erasmus lashed so fiercely.   Such obsession with form rather than with matter was unhealthy and the forerunner, had not other influences stepped in, of speedy decay.   In any case it fostered a spirit of proud omniscience and of contempt for those who could not write good Latin.   Pedantry rather than genuine scholarship was the destined harbour towards which they were steering. *Defective methods of new learning*

It was a single type of culture only which carried the highest approval of those who counted as leaders whilst the movement was at its strongest ; that it should later fertilise other fields, that from it should grow up vernacular literatures and the scientific spirit, would have seemed a matter of slight importance to those eager students of the classical age.   As we have seen the work of Dante and his contemporaries was neglected, while even Petrarch looked on his Latin effusions as the foundation of his fame for after years.   In science no advance had yet been made,[51] and to his contemporaries the experiments and researches of Leonardo were merely eccentricities, because divorced from the ancient world.[52] *Narrow outlook*

A further manifestation of the cramped outlook of the

[49] H. D. Hazeltine in *Camb. Med. Hist.* V. p. 741.
[50] Quoted by Stintzing *Ulrich Zasius* p. 107.
[51] See further *Erasmus the Reformer* p. 6.
[52] Cf. Baron Friedrich von Hügel *Selected Letters* p. 73.

Italian humanists was their inability to appreciate the efforts of less favoured peoples to acquire culture. Those of them who happened to visit Germany, in this period, did not attempt to conceal their scorn for the natives, and the experience of Ovid among the Geti provided a parallel too apt to be allowed to pass unused.

Thus, in spite of many great achievements, the revival of learning, viewed as a movement of the human spirit, was marred by not a few serious limitations. The fundamental defect was the failure of its votaries to attain to a really adequate conception of humanism itself, as something meant for the whole race, and as drawing its treasures from things new and old. The Hellenistic mind tends ever to be exclusive, and to be fostered in narrow circles of those who hold themselves to be aristrocrats in the things of the spirit.

Renaissance art

If learning, however, was thus allowing itself to be confined and limited, the same could not be said of art. The art of the Renaissance carried in its bosom the memories of too wide a series of influences for it ever to become narrow, so long as its spirit retained anything of the first ardour. There was indeed a spirit moving within it, and we owe to Winckelmann our ability, rejecting the temptation to think of art merely in the terms of the artists themselves, to see its essence in the activities of that spirit, rather than in the achievements of the individuals through whom it was manifested.

Byzantine influence

At the back of the conscious tradition lay the great Byzantines ; the representatives of an art which had conquered, before the coming of Islam, the native cultures of Egypt and Persia, and then, through them, had influenced Muslim art itself.[53] This influence had naturally been strong in Italy owing to the link with the Eastern Empire ; in addition the Iconoclast controversy seems to have driven over workers in mosaic.[54] This debt to the East was recognised by the artists of the Renaissance ; for although Vasari's

[53] Byzantine art was introduced into Persia in 528 A.D.—just as the philosophers were being driven from Athens—by Khusraw I ; see De Lacy O'Leary *Arabic Thought etc.* p. 79. As late as the eighth century Byzantine mosaic-workers were helping in the great mosque at Cordova.

[54] See Labarte *Histoire des arts industriels* I. p. 105.

story, that Cimabue neglected his school work to watch the Greek painters at work in Santa Maria Novella at Florence, is impossible on chronological grounds, it records a genuine influence.

Behind influences more recent, however, I believe there was working, especially in Tuscany, an ancient faculty coming down from far-off Etruscan ancestors.[55] It was by no accident that in the artistic movement "Etruscan Florence" stood so central.[56] Thus when Niccolo Pisano took for his earliest models the sarcophagi in the Campo Santo at Pisa he was unconsciously returning to "the natural inspiration of his race". If this was so, the Tuscans shewed the same ability to adapt themselves to new conditions as their distant forebears ; for as the Etruscans were willing to abandon the simple geometric designs which they had brought with them from Asia Minor, and in their work in gold, at Vetulonia and elsewhere, to portray mythological scenes with human and animal figures ; so Giotto and his followers were able to emancipate themselves from the formalism of the Byzantine tradition in which they had been trained.[57]

It is often said that St Francis was the real founder of the artistic Renaissance, and it is a saying with much truth behind it. For Francis saw and recognised the beauty of the world around him, and with his coming a feeling of spring-time returned ; the gap between earth and heaven seemed to be bridged as by another Jacob's ladder. The new feeling can be recognised in the backgrounds of the paintings of the times which followed ; no longer do we find the unrelieved, dazzling gold which isolated the saint from all earthly things,

Marginal notes: Etruscan influence · St Francis as founder

[55] So the characteristics of the Veneti can be seen in Paduan Livy and the great artists of the sixteenth century : see R. S. Conway " The Venetian Point of view in Roman History " in *New Studies in a Great Inheritance* pp. 190 sqq.

[56] See Ruskin *Mornings in Florence* §§ 32 sqq. and cf. Randall-MacIver's description of the Etruscan cities as " a series of beacons of art and beauty lit upon every hill-top in Tuscany . . . sparks from the still gleaming fire were fanned into new flame centuries later by the Renaissance " : *The Etruscans* p. 150.

[57] Though this emancipation was necessary Byzantine Art in its own land was not nearly so lifeless and monotonous as is generally supposed ; it was capable of renewal and change. In the days of the Palaeologi it underwent an amazing expansion and " became living, picturesque, dramatic, emotional, and charming . . . its skilful and harmonious use of colour seems almost impressionistic " : *Camb. Med. Hist.* IV. p: 769.

but a real landscape which set him in the midst of his kind.

Thus did Francis break down the old convention by revealing the beauty of the earth. He did art a further service, for in his own person and the speedy canonisation which followed his death, he provided for the brush of the painter a new theme, devoid of any traditional treatment which might hamper his imagination.[58] And nobly the artist took advantage of his opportunity. The Franciscan legend became the favourite subject for decorating those large open spaces which the revival of religion was to provide in the bare walls of the friars' churches. It has been finely said that the great Church at Assisi, which was built to the honour of St Francis and to be a fortress to guard his bones, was a shrine which " became the cradle of Italian art ".[59]

Rise of Italian art

We cannot here tell of the rise of Cimabue, of Duccio, of Giotto and the other pioneers ; the story has been told in numerous volumes ; but perhaps a plea may be put in for a fuller recognition of the importance of Pietro Cavallini, whom Vasari so strangely called the pupil of Giotto, when actually he was his master.[60] The real pupils of Giotto were men of much less originality and they advanced no way beyond their master. The fourteenth century was indeed a time of arrested development, for Florence, whose wealth and freedom from hampering traditions, made her the obvious leader of the new artistic movement, quite apart from the genius of her sons, suffered from wars, both external and internal ; whilst the default of our own Edward III ruined some of her bankers. The century was indeed a hard one, for Italy as for the rest of Europe, with the Black Death coming midway in its course as a great landmark of desolation.

[58] The gods of paganism had been fashioned by poets and painters, the Catholic pantheon by priests and theologians. Freedom from hampering traditions was a necessary preliminary to artistic advance. The earliest portrait of St Francis is, so far as I know, a fresco in the Sacro Speco of Subiaco (1228) ; there is an altar-piece at Pescia by Bonaventura Berlinghieri (1235).

[59] Julia Cartwright The Painters of Florence p. 14.

[60] It is interesting to notice that Pietro carved the tomb of Edward the Confessor in Westminster Abbey : see Salazzo Pietro Cavallini Pittore, Scultore ed Architetto Romano del XIII secolo. Some of the works which used to be attributed to him are now given to Camillo Rusuti, another Roman painter who also worked in the Upper Church at Assisi : see Cecchelli in Roma II (1925) p. 90.

Furthermore the absence of the Popes at Avignon brought to an end the prospects of a new artistic centre in Rome, whither Boniface VIII and his nephew, Cardinal Stefaneschi, had drawn the painters of his times.

With the new century came a new burst of inspiration The and new wealth to support it.   The dome of Brunelleschi, fifteenth century the gates of Ghiberti, and the sculptures of Donatello, are all signs of it ;   and not least the frescoes of the Brancacci Chapel, painted by that luckless youth, Masaccio, to be the school of all Italy.   So the development went on, with Florence as leader ;   until the firmly established tyranny of the Medici crushed out her heart and the torch was taken by the freer Venetians.

It is strange that those who loved paintings and sculptures, and who spent their substance in the collection of ancient MSS, should have had so little affection for the architectural achievements of their fathers.   But so it was, and even the remains of classical Rome were allowed to decay or were, still worse, deliberately destroyed to provide materials for new buildings or even burnt to make lime.[61]

During the Avignon period and the Great Schism, Rome Renaissance itself had been neglected ; the only real feat of the ' Captivity ', buildings in Rome apart from the rebuilding of St John Lateran, was the erection of the steps leading to Santa Maria Aracoeli.   This neglect gave the Renaissance Popes and their architects the excuse for freely dealing with the buildings which were left to their mercy—they could always plead dilapidation, if they wished to remove some venerable sanctuary, in order to replace it with a temple more after their own conceptions. The greatest offender was perhaps Leo Battista Alberti who had been carried away by the methods and principles of Vitruvius.[62]   He had apparently no religious feelings whatever,

[61] Raphael Riario demolished the arch of Gordian for the sake of its stone and similar things were continually going on.   When Chrysoloras visited Rome and observed the destruction of its treasures he consoled himself with the thought that much still remained buried under the soil awaiting a generation with more taste and reverence.   The older Romans had been much more strict and in 173 B.C. Quintus Fulvius Flaccus was put on trial for sacrilege because, in order to build a temple in Rome, he had plundered one in Magna Graecia.

[62] His writings had been discovered by Poggio.   The palace of San Marco erected by Cardinal Barbo, later Paul II, was the pioneer attempt at a return to classical models in architecture.

to him a building was a building, and that was all. The medieval Church, like the Roman Republic, has left few monuments in Rome ; for just as Augustus could claim that he found Rome brick and left it stone, so the Popes of the Renaissance era could point to an equal achievement in the way of destruction, if not so happy a substitution. The most lamentable act was the pulling down of old St Peter's with all its venerable memories, to give the ambitious builders of the fifteenth century a chance of shewing what they could do if they had an adequate opportunity.[63] Perhaps the Popes were not sorry to have removed from their daily sight the memorial of a time when the Church had been a far different institution.

Joy of creative art

To erect new buildings the old must be removed, and this means destruction. But the art of the Renaissance suffered no such necessity in other directions, it was accordingly joyous and creative. The delightful story of the rejoicings of the citizens of Siena in June 1311 when they heard that Duccio had finished his altar-piece is surely typical of the movement at its best. A public holiday was proclaimed, all the shops were shut, and the painting carried round the streets in triumph, whilst the church-bells sounded joyfully " for the devotion of so noble a picture ". It might be an elemental age, strong in passion as in art, and men have found fitting symbol of its spirit in the roughly hewn stones of its palaces ; but there was a tender and gracious side to it as well.

Effect on the Papacy

Having described at some length the rise and growth of the Renaissance, and tried to suggest something of the atmosphere which it created, I must now pass on to consider its relation to the Church, and their mutual action and reaction.

Pagan and Christian elements

Some Roman Catholic scholars would distinguish two distinct types in the Renaissance, almost two movements—a Christian and a Pagan. But if such existed it is hard to de-

---

[63] A bull of 1451 stated that the Basilica of the Prince of the Apostles was in danger of becoming a ruin (*Bullarum Vaticanum* II p. 188). This is accepted by Pastor and others as evidence of the need for a new structure, but Guiraud says " en réalité, la reconstruction nous apparaît comme une facheuse concession faite par un pape humaniste à l'esprit nouveau de la Renaissance, sans doute sous l'influence d'Alberti " : *L'église romaine et les origines de la Ren.* p. 209.

fine the frontier between them. The very term Renaissance is borrowed from religion, as Croce has reminded us,[64] and in the mystic haze which overhung the movement Olympus and Olivet were easily confused. Some of the greatest minds of the age, indeed, seemed to regard Christianity as a development from Paganism, a higher stage of human progress; and to see in the combination of the teaching of Plato and Christ the great hope of the race.

The challenge of paganism

In the first half of the fifteenth century pagan and Christian elements were struggling together for the mastery; sometimes in strange places, as for example in the Bronze Doors of St Peter's, which were made for Eugenius IV, himself a pious monk and a sincere Christian. Yet the subjects are quite incongruous in such a place.[65] Later the challenge of paganism became more definite. The Renaissance developed into an encounter of vast contraries, Man-god against God-man, as Dostoievsky somewhere says, Appollo Belvedere against Christ. This encounter often enough had to be fought out within the confines of the individual soul; at any rate there was surprisingly little of outward attack on the Church's teaching and practice. There was, of course, the Roman Academy and that quaint figure, Pomponius Laetus, who deliberately ate meat in Lent and declared that St Francis was only a hypocrite and his Master another false prophet.[66] The absence of aggression is perhaps easier to understand if it is remembered that many of the humanists were deriving their means of livelihood from the Church, and that most of them probably felt that nothing was to be gained by attacking Christianity. " The culture of the Renaissance implied a philosophical acceptance of variety in fashion, faith, and conduct; and this toleration was no doubt one

[64] *Theory and History of Historiography* p. 230.

[65] The original doors had been placed there by Hildebrand; one wonders what would have been his opinion of their successors. Perhaps an even earlier example of the mingling of Christian and Pagan elements may be found in the use of a Roman sarcophagus for the tomb of Cardinal Fieschi (d. 1256). It is now in San Lorenzo at Rome.

[66] Cf. Giulio Zabughin *Pomponio Leto* (Rome 1909) and on the liberal movement, Charbounel *La Pensee ital. au XVIe. siècle et le courant liberal* (Paris 1919). More than a century earlier it had been said of Guido Cavalcanti, as he wandered, lost in thought, among the tombs which then surrounded the Baptistry at Florence, that he was trying to discover that there was no God. See Boccaccio *Il Decamerone* VI. 9.

reason why Italian scepticism took the form of cynicism,
not of religious revolution." [67]

Inward decay of the Church If, however, there were no open attacks the Renaissance
spirit did serious damage to the Church.   It was like a magic
potion, and those who drank from it found that life as they
had known it had become suddenly drab and faded ; a new
day had dawned, and the old religion looked a little weary
and tarnished amidst its gleaming lights and blithe songsters ;
the old beliefs and standards thus strangely cheapened and
hollow slipped away.   Even some of the best of the humanists
held that art and freedom were more vital and more religious
than any doctrinal belief.[68]   A sombre hue seemed to have
overspread Christianity, even though the incense still rolled
thick around the altar, and for this the more pious and
sincere among the religious, in their puritan reaction against
the looseness of life around them, were in part responsible.
Even the artists, as we have seen, found religion an unreal
thing, though there were exceptions such as Fra Angelico,
" the painter of eternal love ".   Among the seekers after
knowledge also there was the same tendency to make their
pursuit a substitute for religion.[69]   They forgot that Dante
had left Virgil on the hitherside of the Earthly Paradise,
though the legend of Faust shews that some at least were
conscious that their souls might be the price to be paid for
fuller knowledge and restored powers.[70]

New outlook During the fifteenth century the mental outlook of the
West had been undergoing a gradual change; this process
continued in the sixteenth.   It was not merely that new
facts were added to the sum total of man's experience, even
his dreams and ideals were altered.   This can be seen in
works such as More's *Utopia* and Machiavelli's *Prince*.   A
new world had come into being, a world which was willing

[67] J. A. Symonds *The Renaissance in Italy* III. p. 14.   There were, however, fierce attacks on the religious orders ; Lorenzo Valla going so far as to
affirm that a prostitute was of more use to humanity than a nun.

[68] Cf. Berenson *The Italian Painters of the Renaissance* p. 241 : " Antiquity
was a religion, nay more, a mystical passion, causing wise men to brood over
fragments of Roman statuary as if they were sacred relics ".

[69] Words written of Mark Pattison in *The Times* of Aug. 31, 1884 would
have fitted most of them : " the beatific vision would have been for him, as it
was for Aristotle, rather the ineffable splendour of perfect knowledge than the
opening heaven and the Communion of saints ".

[70] Cf. J. A. Symonds *op. cit.* III. p. 53.   Boccaccio fondly imagined that
the use of allegory would save the Christian soul from pollution.

tacitly to abandon or ignore much of the teaching of the Church. The Church had taught that the world was an evil, a prison house from which the soul would one day escape through the gate of death. But now the world with all its boundless expanses had been rediscovered, and, in spite of all its hardships and its unending problems, men had the joyous sense of finding their home. So too in regard to the body which once, at the Church's bidding, they had despised and buffeted ; it was now seen as a thing of beauty and of power. Men came to have a new pride in themselves and in the earth on which they dwelt ; no longer were they ' miserable sinners ', but craftsmen able to create, and to find joy in the labours of their hands. The views of the middle ages may have been wrong and inadequate ; this reaction certainly went too far in a material direction.

The change of point of view was not slow to make itself *Secularisa-* felt in practical life. The energy and zeal which in earlier *tion of life* centuries had flowed along religious channels, were now diverted into secular ; and the wealth once lavished on the religious orders, save where here and there the pious founded chantries, now went to the endowment of schools and colleges. With the spread of education laymen began increasingly to compete with clerics for all manner of administrative posts ; soon they were to exclude them almost entirely.

Not only so, but the new art of printing furnished the man *Printing* who could read with the materials for applying his own judge- *and private* ment to matters upon which he had grown accustomed to *judgement* take the unquestioned word of his priest. There can be no doubt that the invention made an incalculable difference to the Church's ability to suppress inconvenient opinions. So long as such depended for their circulation upon the work of copyists their multiplication might be checked ; with the introduction of the printing press this was no longer possible, except where the Papacy had complete control. The Fifth Lateran Council made a futile attempt to regulate and bridle the printer, and as late as the end of the sixteenth century St Francis de Sales denounced the presses of Geneva ; [71] but it soon became evident that for good or for ill the printed book must circulate.[72]

[71] See Mark Pattison *Isaac Casaubon* p. 191.
[72] Equally important with printing was the introduction of the manufacture of paper.

Decay of authority

But the growth of private judgement, quite apart from any encouragement which it may have received from the printer, was a characteristic of the age. Everywhere the claims of mere authority were being rejected,[73] and the demand that all things should be tested by reason and experience, was finding utterance, not least among scholars. The older teachers were regarded no longer as tutors, but tyrants; and " even Aristotle, who had been for three centuries more than a prophet, was hurled from his throne ".[74]

Fashion and superstition

Yet for all their boasted freedom and independence men were very much at the mercy of fashion—as in their Latin style—or of superstition—as in their religious practice. The age might pride itself on turning its back on the childish things of the middle ages; but it still retained gross and foolish beliefs such as astrology, alchemy, and the use of mascots and talismans.[75] Even a scholar such as Ficino believed that he received supernatural communications and that man's life was governed by the stars. Savonarola dared to proclaim openly that the Church itself was ruled by astrology, and that every prelate and dignitary had his pet practitioner to assure him of the favourable moment for putting his plans into operation.[76]

Papacy tried to control Renaissance

When the Renaissance spirit first became discernible the attitude of the Papacy towards it was one of encouragement. During the stay of Martin V and Eugenius IV at Florence the bond was drawn even closer. But with the accession of Nicholas V the Renaissance may be said to have ascended the throne of St Peter. Nicholas had much shrewdness, and his aim was nothing less than to gain control of the whole movement, and to make Rome and the Papacy the centre of a great revival of art and learning as well as of

[73] Petrarch already shews signs of independence : " Nam apud Horatium Flaccum, nullius jurare in verba magistri " ; *Epist. Fam.* IV. 10.

[74] Bryce *Holy Roman Empire* p. 359. Gemisthos Plethon strongly attacked Aristotle as being unspiritual and in sad contrast to his own master, the divine Plato.

[75] See Burckhardt *Cultur der Renaissance* pp. 410 sqq. and Burdach *Vom Mittelalter zur Reformation* II. pt. i. pp. 564 sqq.

[76] See his sermon *Utquid Deus repulisti* preached in Advent 1493 (quoted by Horsburgh *Savonarola* p. 103). Schnitzer has also pointed out the extent to which belief in fate, astrology and fortune-telling prevailed in Italy at the end of the fifteenth century (*Savonarola* p. 57).

religion.[77]　He spent vast sums in ambitious building schemes and on MSS ; but his successor, Calixtus III, was not sympathetic, as his one thought was war against the Turk.　In Pius II another humanist became Pope, but even he felt that the recovery of St Sophia was more important than the re-building of St Peter's.　Already the Papacy was beginning to suspect the movement, and the next Pope, Paul II, condemned it as pagan and immoral.[78]　But by this time it had become so strong that it could no longer be controlled, and the Papacy instead of checking it was swept along in its flood.

One strong soul there was, however, who made a deter- *Savonarola* mined stand against the all-prevailing tendency, the Dominican *and art* prior of San Marco, Florence.　Savonarola must not be set aside as " the grave-digger of art " ; he had reason behind him in his condemnation and was swayed by no merely puritan prejudices.　In spite of his later opposition to what he regarded as the excessive paganism of the Renaissance, it is typical of the era that his call came to him, not in the words of the Gospel, but in Virgil's *Heu fuge crudelas terras.*

Savonarola had no objection to art in itself, but to what he considered the debasement of sacred subjects ; to the depicting of saints, for example, in the fashionable clothes of contemporary society, and indeed in the guise of wantons. Perhaps the worst example of this practice,[79] was the representation of Julia Farnese, one of Alexander VI's mistresses, as the Blessed Virgin.　The Pope is also portrayed gazing at her with adoration.[80]

Among those who acknowledged themselves as followers of Savonarola were not a few artists.　Botticelli, Lorenzo di Credi, Fra Bartolommeo, and the robust Michael Angelo were of the number.　This is a testimony to his attitude ; but more striking was his practice of encouraging monks, who had no special aptitude for study or preaching, to devote themselves to art.

[77] Boniface VIII seems to have had a similar ambition : see above p. 273.

[78] As early as 1455 when he was only cardinal, he had accepted the dedication of an attack on the classical poets by Ermola Barbero, Bishop of Verona : see Cod. Vat. Reg. 313 fo. 167.

[79] The Greeks had set the example in classical times, for the model used by Praxiteles for his Venus of Cnidus and by Apelles for his Aphrodite Anadyomene was the famous courtesan Phryne.

[80] The painting was by Pinturicchio and formed part of the decoration of the Borgia apartments in the Vatican.

Behind all the feverish gaiety of the fifteenth century there was, as we have seen, a self-questioning as to the meaning of life and a tacit admission that the soul was not satisfied nor calmed. To such a need and longing Savonarola made his appeal, both as a preacher of righteousness and as a denouncer of corrupt art.

The age of Leo X The protest of Savonarola, however, was unavailing beyond the circle of his followers, and the movement went on. Its point of highest influence in the Church was during the pontificate of Leo X, the son of Lorenzo. This Pope was not ashamed to confess that classical studies were second only to the knowledge of God Himself. As patrons the Popes were exceedingly useful since their resources were so much more ample than those of other Italian despots ; for one thing, through their legates, they were in touch with all the nations of Europe. Some scholars have indeed seen in their patronage the greatest work of the Papacy in this epoch.[81] Others regard it as a degradation of their high office, and Ruskin speaks of Raphael, the Prince of the artists whom they employed, as ministering " with applause, to the impious luxury of the Vatican ".[82]

The Renaissance Popes After all, these Popes were at best a kind of hybrid, but half servants of the God whom they professed to serve, and half patrons of a culture that was largely pagan and often openly immoral in tendency ; and half-breeds have a habit of reproducing the bad qualities of both parent stocks. This was so generally recognised that humanists had no qualms in offering to the Popes works in which the moral basis of Christianity was ignored or even attacked. Eugenius IV might make excommunication the penalty of reading the obscene *Hermaphrodite* of Antonio Beccadelli ; but the condemnation could hardly be taken seriously when his own secretaries were commending it on every hand ; whilst Nicholas V spent more than a week in reading the *Satires* of Filelfo, and excused their obscenities because of the style. Such blindness and levity were surely unpardonable.[83]

[81] So Professor Kraus who says that " the eminence of the Papacy consisted at that time in its leadership of Europe in the province of art " (*Camb. Mod. Hist.* II. p. 8).
[82] *Modern Painters* III. p. 59.
[83] For a severe condemnation see Guiraud *op. cit.* p. xiv.

How different would things have been if the Papacy had been pure, and strong enough really to control the movement. What might have been For there was room within it for all the delights of culture, as well as a place for real beauty ; beauty such as Savonarola perceived in his serener moments, when he allowed the quiet influence of Fra Angelico, as it radiated from the walls of San Marco, to enter into his soul. For the Church, like the Roman Empire before it, was not only a State, but also a culture. Both had shewn on occasion an amazing facility in absorbing other cultures ; but for both a day came when vitality seemed to have gone and creative activity to have ceased—and so cultures remained unabsorbed, and even threatened themselves to absorb. So it was at this epoch. The spirit of man was demanding new institutions in which to find a dwelling-place, for the old were falling out of repair and ceasing any longer to be habitable.

The Renaissance created an atmosphere, not bracing but enervating, and in it that which was worst in the Church as Enervating atmosphere well as outside it most flourished ; whilst the virtues weakened and decayed. Abuses abounded and increased ; the very worship itself became materialistic, for the religious atmosphere itself had become saturated with this alien influence. It was lamentable that this enervation should have spread through the Church just at the moment when all its strength was needed to cope with the Teutonic Revolt.

CHAPTER X

THE POPES AS ITALIAN PRINCES

The rise of
despots

THE fifteenth century, in almost every country in Europe, saw the rise of strong ruling houses; either by the development of already existing dynasties, or by some despot seizing power amidst the ruin of the State. We may find ready instances in Louis XI of France, the Tudors in England, and Ferdinand and Isabella in Spain. In the cities of Italy despotic families, such as the Medici in Florence, the Sforza in Milan, and the Baglioni in Perugia, were emerging. So too the Papacy from the days of Martin V began to assume the appearance of a despotic Italian princedom.

Unrest in
Italy

The rise of despots was a natural sequel in Italy to the chaos brought about by continual conflicts. It was a sword which kept man out of Eden, and by the sword the fairest land in Europe had been turned to desolation. Throughout the middle ages its flame was never quenched, and men looking on their devastated fields and ruined vines almost forbore again to plant or sow. Even the rare interludes between open warfare were filled by private feuds and, as Tacitus would have said, peace itself became savagery.[1] The foreign invader, who was soon to come, would do less hurt; for a great war is not so harmful to a country as innumerable petty feuds carried on in confusing and meaningless succession. As they contributed to the achievement of no considered or comprehensive policy their beginnings and endings were purely fortuitous. Opportunity gave them birth and satiety laid them to rest.

Decay of
communes

By the dawn of the century most of the communes of Italy had been exhausted, and despotism seemed the only way

[1] *Hist.* I. ii. cf. I. i.

to restored stability.[2]   Thus the tyrant came to stand not
only for leadership against foes without, but also for internal
peace.   But since his rule was based on no secure foundation
he had to suppress opposition with relentless cruelty ; and,
by shows and pageants, and by the patronage of artists and
builders, who might glorify his reign, to earn the goodwill
of his subjects.   In this last respect the Popes were behind no
other Italian princes.

The state of Italy at this epoch reveals many parallels Comparison
to that of the Near East in the third and second centuries with Near
B.C., when Rome had not yet decisively intervened.   With third and
Attalus of Pergamon, a citizen who obtained royal power second
without changing his habits, may be compared Cosimo dei centuries B.C.
Medici.   Probably no despot of quite so black a hue as Philip
of Macedon could be found in Italy, though on a smaller
scale Cesare Borgia might run him close.   Affairs in Italy
were certainly on a smaller scale, and there was an absence
of vast pirate fleets and systems of wholesale robbery such as
those practised by the Aetolians.   A slightly later time yields
in Mithradates another giant figure in whom an Italian despot
might have honoured a master, and like him could have
regarded " the experimental study of poisons and antidotes
as an important branch of the business of government ".[3]

From the general prevalence of revolt and civic strife Situation in
Rome was no freer than other Italian cities, and like them it Rome
also suffered from frequent famines and disorders.[4]   It differed, however, in still enduring an ecclesiastical lord and
perhaps also by the greater depth of its iniquity.   Petrarch,
in a well-known phrase, had described Avignon as a sink ;
Lorenzo dei Medici, when writing to his son Piero, uses the
same figure of Rome.   Even the final acceptance of papal
rule—Eugenius IV was the last Pope to be compelled to fly
from the city until the days of Napoleon—did not improve
its moral condition.[5]

[2] The free city state has never had a long endurance in the world of politics,
and tyranny is often the only barrier against chaos.   So men, even enlightened
statesmen such as Seneca, had clung to the Empire of Nero, in spite of its
colossal crimes and deep corruption.   Cf. also St Paul's attitude in 2 Thes.
ii. 8.   [3] Mommsen *History of Rome* III. p. 261.
    [4] See Guiraud *L'état pontifical après le grand schisme*.
    [5] One is reminded of Hort's ironical description of the state of things when
" righteousness became reduced to an optional luxury of private life for
peculiar temperaments " : *The Way, the Truth, the Life* p. 42.

The Popes as rulers   The Papacy, like every other despotic form of government, was greatly dependent on the capacity of the individual holders of the office, and often enough it found them wanting. In general they were advanced in years when elected, and without appropriate experience for ruling a temporal State.[6] There was also a lack of continuity in their work, not indeed in policy, but in personnel. Nepotism was supposed to be justified, because it was a means of strengthening the political power of the Popes ;[7] but it could only be effective during a single pontificate, since one of the first acts of a Pope was to dismiss the " nephews " of his predecessor. In this he was a ruthless, if not as bloodthirsty, as an oriental Sultan towards potential rivals. The change of personnel, however, was not accompanied by a change in the broad policy of the Papacy ; in this there was during the middle years of the fifteenth century real continuity ; for whatever other objects the several Popes might pursue—Nicholas V, the revival of culture ; Calixtus III or Pius II, the idea of a crusade— or whatever meanness of character they might exhibit ; all had one great ambition, the complete recovery of the authority lost during the Captivity and the Schism.[8]

Development of the temporal power   With the origins of the temporal power of the Papacy, the real basis upon which the Italian principate rested, I have already dealt. Innocent III was its founder,[9] although he had no anticipation of the abuses to which his policy was to lead ; but his activities were but a dim foreshadowing of the power and the methods of his successors. Further developments took place in the thirteenth century during the struggle with Frederick II, and later again there is an interesting anticipation of the princes of the fifteenth century in the reign
1277-1280   of Nicholas III. Even upon the throne of St Peter this Pope, who was a member of the noble house of Orsini, was still a great Roman prince and cared for the States of the

---

[6] " The states of the Church," wrote Lorenzo to the Ferrarese ambassador, " have always been the ruin of Italy, for their rulers are ignorant of the art of government, and so bring danger on every side." Quoted by Horsburgh, *Lorenzo the Magnificent* p. 332.

[7] The opinion was expressed at the Council of Basle that it was no bad thing for a Pope to have sons to defend him : see Ranke *Die röm. Päpste* I. p. 30.

[8] See Guiraud *L'état pontifical etc.* p. 2.

[9] See the chapter on " The Italian Prince " in my *Innocent III* pp. 15 sqq.

Church as if they had been an inherited patrimony. He further resembled the later Popes by the favours which he shewed to his relations.

The Popes of the Avignon period had but little opportunity for playing the part of Italian princes ; yet most of them were careful to maintain, so far as they could, the temporal rights of the Papacy in Italy, whilst Urban V and Gregory XI recognised that the preservation of such rights involved ultimately a return to Rome. During the schism, in spite of obvious difficulties, some progress was made, but even Boniface IX, the best of the Popes of this period, was compelled to acquiesce in the seizure of power by various tyrants in the Papal States. His recognition of Ladislas of Naples led to the consolidation of papal power in Rome itself.

With the return of Martin V to Rome the period of the Italian Princes really begins. This Pope, having turned the edge of the Conciliar Movement, found himself faced, when he decided to return to Rome and Italy, with the problem of restoring order to a turbulent city and consolidating the Papal States. This same double problem had also been faced by Innocent III, and like that Pope he found that his family connexions,—he was, it will be remembered, a Colonna, —stood him in good stead. Before his death much had been done, and the policy of the Papacy directed along lines which it was to follow until the end of the era. These lines were narrow, in so far as they regarded only the immediate problem of safeguarding the material basis of the Papacy, often at the cost of its spiritual power. By following them the Popes soon made up for the losses sustained during the years of absence and uncertainty. Over the Church, at any rate, their power seemed stronger than ever, and more and more they realised the natural tendency of the Papacy towards a despotism. Figgis indeed considers that it gave the example to the national monarchs, for Eugenius IV triumphed before Louis XI, or Edward IV, or Ferdinand of Aragon.[10]

This Pope was the immediate successor of Martin V, and as a Venetian he sacrificed much to serve his native city. We have seen already the humiliations which his policy brought upon him from the Council of Basle. As a ruler

Martin V and his work

Eugenius IV

[10] In *Camb. Mod. Hist.* III. p. 738.

he was unpractical, a typical instance of those who do not realise the necessity of cutting their coat according to the material available.[11]

Cardinal Vitelleschi
Eugenius, at the beginning of his reign, owed much to the energy and ability of Giovanni Vitelleschi, another *condottiere* under the purple robes of a cardinal. With the possible exception of Albornoz, Vitelleschi was the most successful of them all, and while the Pope lay in safety at Florence his triumphs gained him the admiration of the Romans who dubbed him the third founder of their city.[12] But the Florentines were hostile, and his speedy rise awakened jealousy both at Rome and amongst those who surrounded Eugenius. At last he was lured by treachery within the gates of St Angelo and thrust, not without wounds, into a dungeon. To such an outrage there could be but one end, for he was far too powerful to be released, and soon it was officially announced that he had died of his wounds. Popular rumour attributed his death to posion. Eugenius made no attempt to punish those guilty of the outrage and may well have been privy to the plot against one who had been his favourite.

Eugenius and Sforza
The rising power of Sforza now drew forth the fears of the Pope.[13] In order to check him he abandoned the cause of the Angevin claimant to the crown of Naples, and went over to Alfonso V of Aragon, who was at last successfully asserting the claims of his house to that kingdom.[14] Several times Sforza seemed on the verge of catastrophe, but each time he was rescued by Filippo Maria Visconti, whose natural daughter he had married. The Duke was not sorry to see his powerful son-in-law humbled; but he could not suffer the loss of so useful a general. In the end Sforza decided to try for a bigger prize than a petty principality in the March of Ancona, and followed the star which was at last to lead him to the throne of Milan itself.

In March 1443 Eugenius left Florence, and reached Rome in the following September. There he received the embassy from Frederick III which enabled Aeneas Sylviʋ to ingratiate

---

[11] See *Vita Eugen. IV.* in RIS. III. pt. ii. col. 890 DE.

[12] Romulus and Camillus were the earlier founders. The same title had been given to Marius.

[13] See his Bull in Raynaldus 1443 No. 11.

[14] For the complicated events in Naples at this epoch see Waugh *History of Europe 1378-1494* pp. 456 sq.

himself with the Pope, and to earn forgiveness for his short-sighted support of the Council of Basle. Before his death in February 1447 Eugenius had the satisfaction of receiving the obedience of the Empire.

A Pope of a very different type now filled the vacant seat. Nicholas V was a scholar first and foremost, and his election seems to have been almost accidental. It was followed a few months later by the death of Filippo Maria which left Milan a prize to be scrambled for. After waiting his time Sforza duly secured it. He had the support of Cosimo dei Medici, who abandoned the traditional policy of Florence in order to assist a fellow usurper. The next event of importance was the visit of Frederick III with his young bride, Leonora of Portugal. They were crowned by the Pope on March 19, 1452 ; the last occasion upon which Rome was to see such a ceremony.[15] It may be said of the visit of the Emperor that it had about as little effect as that of the average tourist, and like the average tourist he bought many trinkets in Venice. These were among the most important fruits of his expedition. *[margin: Nicholas V] [margin: Aug. 1447] [margin: Visit of Frederick III]*

The close of Nicholas's pontificate was disturbed by the conspiracy of Stephen Porcaro, a dreamer and man of letters ; who had, however, shewn unexpected practical ability in a number of official posts. None the less he was quite unfitted to be the leader of so serious an enterprise as the restoration of the ancient glories and liberties of the Roman Republic ; for such was his ambition. Actually he came of a middle-class family ; but conspirators seem never satisfied with the social standing with which nature has provided them, and so he announced that he was descended from the Scipios. The conspiracy came to a head in January 1453 but was quite abortive. It had been badly planned and was equally badly executed. By this time the papal yoke was too firmly fixed on the necks of the Romans to be disturbed by a handful of agitators. None the less Nicholas, who seems to have forgotten the dignity of the Pope in the nervousness of the scholar, became unduly alarmed. The fall of Constantinople *[margin: The Porcaro conspiracy]*

---

[15] Aeneas Sylvius, who took a prominent part in the proceedings, has left a vivid account of all that took place. The last Emperor actually to receive his crown from a Pope was Charles V, who on Feb. 24, 1530, was crowned by Clement VII at Bologna.

March 1455 a few months later was a further blow, and not long afterwards he departed from a world which had grown inconsiderately difficult to manage.

The most important feature of the pontificate of Nicholas, his great scheme for making Rome the cultural centre of the West, has already been considered; in this he was a man of his age, and he might well have anticipated Lacordaire's cry: " I shall be understood by this century, for I have loved everything relating to it ".

Calixtus III
April 1455 to
August 1458
The policy of Nicholas was abandoned by his successor, Calixtus III; who in his brief reign cared for two things only: the driving back of the Turks, and the advancement of his kindred. In order to provide a possible throne for a nephew he refused to recognise Ferrante, the bastard son of Alfonso of Naples; [16] a decision which was reversed by the next Pope, Pius II, the famous Aeneas Sylvius Piccolomini. His support of Ferrante helped to keep the French out of Italy for another generation. During that respite " the fairest flowers of the Renaissance were brought to perfection ".[17] Another consequence, not so happy, was the alienation of Louis XI, who on his accession had abolished the Pragmatic Sanction. In the end he would revive many of its provisions, but in such a way as to injure the Pope and benefit the king.

Pius II and
the crusade
If Pius reversed his predecessor's policy towards Naples and France, his interest in the crusades was just as strong. No sooner was he elected than he summoned a conference of European powers to meet at Mantua to discuss the necessary plans. The response was slow, and not representative. Europe was no longer able to act as a unit, and though Pius might dazzle the assembly by his eloquence, no practical results were to follow. At the end of his life a vague prospect of an expedition against the Turk in conjunction with Venice dragged him, in much suffering, to Ancona. There on August 14, 1464 he died.

Paul II
The conclave which met after the death of Pius II, chose as his successor Cardinal Barbo, a Venetian, noted for his handsome appearance. After vainly suggesting the names of

---

[16] That a king or noble should expect his bastard to be acknowledged as his successor was natural in a century which Gregorovius has described as " das goldene Zeitalter der Bastarde ": *Geschichte der Stadt Rom* II. p. 652.

[17] C. M. Ady *Pius II* p. 191.

Formosus and Mark, he took eventually the title Paul II. The new Pope, like many Venetians, was a lover of pomp and ceremony ; at the same time, although his first act had been to denounce the capitulation which as a cardinal he had signed, he seems to have had a genuine desire for reform.   He achieved little in this direction beyond making the religious orders conform more strictly to their rules.   Perhaps his greatest service was the example which he set of a scrupulous use of his powers as Pope.   He was careful to avoid simony and other questionable means of raising money ; he was careful, too, in his appointments, making no favourites and liking to have about him men of high character and attainments.

Before his death Pius II had decided to take strong measures with George Podiebrad, King of Bohemia, whose craft and deceit were notorious.   Paul now proceeded to depose the king and to release his subjects from their allegiance. In reply Podiebrad demanded a General Council, and strove to form an alliance with Louis XI against the Pope.   In Bohemia the papal censures were almost disregarded, save by a group of Catholic nobles who were already on bad terms with the king ; but in 1468 his own son-in-law, Matthias Corvinus, King of Hungary, at the instance of the Pope and Frederick III, who also had grievances against George, made a vain endeavour to expel him from the kingdom.   This strife between Bohemia and Hungary, barriers both of them against the advancing Turk, was exceedingly regrettable, and the Pope must take some responsibility for it. *Dealings with Bohemia Dec. 23, 1466,*

Towards the Romans, who had just undergone a series of disastrous floods and tempests,[18] Paul shewed much consideration.   His reign, however, was not without its troubles, for a conspiracy was hatched among the disgruntled humanists who formed the Roman Academy.   Plans similar to those of Porcaro, culminating in the murder of Paul himself, were attributed to them ; but it is doubtful whether the whole thing was not the invention of the Pope's own fears, working on the drunken threats of men who felt that they had a grievance against him, since in his reforming zeal he had deprived some of them of their offices.[19] *with Rome,*

[18] Infessura *Diario* RIS. III. pt. ii. col. 1141 B.
[19] Cf. the report of Aug. de Rubeis to the Duke of Milan printed from the State Archives in Pastor *History of the Popes* IV. pp. 492 sq.

19

and with the rest of Italy In Italy, outside Rome, Paul tried to avoid warfare at every cost, and to stand apart from leagues and alliances. His aim was to make the Pope a kind of universal arbitrator. The times certainly called for such an office, for the deaths of Cosimo dei Medici and Francesco Sforza within a few years had left power in the hands of inexperienced rulers, and fresh groupings and fresh misunderstandings were bound to arise. The treacherous seizure of Rimini by Roberto Malatesta, however, forced the Pope from his attitude; but his efforts against Malatesta, who had the backing of Naples and Florence, were unsuccessful. The Pope also had trouble with his native Venice whose policy was definitely anti-clerical, if not anti-papal. The republic even contemplated an alliance with the Turk and an attack on Rome.[20] Paul did his best to preserve peace,

July 26, 1471 and to promote understanding, but when he died diplomatic relations were in a state of suspense. This was the more

July 12, 1470 unfortunate as the Turks, who had captured Negroponte, were threatening Italy itself. But men said that Venice had an understanding with the Sultan, and cared more for preserving its commerce than for anything else.

Sixtus IV If the era of the Popes as Italian princes begins with Martin V, the first who shewed what could really be made of the situation was Sixtus IV.[21] This Pope had been a reformer before his elevation; but once in possession of power he used it to the full, and in his feverish desire to increase the temporal power of the Papacy, or more correctly to advance that of his nephews, he seemed blind to all moral considerations. It was said of him that he was " the pilot of the Church's bark who steered it to the island of Circe ".[22]

His nephews Of the nephews whom he favoured, Giovanni della Rovere married the daughter of Federigo da Montefeltro, Duke of Urbino, and founded a dynasty; whilst Girolamo Riario married Caterina Sforza and was murdered in an outbreak at Forli in 1488. Two others became cardinals; Piero Riario, whose brief and evil life shocked even that lawless age, and

---

[20] See *Mon. Hung.* II. p. 14.

[21] " This pontiff," wrote Machiavelli, " was the first who revealed the full extent of the papal power, and demonstrated that many things which hitherto had been regarded as misdeeds, might be hidden under its authority " : *Hist. Flor.* VII.

[22] Quoted by Creighton *History of the Papacy* IV. p. 92.

Giuliano della Rovere, the future Julius II. During the lifetime of Sixtus the nobles and people of Rome had to endure much from their excesses; but on the death of the Pope there was a rising, led by the Colonna who had suffered more than the rest; their palaces were sacked and they themselves driven from the city.

If Sixtus was successful in his dealings with the local nobles, the same could not be said of his relations with the other powers of Italy. In the plots and counter-plots against Ferrara Venice gained more profit than the Pope, in spite of excommunication. It was, however, against Florence that his chief activities were displayed. *Sixtus and Florence*

On his accession Lorenzo himself had been the envoy who had borne the congratulations of the republic. He shewed his Medici blood by combining business and politics, and returned with the confirmation of the banking privileges of his house, and, in addition, the office of receiver of the papal revenues. But the good feelings thus manifested were not to continue. In 1474 Lorenzo abandoned the policy of Cosimo, which had seen in Venice the chief enemy of Florence, and joined it in an alliance with Milan. This drew Naples and the Pope together as they seemed to be threatened. The Pope had other causes for grievance against the Medici, for they were thwarting his plans for the advancement of his nephews. He shewed his resentment by displacing them in the office of papal receivers by the rival family of the Pazzi. Another dispute arose in 1474 over the appointment of Salviati to be Archbishop of Pisa, in defiance of the express wishes of Lorenzo.

Four years later came the famous Pazzi conspiracy which aimed at the murder of Lorenzo and his brother Giuliano in the Duomo at Florence. The plot was only partly successful, as Lorenzo escaped, and the attempt at a revolution failed miserably. The conspirators were seized and put to death. The Archbishop of Pisa, who was among them, was lynched by the mob, as well as the priests who were actually to have carried out the murder. Sixtus, infuriated by the breakdown of his plans (it is not certain that he knew that the murder of the Medici was part of the plot) and at the lynching of the archbishop, commanded the Florentines to expel Lorenzo. On their failure to do so, he declared war in conjunction with *The Pazzi conspiracy April 26, 1478*

Ferrante of Naples.[23]   Florence had the support of her allies,
Milan and Venice.

Desperate position of Florence

But these allies were not very effective, for Milan was
still in a state of unrest following the assassination of Galeazzo
Maria Sforza in 1476, while Venice was occupied by a Turkish
attack on Scutari.   The position of Florence soon became
desperate, and Lorenzo determined to put his fortunes to the
test, and either to save the city, or by his death or imprisonment, to remove the cause of papal hatred.   He suddenly
fled to Naples and threw himself on the mercies of Ferrante.
This dramatic act completely justified itself, and he succeeded,
not merely in gaining the mercy of the Neapolitan sovereign,
but his favour in addition.   How far this was the result of
the threat of the Turks, who in 1480 had landed at Otranto,[24]
and how far it was due to the personal qualities of Lorenzo
it is impossible to say ; but Florence was saved, and so was
Lorenzo.

Innocent VIII

Sixtus was followed by Innocent VIII.   If the former had
been a pioneer in demonstrating the use which could be made
of the temporal power, and, incidentally, the extent to which
nepotism could become a political principle ; Innocent, in his
way, was also a pioneer ; he was the first Pope openly to acknowledge his children.   His chief characteristics were indeed
those of an amiable father of a family ; for he was no statesman,
and did nothing to further the interests of the Papacy in Italy.
He did, however, set a good example by respecting the rights
of others, and in providing for his son, Franceschetto, actually
paid for a principality.   It was the marriage of this son with
a daughter of Lorenzo that led to the bestowal of a cardinal's
hat upon her brother Giovanni, then only fourteen years of
age.[25]

and Naples

The rebellion of the Neapolitan nobles gave Innocent an

---

[23] There is a parallel to the action of Sixtus in that of Urban V, who,
in September 1368, placed Perugia under an interdict because it had thwarted
a conspiracy to massacre the Raspanti and to seize the city.   In this case,
also, the conspirators had been put to death.

[24] For the panic in Italy over the presence of the Turks see Vesp. Bisticci
Lamento per la presa d'Otranto in Arch. Stor. Ital. IV. p. 457.

[25] This was the future Leo X.   His youth recalls the case of Benedict IX
who became Pope in 1033 at an age still younger.   Rodulfus Glaber *Hist. sui
temporis* IV. v. 17 says that he was " puer ferme decennis ".   R. Lane Poole,
however, thinks that there may be an error in this : see " Benedict IX and
Gregory VI " in *Proceedings of the Brit. Academy* VIII. p. 217.

opportunity of trying to regain the customary tribute. His claim was allowed as an act of grace, for the rebellion was crushed. The cruelty and treachery shewn by the King of Naples was so great, however, that it created a permanent source of disaffection, which facilitated, if it did not originate, the attempt of Charles VIII to seize the kingdom.

The Pope died in 1492, and in the same year Lorenzo also Death of passed from the earthly scene. This last was a tragic loss, Lorenzo dei Medici and had he lived the whole history of the West might have been changed ; Lorenzo was the only person capable of keeping out the French and controlling the Borgias, who in the person of Alexander VI now mounted the papal throne.

The election of Alexander was due to shameless and open Alexander bribery. The cardinals might be shut up in conclave away VI from outside influence ; but the stream of gold managed to get to them, just as it penetrated the tower of Danae in the Greek legend. If, however, Alexander gained the Papacy by unlawful means, and if his morals were scandalous, he served it well in other ways. It cannot be denied that he had statesmanlike instincts, or that he was tolerant in face of personal attacks—his treatment of Savonarola, as we shall see, was marked by very great restraint and consideration. Furthermore he was entirely orthodox and careful to maintain the services of the Church. Alexander was no John XII in his attitude to the faith, although he might imitate his morals ; if he gave a dinner to the prostitutes of Rome, one cannot imagine his drinking to the old heathen gods as John had done. I think that sufficient importance has not always been attached to the orthodoxy of the Renaissance Popes, at least in outward profession, whatever private views they may have held. The glaring contrast of their morals has obscured it. But so long as the faith was preserved in its purity there was always the possibility that once more it might become operative. Had Christian faith followed Christian morals then the chance of recovery might well have gone for ever.

The Pope was accepted as the successor of St Peter, the His vicegerent of Christ ; one who ought to have been exalted character above the consciousness of desire or regret on personal grounds. This office was now held by Roderigo Borgia. To us the contrast is so startling as to be ludicrous ; but to the men

of the late fifteenth century the disparity, though it may
have been recognised, was not nearly so striking ; for they
too desired to be religious without being moral—and the
Pope exactly suited their ideas.   The practical effect, therefore, was very slight, and served to confirm prejudice where it
already existed, as among the followers of Savonarola, rather
than to originate it.   Certainly the sacrifice of that prophet
was no testimony to the corruption of the Roman Church
as Villari seems to think.[26]

The career of Savonarola   I cannot avoid the feeling that Savonarola has received
much more notice than his career and influence really justify.
This is probably due to the notion, once current, that he was
a forerunner of the Reformation.   Such a notion is erroneous ;
for while it is perfectly true that he defied Alexander VI,
it was the individual, and not the institution against which
he made his stand.   Savonarola was absolutely loyal to the
Church and its teaching ; he merely withstood a papal condemnation which he felt to be unjust, and based on imperfect
information.

Savonarola has also been unduly isolated from his times,
and made to appear far more original than actually he was.
In his methods he was by no means unique.[27]   The early
thirteenth century had had in St Antony of Padua a preacher
who denounced the Church just as strenuously for its abuses,
its luxury, its immorality.[28]   A similar line of attack had been
taken by the Dominican preacher, Venturino of Bergamo, in
the next century.[29]   Later there came famous preachers such
as the Franciscan, Fra Ricardo and the Dominican, St Vincent
Ferrer.   In the fifteenth century itself there were many
preachers who boldly held up the Christian standard of living
in an age which might recognise it, although it did not observe it.   A generation before there had flourished perhaps
the best known of them all, Fra Bernardino of Siena ; [30]

[26] *Life and Times of Savonarola* p. 771.
[27] Joan of Arc has been similarly isolated and misunderstood ; cf. Anatole
France *On Life and Letters* III. pp. 246 sq.
[28] He even ventured to maintain that religion had deserted the clergy
—" clerici sunt infructuosi et laici fructuosi ".
[29] See Giuseppe Clementi *Un Savonarola del secolo XIV* and *Il Beato
Venturino da Bergamo*.
[30] There is an excellent study of this saint by A. G. Ferrers Howell.

whilst another Fra Bernardino, this one from Montefeltro, was a contemporary. These names could be supplemented by those of many other mission preachers.[31]

If the career of Savonarola was not so significant as some would have us believe, none the less it is worthy of consideration ; not only on account of the personality of the man himself, but also because he was the centre round which played the chief movements and influences of his time. Moreover there are minor lessons to be learned from his career, such as the almost unique position of the priesthood as a way of advancement. The only rival of the Churchman was the *condottiere*. In the court of a despot some low-born favourite might suddenly be exalted, but in a commune this was well-nigh impossible for a ' foreigner ' ; yet Savonarola, the Dominican from Ferrara, became the virtual ruler of Florence.

It was in 1491 when a course of his sermons in the Duomo In Florence turned the city upside down, that Savonarola first became prominent. He was then nearly forty years of age. He had become a friar because, like the hermits of old, he despaired of the world and desired to save his soul. In spite of his affection for St Francis he finally became a Dominican.[32] His appearance as Lent preacher in Florence in 1483 was a failure ; he was too earnest and too provincial in style for the literary Florentines ; [33] but a renewed study of the Hebrew prophets and a successful mission in Lombardy restored his confidence.

That Savonarola should have turned to the Old Testament His ideas prophets is natural and revealing, for his own message was the same as theirs—the Church and the nation were alike corrupt, God was preparing a scourge for His rebellious people, repentance would follow and the conversion of the heathen.

[31] For mission preachers in Germany see Pastor *History of the Popes* II p. 129.

[32] The deciding factor was St Thomas Aquinas : see Schnitzer. *Savonarola* p. 23. This shews that Savonarola was no merely emotional preacher, but a philosopher as well.

[33] Letters recently discovered by the Marchese Ridolfi shew that on his arrival from Ferrara Savonarola's style was disfigured by quaint provincialisms : see his *Lettere di G. Savonarola etc.* It seems to me that these provincialisms may have also come out in his sermons. The Romans had also criticised the bad Latin of Venturino da Bergamo, and in earlier times Epictetus had evidently been despised for his poor Greek : *Moral Discourses* III. ix. 1.

Savonarola did not spare even the Medici; but Lorenzo refused to be provoked, and merely advised him not to stir up bad feeling. On his death-bed he seems to have desired to be on friendly terms with the intransigent Prior, and after he had made his confession and received the last sacrament, he sent for Savonarola.[34]

The French in Italy

Two years later died Ferrante of Naples; the same year the French invaded Italy. With their advent began a period of three centuries during which the unhappy land " became in turn the battlefield, the spoil and the plaything of the stranger ".[35] Their coming was largely due to Ludovico of Milan, though the intrigues of the Venetians and the presence of Cardinal della Rovere at the French court no doubt were contributory causes. Ludovico feared Naples and France alike, and wished to set them by the ears. He therefore bribed the advisers of Charles VIII to urge him to press his claims to the throne of Naples.[36] The king, who was full of wild dreams of conquest, readily responded to the suggestion. He desired to be another Louis IX and to make the conquest of Italy a step to coronation at Constantinople and the recovery of the Holy Land.[37] Charles was weak in both mind and body, and his schemes were like the ravings of a lunatic; unfortunately this lunatic had immense power at his disposal, and so became a danger to Europe as well as disastrous to Italy.[38]

Welcomed by Savonarola

To others the French invasion was a grave threat to

[34] Strange and absurd stories concerning this interview were circulated by the Dominicans : see Creighton *op. cit.* IV. pp. 174 and 340 sqq. : also Horsburgh *Girolamo Savonarola* pp. 76 sqq.

[35] Horsburgh *op. cit.* p. 108. The evil consequences of their coming were anticipated by men of vision. Matteo Boiardo, the author of *Orlando Innamorato* heard of it just before his death with foreboding :

> " Mentre che io canto, o Dio Redentore,
> Vedo l'Italia tutta a fiamma e foco,
> Per questi Galli, che con gran valore
> Vengon, per disertar non so che loco."

[36] The evidence for this is contained in the State Archives of Milan : see Batiffol *Le siècle de la Renaissance*, p. 12.

[37] There was a poem widely current at the time in which Joan of Arc led a French king to the conquest of the Holy Land ; see Anatole France *On Life and Letters* II. p. 332.

[38] For a generation the French had been approaching the frontier of Italy through their gradual absorption of the Kingdom of Arles ; Dauphiné had been acquired in 1457 and the whole of Provence by 1486.

Italian liberty; to Savonarola it was the fulfilment of prophecy. He gave therefore to Charles the strength of his support and the prestige of a divine agent. After Piero Medici's cowardly, if not treacherous, surrender to the invaders, Florence was quickly occupied by the advancing Frenchmen.

Meanwhile the Medici had been expelled and Florence had come under the rule of Savonarola and his supporters. He aspired to make it a veritable kingdom of God with Christ Himself as king. His rule was naturally puritanical, and the carnivals of 1496 and 1497 were turned into religious festivals. At them occurred the famous Burning of Vanities in which, amid much that was evil and worthless, some priceless works of art probably perished.[39] *Savonarola as ruler of Florence*

The activities of Savonarola had already alarmed Alexander VI. So long as a moral reformation was in question, or even the Pope's personal character, he cared but little; but in the tense atmosphere of the times it was exceedingly dangerous to have wild and reckless statements, statements which claimed moreover to foretell the future, proceeding from the pulpit of the Duomo at Florence. Above all that city was being prevented from coming into line with the rest of Italy so as to oppose the invaders with an unbroken front. As Cardinal della Rovere was in favour with the French their success might lead to his own displacement from the Papacy. *Alexander takes action*

In 1495 Savonarola had been cited to Rome. He refused to obey, on the double ground of his own poor health and the need for his presence in Florence. He gave up, however, his preaching; though only for the time. In the following February at the request of the Signoria he resumed it and made bitter attacks on the Pope and Rome. But he himself was not without antagonists even in Florence; while in Rome an old enemy and rival preacher, the Augustinian, Fra Marino, was commissioned to denounce him.[40]

With such measures the Pope, for the moment, was content; but in May 1497 they were followed up by the excom-

---

[39] These burnings were not a new thing. Fifty years before, the preaching of Fra Bernardino of Siena had moved men to a hasty penitence which among other symptoms had resulted in such destruction. They seem to have been a frequent consequence of revivalistic preaching.

[40] Creighton *op. cit.* IV. p. 173, by a slip, calls him a Franciscan.

munication of Savonarola.   He respected the sentence so far
as to abstain from preaching or performing any priestly act ;
but he openly declared that it was invalid because based on
false accusations.   At length, to the consternation of some
among his own followers, he defied the ban and on Christmas
Day celebrated mass.   In the following February he resumed
his preaching.

Savonarola loses influence   But already his position in Florence was becoming precarious.   In April 1497 there had been a futile plot to restore
the Medici, and some months later five of the leading citizens,
members of the party opposed to Savonarola, were put to
death as having been privy to it.   To make things worse they
were denied the right of an appeal to the people which was
theirs under the constitution.   Moderate men were shocked
by this arbitrary conduct and Savonarola was blamed.   Thus
when the Pope launched his final blow, and threatened Florence
with an interdict and the seizure of its merchants in papal
territories, the city gave way and compelled their prophet to
become silent.

His downfall and death   Then came the Ordeal by Fire in Lent 1498.[41]   This was
the result of a Franciscan challenge to the Dominican followers
of Savonarola.   It was a skilful move for the latter had everything to lose, and nothing to gain by the test.   In spite of
a papal prohibition the two bodies of Friars met before an
expectant crowd in the piazza on April 7.   But there was
a breakdown over the conditions, and then rain came on and
made the whole thing impossible.   The disappointed mob
turned its fury on the Dominicans, and when on the following
day, Palm Sunday, Savonarola defied the Signoria and
preached, the crowd stormed his convent and he himself,
with two friars, was arrested.   Then followed a trial in which
torture and false evidence played a big part.   The prisoners
were condemned for heresy, schism, deceiving the people
and inciting them to rebellion.   A request by the Pope that
they should be handed over to him having been refused, they
May 23, 1498 were hanged and their bodies burnt.   Before his execution
Savonarola was degraded from his office by the bishop.
The latter inadvertently added separation from the Church

---

[41] The ordeal may have been suggested by the earlier case of Fra Pietro
Igneo who successfully endured it in 1068 : see Villari *History of Florence*
pp. 78 sq.

Triumphant as a consequence; to this Savonarola protested, and the bishop admitted his error.[42]

It is, as I have said, easy to exaggerate the importance of Savonarola—but he was at least a straw which shewed the set of the wind, and the flames of his funeral pyre lighted up more than the piazza at Florence. He died, so Lord Acton believed, " for his belief that the way to make men better was to make them free ",[43] and if Florence is the Athens of Italy, Savonarola is its Demosthenes. He had aroused the ancient Guelf spirit, austere and puritan, against a Pope who had deserted the cause of freedom. His destruction is symptomatic of the breach, already an old one, between the Papacy and the communes. His failure to keep the favour of the Florentines was due, as one of them, Guicciardini has observed, to man's willingness to sacrifice apparent liberty for justice. The history of Florence in the subsequent centuries is a commentary on that doctrine. But he died because he was the enemy of Italy, the barrier to its unity.[44] So within and without the city support was withdrawn and all save a few personal adherents deserted him. In 1527 Florence was to see a brief revival of his ideas, and in a form even more fanatical than that of his own day—but it was suppressed for ever by the Medici Pope and the Medici arms. Yet Savonarola is a name which adorns, and will adorn the city, for which he strove so courageously and in which he perished so nobly.

The weak rule of Innocent VIII had left Rome in a state of lawlessness; his successor quickly endeavoured to assert the claims of justice and order. To make his position within the city more secure Alexander strengthened the fortifications

(marginal notes: Significance of Savonarola; Alexander and Rome)

---

[42] Gebhart *Mystics and Heretics in Italy* pp. 268 sq. has pointed out that Dante makes Manfred utter the same protest against any attempt by the Church to anticipate the Final Judgement :

> " Per lor maledizion sì non si perde,
>   Che non posse tornar l'eterno amore,
>   Mentre che la speranza ha fior del verde."
>   —*Purgatorio* iii. 133-135.

[43] *Letters of Lord Acton to Mary Gladstone* p. 97.

[44] By a strange irony the very men who brought about his downfall were found within less than a year adopting his policy, and the Pope himself was allied with France.

of St Angelo and improved its communications with the Vatican. In ecclesiastical matters also he began to secure himself. This was done by the creation of new cardinals, among them a number of Spaniards, some of whom were his own relations. It was the beginning of the great age of Spain. On January 2, 1492 the last stronghold of the Moors had fallen, and in the following October the Genoese seaman, Christopher Columbus, sailing in Spanish ships, had discovered the New World, and it was to a Spanish Pope that application was made for the disposal of the territories thus made available.

His alliances   At first Alexander tried to preserve peace in Italy, but in April 1493 he entered into an alliance with Venice, Milan, and other cities, which seemed a threat to the rest of Italy. The aged Ferrante of Naples warned him against the danger of this policy, and though his warnings were not heeded, immediately before his death he had gained over the Papacy to an alliance against Milan. He breathed easily at the last for his dynasty now seemed secure. Peace of mind comes often from a merciful ignorance of the future and what it is to bring.

Relations with the Sultan   When Charles VIII entered Italy the Pope was so terrified that he opened negotiations with the Sultan. Bayazid II promised him 300,000 ducats for the head of his brother Djem, who had been handed over to the custody of the Papacy in the days of Innocent VIII—he suggested that the money would be useful to Alexander for buying new lands for his children ! The documents containing the details of these transactions fell into the hands of Cardinal della Rovere, and, to the scandal of Christendom, he made them public.[45] However, when the French reached Rome at the end of 1494 Alexander came to terms with them. A month later Alfonso of Naples had abandoned his throne leaving the French to take possession. So speedy a conquest alarmed the States of Italy and even Maximilian, the King of the Romans. The league which they formed was a threat to Charles' line of retreat which could not be ignored, so, leaving a small army of occupation, he began his retirement in May. Nothing but the feebleness and half-heartedness of the Italians saved him

January 28, 1495

League against the French

---

[45] The Pope denied their authenticity. For a discussion of this question see Creighton *op. cit.* IV. pp. 345 sq.

from complete disaster, and though he sustained a technical July 5, 1495
defeat at Fornovo his march was not checked.

The troops left in Naples were in a sorry plight, as they The
were insufficient to hold the conquered territories, and cut Spaniards in Naples
off from reinforcements. Their fate was soon decided, for
Ferrante II landed with Spanish troops under Gonsalvo de
Cordova, and by November 1495 the last of the French
opposition had been overcome. This gave Alexander an opportunity of attacking the Orsini and other Roman nobles
who were obnoxious to him. His efforts, however, were
not successful, and led to the strange spectacle of the two
inveterate rivals, the Orsini and the Colonna, uniting against
him.

Charles VIII died on April 1498, and was succeeded by Louis XII
Louis XII, who had claims on Milan as the representative of and Alexander
the Visconti. A desire to obtain papal dispensation for a
marriage with the widow of the late king, and for permission
to put away the wife whom he had already, made Louis
anxious to be on good terms with Alexander. The negotiations were undertaken on the Pope's behalf by his son Cesare,
who had just renounced his cardinalate, since a secular career
was now open to him through the murder of his brother,
the Duke of Gandia.[46] The divorce was duly granted and
Cesare was given the hand of a French princess. Thus the
Pope and the French were leagued together and the obvious
victim was Milan. Soon Venice also joined the alliance as she
wished to have a share of the spoil. The position of Milan
was so hopeless that Ludovico fled across the Alps and the
French entered the city in October 1499. Their coming into
North Italy gave to Cesare Borgia, who was high in favour,
the opportunity of beginning his short but amazing career.

It was the policy of Alexander to consolidate the States Cesare
of the Church by means of his own children, and by placing Borgia
power in their hands to prevent a piecemeal absorption of
papal territories.[47] It was Cesare, of course, who mainly

[46] This event filled Alexander with such remorse that for a time he contemplated really drastic reforms in the curia and Church.

[47] Whilst the Pope was away from Rome in 1501, he left his daughter
Lucrezia in charge of affairs to the no small scandal of the official world. She
was even empowered to deal with the papal letters, consulting when necessary
one of the cardinals. "It was an unheard-of thing . . . that a woman should
be seated in the Vatican as the Pope's representative" : Creighton *op. cit.*
V. p. 20.

benefited from this policy. With the aid of French troops he made, in the early months of 1500, a series of speedy conquests ; and although the sudden return of Ludovico to Milan checked him for the moment—his auxiliaries were withdrawn—he had done enough already to enjoy a triumph on his return to Rome. His triumph, which was compared by flatterers to that of his namesake, the great Julius, coincided with the year of Jubilee, and no doubt the pious pilgrims from across the Alps were duly edified by the achievements of the Pope's offspring.[48]

Death of Alexander

Ludovico's occupation of Milan was as brief as it had been unexpected, for he was betrayed into the hands of the French by his Swiss mercenaries. The disappearance from Italian politics of so prominent a figure left to Cesare the centre of the stage. A further happy omen was his friendship with Venice. These advantages were backed up by real talent for warfare and intrigue. It is not surprising therefore that by the early summer of 1501, he had made large conquests in Romagna, and that even Florence had been compelled to buy him off. But fate was against him, and his hopes of creating an Italian principality were cut short

Aug. 18, 1503

by the sudden death of the Pope and his own illness. Men said that poison was the cause, but probably without justification.[49]

Partition of South Italy

In the meantime Spain and France had made a clean job of South Italy by dividing up the kingdom of Ferrante II between them—an act of injustice which was to be the source of strenuous disagreement between the spoilers. But such a sequel is too common to deserve comment. For Italy it was a further step to enslavement beneath the foreign yoke.

Election of Pius III

The continuance of Cesare's princedom was dependent on the successor to his father. His efforts, much curbed by his illness, were spent in trying to obtain a Pope who would be favourable ; in this he had the sympathy of the seventeen Spanish cardinals. Above all Cardinal della Rovere must

---

[48] Apart from this the Jubilee of 1500 wrought immense harm to papal prestige in the North. Abuses and corruptions when actually seen or reported by eye-witnesses gain much force and the worst rumours which might have reached it were amply confirmed.

[49] The illness in each case seems to have been a clear case of fever and the recent attempt of Schnitzer *Der Tod Alexanders VI* to revive the poison theory cannot be held to have succeeded.

be kept out. Cesare actually tried to prevent his returning to Rome ; [50] but the resolute cardinal succeeded in avoiding his intercepters. He at once began to take measures for the foiling of Cesare's plans in the conclave ; but the battle was not yet to be fought out, and by the choice of Cardinal Piccolomini, who took the title of Pius III, a breathing-space was obtained. It proved to be but a short one, and the schemes which the new Pope had contemplated for the reform of the Church and for the peace of Italy were doomed never to be attempted. He died within a month of his election.[51]

The conclave which now met was held amidst disorders ; for the partisans of Cesare and the Orsini engaged in open conflict in the streets of Rome. *and of Julius II* But Rovere determined that this time there should be no mistake, and his promises and bribes were notorious ; the Papacy seemed to be put up for sale to the highest bidder.[52] He even came to secret agreement with Cesare himself. The latter saw that he had no chance of obtaining a Pope entirely favourable, and decided that an agreement with the old enemy of his house was the only way of preserving a remnant of his powers. Rovere, for his part, recognised that Cesare controlled the Spanish votes, and that he was moreover a useful check on the Venetians for whom already he had a hostile regard. Rovere was duly elected, with only one dissentient vote, and took the style of Julius II ; he thus followed the example of Roderigo Borgia in choosing the name of a heathen soldier and conqueror.

In spite of the agreement the accession of Julius marked the end of Cesare Borgia's power. *Downfall of Borgia* He had to surrender his conquests to the new Pope, and a safe-conduct did not save him from arrest at Naples. Thence he was transferred to Spain and lodged in prison. In October 1506 he succeeded in regaining his liberty, but within a few months he had been slain in a skirmish. So ended the vast and ambitious schemes of Alexander VI for his resolute and ruthless son.[53]

[50] Giustiniani *Dispacci* II. p. 138.
[51] Pius III, like the three Popes who had gone before, was the father of a large family ; in spite of this he may well have been sincere in his wish for reform.
[52] Giustiniani *op. cit.* II. p. 225.
[53] The Venetians had waited patiently for the death of Alexander to bring Cesare to nought ; his career, they saw, was but " foco di paglia."

Character of
Julius II

Julius II was a strong man—strong both in character and in physical power. But his strength led him into acts of violence, and in dealing with others he would never try the smooth way. Men said that he had thrown the key of Peter into the Tiber, but had kept the sword of Paul. He was, in fact, a kind of priest-king like the Hasmoneans of the days before our Lord. The great aim of his pontificate was to complete the task of consolidating the States of the Church. In carrying out his plans, however, he shewed one noticeable difference from the methods of his predecessors, he made no use of his relatives ; nepotism as a political weapon was abhorrent to him.[54]

In order to provide funds for his campaign the Pope began a drastic revision of the finances of the Papacy. He cut down expenses wherever possible, and earned for himself the reputation of a miser. He even tried to put an end to the simony which had been one of the means of his own election. One cause only was allowed to divert money from his wars— and that was equally calculated to give him permanent fame —the beautifying of Rome.

Julius and
his wars

The two objects of Julius in his campaigns were the pacification of the Papal States, and the humiliation of Venice, which he regarded as the real enemy to their peace and security.[55] In the latter part of 1506 he managed to get a full recognition of papal rights in Perugia and Bologna, and thus was in a better position to attack Venice when the time came. Meanwhile the great dynastic struggle of the next quarter century was developing. The rivalry of France, Spain, and the House of Habsburg was patent to all ; and equally patent was the fact that Italy was to be the chessboard. Julius was probably a sincere patriot ; but his policy demanded the elimination of the Venetian danger, and for that he was willing to sacrifice everything. Venice after all

[54] Julius had only one child, a daughter, Felice. She came to Rome, and was married to one of the Orsini in 1506. The statement in the text does not mean that Julius failed to grant favours to his relations ; but in his self-reliance he gave them little power.

[55] The attitude of Venice to the Holy See had always been one of independence. A symbol of it is San Marco, the magnificent private chapel of the Doge, which must be compared with the tiny cathedral of San Pietro di Castello tucked away on its small island. San Marco did not become the cathedral until 1807, when Venice had lost its independence.

was insufferable, not only to the Pope, but to the other powers, and needed to be taught her place.[56]

There seems to have been some thought among the rival powers of dividing up the Papal States, and ending the temporal power, but they were too disunited to agree upon it. Maximilian even proposed to combine the functions of Pope and Emperor in his own person. In 1508 he invaded Italy, only to be compelled by the Venetians to make a three years' truce after his troops had received a number of defeats. This success was fatal to the Venetians, as it drove the Emperor into the hands of those whose one immediate object was to bring about their downfall. The chief of these was the Pope. *Maximilian in Italy* *June 1508*

In the following December the League of Cambrai, from whose effects Venice was never fully to recover, was formed between the Emperor and France. It included provisions by which the Pope, as well as Spain and Hungary, were to have their pickings from the Venetian carcase. Creighton has quite fairly condemned the League as " a great political crime," a combination, entirely unprovoked, " for the purpose of international robbery ".[57] Julius openly joined it in March 1509 and supported the French offensive by excommunicating their victims. Venice was clearly in a state of panic, and after one slight set-back—at Vaila on May 14—made her submission. *League of Cambrai*

That was all the Pope wanted, and with continued treachery he deserted the French lest they should become inconveniently strong. He rejoiced, as he himself said, at having thrust a dagger into the heart of Louis with whom he was now on bad terms. But the Venetians did not get off lightly, and had to purchase dispensation on very hard terms.[58]

Julius now turned against another of his late allies, the Duke of Ferrara. Again the offensive was preceded by excommunication; but this time it was a partial failure, as his *Papal reverses*

[56] On one occasion the Pope threatened to make the Venetians fishermen again. The proud envoy replied that Venice could much more easily reduce the Pope to a curate : Luigi da Porto *Epist.* III.

[57] *Op. cit.* V. p. 115.

[58] Julius insisted on the surrender of usurped powers, such as the appointment of its own bishops and jurisdiction over clerics. The Council of Ten made a secret protest that it agreed only under duress and later used this protest in the quarrel with Paul V.

20

Swiss mercenaries were bribed by the French to return to
their homes.   To be near the scene of hostilities Julius had
moved to Bologna.   A sudden French offensive drove the
Pope back—he escaped by a narrow margin—and had they
pressed home their victory Rome itself might have fallen into
their hands.   But Louis XII was weak and overscrupulous
and his troops were ordered to retire on Milan.

Julius threatened by a council — The Pope was beside himself with rage over the failure
of his military projects.   Further fuel for his anger was
provided by the attempt of a body of cardinals, led by
Carvajal, to summon a General Council.   This might have
been a serious threat to the power of Julius had it received
stronger support.   As it was Louis alone recognised it, and
the Council after a short sojourn at Pisa—not entirely happy
owing to the uncordial attitude of the inhabitants—passed
on to Milan, and finally expired at Lyons.

The Council of Pisa was much more important than has
sometimes been supposed ; it has its interest as being the
last attempt to force the Pope's hand by such a method.[59]
Julius countered it by convening a Council of his own.

The Holy League — In 1511 yet another League was formed, this time France
was   the common enemy.   Its members included Ferdinand
of Spain, Henry VIII of England, Venice and the Pope.   It
is known to history as the Holy League.   At first the French
April 11, 1512 were successful, and the Battle of Ravenna is among their
most famous victories.   But the loss of experienced commanders, including the youthful Gaston de Foix, in that
engagement made it more disastrous than a defeat might
have   been.   With   characteristic   indecision   Louis   again
ordered his troops to retire, and a space was given for the
League to raise fresh armies.

The Fifth Lateran Council — The pause gave Julius time to attend the meeting of
his council, the Fifth Lateran, which assembled in May 1512.
It was opened by a noble and moving speech by Egidius of
Viterbo in which the Church's needs and failings were plainly
exposed.[60]   But the Pope was in no mood for such trifles

---

[59] See Imbart de la Tour *Les origines de la réforme* II. pp. 126 sqq.   He
remarks that " M. Pastor ne s'appuie que sur les documents favourables à
Rome " : *op. cit.* p. 137 n. 3.   In the Florentine Archives he discovered a
number of documents which Pastor had missed.

[60] This speech was printed soon after its delivery ; an early instance of
what has now become a common practice.

when war was to be waged. His only object in summoning
the council, it would seem, was the desire to stultify that at
Pisa, and to demonstrate the papal power. It was significant
that the procession to the Lateran on the eve of the Council
was brought to an end by a body of armed men and nine
cannons.

In June the Pope was back again in Bologna from which Death of
the French had withdrawn. But Ferrara still held out. In Julius
spite of difficulties the papal policy was proving successful,
according to his standards. But he was now an old man,
and his bodily powers could not much longer carry the burden
of his astounding mental vigour. The new year saw the
beginning of a breakdown ; mercifully for Julius it came
swiftly, and after being confined to his bed for less than a
month he died on February 20, 1513. At the end he seems
to have been troubled by remorse and begged the cardinals
for their prayers. He also feared that his body might be
deserted when he was no more. But such fears were groundless. He had been popular with the Romans, and the whole
city crowded to see him lying in state, and many as they
passed stooped down to kiss his foot.

There can be no question that Julius accomplished a His
magnificent work in bringing order and peace into the Papal achievements
States. By his various devices, his swiftly changing alliances,
his uncanny and unscrupulous ability in playing off one power
against another, he had enormously increased the temporal
prestige of the Papacy. Its moral and spiritual prestige
could hardly be lowered.

We have seen already the disastrous effect which the Evils of the
continued attempt to hold Italy had upon the Empire ; its principate
effect upon the Papacy was equally grave. For it diverted
the Popes from their true mission, that of spiritual leadership, and led them to depend upon force for the maintenance
of their influence. To carry out their numerous schemes of
conquest or defence, large financial resources were necessary,
and it was to raise such funds that the Popes were compelled
to tax those who accepted their authority. This heavy taxation aroused serious resentment. The Papacy also was not
above making use of its spiritual weapons in this warfare,
after all bulls were cheaper than mercenaries, and often
created grave complications for those who recognised its

claims. But it was not long before men began to realise
that such weapons, from too frequent usage, had lost their
edge.

The attempt to maintain an Italian princedom had a
further effect, however, for not only did it arouse the rivalry
of other Italian states, but it robbed the Papacy of the
sympathy of a great part of Europe. To the nations beyond
the Alps it was not the presence of abuses in the papal court,
not its secular spirit that really mattered, but the fact that
it was devoted to a narrow and selfish policy.

The acquiring and retaining of temporal sovereignty involved " power, compromise and display ", all of which were
condemned and rejected by our Lord in His temptation,
both for Himself and, by implication, for His Church. But
the age had a marvellous power of separating the spiritual
and the temporal, the prince and the pontiff ; and from a philosophical point of view, it saw nothing wrong in the Pope
holding an Italian kingdom, any more than an earlier generation had seen anything unusual in a bishop being a feudal
noble. This ability to distinguish between the individual
and his office, also explains the small significance which was
attached to the low morals of several of the Popes.[61] That,
and the regrettable fact that many religious men were guilty
of similar lapses. Religion and sexual morality might, with
little exaggeration, have been said to belong, in the estimation
of the age, to watertight compartments.[62]

Forgeries
It was in this period that the discovery was made that
some of the documents on which the papal claims were thought
to rest were forgeries. To pious souls such as Luther this
discovery might come as a great shock ; [63] but it did little
to shake papal prestige, for to many it seemed only natural
that such a corrupt institution should have such a basis.
Others accepted its claims on grounds independent of docu-

[61] It is true that protests were lodged from time to time by the representatives of the powers against the state of morals in the Roman curia ; but these
were hypocritical and the work of enemies.
[62] It is interesting to notice Pasolini's comment on Caterina Sforza whose
robust piety, although she had been " the idol of one pope and the victim of
another . . . never permitted her to doubt the divineness of their mission while
she ascribed to human frailty the manner in which they exercised it " :
Catherine Sforza p. 46.
[63] See his letter to Spalatin in Enders *Luther's Briefwechsel* II. p. 382.

ments.[64] The most notorious document was the so-called
Donation of Constantine. At various epochs its claims had The
been derided or challenged ; but its genuineness had not been Donation of
doubted. Suddenly in different quarters it began to be Constantine
questioned ; by Nicholas of Cusa, by Reginald Pecock, Bishop
of Chichester, and most famous of all by Lorenzo Valla.[65]
In a treatise entitled *De falsa credita et ementita Constanti
donatione declamatio* the latter exposed the forgery, and
called upon the Pope to renounce his usurped dominion,
and confine himself to purely spiritual functions. He denounced the Papacy as the root of Italy's misfortunes and the
donation as the cause of its disasters.[66] This act did not
prevent Valla being employed as a papal secretary. But
by this time the Donation had become a source of embarrassment rather than of strength ; for had it not been held,
from the days of Innocent IV, if not earlier, that the Pope
was the supreme disposer of earthly power, and such a gift
on the part of an Emperor would have been presumption.

In considering the Popes of this period one is tempted The failure
to forget their high office and responsibilities, to regard of the
them simply as interesting types of character. This is a Papacy
mistake, for it was the Pope, and not the man, which really
counted, or rather the man counted because he was the Pope.
They have long ago passed before the only judgement-seat
whose competence they would have recognised. The verdicts
of that high tribunal are hidden from the historian ; but he
may perhaps be allowed to surmise the charges to which these
great Churchmen might be called upon to answer. Some
among them had definitely been guilty of gross crimes and
serious offences ; but the temptations which had led others

[64] Forgery was a regular device throughout the middle ages. Every
monastery had its forged charters and even papal Bulls had to be protected
by special devices. The Archbishop of Cosenza, secretary to Alexander VI,
was found guilty of forging no less than 3000 Bulls giving various exemptions.
[65] See C. B. Coleman *The Treatise of Lorenzo Valla on the Donation of
Constantine.* Valla was an acute critic and his notes on the text of the Vulgate
were used by Erasmus himself.
[66] Dante held a similar opinion it will be remembered :

> " Ahi, Constantin, di quanto mal fu matre,
> Non la tua conversion, ma quella dote
> Che da te prese il primo ricco patre."
> —*Inferno* xix. 115-117.

astray were not in themselves evil, save that they were inconsistent with the high office which they held.   The desire, for example, to found a family is praiseworthy in a layman, and is one which appeals strongly to most Englishmen; but it was hardly fitting in the celibate head of a spiritual society.   The Popes were bishops of the souls of men, and, as such, pledged to uphold a high moral standard; because of this their failure was all the more pitiful and damning, for those who profess noble ideals cannot abandon them with impunity, and judgement against them must be severe.   Not only did they degrade a high office, they lowered the self-respect of humanity.

CHAPTER XI

THE NORTHERN RENAISSANCE

HAVING considered the Renaissance in Italy we must Character-now turn to the North where the movement took a istics form which in many ways was distinctive. In one sense it is inaccurate to speak of a Northern Renaissance; for whereas in Italy there was a definite revival of native culture, the culture of the North had never been native, and its learning, even in Carolingian times, had been mainly classical. It is true that there were vague traditions among the people and a mass of folk tales; but these had but little influence among the educated,[1] and as they were gradually redueed to writing they tended to imitate classical models. Neither in number nor in quality were they adequate to form a culture. The Northern Renaissance was definitely a movement effected by outside influences although, as we shall see, these influences were modified and changed, were not received without discrimination or criticism. Gregorovius indeed would have us believe that the real Northern Renaissance was the Reformation.[2]

That the Northern peoples in accepting the culture of the South should, each in its different way, modify it was but natural; for nations are like individuals, they must work out their own salvation, once they have attained to maturity, and cannot be expected to adopt ready-made the laws, the constitution, or the culture of another people.

---

[1] G. M. Trevelyan suggests that if these stories had been better known in England—and the same is true of Germany—" they might have changed much in the history of letters ": *History of England* p. 143. Christian teachers among the Teutons had discouraged the spread of stories of the old gods as they had not done in the South. In Italy such stories had become part of the general culture and were no longer taken seriously.

[2] *Geschichte der Stadt Rom* II. p. 579 and 874. A similar idea is held by Christopher Dawson *Progress and Religion* p. 178. Mr Dawson would postpone any literary Renaissance to the end of the eighteenth century and the rise of the Romantic Movement (*op. cit.* p. 29).

That is why the attempt of one people, even with the best of good intentions, to impose its culture upon another is an act of tyranny; though the desire to share it is an act of grace.   Unfortunately it is hard to distinguish between the two processes in practical life.

Comparison with the Italian Renaissance It has often been pointed out that Italian institutions gain strength when they have left the land of their origin; [3] this was, I think, true of the revival of culture in the fourteenth to the sixteenth centuries.   In Italy the movement had but lightly concerned itself with religion; but when it crossed the Alps, though it may have lost some of the languid sweetness which marked it in its first home, yet the passage over the mountain snows seemed to give it a new vigour and purity.   The men of the earlier Renaissance had seen in culture an end in itself; the Teutons, with deeper insight, extended its scope, and thereby its usefulness, and applied it to the great mysteries of man's being and to the conduct of his life.   They recognised, in other words, that the spiritual side of his complex nature was as worthy of cultivation as the intellectual.[4]   Its effect in Italy had been to set before men as the object of their mental pilgrimage no longer the tombs of the Apostles, but the more distant shrines of Athene and Apollo beneath Hellenic skies; it taught them to seek, not Calvary, but Olympus.

Italian culture in Germany Historians may quarrel over the political effects of the link between Germany and Italy during the middle ages; [5] from the standpoint of culture its value was undeniable; at every stage the mind of Germany was quickened and fertilized by the contact.[6]   The spread of Italian culture was indeed a step towards " the necessary intellectual equilisation of

[3] This is true in particular of the Benedictine Movement; see Luigi Salvatorelli *San Benedetto e l'Italia del suo tempo* (Bari 1929).

[4] The above passage, with a few verbal alterations, comes from my *Erasmus the Reformer* pp. 80 sq.   It is possible to exaggerate the dependence of the North, for the modifications were so drastic as almost to constitute a new movement : cf. Dr Whitney *Eng. Hist. Rev.* XXXV. p. 3, who says " In the Netherlands and not in Italy is to be sought the true birthplace of the German Renaissance, which was not artistic, was certainly not pagan, but was from first to last practical and educational in its aims ".

[5] Von Sybel condemned the connexion and his views have recently been restated by Von Below *Die italienische Kaiser-politik des deutschen Mittelalters*. On the other side were Giesebrecht and Ficker, and more recently Hampe and J. Haller.

[6] Ranke *Deutsche Geschichte im Zeitalter der Reformation* I. p. 15 (E.T. p. 20).

the nations," to borrow a useful phrase from Mommsen.[7] It
gave to the artists and thinkers of the North new ideas as
well as new materials upon which to feed their imagination.

In the earlier middle ages the repeated expeditions of Germans in
the Emperors to be crowned at Rome had not so great an Italy
effect as they might have had, since those who accompanied
him, even the ecclesiastics, were commonly men of the sword,
and as such, in that age, not greatly interested in culture.
But when the Emperors had ceased to descend in warlike
array, they naturally attracted around them those who could
better appreciate the wonders of their titular capital.[8] But
it is to those who undertook the journey from religious
motives that the greatest debt for bringing back the seeds
of new ideas is due. Such was the visit of Roger van der
Weyden in 1450 and of many other artists and pilgrims.
The men of letters, indeed, had probably been before the
painters, if not in religious motive, at least in appreciation
of the treasures which lay hidden behind the southern mountain chain. By the latter half of the fifteenth century it was
the exception for a humanist, particularly if he knew Greek,
not to have been to Italy. Some, indeed, went further afield;
Johannes Wessell, for example, had seen not only Italy,
but Greece itself, and even Egypt. These men did not
travel in the train of princes, but on foot. They were thus
in a better position to study the country and its riches,
and were less attracted by the lighter side of life, which was
exhibited to distinguished guests.

Many of those who returned to their native land found
the atmosphere a little chilling and uncongenial,[9] or affected
to do so. Rudolf Agricola even dared to affirm that after
he left Italy he had forgotten everything, " the classics,
history, even how to write with any style ".[10] But the

---

[7] *History of Rome*, II. p. 243. He uses it, of course, of the spread of
Hellenism in Italy.

[8] Muffel, the Burgomaster of Nuremberg, who accompanied Frederick III
on his journey to Rome in 1452 has left in his *Beschreibung der Stadt Rom*
(Tübingen 1876) a vivid description of the city and its marvels.

[9] Many, especially among the artists, did not return at all ; but like some
of the Emperors forgot their home for the sake of Italy. A large number of
works from the hands of these Northerners, and in particular from the
Flemings, still exist in various Italian churches : see T. H. Fokker *Werke
Niederländischer Meister in den Kirchen Italiens* (The Hague 1931).

[10] See his letter of September 20, 1480 to Hegius in Allen *The Age of
Erasmus* p. 25.

travellers were glad to share with their countrymen the treasures which they had brought back. Among them a high place deserves to be given to our own scholars; Hadley and Selling among the pioneers, and later Grocin, Linacre, and Colet, to name but a few among the more prominent who made the long journey. To them the nation owed new knowledge and widened experience.

Northern culture   But if at this epoch the North derived so much from Italy, it must not be forgotten that behind it there was a long record of culture; now strong and now lapsing almost to nothingness, but never entirely lost. The lands which had produced " the literature of Provence, the romances of chivalry, the cycles of Charlemagne, the Round Table, the Nibelungen Lied, innumerable ballads, and the splendid cathedrals "— to repeat Villari's catalogue [11]—could not be held to have been devoid of culture. But in addition there had been a continual tradition of classical learning.

In the early middle ages   The political stability which Charlemagne gave to Germany brought about a rapid development of culture and education; in the tenth century the North was in advance of Italy. In the latter country the clergy, at any rate in Rome, were scornful and suspicious of what they regarded as pagan learning.[12] The extent to which the love of the classics spread was amazing. In the convent schools women and girls knew Virgil and the legends of Rome better than their own folk-lore; while the famous nun, Hroswitha, wrote comedies after the manner of Terence.[13] The century which followed, in spite of the work of Otto III and some of the Henries, saw learning decay in Germany, although some ecclesiastics paid visits to the growing schools of Northern France, and some quickening influence came from Italy.[14]

[11] *History of Florence* p. 310. He might have added the *Speculum Regale* (*c.* 1250) which reveals the advanced state of culture in Scandinavia.
[12] " Gerbert in Rom ist wie eine einsame Fackel in tiefer Nacht " : says Gregorovius *op. cit.* I. p. 847.
[13] Light is thrown on the times by the story of the monk Ekkehard who taught Virgil and Horace to Hedwig of Swabia : an episode which inspired one of the best of historical novels—Von Scheffel's *Ekkehard.*
[14] Wippo was greatly impressed by the zeal of the Italians for culture, especially when compared with his own countrymen :

" Hoc servant Itali post prima crepundia cuncti
Et sudare scholis mandatur tota juventus."
—*Tetralogus* (MGH. SS. XI. p. 251).

But both Italy and Germany soon became too busy with French leadership the struggle of Pope and Emperor, to give much attention to culture, and it was upon France, the mother-land of typical medieval things, that the burden of its maintenance now fell. From the days of Philip Augustus it took the lead in Europe— 1180-1223 even Italy came under its influence [15]—and Germany and all things German came to be despised.[16]   This was due in part to racial and political prejudice, partly to sheer ignorance. To this ignorance of German literature, and contempt for it, there is an interesting exception in Tommasino dei Cerchiari, Canon of Aquilea, who himself actually wrote in German, and whose *Welschen Gast* is one of the masterpieces of early German literature.[17]

The same epoch, that of the wars between Otto and Philip Literary activity of thirteenth century of Swabia, at the beginning of the thirteenth century, was a time of great activity in German literary annals.   To it belong the great epics, as well as the best songs of the Minnesingers.   Hermann of Thuringia might cut a queer figure in politics, with his frequent change of side, but his court on the Wartburg was a gathering point for writers and poets whose work will never be forgotten.[18]   The Hohenstaufen age which followed had a profound influence on German culture, and it brought " a real blossoming of song and vision, of fairy tale and epic, of painting, building and sculpture ".[19]

[15] In the middle of the thirteenth century Martino da Canale wrote his *Cronaca dei Veneziani* in French because " lengue franceise cort parmi le monde et est la plus delitable a lire et oir que nule autre ".   Brunetto Latini uses almost identical words in explaining why he used French for his *Trésor*, whilst another contemporary, the famous Marco Polo also chose the same medium.   The use of French architects in this age is noteworthy ;   Milan Cathedral (not the present one) was built by them and in the South both Frederick II and Charles of Anjou employed them : see Funck-Brentano *Le Moyen Âge* p. 228.

[16] Cf. the opinion of the twelfth century Provençal poet : " Their speech seems like the barking of dogs, and for this I would not be the Lord of Frisia because I should have every day to hear the voices of the damned " : quoted by Fisher *The Med. Empire* II. p. 256.

[17] On this interesting Churchman see Burdach *Vom Mittelalter zur Reformation* I. pp. 15 sqq., II. pt. i. p. 8.

[18] It is a striking instance of Italian ignorance of things German that Dante at the end of the century was apparently unaware of the existence of Walter von der Vogelweide.

[19] Kantorowicz *Frederick the Second* p. 80.   This epoch saw a fresh attempt to render Latin poets into German,—the last had been Notker's Virgil in Carolingian times,—when Albert of Halberstadt translated Ovid.   It was, however, an isolated effort and nothing more was done until the fifteenth century.

The papal court at Avignon

The opening years of the fourteenth century seemed to promise a revival of art and learning when the papal court was moved beyond the Alps to Avignon, and for a time the city seemed likely to draw to it the best of Italian artists and scholars. But after Clement VI Italians were no longer encouraged and no fresh advance was made.[20]

But learning in Germany was not entirely dead, and Abbot Bartholomew has left on record his admiration for the erudition of certain German Benedictines who came to Subiaco in his day.[21] Such savants, however, were but rare in Germany during the fourteenth century, and it is significant that the first university to be established in the Empire was that of Prague founded by Charles IV in 1347-1348.

Charles IV and culture

The work of Charles as a patron of culture [22] is so important, that more must be said of him and the men who were his principal helpers.[23] His university was modelled on that at Paris where he himself is said, perhaps without sufficient warrant, to have studied. The first chancellor was Ernst Pardubitz who was also the first Archbishop of Prague. Archbishop Ernst had spent fourteen years in Italy and he did much to foster classical studies in the Empire,—Prague itself became a centre for the radiation of such influences.[24] Another potent influence was the Chancellor, Johann of Neumarkt (Noviforensis) who had a profound knowledge of the works of Dante and did much to promote learning.[25] They were both correspondents of Rienzo, and it is to this remarkable man that the real inspiring force must be traced back. His coming to Prague was the beginning of an epoch, and little as it has been recognised his literary activities were more significant for the future than his fanciful political dreams.[26]

---

[20] See Guiraud *L'Église Romaine etc.* p. 47.

[21] *Cronaca Sublacense* pp. 394, 396 sq.

[22] " Karl IV ist der Vater der deutschen Renaissance " says Burdach *op. cit.* I. p. 63.

[23] Earlier still in 1318 John of Drazice, Bishop of Prague, had visited Avignon and brought back illuminated MSS which stimulated Bohemian ideas and practice.

[24] See Ferdinand Tadra *Kulturní styky Čech s cizinou až do válek Hisitských.*

[25] See Burdach *op. cit.* I. pp. 30 sqq., II. pt. i. pp. 12 sqq. and VI.

[26] " Die Ankunft Colas in Prag darf der eigentliche Anfang der Renaissance-bewegung in Deutschland gelten, und das Jahr 1350 bewährt wiederum seinen Charakter : es macht Epoche " : Burdach *op. cit.* I. p. 88. For the admiration aroused by the literary powers of Rienzo see *op. cit.* II. pt. i. p. 19.

The North was not without its literary treasures ; but they were hidden away in monastic libraries, and no one knew or cared about them. The extent to which writing had become almost a forgotten art is illustrated by the experience of Petrarch who, when he discovered a MS of one of Cicero's speeches in Liège, had to search almost the whole city before he could find any ink with which to copy it.[27] Later many MSS were to be unearthed by the untiring Poggio.[28] He it was who found a copy of Petronius in Cologne, and other valuable MSS in Lübeck and Roskild. At Hersfeld he got possession of a copy of Tacitus by promising to push the interests of the monastery at the papal court where a law-suit was hanging fire. Another famous discoverer was Nicholas of Trier who might almost be called a professional searcher after MSS.[29]

Neglect of literary treasures

The event which brought the North into close touch with the culture of the South was the Council of Constance, for many scholars were among those who attended it. The same was true of the Council of Basle.[30] Aeneas Sylvius found that among the natives of the latter town the level of culture was low ; there was some study of grammar and rhetoric, but poetry was ignored, and even the name of Cicero seemed to be unknown. It is significant of the influence of Prague that among the few congenial spirits whom Aeneas met north of the Alps, there were no Germans, but several Bohemians and Poles.[31] When in later years he served in the Imperial Chancery he was disgusted by the inferiority of his German colleagues. But if he despised them it was in the Chanceries of Germany that Humanism was to develop, and among this same official class.[32] One of the finest examples was Aeneas's inveterate enemy, Gregory Heimburg. This man had been in

Effect on culture of the Councils

---

[27] See H. C. Hollway-Calthrop *Petrarch* p. 44.

[28] He paid a fruitless visit to England on the invitation of Henry Beaufort.

[29] He has been identified by some with Nicholas of Cusa : see *Camb. Mod. Hist.* I. p. 599.

[30] John of Ragusa brought a number of books, including some Greek MSS to Basle and left them in the Dominican convent. They were much used by later scholars including Erasmus.

[31] Cf. C. M. Ady *Pius II* p. 109.

[32] A recent writer suggests that the dullness of their labour drove them to literature to find relief ! " Denn diese Personen suchten in dem Humanismus gerade Erholung von ihren trockenen Amtsgeschäften " : Molitor *Die Reichsreformbestrebungen* p. 172.

Italy in his youth, but his temperament and outlook were so typically German that opposition between him and Aeneas was instinctive and inevitable.[33]

The new learning in the Netherlands

By the second half of the fifteenth century the new learning was well established in the Low Countries. The great centre was an interesting group of scholars connected in one way or another with the " Academy " which Henry of Rees gathered round him at the Cistercian monastery of Adwert near Gronigen of which he was abbot. Included among them were men of famous name, such as Rudolf Agricola (Huysmann) who died in 1485, when at the height of his powers, leaving an example which provoked enthusiastic devotion to learning in others.[34] Hegius, the rector of the famous school at Deventer and the teacher of Mutianus Rufus and Erasmus,[35] was another. On his death in 1498 he left nothing but his books and clothes. But most important of all was probably Johannes Wessell, who ended a long life in the same year as Hegius, worn out with his studies. He had been attached to Sixtus IV, and on his departure for Friesland the Pope wished to give him a parting gift. He asked for Greek and Hebrew volumes. The Pope was astonished and said : " What ? No benefice, no grant of office or fees ? Why not ? " " Because I don't want them," came the quiet reply. The books were forthcoming—one, a Greek Gospels, was perhaps the parent of a copy which reached Erasmus for the second edition of his New Testament.[36] This incident is important as an illustration of the inability of the Italians to understand the stern, upright German character ; a serious consequence was papal miscalculation in the treatment of Germany. Wessell was one of the simple souls, though learned, to whom the Reformation doctrines were in the next generation to make so strong an appeal.

Art in the North

The artistic development of the North, and of Germany in particular, did not lag behind the literary. In architecture

---

[33] On Heimburg see C. Brockhaus *Gregor von Heimburg* and Joachimsohn *Gregor Heimburg.*

[34] On his writings and importance see Allen *Erasmi Epistolae* I. p. 106.

[35] Erasmus did not, however, receive a great deal of instruction from him, he says in *Compendium Vitae* " post aliquoties audiuit Hegium, sed non nisi diebus festis quibus legebat omnibus " (in Allen *Erasmi Epistolae* I. p. 48).

[36] Allen *The Age of Erasmus* p. 11.

indeed the North had been supreme, and if the first flowering
of the Teutonic mind had been " barbarous," it was touched
with grace and refined with beauty. The aspirations of the
Teutons towards the God Who had found them in their
native forests took shape in stone, and Italy herself was
not ashamed to follow where they had led.[37] In other departments also the North had its lessons to teach. As far
back as the Council of Lyons in 1245 Innocent IV had admired
the copes of the English bishops ; [38] they were but samples
of the art of needlework which was much cultivated in
English nunneries.[39] But in time zeal for architecture, for
illuminated MSS, and even for stained-glass spent itself
and artistic deterioration followed.

In England, and even in France, during the period of Its
their growing intellectual life art was neglected.[40] But in character-
Germany and the Low Countries it was far otherwise, and if istics
Italy had its Assisi to be the cradle of a new birth of painting,
Germany had Cologne. Cologne was in a peculiar sense a
sacred city to the Germans, hallowed alike in history and
in song ; it was the seat also of a mighty growing cathedral.
In it mystics and scholars had found a home, Albertus Magnus,
Eckhardt, Tauler of Strassburg, and above all Suso.[41] But
if Assisi found its parallel in Cologne, the Brancacci frescoes
which served as a school for Italian artists found its counter-
part in the great altar-piece of Hubert van Eyck at Ghent.
Art in the North reflected the religious feeling and enthusiasm
for the things of the spirit which flowed from the pages of
Thomas à Kempis. This can be well seen in the canvasses
of Memling. What, however, is strange and inexplicable in
Northern Art, even in this period of its greatest strength,

[37] Cf. Bompas *The Cathedrals of Central Italy* p. 150 : " At Pavia and in
Bergamo we are in the presence of the same art as at Mainz, Coblenz and
Cologne ".

[38] Matthew Paris *Hist. Major* IV. p. 547 (RS.).

[39] " It is not generally known . . . that some of the most famous em-
broidered vestments still preserved in Italy are the work of English nuns
. . . such as the Lateran cope in Rome, the Piccolomini cope at Pienza . . .
and some at Anagni, Florence and Bologna." Stevenson *Robert Grosseteste*
p. 165. The fame of English needlewomen went back at least as far as the
Conquest : see *Gesta Willelmi* PL. CXLIX. col. 1267.

[40] Ruskin *Modern Painters* IV. p. 380.

[41] On the influence of Suso on art see Muther *History of Painting* I. pp.
17 sqq.

is an absence of the highest perception of the beautiful, and a delight in actual ugliness, in distorted and unnatural forms.[42] The Northern Renaissance was, after all, not really æsthetic, in spite of some striking achievements in the realm of art ; and to this it owed its freedom from pagan influences. None the less it would have been well for the North, from the artistic standpoint, if it had come earlier under the influence of the Italian painters.

Out of main stream of development   The main stream of development which arose from Giotto and his followers left the North untouched until well into the fifteenth century, when artists, as we have seen, began to travel south. They did not go empty-handed, for one of the first of them, Piero di Burges,[43] probably taught Antonello da Messina the technique of oil-painting. Later still the realism which was characteristic of Flemish art, was to influence Italian painters, such as Ghirlandaio, " whose temperaments inclined them to literalism ".[44] Thus in their isolation the Northern artists had developed on their own lines. The chief difference between them and the Italians was that the latter were more scientific, and the former more dependent on direct observation. " Van Eyck and his followers appear to have [depended upon] careful and precise observation of each successive situation ; Brunelleschi in Florence instantly sought for the general law and stated it mathematically." [45] The weakness of the Flemish method was that it did not allow a definite artistic tradition to grow up, a body of knowledge to which each successive generation could make additions ; and so the influence of a great painter tended to be merely individual and transitory.[46]

Learning in England   We must now consider the development of learning in the several countries of Europe. In England it tarried unaccountably. It is true that in Richard of Bury, we had an early collector of MSS,—but he was hardly a humanist ; [47] and that in the middle of the fourteenth century, Nicholas V

---

[42] See Ruskin *Modern Painters* III. pp. 348 sqq.
[43] Perhaps the same as Petrus Christus, a pupil of Van Eyck. Vasari says that Antonello went to Bruges and learned it from Van Eyck himself.
[44] Roger Fry *Flemish Art* p. 29.
[45] Roger Fry *op. cit.* pp. 3 sq.
[46] Cf. Holmes *Introd. to Ital. Painting* pp. 4 sq.
[47] See Creighton *Hist. Lectures and Addresses* p. 194.

could express his admiration for the learning of William Grey, whom he made Bishop of Ely. The suppression of Lollardy and the gagging of Oxford University by Archbishop Arundel, at the beginning of the fifteenth century, initiated a period of intellectual barrenness which the isolated efforts of Humphrey, Duke of Gloucester, did little to check. The time of England's Renaissance had not yet come in spite of numerous visitors to Italy. The bulk of the great men were still as Poggio had found them, more interested in agriculture than in the promotion of letters; and even the encouragement of patrons and the example of foreign nations did little to rouse the English [48] until Shakespeare and his contemporaries came upon the scene.

In Spain also the Renaissance was delayed and checked, in Spain one might almost deny its existence there.* In the latter half of the fifteenth century Arias Barbossa, who had been a pupil of Poliziano, and Antonio Lebrixa, brought some learning from Italy ; but it really never spread. The work of Cardinal Ximenes in producing the first printed Greek Testament at Alcalà in 1514 must not, however, be forgotten.[49] But though the New Learning seemed never to take firm root in the Peninsula, a great writer, as in England, was to arise. Cervantes and Shakespeare both died on April 23, 1616.

A new interest in letters began to manifest itself in France in France after the desolations of the Hundred Years' War, and at the beginning of the fifteenth century there was an interesting group of humanists, who in the manner of their successors later in the century carried on a varied correspondence ; one of the most prominent in this group was Nicholas de Clémanges. Their influence does not seem to have been lasting, and no advance is seen until the second half of the century, when lectures in Greek were given in Paris. Later 1458 both John Lascaris and George Hermonymus paid visits.

[48] Creighton *op. cit.* p. 203.

* [This is the view of many scholars, e.g., A. Wantoch, *Spanien : Das Land ohne Renaissance* (1927). Mr H. O. Evennett, however, has drawn my attention to the article " Notes on the Spanish Renaissance " by A. F. G. Bell in *Rev. Hispanique* (Dec. 1930), pp. 319-653 which suggests that some modification is necessary.]

[49] A delay in publication prevented it from being the first actually to appear as Erasmus anticipated it.

21

Useful service was done by Guillaume Fichet, who also introduced printing,[50] but it was to Robert Gaguin that the real beginnings were due.[51] Upon these foundations Aleander who lectured in Paris from 1508 to 1516 in the three languages —Greek, Hebrew and Latin—began to build up.

In the meantime, the expedition of Charles VIII into Italy had brought Frenchmen face to face with the New Learning, and the spoils which they brought back introduced into the country a manner of life more luxurious and refined than that to which it had been accustomed. The effect of the expedition has been questioned by Batiffol, who can find no evidence for it ; [52] but surely Creighton is nearer the truth when he writes that " Charles carried beyond the Alps a vague yet powerful fragrance of the Italian Renaissance ".[53]

Italian influence in France It is interesting to notice that when the Renaissance had spent its force in Italy, it found a brief renewal of life in France, where a generation arose which took for its model and inspiration in verse, not the poets of Greece and Rome, but those of Italy.[54] For a time Greek flourished in France. Anne of Brittany, the wife of Charles VIII, encouraged it and was herself not without some knowledge of it—but it never went very deep ; the Latin mind seemed unable to give to Greek that place which was found for it by the Germans. It is true that Budaeus, who died in 1540, was the greatest Greek scholar of his day, but after the departure of Scaliger in 1593, the culture and civilisation of France became almost exclusively Latin.[55]

The new learning in Germany and the Netherlands It is time we returned to what is the really important line of our study ; the growth of the New Learning in Germany and the Low Countries. We may perhaps best resume by glancing at the effect of the new life upon the universities. The foundation of Louvain in 1426 had been an important

---

[50] See Philippe *Guilliaume Fichet.*

[51] See Thuasne *R. Gaguini Epist. et Orat.* Of this scholar, who gave encouragement to Erasmus at the beginning of his career, Imbart de la Tour has written " la Renaissance française élargit ses horizons et se rattache à la Renaissance européenne " : *Les origines de la Réforme* II. p. 350.

[52] " Il est donc malaisé de savoir en quoi l'entreprise de Naples a contribué au mouvement des arts en France " : he writes : *Le Siècle de la Renaissance* p. 20.

[53] *History of the Papacy* IV. p. 246.

[54] See *Camb. Mod. Hist.* III. p. 55.   [55] *Op. cit.* III. p. 60.

step, for it diverted to some extent the stream of students from Paris and Cologne, and helped to give new confidence and scope to native scholarship. In Germany itself there was an increased interest in the universities towards the end of the fifteenth century ; Heidelberg, which had been founded in 1385, took on a new lease of life under the Elector Palatine Philip, and the new foundation of Wittenberg (1502) was a centre of activity. Even at Leipzig, where the New Learning met with opposition, it managed to make progress. At the beginning of the sixteenth century Erfurt (1392) took a prominent place, and Luther could say that in comparison the other universities of Germany were like infant schools.[56]

The universities

Behind the universities new ideas were spreading through the influence of the schools founded to teach the New Learning. Of these one of the most famous was Schlettstadt, founded by Dringenberg (d. 1490), which drew students from South and West Germany ; among its headmasters was Sapidius (1490-1561), who resigned in 1525 when the school rejected the Reformation doctrines. The students of North Germany and the Low Countries went to the equally famous Deventer, of which mention has already been made.

The schools

In addition to schools and universities the new ideas were propagated by groups of scholars (*sodalitates literariae*). The two most famous were the *Danubuana*, founded by Conrad Celtes in imitation of the Roman Academy of Pomponius Laetus, whom he had met in Italy ; and the *Rhenana*, of which the moving spirit was Johannes Trithemius, Abbot of Sponheim, alchemist, politician, and humanist.[57]

Sodalitates literariae

The movement in the North, like its fellow in Italy, owed much to the support of the great and wealthy ; [58] the Emperor Maximilian was a patron of learned and cultivated

Its patrons

[56] The following list of German universities, with the dates of their foundation, is taken from Geiger *Renaissance und Humanismus in Italien und Deutschland.* Prague (1348), Vienna (1365), Heidelberg (1385), Cologne (1388), Erfurt (1392), Leipzig (1409), Rostock (1409). These may be said to belong to the middle ages. Then later came Greifswald (1456), Freiburg and Basle (1460). Ingoldstadt (1472), Mainz and Tübingen (1476), Wittenberg (1502), Frankfurt-am-Oder (1506), Marburg (1527).

[57] He was the teacher of the notorious Paracelsus.

[58] Among noble patrons were Eberhard of Würtemberg (1445-1498), who had himself visited Italy ; Frederick the Wise of Saxony (1463-1526) ; and Albrecht of Mainz (1480-1545).

men, and as early as 1497 he summoned Conrad Celtes to Vienna, where he remained until his death in 1508. But **The towns** it was to the towns that it owed the greatest debt. Behind their strong walls they had a high measure of security which enabled them to give attention to the luxuries of life, as well as its necessities. Their wealth was increasing fast in the fifteenth century, for the Hundred Years' War had diverted the trade routes from the Rhone valley, and in addition the mineral resources of their own rich land were being exploited for the first time in real earnest. Thus they had ample resources for the patronage of art and culture,[59] and prosperous merchants thought it no ill way to spend of their substance in encouraging painters and men of letters. Strassburg, from its nearness to France, took the lead in such matters, under the direction of Jacob Wimpheling (1450-1528), the preceptor of Germany as he was called. Another famous citizen was Sebastian Brandt, the author of the *Narrenschiff*.[60] At Augsburg, the home of Hans Holbein, the painter, the leading spirit was Conrad Peutinger (1465-1547), who after being educated in Italy returned in 1485 with an intense love of antiquity. At Nuremberg was the famous Willibald Pirkheimer (1470-1528), the patron of men of letters and the adviser of kings.[61] He too had been to Italy, when he studied at Padua and Pavia, and he too brought back a love of humanistic studies. His house in the Market Place was close to that of Behaim (1459-1506), the maker of maps and globes, and facing the clock which had been put up to commemorate the Golden Bull of Charles IV.[62] At Erfurt, Mutianus Rufus (1471-1526) gathered round him a group which included Eoban Hesse, Ulrich von Hutten, and Crotus Rubeanus.

Greek in the North   The scholars of the North were even more ambitious to

---

[59] As in Italy men of letters found employment as secretaries, even a small town like Gronigen required that its documents should be in correct Latin and appointed Rudolf Agricola as Town Secretary.

[60] There is an interesting letter from the Strassburg *Sodalitas Literaria* to Erasmus containing the names of many of its members : see Allen *Erasmi Epistolae* II. p. 7.

[61] Amongst others whom he encouraged was Albrecht Dürer.

[62] For earlier developments in Nuremberg see Joachimsohn *Gregor Heimburg* p. 101. One other name deserves mention, that of Johannes Müller (1436-1476), who took the name of Regiomontanus. He settled there in 1471 and gave himself to astronomy.

acquire Greek than those of Italy, and their task was harder, since the North lacked native teachers. In the case of some, Greek was desired merely as a distinction,—the gold-lace of Dr Johnson,—and after its novelty had worn off something else was sought. Even so sound a scholar as Rudolf Agricola confessed to this failing and, in a letter to Hegius of January 1485, wrote that he was now turning his attention to Hebrew, in order to have something new on hand.[63]

It has been pointed out that before the beginning of the sixteenth century there was no Greek type in the North,[64] and Greek words were inserted where necessary by hand. The first book to be printed in the language was the New Testament of Erasmus which came from Froben's press at Basle in 1516.[65] After the Sack of Rome in 1527 the study of Greek in Italy began to languish; the great men were all dead, Ficino in 1499 was the last of them; and Bembo and his like were poor successors. The scholars of Germany now began to gain the pre-eminence, and Erasmus has recorded the vast change from his boyhood days when the North seemed barbarous and culture to be found only in Italy. His own visit to Italy in 1509 revealed to him the decay which had already set in. Before the middle of the century there were even found Italians who acknowledged the superiority of the Germans.[66]

But the New Learning by no means had it all its own way Opposition in the North. In fact opposition, especially in some of the to the new universities, was exceedingly fierce, fiercer even than in Italy. learning This is not altogether surprising, when it is remembered that Scholasticism had been, in the main, a product of the Northern mind;[67] even St Thomas himself was, by descent, a Norman and a Teuton. When the humanists of Italy despised the Schoolmen for their barbarous style, the Churchmen and the universities of the North were still loyal. In any case, with certain exceptions, the North did not pay that exaggerated homage to good style which was characteristic of the Italians,

[63] See Allen *The Age of Erasmus* p. 29.
[64] Geiger *Renaissance und Humanismus in Italien und Deutschland* p. 482.
[65] The desire to read the New Testament in the original was a strong motive with many Germans for learning Greek.
[66] See the end of Paulus Jovius's *Elogia Literaria*.
[67] Cf. Allen *The Age of Erasmus* p. 253.

and the Dominicans, in particular, were jealous defenders of their great theologian.   But none the less scholars of humanistic sympathies tended more and more to approximate to the Italian point of view, and Rudolf Agricola could bemoan the fact that he had wasted seven precious years in the study of Scholasticism ; whilst Johannes Wessell actually gained the title of *Magister Contradictionis* from his criticisms at Paris in 1455.   The scorn which Colet poured upon the Schoolmen is well known, and in it he was followed by Erasmus who had, however, a little kindness for Aquinas, a testimony to his loyalty and also, I think, to his insight.[68]

The case of Reuchlin   The battle between the old and the new was joined over the famous case of Reuchlin.   Reuchlin had drunk deep of the new spirit during a visit to Italy ; and John Argyropaulos, whose lectures on Thucydides he had attended in Rome, is reported to have exclaimed on his return to Germany that Greece had now flown beyond the Alps.[69]   It was not, however, on the question of Greek studies, but of Hebrew, that the quarrel arose.   The converted Jew, Pfefferkorn, was the protagonist on the other side, and leading representatives of the old and the new learning were gradually drawn in ; a vicious war of pamphlets at once sprang up. Each set of combatants sought to obtain political and ecclesiastical support, and an attempt was made to drag the Emperor into the dispute.   Fortunately for the humanists they had to deal with a humanist pope, Leo X ; and the commission appointed by him to enquire into the matter gave a decision in favour of Reuchlin and freedom.   But so great was the power and indignation of the Dominicans who had already " abused Cardinal Grimani, called the Pope a schoolboy, and threatened in case of an adverse decision to appeal to a council, or even to rebel against the papal seat ",[70] that Leo was afraid to act upon it ; and in fact, after a long delay, he actually issued a belated condemnation in 1520.   But the contest was a victory for the humanists, since the effort to

[68] See *Erasmus the Reformer* pp. 70 and 125.
[69] Geiger considers that he and Conrad Celtes were alone, among the older generation of German scholars, in possessing a real knowledge of Greek : *op. cit.* p. 481.
[70] Strauss *Ulrich von Hutten* p. 114.

silence their champion had failed, and from the publicity which the struggle had aroused an abundant harvest had been reaped. A generation was growing up of which the Pope and his advisers were ignorant and apparently content to remain so.

At this epoch, as at every epoch when new life is flowing strongly, the most strenuous opposition came, not from the incurable ignorance of the foolish,—for to seek for the weaknesses which inevitably lurk in every novel project was a task beyond the mentally obtuse,—but from the inertia and prejudice of men of learning who took their stand in the old ways and refused to advance. Their opposition did not mean, however, that there was to be no advance, although it may have a little retarded it ; the advance came inevitably and the stand against it served only to mark its extent.

In Italy as we have seen the New Learning, if it did not Heretical actually attack Catholicism, was in its attitude a little scorn- views in the ful of such old-fashioned notions as the traditions of the North Church. To a much smaller degree this spirit spread into Germany. The Neo-Platonic ideas of Pico della Mirandola, in particular, found favour, and his disciple Mutianus could write to Henry Urban that there was " only one God and one Goddess though they had many names—Jupiter, Sol, Apollo, Moses, Christ, Luna, Ceres, Proserpina, Tellus, Mary ".[71] Reuchlin, also, had been influenced by Pico, especially in the direction of Jewish mysticism ; he called the Kabbala " the great mystery of the speech and words of God ".[72] Another writer of a disintegrating tendency also carried much weight in the North, Lorenzo Valla.[73] His style seems to have made an especial appeal to German Humanists : " How brilliant Valla is," wrote Langen to Vrye in a letter of Feb. 27, 1469, " he has raised up Latin to glory from the bondage of the barbarians ".

The spread of such views, even if they never attained Growing to the popularity which they enjoyed in Italy,—the North seriousness was in general suspicious of pagan tendencies,—was bound

[71] Quoted by Strauss *Ulrich von Hutten* p. 25.

[72] For the influence of Pico on Erasmus see Pusino " Der Einfluss Picos auf Erasmus " in *Zeitschrift für Kirchengesch.* (1928) pp. 75 sq.

[73] Hutten published the *Donation* of Valla for use in Germany and, with amazing audacity, dedicated it to Leo X, with a request that he would publicly commend it. Hutten's *Opera* I. pp. 155 sq. (ed. Böcking).

to react unfavourably towards papal authority. An even more serious reaction, however, came from the opposite quarter ; the growth of deep religious convictions, and the realisation of profound religious needs. In the Northern Renaissance the desire for culture and for religion were closely allied. The growing religious spirit was disgusted by the levity and the inveterate abuses of the papal system.

We have séen that the Transalpine Renaissance can be traced back to Prague and the latter half of the fourteenth century. Even in its earliest manifestations it was associated with a religious movement, for in addition to the Hussite revolution there was a stirring among the orthodox, and in particular among the Augustinians. From Bohemia this movement spread to the Low Countries and Westphalia, where it stimulated similar attempts at spiritual revival. Such were those of the Friends of God and a movement associated with the Dominicans of the Rhine district with their mystics, Eckhardt, Tauler, Suso. Ruysbroek, the master of Gerard Groot, had himself been affected by Bohemian influence.

It will be convenient here to say something of the numerous efforts to reform the monastic orders north of the Alps in the fifteenth century. In 1422 the Benedictine Houses of the province of Trier introduced a stricter rule ; a little later this rule was adopted by John Dederoth, Abbot of Bursfeld, and a group of neighbouring monasteries. By the end of the century some hundred houses had joined this " Bursfeld " Union. A similar Union or Congregation was formed round the reformed Augustinian house of Windesheim, near Zwolle. In this last community the cultivation of mysticism and humanism went on side by side, and from the Brethren of the Common Life, as they called themselves,[74] arose a movement which left permanent traces on the education and the religion of the North.[75] One characteristic of the movement

---

[74] More correctly " of the Common Lot " (see *Erasmus the Reformer* p. 79), but the usual form is too widely accepted to allow of revision.

[75] Thomas à Kempis, who wrote the lives of the founders of the " New Devotion " as he called it, shewed no great anxiety to promote secular learning. On the religious side, of course, he was its best known product. Luther also came under its influence, though the school at Magdeburg which he attended, did not actually belong to the Order : see Scheel *Luther* I. pp. 67 sq.

was its anxiety to promote the reading of the Scriptures in the vulgar tongue.[76]

The piety of the North, a little comfortable and a little tinged with self-satisfaction, is well seen in the paintings of the Flemings. Even in the primitive artists, who worked in an age which the Chroniclers depict as one of almost unrelieved cruelty and misery, there is found " a vision of pure and naïve beauty, of religious fervour and profound mystic peace ".[77] With Roger van der Weyden we arrive at a painter, who, like a Flemish Fra Angelico, found in art the means of expressing his intense religious emotions. And it was his influence which became predominant in the fifteenth century and persisted through followers such as Memling and Metsys. The latter, indeed, tends to replace true devotion by " the new tendency to exploit the sentimental aspects of life which we find contemporaneously in Perugino ".[78] *Northern piety*

In the person of Johannes Wessell we have had already an example of the man of letters who was genuinely religious; in the North he was by no means an exception; did not Rudolf Agricola intend to devote the remnant of his life to the study of theology ? [79] But the most significant testimony to the different spirit which characterised the Renaissance in Germany, is revealed by a comparison of the earliest books printed in that country and in Italy. The printers in the latter country, Germans it is true, produced hardly anything but classics; [80] those who remained in their native land, on the other hand, published editions of the Fathers, and the works of the Schoolmen. Even at this early stage the taste of the readers was the standard to which the printer had to conform. *Interest in theology*

The widespread publication of theological books in Germany provided men with material for private judgement on such questions, as elsewhere, and made them feel that they *Intellectualism of religion*

[76] Cf. Gasquet *Old English Bible* p. 120.

[77] Huizinga *The Waning of the Middle Ages* p. 222.

[78] Roger Fry *Flemish Art* p. 25.

[79] Allen *The Age of Erasmus* p. 29. Heimburg had expressed a similar desire in 1454 : see Joachimsohn *Gregor Heimburg* p. 110.

[80] The first Vulgate to be printed appeared in 1471 ; but before that Lactantius *De divinis institutionibus* and Augustine *De civitate Dei* had appeared.

were no longer so dependent on authority. This growing knowledge led to an increased exercise of private judgement, especially in Germany where individualistic tendencies were marked. This same tendency fostered another danger, an excessive intellectualism in the religious life.[81] Learning in the North was not to serve merely cultural ends; it was also to dissipate the clouds of ignorance, and be a means of combating the evils which sheltered beneath them. By education the world might be saved; but it must be of a religious nature.[82]

German nationalism

Mommsen tells us that the spread of Hellenism in Italy, during the two centuries which ended the pre-Christian era, had a revolutionary and denationalising tendency;[83] the spread of the New Learning from Italy into the North, in the age of Renaissance, although it may have had a revolutionary effect, carried with it no denationalising tendency; in fact its effect in this regard was exactly the opposite. It served to emphasise the difference between the two peoples, and to arouse the Germans to emulation.

The attempt to shew the value of things German took many forms, some of them distinctly humorous. In adopting the New Learning the Teutons were definitely encouraging a foreign form of culture which threw no light on their own customs and traditions. To compensate for this they made it a point of honour to bring into their poems as many place-names as possible; thus they were able, not only to exhibit their skill, but also their patriotism.[84]

There were also various efforts made to shew that Germany, in the past, had been quite as great as Italy; and that, in

---

[81] The fact that the tendency was recognised rendered it less ominous, for as Erasmus insisted " Vita est magis quam disputatio " (*Opera* VI. p. 3).

[82] In France and Italy the divorce between culture and learning on the one hand, and religion on the other, has, with few notable exceptions, persisted. In the North religion and culture have been much more closely allied.

[83] *History of Rome* II. p. 243.

[84] This was also a characteristic of the Carolingian Renaissance. Theodulf, for example, made up a distich on the rivers which watered the dominions of Charles :

" Rura Mosella Liger Vulturnus Matrona Ledus
Hister Atax Gabarus Olitis Albis Arar."
—*Versus contra Iudices ll.* 105 sq. in MGH. *Poet* I. p. 496.

the present, its beauties were equally worthy of praise.   This
last tendency was a counter-blast to Flavius Biondo and his
descriptive writings.[85]   Amongst the protagonists were many
whose knowledge and taste were far inferior to their patriotism ;   and their productions, it must be confessed, in striving
after the sublime, fell too often into the ridiculous.   But
there were others of a different stamp, men like Wimpheling [86]
and Beatus Rhenanus ;   the *Res Germanicae* of the latter
is a really noble attempt to vindicate the achievements of
the German people in the past and their possibilities in the
future—the latter aspect was ignored by many.   The Emperor
Maximilian was naturally forward in promoting any movement which would add to his own glories, and he was
genuinely interested in German antiquities.   Around him
there quickly gathered a group of scholars who did much
to foster this interest.[87]   Among them were Brandt and
Trithemius, Cuspinian and Stabius, as well as Pirckheimer
and Peutinger.

The patriotism of the Germans was not proof, however,
against the temptation to exchange their perfectly good
native names for classical equivalents.   Reuchlin was an
exception to the rule which made nearly all men of letters
succumb, though even he was addressed by Erasmus and others
as Capnio, and he turned the terrible Schwartzerd of his
pupil Philip to Melanchthon.[88]

Intercourse between the two peoples seem to have in- Antipathy of
tensified their mutual dislike.   In the early days of the Germans and
Renaissance German scholars, who went to the south, were Italians
regarded as barbarians, and scorned for their lack of culture.
Conrad Celtes, on his return from Italy in 1492, wrote that
" The ancient hatred between us can never be dissolved.
But for the Alps we should be eternally at war ".[89]   There

---

[85] These were *Italia Illustrata, Roma Instaurata,* and *Roma Triumphans.*

[86] Wimpheling scored a good point by making much of the German invention of printing and its spread by German craftsmen : see Geiger *op. cit.*
pp. 325 sq.

[87] On the study of German antiquity see Horowitz in Sybel's *Hist. Zeitschrift* XXV. pp. 66 sqq. and Joachimsohn *Geschichtsauffassung und Geschichts-
beschreibung in Deutschland unter dem Einfluss des Humanismus.*

[88] Another instance was Ulrich von Hutten.   In his case the possession
of a noble and ancient name may have been his reason for retaining it.

[89] Quoted by Allen *The Age of Erasmus* p. 265.

was indeed something irreconcilable in the spirits of the Germans and of the Italians, and its persistence in their cultures, even though Germany was the debtor, was not surprising.   It was to find a further manifestation in the sphere of religion, where it was reinforced by economic causes, the dislike of the Teuton to being taxed for the benefit of the Latin Church.

CHAPTER XII

THE TEUTONIC REVOLT

CREIGHTON began the last volume of his *History of* the Papacy by remarking that " The religious revolt, originated by Luther, fell like a thunderbolt from a clear sky ".[1] This statement is true ; although the common habit of reading back after-developments into the past has blinded us to it. Revolutions in thought mature much more slowly, and come to a head less suddenly, than political revolutions ; for this reason they generally effect or register changes more profound and more permanent. It has often happened that a religious or social commotion, even when it has long been preparing, is preluded by an uncanny stillness, the calm before the cataclysm.

It must be remembered that the real crisis arose, not with the publication of the Theses in 1517, but with the burning of the papal Bull in 1520.[2] When Ulrich von Hutten, the famous humanist, who was himself to become for a time a violent advocate of Reformation views,[3] heard of the dispute aroused by the Theses, he made light of it, it was merely another squabble between different friars, similar to that between the Franciscans and Dominicans over the Immaculate Conception.[4] But humanists and papalists alike were soon to see that no merely academic question was at

Suddenness of the revolt

The real crisis not the Theses

---

[1] *Op. cit.* VI. p. 3. The same was true, in a sense, of the French Revolution. The real revolution took place, as Lord Morley has said, between 1727 and 1781 (*Miscellanies* II. p. 41).

[2] See *Erasmus the Reformer* p. 41.

[3] The views of Strauss must be modified by later work, in particular that of Kalkoff, who in his *Ulrich von Hutten und die Reformation* and *Hutten's Vagantenzeit und Untergang* criticised the older conception of him as a co-worker of Luther. See further Mackinnon *Luther and the Reformation* III. p. 165.

[4] Letter to Count Hermann of Neuenahr April 1518 in *Opera* I. p. 167 (ed. Böcking).

stake ; for in Luther the dim strugglings and aspirations of myriad obscure souls had become vocal, and with his utterances the lips of the dumb were at last unsealed.

Luther's development Luther himself began as a loyal servant of the Church and its visible head the Pope ; though even as early as the Augsburg dispute of 1518 he recognised that there was something higher than he.[5] It was the mishandling of the whole situation by the Papacy which forced him on ; the realisation that the Church had become so corrupt that the highest loyalty demanded denunciation of its rulers, and at last open rebellion. Luther's progress can be traced, as I pointed out in my Hulsean Lectures,[6] by the different authorities whom he was prepared to accept, ending with the territorial prince.

The recognition of the prince as *summus episcopus*, however, and the virtual, though qualified substitution of the State for the Church, a substitution which naturally widened the breach with the Papacy, had become necessary owing to the Peasants' Revolt, and the growth of fanatical sects such as the Anabaptists. Religious revolution might otherwise have become political revolution.

It is, of course, permissible to argue that Luther when once launched on his career as a reformer, was bound in the end to break with Rome. His strength and weakness alike lay in the belief that God's grace was everything, man's will nothing. In other words he had an intense belief in his own inspiration. This belief led straight to the corollary that all who opposed him were opposing the divine will. Luther, by temperament, was probably conservative ; but his conscience hurried him into opposition when he found that his own liberty and that of countless others was being threatened. The internal struggle between his temperament and his conscience was the cause of those frequent outbursts of rage, the fruit of overstrained nerves, which brought no little harm to the cause which he tried to serve.[7]

Different opinions of Luther There are few characters in history of whom such different opinions have been formed as Luther. Those who

---

[5] " Veritas divina est etiam domina papae " : *Werke* II. p. 18.
[6] *Erasmus the Reformer* pp. 40 sq.
[7] Emil Ludwig has said, without any reference to Luther, that it is " not ideas but emotions which make revolutionaries " (*Genius and Character* p. 55). Perhaps it would be truer to say that the combination of ideas and emotions make the revolutionary ; the case of Luther certainly tends to this conclusion.

attempt to assess him, in one direction as in the other, by inconsidered praise or by blame absolute, ignore the canon that nothing can be said of the character and doings of any man except relatively. It would seem that the estimate which each critic forms, ultimately depends upon his theological or temperamental sympathies. To the Protestant Luther is a saint and hero ; to the extreme Roman a case for the pathologist. One thing, however, cannot be denied— the immensity of the influence which he has exercised on the mind and destinies of Europe, and in particular of Germany. Others had had similar experiences and arrived at similar ideas, but they had not the same force, and did not strike the same happy combination of circumstances. Fortunately we are here concerned with Luther only in his relations with the Papacy and as the symbol of the Teutonic peoples in their revolt against Latin influences and Latin exploitation ; many problems connected with him can therefore be passed by.

In the past there has been a tendency to exaggerate the extent to which Luther broke away from the old religion, and to regard him too much as a modern. Both these tendencies are mistaken as recent work and the discovery of fresh material have shewn.[8] Luther was rooted in the old religion and was greatly influenced by the later Schoolmen, especially by Ockham and Biel. The great German mystics, in particular Tauler and the author of *Theologia Germanica*, affected him profoundly ; later he came to feel that they were inadequate.[9] Luther was not really a mystic, hence his misunderstanding of Carlstadt, and his unsympathetic treatment of similar teachers ; some of them, indeed, slipped over the border which divides mysticism from sheer fanaticism. Luther does not seem to have owed much to the so-called reformers before the Reformation ; if his position was much like that of Hus or others, his own experiences had led him to adopt it.

[8] In 1889-90 Bushwald discovered in the Municipal Library at Zwickau copies of St Augustine, Peter Lombard, Anselm, and Tauler which Luther had used, and which contained his marginal notes made in 1509 and the years following. As late as 1908 the original MSS of his Lectures on Romans were found in the Royal Library at Berlin.

[9] The German mystics were forerunners of Luther in more senses than one. Not only did they exhibit a like independence and a tendency to minimise the value of good works, but some of them actually wrote in German.

His religious struggles

Luther's struggles began after he became a friar in 1505. He gave himself up to the study of theology, in which he attained a certain proficiency; but self-questionings arose, and much spiritual conflict and misery.   Fits of terror came upon him, no doubt partly physical and nervous in their origin but terribly impressive.   The shrewd and sympathetic handling of Staupitz, the Vicar-General of his Order, did little to meet them; his troubled spirit refused to receive comfort.   At last in 1508 or 1509 he found a clue in Romans i. 17 " the just shall live by faith ".   With this clue in his hand he was at length to find his way out of the labyrinth, but not for many years.

At the end of 1510 a visit to Rome shewed him that abuses in Germany were matched and surpassed by those in the Mother Church of the West.   But at the time he was not turned definitely against the papal system though probably he had received unconscious impressions which worked strongly within him.

Indulgences

In the meantime Luther had succeeded Staupitz as Professor of Biblical Theology at Wittenberg; whilst there his attention was drawn to the traffic in indulgences.   Out of his interest in the question vast consequences were to flow; but at first it was almost purely academic, the desire to get at the meaning of the whole system, but not to challenge the Papacy over it.   There can be no question that many abuses had grown up in connexion with the traffic : they were doubtless discussed in every tavern, and attempts had been made to end them.   Probably the Papacy was largely ignorant of what was actually going on, and only indirectly responsible for the worst features.

Scandal in Germany

In Germany things were especially bad.   Albrecht of Brandenburg, who at the age of twenty-three already possessed the Archbishopric of Magdeburg and the Bishopric of Halberstadt, desired in addition the Archbishopric of Mainz.   He was, of course, under the canonical age, and such excess of plurality was more than even Leo X could stomach.   However, the golden key worked as usual, and Albrecht took possession of his preferment.   But he owed an enormous sum to the Fuggers who had advanced the money for the bribe.   In order to meet it he made a deal with the Pope by which he was to take half the proceeds from the sale of indulgences. Albrecht was a shrewd man of business, and would, as Mr Wyndham Lewis has remarked, " have done well on the Stock Exchange " ; [10] but he was not one to increase the spiritual prestige of the Church, nor to commend the cause of Indulgences.[11] In many parts of Germany the sale was forbidden ; but wherever it could be carried on, the hawkers of these privileges spared no effort to push their wares, and in order to do so were not always careful to observe the teaching of the Church. One small matter aroused particular indignation. The Papacy made a special declaration that wives were permitted to buy Indulgences with their housekeeping money, without informing their husbands ! It has been conjectured that the discovery of this privilege had much to do with arousing German feeling against the practice.[12]

When Luther nailed his Theses to the door of the Castle Church at Wittenberg, he was merely challenging other scholars to a discussion of the whole question. There followed four years of discussion, as futile as such exercises tend to be as a means of reconciling divergent opinions. They served, however, to clear the air, and to make more definite the position of both parties. At the dispute with Eck at Leipzig in June 1519, Luther was specifically accused of holding Hussite views ; at the time he indignantly denied the charge, later he came to see that it was legitimate, and to rejoice over it. Leo, who had reasons for keeping on good terms with the Elector Frederick, Luther's patron, postponed action for a time ; but on June 15, 1520 by the Bull *Exsurge Domine* he excommunicated him. At the same time the works of the reformer were burnt in the Piazza Navona at Rome. Moderate men, such as Erasmus,[13] felt that the act was an unfair attempt to crush free discussion, and Luther received their sympathy, if not their agreement.

But Luther was not to be checked by a papal Bull or by the burning of copies of his writings. On December 10 of the same year he retaliated in kind. The Bull was burnt

The Theses Oct. 31, 1517

The burning of the Bull

---

[10] *Emperor of the West* p. 188.

[11] It should be remembered that the Council of Trent, among many other reforms, separated the granting of indulgences from financial considerations.

[12] I owe the point to D. B. Wyndham Lewis *op. cit.* p. 173.

[13] See Luther *Opera Lat. Var.* V. pp. 241 sq. and Erasmus' Letter to Campeggio in Allen *Erasmi Epistolae* IV. pp. 400-411.

22

and with it other literature including a copy of the Canon
Law.   The matter had now become extremely serious.

The Diet of Worms 1521   In the following January the youthful Charles V held at
Worms his first Diet as Emperor, and the affair of Luther
was one of the subjects down for consideration.   Luther
himself arrived in April under safe-conduct, and backed by
no little political power, as well as the support of many
German clerics who, as Cardinal Aleander reported, were
moved more by hatred of Rome than love of Luther.[14]   The
Diet, as was natural, condemned the opinions of the reformer ;
but he himself left the city in safety.   On the way from it,
however, he was abducted by friendly knights, and taken
to a secure hiding-place in the Wartburg.   That an Edict
of the Diet should put him under the ban of the Empire
and order his writings to be destroyed troubled him but little.

Decr. 1, 1521   Before the effect of this pronouncement could be seen Leo
Jan. 9, 1522   was no more, and Adrian VI reigned in his stead.

Adrian VI and Erasmus   In the following December the new Pope summoned
Erasmus to Rome.[15]   Erasmus asked to be excused ; but he
did not lose the opportunity for giving publicity to his views
on the situation.   He urged the Pope to call a council, and
to consult wise and judicious scholars who would be able to
rise above the passions of the moment, and in the calm air
of the study to reach true conclusions.   He pointed out that
a settlement could only be reached by sacrifices on the part
of both sides.[16]   It was at this very point that all Adrian's
short-lived efforts at reform were to be shipwrecked ; the
curia, at any rate, were not prepared to make any sacrifices.[17]
As to the calm, passionless scholars they too would not be
easily found, neither among the conservatives nor among
the reformers themselves.

Clement VII   Adrian died in September 1523, and Rome rejoiced at
the end of the Cimmerian darkness.   The election of another
Medici, in Clement VII, seemed to promise a return to the
golden days of Leo.   A reaction against Lutheranism now

[14] At the Diet the grievances of Germany against the Pope were brought
to the Emperor's notice ; as in France they were concerned with taxation,
patronage, and jurisdiction.

[15] The letter is in Allen *Erasmi Epistolae* V. pp. 145-150.

[16] See Allen *op. cit.* V. pp. 257-261.

[17] The best of them would have agreed with Livy I. Praef. 9 : " nec vitia
nostra nec remedia pati possumus ".

began to set in. A visit of Campeggio to the Diet of Nuremberg in January 1524, was followed by the formation of a League of Catholic Princes at Ratisbon in the following June. The same year saw the publication, by Erasmus, of his *Essay on Freewill*, which manifested his disagreement with the reformers and earned a bitter attack from Luther. The movement also suffered from the Peasants' Revolt,[18] and the Anabaptist Rising, both of which owed to it in some measure their origin. Things were by no means going well.

Then came the important Diet at Speier in 1526, with Ferdinand as president in the absence of his brother.[19] This diet saw the establishment of the famous rule *cuius regio eius religio*, by which each prince was to decide on the religion in his own territory.[20] It was, of course, simply a legalising of anarchy, and not intended to be a permanent solution of the religious problems of Germany.[21] As Charles was absent something had to be done to enable affairs to proceed until he could attend in person. But in effect the rule became permanent, for when the Diet met three years later, again at Speier, in spite of the breach in the ranks of the Reformers through the disagreement of the Lutherans and Zwinglians, the proposal for its abolition brought forth a strong protest from a minority too powerful to be disregarded. They asserted the right of private judgement—that is for those who happened to be ruling princes or magistrates of important municipalities. Protestantism had come to the birth, and the breach between Roman and Teuton was past filling.

Diet of Speier 1526

Diet of Speier 1529

The Lutherans, however, did not at once give up hope that they might still retain their place as a reformed Church in union with Rome ; and the Confession presented to the Diet of Augsburg in 1530 was intended to be conciliatory.

Further developments

[18] The revolt was rife in the ecclesiastical provinces, but Electoral Saxony was unaffected. The Catholic princes made it an excuse for slaughtering Lutherans. This was an old trick ; cf. the letter written on 15 July 1233 by Gregory IX in which he accused Frederick II of slaying his political opponents as heretics (in Huillard-Bréholles *Hist. Dipl. Frid. II* IV. p. 444).

[19] Charles wished to be on good terms with the Lutheran princes as he had quarrelled with the Pope who was scheming against him.

[20] This rule was the culmination of a long process by which the local nobles, many of whom were actually ecclesiastics, had been consolidating their control over their territories.

[21] Ranke considers that the rule was intended to be permanent ; *Deutsche Geschichte im Zeitalter der Reformation* II. pp. 261 and 290 (ed. 1925).

But such a hope soon proved to be groundless. Further attempts at reconciliation, sponsored by Charles V himself, failed at Ratisbon in 1541, and warfare followed. It was ended for a time by the Religious Peace of Augsburg in 1555 ; only to break out again in the disastrous Thirty Years' War. The Peace of Westphalia in 1648 at length recognised that division was permanent.

Origins of the revolt

The Reformation, although it seemed to arise with the suddenness of a breaking wall, had long been preparing,[22] and like all great movements it had its origins in diverse quarters ; the main stream drew to itself many lesser tributaries. In considering the problem of its origins two questions have to be faced. Why did revolt arise and why, when it had arisen, was it allowed to assume such proportions that finally it became incurable ? The answers to these questions overlap considerably, for the persistence of the abuses which had provoked the original movement worked for its continuance. It will be best therefore to consider them together.

Its chief causes

The year 1520 saw the production of three important pamphlets by Luther ; *The Appeal to the Christian Nobles, De Captivitate Babylonica Ecclesiae and De Libertate Christiani.* In these pamphlets the three chief causes of the revolt are fully exposed ; German national feeling, the loss of papal prestige, and the religious needs of the German people. Underlying them all was the insistent demand for freedom from the bondage of tradition and the control of an alien power.[23] National and racial characteristics were the ultimate cause of this demand. The Teuton is by nature independent and individualistic,[24] and from of old, critical in his attitude towards authority.[25] There were, moreover,

[22] The desire for some new movement, and the hope that it was at hand, can be seen in popular literature, and in particular in Hans Sachs' *Die Wittenbergische Nachtigall*, parts of which recall inevitably the spirit of Swinburne's *Songs before Sunrise* ; e.g.

" Wake up ! Now may the dawn be seen ;
And singing in the thicket green
I hear a tuneful nightingale."

[23] In 1517 Luther signed himself, by an obvious pun, Martin Eleutherius, Martin the Emancipator.
[24] Cf. Villari *History of Florence* p. 897.
[25] This has recently been pointed out afresh by N. P. Williams *Northern Catholicism* p. x. " The normal attitude of the free Northern races towards executive authority and its depositories is respectful, but always potentially,

concrete grievances of a fiscal and economic character. When the first symptoms of dissatisfaction became manifest the irresponsibility of the Popes and their advisers widened the breach and made understanding impossible. Into these various factors we must now enter in some detail.

In the struggle with the Empire the Popes had made National use of racial feeling to drive the Germans out of Italy. feeling Even a great Pope like Innocent III, whose name Lothar [27] was itself German and who came of Teuton stock, employed it. The revival of learning, as we have seen, helped to perpetuate the antagonism ; for the new-found glories of Latin culture increased the pride of the Italians, and made them contemptuous towards the " Gothic " barbarians. Luther was strongly aware of this ; " The Romans have too long mocked us as blockheads ", he wrote to Staupitz in September 1518.[28]

The truth was that Latin culture and the Latin Church had done their work ; they had been tutors to bring the Germans to civilisation and to Christ. The Germans now began to feel that their own development was being hampered by further dependence ; they were conscious of their powers and avid to express them in their own way. There was moreover throughout Christendom a consciousness of differences which, as Creighton has said, " were sure to find expression sooner or later in religious matters ".[29]

In its early days the Roman Church had gained strength Roman by taking into itself elements from the soil in which it had Church too Italian been planted ; as it continued to develop this process went on, and by the fifteenth and sixteenth centuries it had acquired much that was pagan and Italian.[30] In fact the Teutons were coming to regard it not as a Catholic, but as an Italian, Church.

and often actually, critical." Professor Williams quotes Tacitus *Germania* VII. i. for similar traits in the ancient Germans : " nec regibus infinita aut libera potestas, et duces exemplo potius quam imperio . . . admiratione praesunt ".

[27] The curious reader may like to know that Lothar is really the same name as the later Luther : see Köstlin *Martin Luther* I. p. 21.

[28] De Wette *Briefe, Sendschreiben und Bedenken* I. p. 188.

[29] *History of the Papacy* V. p. 192.

[30] There are some interesting admissions by Guiraud *L'Église Romaine* pp. xvii sq. Some critics see in its later developments the outcrop of a " magical sacramentalism " which was far older than Christianity itself, a return to what Santayana has called Mediterranean religion.

Effect of the Schism   Signs had not been wanting, in the century before the Reformation, of dissatisfaction with Latin control. During the Great Schism there had been a loosening of the bands which linked Germany and the Papacy, and when unity had been restored the Northern clerics were by no means anxious to have them tightened up again.[31] The declaration of neutrality in 1438 [32] revealed a drift away from the Papacy, and the desire to organise the Church on national lines; though such a movement was checked by the Diet of Mainz in 1461, it had a significance for those who could perceive the signs of the times. The large circulation enjoyed by the writings of Gregory Heimburg, with his pro-German and anti-papal outlook, is evidence of the feeling of his contemporaries.[33]

Loyalty to Rome of older humanists   What is strange about the movement is the fact that while the younger humanists, such as Bucer and Melanchthon, went with the Reformation ; the majority of the older scholars remained loyal to the Church of their baptism, and that in spite of their avowed dissatisfaction with much within it. To mention the names of Reuchlin, of Erasmus, of Wimpheling, and of Willibald Pirkheimer,[34] will be enough to illustrate the point. It may have been that, like their contemporaries in England, they were anti-clerical rather than anti-catholic. But still more was it due to the natural conservatism of the scholar. When the Reformation movement got on its way they must have felt that it was travelling too fast and too far for their sympathies. They had been at home in the Renaissance world, for that was an age of counsel ; now there had come upon them an age of execution, when men had their feet firmly planted on a new road, and demanded from their guides a stout heart and an unwavering confidence.

Criticism of the Papacy   If the humanists, for the most part, remained loyal to the

---

[31] For anti-papal feeling in the middle of the fifteenth century see Chmel *Kirchliche Zustände* pp. 43 sq. and *Epist.* of Vincent of Anspach in Pez *Thes. Nov.* VI. pt. iii. pp. 327 sq. It was especially strong in the monasteries, perhaps on account of their laxity.

[32] See above p. 212.

[33] Pastor states that numerous copies of his writings can still be found in German libraries : *op. cit.* III. pp. 188 sq.

[34] He has been suspected of writing the *Eccius dedolatus*, a coarse satire on Luther's opponent, but probably wrongly : see Merker *Der Verfasser des Eccius Dedolatus* (1923). When his name was included in the Bull against Luther he took alarm and recanted.

Papacy, they reserved to themselves the right to criticise it. In this they were not alone, for in the case of the quarrel over Reuchlin, as we saw above, even the Dominicans could threaten the Pope. Their threat need not be taken seriously, but it was an indication of the loss of papal prestige in quarters where once it had stood very high.

In other quarters, too, there was an ever-increasing tendency to disregard papal leadership or even to consider it definitely harmful. The French expedition into Italy in 1496, had opened the eyes of the dwellers North of the Alps to conditions as they really were in Rome, and growing intercourse had robbed men's minds of that reverential awe which is often best preserved by distance, or an impenetrable veil. The German artists who swarmed into Italy from the fifteenth century onwards, would not be silent about their experiences when they returned. Even the pilgrims could narrate strange stories, and express their dissatisfaction ; at the Jubilee of 1500 they complained of the stench of the corpses hanging from the Bridge of St Angelo. Outwardly, of course, there was much to admire ; but the external magnificence of Rome and the papal court went to conceal its spiritual squalor. The eyes of Luther pierced through it and his soul was revolted. When first he caught sight of the venerable city " sacred with martyr blood " he fell on his knees ; but when he entered he found it was the home of countless abominations. So great was the impiety and wickedness that nothing but the evidence of his own eyes would have convinced him of its existence.[36]

The discovery that the moral basis of the Papacy had been undermined carried far more weight in Germany than in Italy. To the latter country it had come gradually, and was at length regarded as a commonplace ; to the Germans it came with the shock of a discovery. Moreover the Germans had a much higher sense of moral decorum than the Italians ; and at this period there was a growing seriousness, as can be seen from the restrictions set on the licence of the carnivals, and in the sobering effect of the outbreak of the

---

[36] See *Tischreden* III. pp. 451 sq., and, for a description of the state of the city as Luther found it, Böhmer *Luther's Romfahrt* pp. 99 sq. The visit took place at the end of 1510, not as is sometimes stated in 1509 or 1511 : see Scheel *Luther* II. pp. 415 sq.

terrible new disease of syphilis.[37]   To them the excuse that the state of society in Italy was low, and that the Papacy was merely carried away with the rest, would have sounded very inadequate ; was it not the Church's task to uphold the moral standard, and not to fall with it ?   The Reformers might well have said, from their knowledge of the papal court, with the English Evangelical leader, John Newton, that if the Pope was not anti-Christ he had bad luck to be so like him.

Distrust of Papacy   Germany certainly objected strongly to paying excessive taxes for the benefit of Italy—a subject to which we shall return—but fiscal abuses alone would not have caused a revolt ; it was the moral revulsion which led the better minds to rebel.   This is in accord with general political experience, for distrust and loss of respect on the part of the governed, is generally a more potent fountain of revolt than oppression on the part of the ruler.

This loss of prestige had come about slowly ;   it may indeed be traced right back to the beginnings of our period, in the rise of the temporal power.   For it was this, according to Lord Acton, which was its root, for it brought the Popes " into degrading and contaminating rivalry with wicked statesmen " ;   as a result they learned " to expend spiritual authority in exchange for worldly gains, until at last, when they have to face new antagonists, their dignity is tarnished and their credit gone ".[38]

Religious needs of the German people   The German people were at last in deadly earnest.   Their religious needs were not being satisfied, and they were crying out for light and leading.[39]   Efforts there had been to cope with such demands, but they had not been on any considerable scale, or had even been suspect as heretical.[40]   Now the demand was becoming so urgent as to be threatening.   This can be seen in the paintings of Roger van der Weyden which spoke " in tragic convulsive tones such as never before . . .

[37] Cf. P. F. Schmidt *Frankfurt* p. 88 : " Die Natur setze mit jener Krankheit gleichsam einen Merkstein, dass es mit der alter Welt zu Ende gehe und ein anderes, ernstschafteres Zeitalter heraufkommen."

[38] *Historical Essays and Studies* p. 434.

[39] Mackinnon is very insistent that the Reformation was not merely a nationalistic movement but " the revival of the Pauline type of religious thought and experience " : *Luther and the Reformation* II. p. 337.

[40] See Pastor *History of the Popes* I. pp. 157 sqq.

had been found in art ".[41]   Sin to the German was something
serious, " something ineradically ingrained . . . and never
to be removed by any piecemeal operations " such as might
suit the Latin.[42]   Until Luther came, darkness hung low
over Germany.   His teaching pierced the gloom and men
when they saw the light hurried to it.   They found in him
the fragment of truth which their souls needed, and so in
countless hearts he met with response.

At every epoch of the middle ages the cry for reform was Delayed
heard ; not only in Germany, but throughout the Church ; [43] reforms
the long delay, however, and the general hopelessness of any
remedy from within the Church, led men's thoughts to reform
at any cost, even the cost of leaving the Church.   Freeman
once wrote of the allies of ancient Rome that they " did not
seek to get rid of Rome as their ruler " but to have a share
in the government of themselves and others ; it is only " in
some desperate moment when every demand is refused that
they resort to the extreme measure of secession."   The same
was true, on the whole, of the relations of the Germans and
the Papacy.   For long they had borne the consequences of
papal neglect and papal exploitation ; now at length they
would bear them no more.   Unity ceased to be valued
when its most impressive representative was the papal
collector.

In the middle of the fourteenth century there had been
a good deal of opposition to the Papacy in both France and
Germany, and although heresy existed it did not furnish
the cause ; there was no question, as in Bohemia, of differences
of doctrine.   That the reforming movement in Germany
became critical of the Church's doctrine, as well as of its
administration, was due in no small degree to the refusal of
the Papacy to grant reforms.   It failed to recognise that the
spirit of change, ever at work both in individuals and institutions, had to be conciliated and guided into safe channels ;

---

[41] His art " is no longer the soft, rather thoughtless and phlegmatic piety
of the Middle Ages . . . but the thunder preceding the storm, an earthquake
which convulsed the nations " : Muther *History of Painting* I. pp. 106 sqq.

[42] Cf. William James *Varieties of Religious Experience* p. 184.

[43] See Haller *Papsstum und Kirchenreform* I. pp. 3 sqq.   He ends his
survey of the middle ages with the remark : " wer Paradoxe liebt, mag sagen,
das Problem der Reform beginne mit Ananias und Saphira ".

that to meet it face to face, and try and drive it back was a means of inevitable disaster.[44]

Excuses for this   To this as to every question there are two sides, and something may be said in excuse for the delay. It has always to be remembered that any existing situation is invariably complex, and the risk of disturbance by hasty action is correspondingly dangerous. Change often makes for uncertainty and loss of confidence, especially in an institution which claims a wide authority over the beliefs and thoughts of men. There is also the temptation to delay reform in order to make it more comprehensive. All this might be urged in palliation of the charge against the Papacy; unfortunately no unprejudiced student of the early sixteenth century can feel that it is applicable, for, as we shall see, the policy adopted by that august body was based on no principles, but was due almost entirely to ignorance of the situation, and a desire to raise the maximum amount of revenue from Germany.

Resistance to taxation   We saw above that in the Avignon period the exactions of the Papacy and its collectors met with deep resentment in Germany, and even with forcible resistance. In England and Spain during the Schism, national feeling resisted taxation ; as a consequence increased burdens were laid on Germany. But there, too, resistance grew. In 1487 an attempt to impose a tithe was thwarted, and as late as 1500 the imperial government kept back two-thirds of the money raised ostensibly for war against the Turk.[45] Concrete grievances, such as over-taxation by a foreign power, are more cogent arguments in favour of revolt than abstract differences. Heavy taxation by a native ruler may be endured, for most of the proceeds are spent in the country itself. Payments to a foreigner, even when they are not resented as a mark of servitude, bring no such benefit.

Changing social and economic conditions   Quite apart from the resentment felt against papal taxation social and economic conditions in Germany were making

---

[44] Sir Robert Morier, a shrewd diplomatist of the last century, used to say of the art of governing : " The banks must be ameliorated and strengthened where the stream threatens to overflow and destroy them—but they must neither be drawn too close . . . nor kept too far apart : above all the attempt must never be made to throw a dam across the bed inasmuch as it would accumulate the waters and necessarily bring about a general inundation " : see *Memoirs and Letters of Sir Robert Morier* I. p. 232.

[45] See Ranke *Päpste* I. p. 27 (E.T. p. 31).

for discontent. The nobles were rapacious, and forced huge sums from their dependents to spend on their own pleasures ; the middle classes were growing in wealth and influence, and in consequence impatient of all authority, and intent on material prosperity ; whilst at the bottom the wretched peasants were subject to insufferable burdens. Wealth and power were getting into fresh hands, as the nobles dissipated their substance, and the traders kept a close hand on all that came their way. This is ever a frutiful source of unsettlement, as the old endeavour to defend their privileges and the new strive to usurp them. A changed attitude towards the Church was almost inevitable ; grievances over excessive taxation made it all the more bitter when it came.

The failure of the Papacy to deal adequately with the situation can be traced back to three causes. Ignorance of what was really happening ; [46] refusal to see the seriousness of it ; mistakes in handling Luther and those who felt with him. *Causes of papal failure*

The Church, like the ancient Empire, had become unwieldy and out of touch with its extremities,[47] though the methods for raking in revenue were up-to-date and well organised. It did not realise that forces had been mustering secretly behind the sombre shadow of the past, and such warnings as were conveyed to it in the fifteenth century seemed unduly pessimistic. Nicholas of Cusa, indeed, declared that the legates in Germany knew of its state but did not inform the Pope. He suggested as a remedy the formation of a council to keep him up to date, and so prepare for reform.[48] It is, however, doubtful if such a body would *Ignorance of situation*

[46] When the Umayyad party fell in 750 a sheikh, who belonged to it, gave as one reason for the catastrophe " ignorance of how we stood " : see Masudi *Prata Aurea* VI. pp. 85 sq.

[47] The Roman Empire fell because the provinces decayed and decay spread to the centre. The Papacy declined because the provinces grew in strength and broke away owing to their lack of confidence in the central authority.

[48] *Opera* p. 742. His own appointment as legate in 1450 had aroused resentment and opposition, and as late as 1458 alarming reports were still being sent to Rome of the state of Germany. But nothing was done and " ultimately the opposition died a natural death ", as Pastor writes (*History of the Popes* II. p. 422) ; and so, no doubt, the Popes were glad to believe. The actual facts were probably far different ; opposition had merely been driven below the surface.

have made any difference ; the age was one which loved
talking and discussing, which set theoretical problems above
practical.   When the revolt broke out at last, there was a
sudden interruption to the quiet and calm, and the Papacy
was faced by urgent realities.   But even then it failed to
cope with them, and lapsed again into a state of foolish
optimism.

Such a failure can be accounted for on one of two grounds :
it may have been due to mere indifference and foolish security ;
it may have been due to weariness in upholding high traditions ; such as Seneca had foretold would afflict the Roman
Empire after his day.[49]   The candid student of the history
of the Papacy has to admit that it was the former, less noble,
sentiment which was mainly responsible for the neglect of
the Papacy to undertake the task thrust upon it.

Undue optimism   Croce tells us that tragedies are an inseparable consequence
of spiritual revolutions ; [50] but in the Reformation story,
as viewed from the side of Rome, there was, in the early
stages, no idea of tragedy at all.   When the old Empire
collapsed after its long agony, the sense of tragedy was overwhelming, of a brooding fate hanging over men ; the Papacy
was too shallow to realise what was at stake, and met the
whole crisis in a spirit of levity ; Luther's solemn outbursts
were but " the vapourings of another tipsy German who would
soon be sober and change his mind ".[51]

There are times when the wisest policy of a ruler is to
avoid danger, and to leave undisturbed the sense of security
and peace ; but at this epoch the dangers were unavoidable,
and to preserve the sense of security was only to postpone
the coming crisis, and to aggravate it.   Leo may have felt,
like Louis XV, that things would last his time ; he had an
immense faith in his own fortune, and if he did not actually
utter the remark attributed to him, " The Papacy is ours
let us enjoy it ", his attitude is revealed in it ; others, too, were
content to enjoy it with him.   The Popes had little interest

[49] " Nature's stern law requires that all high achievements shall end in a
fall swifter than our ascent to the heights " : *Controversia* I. preaf. vii.

[50] *Theory and History of Historiography* p. 271.

[51] *Tischreden* II. p. 567.   At the time Luther had a pathetic belief in the
good intentions of Leo and put down all evils to the bad influence of the
curia.   The Pope was like Daniel in Babylon : see *Werke* I. p. 679.

in the spiritual responsibilities of their high office,[52] and exhibited an admirable patience under abuses which mainly afflicted other people.

When at last the Papacy was compelled to act, its efforts were marked by a series of blunders, "the result of the triumph of officials over statesmen in the Papal court" Creighton would say.[53] There was no real attempt at understanding, but only at suppression of what was annoying and inconvenient. It is sometimes asked why Leo did not shew to Luther the consideration which, in spite of many obstacles, he had done to Reuchlin. The answer is obvious; the Reuchlin controversy left revenues unaffected. The whole papal system of diplomacy unfitted it for dealing with a truth-loving and straightforward people like the Germans.[54] In Italy it was different and Leo's own maxim, "When you have made a league with one party you should keep in constant negotiation with the other", was a recognised method of playing the game of politics. But Germany was not "playing a game" at all; the German people were face to face with sin and death. *Mistakes in handling situation*

Part of the papal failure was due to the choice of wrong instruments for conducting negotiations. Tetzel was, of course, not really an instrument of the Popes at all, and was quickly thrown aside to die in shame with nothing but a kindly message from his late antagonist to console him.[55] Cajetan [56] made some kind of an effort to get Luther to recant, but he was so bound up in the old Scholasticism that they found no point of contact. Miltitz promised to bring in a better state of affairs; but he had no authority, and was, moreover, a feeble person and unable to grasp the real significance of things. Aleander as an Italian was unacceptable to the Germans.[57] *in choice of agents*

[52] Cf. Pastor *History of the Popes* VII. p. 4 : " With unprecedented optimism Leo X looked into the future without anxiety, and frivolously deluded himself as to the importance of the times ".

[53] *History of the Papacy* VI. p. 91.

[54] This was true of the people in general though not of their rulers ; the Elector of Saxony, Luther's protector, was himself a skilled ' diplomatist '.

[55] Enders *Luther's Briefwechsel* I. p. 413.

[56] His real name was Thomas de Vio. He was called Cajetan from his birth-place, Gaeta.

[57] Erasmus did not conceal his opinion of the papal agents. In a letter to Nicholas Everard in the spring of 1521 he wrote : " Quin et illud demiror,

Effects of revolt

To the men of the early sixteenth century the dramatic significance of the events of their day must have been obvious ; but the Reformation set in motion vast forces which are still operative, whose final goal cannot even be foreseen. The complete significance of what then took place will only be known to generations that lie waiting within the dark womb of time.   Enough, however, has been made plain in the centuries that have already passed to shew that immense changes came as a result of the movement ; these can best be considered under the headings of religious, intellectual, and political.

The Schism

The most obvious result in the religious sphere was the schism of the West by which the Roman communion lost wellnigh half, and that certainly the mentally more active half, of its adherents.[58]   Thus alongside the great division of East and West there was another into South and North, for the frontier of Protestantism when finally it became stable corresponded almost exactly with that of the old Roman Empire.   To some this split was providential and calculated ultimately to work for the enriching of Christianity in the West.[59]   But to others it was a grievous rending of the unity of the Church.   The revolt in Germany led the way, and without it there would probably, if one may venture on a hazardous judgement, have been no breach in England or elsewhere.   It had one good effect, for Rome at last was shamed into reform.[60]

Loss of clerical privileges

The Reformers were mainly concerned with the salvation of the individual soul, and it almost seemed as if the Church was for most of them little more than a voluntary association for that end.   Luther's novel doctrine of a Church which

Pontificem tale negotium per tales homines agere, partim indoctos, certe impotentis arrogantiae omnes . . . Omnibus placet illud iuuenile consilium : Minimus digitus meus maior est dorso patris mei." Allen *Eras. Epist.* IV. pp. 446 sq.

[58] See Von Hügel *Essays and Addresses* II. p. 15.

[59] Cf. the words of Alexander Knox quoted by Brilioth in *The Anglican Revival* p. 49 : " Was it not, then, worthy of Providence, when the ripeness of time came, to set one half of the Western Church loose, to go in search of new benefits, and to leave the other half on its old unaltered ground, in order that by retaining everything, it might lose nothing ".

[60] See *Erasmus the Reformer* p. 46 with references.   Fogazzaro actually calls Luther " that great healer of Catholicism " : quoted in *Life of Antonio Fogazzaro* p. 77.

was invisible,[61] alongside that which could be seen and whose membership could be enumerated, made an appeal to the strongly individualistic attitude of the times, as well as to the individualistic Teutonic spirit.[62] This involved a new attitude towards the clergy and towards that decaying in-stitution of the middle ages, monasticism.

The doctrine of justification by faith, and the general protest against any idea of a mediating priesthood, at once reduced the clergy to a position of small importance, save so far as they were capable of becoming effective preachers. To those who still clung to the old conceptions there was distinct hostility, which at times broke out into actual violence, as at Erfurt in the spring and summer of 1521. In the autumn of the same year a bitter attack on the clergy appeared with incitements to spoil their goods. This was contained in a tract entitled *Neukarsthans*.[63] It need hardly be said that benefit of clergy, which Maitland has described as " one of the worst evils of the later middle ages " was practically abolished.

As to monasticism, it was opposed not merely because it had become corrupt, or even because the monks were papal agents, but on political and social grounds, as setting forth an ideal which was liable to clash with the authority of the ruler, and the supremacy of family life. With it went the idea that celibacy was more honourable than the married state, a view which was strongly condemned by Luther.[64] The opinion of a recent writer on social subjects that the sterility of monks and nuns " for so many centuries turned the laws of heredity against the moral progress of the race " [65] is true in part, but it cannot be widely applied, as it is based

Opposition to monasticism

[61] It was not entirely novel, for Augustine *De Doctrina Christiana* III. 32 seems to recognise the distinction.

[62] Inge considers that the idea of ' personality ' culminating in the im-pervious selves of Kant, was not part of the original Christian tradition : *Personal Idealism and Mysticism* pp. 95, 97.

[63] It used to be attributed to Hutten and is printed among his works by Böcking (IV. pp. 651 sqq.). But it is more probably by Bucer : see Kalkoff *Hutten und die Reformation* pp. 537 sq.

[64] *Werke* XII. p. 99. Luther and the reformers really held an entirely different view of the Christian life to that of the Catholics ; this, and not differences of doctrine, was the insuperable barrier to agreement (cf. Harnack *Monasticism* pp. 115 sq.). The one saw in the monk the ideal Christian, the other held that the ideal Christian must live a more normal life.

[65] Rauschenbusch *Christianity and the Social Crisis* p. 174.

on too optimistic a view of the character of the average monk or nun, which was probably not much higher than that of their contemporaries in the world.

Luther regarded marriage, indeed, as a physical necessity, since sex was a divine ordinance ; [66] though he would admit that certain exceptions were allowable in view of Christ's decláration.[67] His own outlook on the married state was unfortunately almost purely animal, and this led him to permit practices which suggest the moral standard of the Old Testament, rather than the higher teaching of Christianity.[68] In view of this, it is not surprising that the spread of the reformation doctrines was accompanied by a decline in morals which at times almost threatened a breakdown. But for this the Reformers were not entirely to blame.

Decline of morals

It has to be remembered that habit and custom are potent influences in settled communities and quiet times ; a sudden uprising not seldom reveals the feebleness of their hold. Under the old system there had been rigid control, and men and women were not yet ready for freedom and inevitably they abused it. They had not been trained to move alone, and anti-nomianism of one shade or another might easily infect the mind of the less stable folk who felt that they were ' saved.' The dissolution of the monasteries, moreover, had let loose on society whole swarms of monks and nuns who became Lutherans " for the sake of their bellies and in order to indulge the flesh ".[69] The low moral tone which prevailed was a condemnation, not of the new, but of the old system under which characters had been formed. The bigamy of Philip of Hesse and of an even greater man, William the Silent, is a heavier condemnation of the Pre-Reformation Church than any number of papal ' nephews '. Ultimately the efforts of Melanchthon and Calvin were to shew the real power of the Reformation teaching to enforce a high moral standard.

---

[66] *Werke* X. pt. ii. pp. 276 sq.

[67] Matt. xix. 12.

[68] In case of impotence " he would allow the married woman to seek satisfaction by agreement with her husband " (Mackinnon *Luther and the Reformation* III. p. 135), and if a wife refuses co-habitation " he holds that the husband is justified in repudiating the wife and taking another, and vice-versa " : (*op. cit.* p. 137).

[69] This is Luther's own admission : see Enders *Luther's Briefwechsel* III. pp. 323 sq.

Intellectually also the application of the principle of free-_{Private} dom had a startling effect. Luther himself is not always ^{judgement} quite consistent in his attitude towards private judgement. He certainly would not have allowed such absolutely, since he regarded the authority of the Scriptures as supreme ; but it was for each to accept them. In some ways there was less room for the reason in Lutheranism than in the old Scholasticism. Private judgement is really a modern luxury coming from scientific studies and the philosophical systems based on them.

In many quarters private judgement was carried to excess, and men without any proper training regarded themselves as qualified to decide upon theological questions by the light of nature and the Bible. This tendency opened the door to numerous differences, and to the eventual growth of count-less petty sects, " the maggots of corrupted texts " as Samuel Butler has called them.

The earnest and aggressive assertion of great principles _{Excesses,} is always accompanied by the risk that they may be extended ^{political} into undesirable quarters. Leaders vie with one another in bold inferences, and take delight in startling utterances. So it was with the Reformation. It brought forth many extreme leaders, and as a whole suffered from the tendency almost inseparable from a living and vigorous movement, the tendency to resent even necessary barriers and to push matters too quickly. Such teachers aroused in Luther only disgust and opposition ; but they also aroused the same feelings in others, who were not so strongly pledged to the movement. In this lies their importance for our purpose ; for the reaction towards Rome which followed the outbreak of the revolt was partly due to the excesses of the Reformers, and to the chaos of beliefs which ensued.

A successful revolutionary, unless perchance the scene of _{and} his operations is a South American Republic, is always sur- ^{theological} prised that there should be a revolution after him. So Luther could not understand why other people should wish to extend his principles beyond the point to which he himself applied them. Froude once suggested that he " would have gone to work with less heart, could he have foreseen the Thirty Years' War, and in the distance the theology of Tübingen ".[70]

₇₀ *Short Studies in Great Subjects* I. p. 28.

But had such a vision been vouchsafed to him, surely his answer would have been in words which, even if they were not actually used by him, represent his spirit—" I can no other ".[71]

Protestant Scholasticism

The position was, of course, intolerable, and soon Melanchthon, and Calvin, and the other Protestant Schoolmen, faced the need of resolving the chaos, and giving to their cause a dogmatic foundation, which would incidentally place it in a firmer position for meeting the attacks of the Roman advocates. Thus the Reformers were forced to become as narrowly dogmatic as the Romans. Yet to their work the modern spirit of toleration is indirectly due ; for in the lapse of centuries it came to be seen that differences of belief did not after all make the difference which the medievals had imagined. When the secular prince, in particular, found that the Protestant was as good a citizen as the Catholic, and vice versa, every excuse for persecution was gone. The fact that no one religious creed had the predominance worked in the end for universal tolerance.

Growth of toleration

Decline of learning

Although Luther himself was anxious that education should spread, many of his followers, especially in the excitement of the first preaching of the Reformation doctrines, were inclined to rest on a kind of divine inspiration. Learning thus came to be despised, and the number of students in the German universities dropped enormously.[72] One of the reasons which Erasmus gave for his disapproval of the movement was that it was detrimental to scholarship. It is probably not true, as is sometimes stated, that the Reformation was responsible for the loss of Latin as a universal language among scholars. It would in any case have decayed before the rising vernaculars and the effect of printing.

Political elements

Religious quarrels are seldom fought out apart from political complications, and often indeed have their origin in the sphere of politics. So it was with the Reformation. To many the movement seemed the natural sequel to earlier struggles, and Luther the successor of Hildebrand in severing, this time from the side of Germany, the link between it and the Papacy. At first the current of reform flowed so swiftly that many of the princes were persuaded to support

[71] For the origin of this well-known phrase see Mackinnon *Luther and the Reformation* II. p. 302.

[72] See Mackinnon *op. cit.* III. pp. 212 sqq.

it, without having any real sympathy ; political reasons swayed them as they swayed many who joined the opposite camp. But Germany was not sufficiently united even for religious agreement, and the balance of power led one ruler to take up the Protestant side or the Catholic, because his neighbour and rival had taken the other.

But if the Reformation owed much to political complications, the movement in its turn had deep political repercussions. Although Luther cared greatly for religious freedom, he had no sympathy with those who sought political liberty, which he seems to have regarded as dangerous to society ; and Calvin held the idea of a theocracy, which would have meant in the long run the rule of the pastor, the position dreaded by Erastus. None the less it is " not too much to say that political liberty would not nowadays exist anywhere but for the claim to ecclesiastical independence ".[73] The Church was certainly a heavy loser by the political changes within the various States which followed the Reformation ; it was not merely that benefit of clergy was abolished, but the very spheres of Church and State seemed to be transposed, and civil authority substituted for ecclesiastical as a final court of appeal.[74] The burning of the Canon Law with the Bull in 1520 had a deeper significance than contemporaries realised, for from that time it was to cease to be an international code.[75] In future the civil rulers, with few exceptions, would reserve to themselves all coercive power and refuse to act at the Church's bidding.[76]

National feeling had played a large part in the rise of the National Reformation, and it continued to function as the movement divisions progressed, though peoples were divided by the new doctrines, German against German, Swiss against Swiss. New sympathies and new alignments were demanded by the changed religious conditions, and in many cases the appeal to arms was the direct sequel to the attempt at new combinations, and the assertion of new liberties. The ill-feeling between Spain and England, and the revolt of the Netherlands, are instances of this as well as the Thirty Years' War. One interesting

[73] J. N. Figgis *From Gerson to Grotius* p. 151.
[74] *Op. cit.* p. 5.
[75] Its study was forbidden in England by Henry VIII.
[76] Figgis *op. cit.* p. 81.

feature was the drawing of Denmark and Sweden once again into the orbit of European history.[77]

Papacy and Empire driven to unite

In Germany the crisis had revealed the real weakness of the Empire, and in its weakness it had been driven into an alliance with its old enemy, the Papacy. These two venerable opponents were thus forced to make a tardy peace by the descent of other combatants into the arena. It was, indeed, a tardy alliance, for it came, as Bryce has said, " when faith had forsaken the one and grown cold towards the other. From the Reformation onwards the Empire and the Papacy fought side by side for existence." [78]

The end of Medieval Europe

Thus the German people had asserted their right to think as they wished, and to control their own destinies. With that assertion the old Europe came to an end. No longer would there be a single religious, or even a single cultural, system. But the full end was not yet so far as the Medieval Papacy was concerned, it had still to be uprooted in Rome itself.

[77] From the thirteenth century onwards, when they were assisted by German capital, the Scandinavian countries had been in touch commercially.
[78] *The Holy Roman Empire* p. 432.

CHAPTER XIII

THE SACK OF ROME : THE END OF AN EPOCH

BETWEEN the death of Julius II and the Sack of Rome The by the imperialists a period of fourteen years elapsed. Medician This period may well be called the Medician era of the Papacy Papacy, for to Leo X, the son of Lorenzo, succeeded, after a very short interlude, his cousin, the bastard son of the murdered Guiliano. The period began in an outburst of magnificence ; it was, before it closed, to experience the loss of the allegiance of Germany and to see the end of the Italian Renaissance.

The choice of Giovanni Medici in the room of Julius II, Election of was most unexpected. He was not yet forty years of age Leo X and, except for his mild and conciliatory nature, in no way distinguished. It is true that when Julius, as a means of gaining influence in Florence, had pushed him forward he had shewn efficiency and tact ; but he could not be regarded as a strong candidate. His election was due to a desire, in particular on the part of the younger cardinals, for a change of papal policy. They were weary of Popes, who by their choice of title, gave it out that they looked upon themselves as great conquerors and statesmen.[1] The curia wished for peace and the character of Leo X, as the new Pope called himself, seemed to assure it ; so far, that is, as any such assurance was possible in the state of contemporary Italy.

Italy was indeed in a condition when peace seemed un- State of likely. North of the Apennines Brescia was occupied by Italy a Spanish army ; the Swiss were in Milan ; France and Venice had an understanding ; whilst the disputed possession of

---

[1] Cf. Colet's reference in the famous Good Friday Sermon of March 25, 1513 : " Addidit ut Christum Principem suum imitarentur potius quam Julios et Alexandros ". We owe the preservation of the remark to Erasmus' letter to Justus Jonas : see Allen *Erasmi Epistolae* IV. p. 525.

Parma, Piacenza, Modena and Reggio was bound to cause a clash of papal and imperial interests.

French invasion June 6, 1513

Leo had been but a few months on his throne when the French invaded Italy once more ; but only to suffer a severe and unexpected defeat at Novara from the sudden onslaught of a body of Swiss infantry unsupported by either cavalry or artillery. The French offensive had been provoked by the formation of a league against them to which Henry VIII, Maximilian and Ferdinand were parties. Leo was not anxious that France should be weakened too greatly, and the defeat gave him the opportunity of restoring his own influence. The schismatic cardinals had already submitted and received pardon ; France now recognised the Lateran Council.

Francis I

In January 1515 Louis XII closed a somewhat inglorious reign and was succeeded by his nephew Francis, a young man burning with the desire to revive the prestige of the French arms and to emulate Gaston de Foix. It was significant that he at once adopted the title of Duke of Milan. This was an open challenge, and a league was immediately formed against him by Maximilian, Ferdinand, Milan, and the Swiss, together with Florence and Genoa. A secret member of the league was Leo himself.

Victory of Marignano

September 14, 1515

Things began well for the French, and after forcing their way over the Alps by a new passage, they won the splendid victory of Marignano over the Swiss, and thus brought to an end the belief in Swiss invincibility which had become almost a superstitution.[2] The struggle was a fierce one and lasted nearly two days ; it was finally decided by the arrival of Venetian cavalry to support the French. The Swiss then drew off. Francis was knighted on the field by Bayard.

The victory was a staggering blow to Leo ; but he proved equal to the occasion, as in accordance with his usual policy he had not fully broken with Francis. The Popes were accustomed to follow the victors,[3] and Francis, as others in the same case before him, was not slow to respond to the papal advances. There is something intensely ironical in such an attitude on the part of the secular rulers ; none of them was

---

[2] So the Battle of Rocroi in 1643 was later to end the supremacy of the Spanish infantry.

[3] " E costume de' papi moderne de tenire sempre da chi vince " : Prato *Storica di Milano* in Arch. Stor. Ital. III. p. 344.

under any illusion as to the good faith or honesty of his new and unwilling ally.

Leo and Francis met at Bologna in December 1515 and took the opportunity of arriving at an understanding on the question of the Pragmatic Sanction.   The substance of their agreement, which was to benefit both at the expense of the French Church, found expression in the Concordat of the following August.   But if the king and the Pope were the obvious beneficiaries, the French people could feel that they were not without compensations, even if Gallicanism, for the moment, was suppressed.   The subjects in dispute between the Pope and the nation were those concerning patronage, taxation, and jurisdiction.   The solutions reached were only rough, and subject to many exceptions ; but the right of royal patronage was recognised, subject to papal approval of the candidates.   In fiscal matters the Pope was a distinct gainer, for annates were restored and remained in force until the French Revolution.   The question of jurisdiction, always a difficult one, was met by mutual concessions ; those cases which, under the Canon Law were classed as major, were to be reserved to the Pope ; but the lesser, and more common, cases were to be tried by the French Church, though the right of final appeal to Rome was not forbidden ; the Roman curia, however, was not to be a court of first instance in such cases.

Leo and the French

Leo had inherited from his predecessor the Lateran Council, a feeble successor of the great Lateran Councils of older days. Before it finally sank into silence, it passed a number of resolutions dealing with the wickedness of those who question the immortality of the soul, the desirability of curtailing the exceptions enjoyed by monastic bodies from episcopal control, and the necessity of checking unlearned and sensational preachers whose absurdities and eccentricities shewed up badly in the era of the New Learning.   In addition it received the report of the Committee appointed to consider necessary reforms.   This report was a vague document, and the resolutions based on it were equally vague ; nothing tangible was done to meet the legitimate complaints of Christendom and of Germany in particular.   The Council's effectiveness had undoubtedly been damaged by the strife which arose

The close of the Fifth Lateran Council

between the cardinals and the episcopate. But this was no excuse for its pitiful failure on the very verge of a catastrophic movement which, by a genuine effort to remove grievances, it might have delayed, and possibly have rendered unnecessary. The Council was finally dissolved on March 16, 1517, in spite of the protests of many of its members who realised the futility of what had been done and the needs of the Church.

Charles V Early in 1516 died Ferdinand of Aragon full of years and duplicity. To him succeeded his grandson Charles, and thus the destinies of Europe were in the hands of three young rulers—for Maximilian was hardly taken seriously, and in 1519 he was to leave a world which had been a little hard on him, and in which his brilliant schemes had had the unhappy knack of just failing of success. Leo, at this juncture, played his usual subtle game, and no one trusted him in the least. In spite of this he made the most amazing, and what in a less exalted personage would have been deemed the most impudent, protestations.[4] In December 1516 the war of Cambrai was finally ended by the Treaty of Brussels. Venice in spite of years of warfare was left in possession of her territories ; but her resources had been strained, and her commercial supremacy was threatened. The Treaty restored some kind of equilibrium, but it was only an interlude before another period of warfare.

The Imperial election When Maximilian died, the elaborate arrangements which he had made for the choice of Charles as King of the Romans fell through, in spite of the vast sums which he had spent in making them. The process of bribery had to be begun all over again. The King of France had the deepest purse, but his possession of such resources made him an object of suspicion ; as Emperor he would be too independent. Henry of England was hardly regarded as a serious candidate outside the circle of his own dependents ; whilst a German prince, especially a member of the electoral college, might be a possibility. The real struggle, however, was between Francis and Charles.

[4] A good example is the message sent to Francis avowing that suspicion and double-dealing were " alien to the Pope's nature which wished to give itself without reserve and to meet with a like return ". Creighton remarks that the delivery of this message by the Bishop of Bayeux, hardened diplomat though he was, must have been a severe trial : *History of the Papacy* V. p. 258.

Leo came of a trading stock and his motto, quite evidently, Duplicity of was quick returns and small profits. Dissimulation was the Leo very air he breathed, and some of his mystifications seem so purposeless and so obviously futile, that one can only suppose that he entered upon them from sheer inability to act in a straightforward manner. This election gave him a splendid chance of exercising his powers, and at the same time it promised no small pickings for the Papacy. He pretended to support each candidate in turn ; but probably he would have been best pleased by the choice of neither of them, but of one more dependent upon himself. At last in June 1519 Charles was elected,[5] and one result of the incessant scheming of Leo was to manifest the absolute weakness of the Papacy in the counsels of Europe.[6]

In the following year Leo, by an unexpected combination Leo and of force with his habitual craftiness, succeeded in gaining Spain possession of Perugia, after failing in an attack against Ferrara. He was by this time beginning to feel the restraint of the Spanish hold upon him, and would gladly have got free if he could. However there was no way out, and in May 1521 he had to enter upon a definite alliance with Spain. After all it was a choice of two evils, and Spain was less dangerous than France. In spite of the efforts of Wolsey, who wished to preserve the neutrality of England, and so to play the part of arbiter that country also joined the alliance. In Novr. 24, the same month the French hold on Milan was relaxed and 1521 they were reduced to the citadel. This success filled Leo with joy ;[7] but he survived it only a week.   Decr. 1, 1521

The conclave which followed had some difficulty in reaching Election of a decision. The obvious successor to Leo was his cousin, Adrian VI Giulio ; but for the present he was set aside, owing to Italian jealousies and the opposition of France.[8] There was an attempt to obtain the Papacy for Wolsey, and Charles gave

---

[5] He was advanced enormous sums by the Fuggers whose patriotic feelings could not stomach the thought of a French Emperor.

[6] It is possible that Leo's schemes were intended to conceal papal weakness : cf. Creighton *op. cit.* VI. p. 117.

[7] He is reported to have said that it pleased him more than his election to the Papacy : Creighton *op. cit.* VI. p. 188.

[8] Francis assured the cardinals that the election of Giulio would mean the withdrawal of obedience ; see the letter of Fitzwilliam to Wolsey in Brewer *Calender* No. 1947.

a lying promise of his own support.[9] But the Englishman
was too powerful already for his claims to be admitted by
his fellow cardinals. At last as absent cardinal, Adrian,
Bishop of Utrecht, was chosen. As he had been Charles'
tutor, and was at the time of his election his viceroy in Spain,
imperial influence had evidently been at work. Adrian was
a stranger to many in the conclave but his upright character
was in his favour. For once the cardinals, finding that their
schemes to elect on political grounds had reached a condition
of stalemate, turned to one whose main qualification was
personal. In some ways the situation was parallel to that
which led to the choice of Celestine V ; though Adrian was
no hermit, but a man of affairs. But the appointment proved
hardly less propitious, and led to a pathetic attempt of the
new Pope, who retained his own name and so became Adrian
VI, to raise the standard of virtue in the midst of almost
universal corruption. The truth was that although Adrian
had an ardent desire for reform, he was unpractical, and,
moreover, one of those natures which may be described
as non-conducting—he was unable to make others share in
his own ardour.

His peaceful policy   The new Pope wished to keep himself free from political
commitments, and hoped that the threat of a Turkish advance
would unite the monarchs of Christendom. But Charles was
unwilling to forget his quarrel with France so long as French
troops remained in Italy. The only result therefore of his
policy was to isolate the Papacy, and to make men ignore
it, since it was no longer of use to them as an instrument.
In Italy itself Adrian had difficulties to face, for on the death
of Leo the petty lords, who had been driven from their usurped
possessions, began to return. In the end he found himself
compelled to side with the Imperialists, and in August 1523
Sept. 14, 1523 he joined the league against France. Within less than a
month he was dead.

Election of Clement VII   The conclave for the election of the next Pope met in
the Sistine Chapel on October 1. It was long drawn out
and to expedite a decision the Roman magistrates cut short
the food-supply. There was a good deal of outside influence,
for there were many who desired a Pope subservient to their

---

[9] On Charles' duplicity on this occasion see Campeggio's letter to Wolsey :
Brewer *op. cit.* No. 1952.

interests. At last the French realising that they could not get their own candidate decided to support Giulio Medici as a harmless alternative.

Clement VII, as he was styled, had had much experience, **His** he had been the right-hand of Leo, and Rome and Italy hoped **character** for a revival of the splendid days of the previous Medici Pope. But the circumstances had changed since Leo had smiled down on a world of charm and delight. Clement was in reality quite unfitted to meet a crisis, and his pontificate has been described as one of the most unfortunate in history; the reason must be sought in the Pope's vacillating character.[10]

The new Pope began by reverting to Adrian's original **Relations** policy of trying to keep out of political complications. **with the** Natural gratitude to the French for aid in the election was **French** probably responsible for his abandoning action against them; and in December 1524 he actually entered into an alliance. In 1523 the position had been much changed, through a family quarrel between Francis and Charles, Duke of Bourbon, which led the latter to take service with the Imperialists. Receiving the chief command in Italy he quickly shewed his worth by driving the French once more from Lombardy. In this campaign Bayard was killed.

Bourbon followed up his success by crossing the Alps, **Battle of** and threatening Marseilles; but trouble with his mercenaries **Pavia** forced him to retreat, and the French again occupied Milan. **Feb. 24, 1525** Had they pressed home their advantage, considerable results might have followed; but they allowed themselves to be delayed by the siege of Pavia. This enabled Bourbon to collect fresh troops, and with nearly equal numbers once again to face the invaders. A fierce battle was fought in front of the invested city, but the French were deserted by some of their Swiss mercenaries, and in the end a panic broke out through a sally from the garrison in their rear. Francis fought to the last and then surrendered.

This surprising victory left France at the mercy of Charles. **Its** But he had no wish to crush a beaten enemy and held his **consequences** hand. He and Francis met in Spain, and at length the French king recovered his liberty after signing the Treaty of Madrid. **Jan. 13, 1526** By its provisions France was to withdraw from Italy, and to

[10] Cf. Pastor *History of the Popes* X. pp. 330 sqq.

restore to Charles his ancestral dominions in Burgundy, as well as Tournai.

No sooner was Francis his own master, than he repudiated his promises on the ground that they had been forced upon him. In this course he was supported by Wolsey; whilst the Pope, who wished to weaken Charles lest Medici interests should suffer, granted him absolution. A League was now formed between Francis, Clement, Venice, Florence, and Milan, with the sympathy of the Turk, who on August 28 had won the battle of Mohacs, in the background.

Charles and Clement Charles tried to detach Clement from the alliance, and sent Ugo da Moncada, an old soldier from the days of Cesare Borgia, to remonstrate with him. The envoy met with a haughty refusal. For a time he held his hand, and then in the following September, in agreement with the Colonna, attacked Rome, looting the Vatican and St Peter's itself.[11] Clement was so terrified that he submitted, especially when he saw that the Romans were not disposed to help him.[12] This was a mild rehearsal of what was to come. Charles cannot be held to have been responsible for the outrage any more than for that of 1527; but he seems to have regarded it as a natural sequel to the continual double-dealing of the Papacy.

The Imperial troops in Italy Early in 1527 the Imperial troops in Italy, which consisted of Spaniards and a strong body of German *landsknechte* under Frundsberg, suddenly determined to fend for themselves on a large scale. Their pay was long overdue, the country was desolated already, and the weather was atrocious. Taking Bourbon, their general, with them, they made an unsuccessful attack on Florence. This led them to an even greater enterprise. Mercenaries had never been noted for their respect for ecclesiastics, and round the camp fires stories of papal wealth and luxury must have been common talk, as well as the feebleness of the disarmed Roman people. They therefore moved south against Rome itself, resolved to recoup themselves from the accumulated treasures of the Church. They had no proper transport or supplies, and little artillery;

[11] Guicciardini remarks that they shewed as little respect for sacred buildings as the Turks for the churches of Hungary: *Istoria d'Italia* XVII. v.
[12] See the extracts from the Diary of Marcello Alberino printed by Creighton *op. cit.* VI. pp. 421 sqq.

but so weak was Italy at the time that their march was uninterrupted, and after being joined by numerous outlaws
and riff-raff they burst into the city early in May 1527.

The unfortunate city was given up to pillage ; nothing Sack of
was spared by the mercenaries, not even the houses of their Rome
Spanish and German fellow countrymen. Relics were stolen,
tombs violated, libraries destroyed. Spaniard vied with
German, Catholic with Lutheran in outrage and brutality.
The Pope managed to escape, though with difficulty, and
from the shelter of St Angelo looked down on the spoiling
of Rome. Here he remained until June 7th when he surrendered to the Prince of Orange who was nominally in command of the Imperial troops. Bourbon had been killed in
the attack on the city. Thus the Pope's foolish diplomacy,
and general shiftiness had turned to his hurt, and brought
grave disaster not only to himself, but to Rome and the
Church.

The city had indeed suffered terribly. During the prosperity and security of Leo's reign, many had been drawn
within its walls, and the population had increased to more
than 80,000. But in the sack some 13,000 houses were
destroyed and more than 30,000 people are said to have lost
their lives by murder, by plague, or by famine. Perhaps
those who suffered most were the humanists, the scholars
and the artists. Many of them had been imported into the
city ; and they now fled from it, that is those who survived.
Many had been subjected to violent treatment and robbery,
some died as a result, and it was hard to obtain news of their
fate.[13] Thus ended Rome's brief resumption of her place
as the centre of magnificence and artistic achievement, of
classical culture and refinement of life. From this time forward scholarship in Italy begins definitely to decline and art
itself to take refuge amidst the lagoons of Venice. The new
Augustan age did not equal in length the reign of Octavianus.

The Imperial victory did not bring peace to Italy. For
another thirty years she was to be the victim of Spanish
and French rivalries, until the Peace of Cateau-Cambrésis

---

[13] For the sufferings of artists and men of letters see Valeriano *De
Literatorum Infelicitate* and for the uncertainty of their fate Erasmus's letter
to Sadoleto of 1 Oct. 1528 : in Allen *Erasmi Epistolae* VII. pp. 509 sqq.

(1559) ushered in a period of respite. Wars of Religion in their own territories occupied the two great rivals.

End of Medieval Papacy

The sack of Rome in 1527, not only marks the end of the Renaissance in Rome, that " guilty, glorious Babylon " ; it is also the terminal point of the Medieval Papacy ; [14] which in its downfall, as in its rise, seemed to have a mystical affinity with the fortunes of the city. Not only so, but in its very history, again in its rise and in its downfall, it seemed to repeat the story of its pagan predecessor. Ancient Rome had fallen because it had drained the provinces to beautify and adorn itself ; and because, at last, its own life-blood had ebbed away through luxury and corruption. Much the same was true of Papal Rome, and now it had fallen before the mercenaries of an imperial master.[15] In both cases the final fall had been heralded by warning voices ; the consequences of pride and luxury had been foreseen by Horace and Seneca, even when vast and magnificent schemes for the adornment of the city were being carried out, and before the onward march of the legions had yet been checked.

Responsibility for the tragedy

The guilt for the tragedy was almost universally attributed to the Popes [16] and the clergy.[17] The state of the papal court was itself enough to account for the judgement which had fallen upon the city. When Alaric sacked the city in 410 the pagans declared it to be the punishment of Jove for the neglect of the traditional deities ; the sack by the Imperialists might equally well have been the punishment of Jehovah on the faithless city. But the view that the Almighty thus takes vengeance is part of the old Jewish-Pagan belief that prosperity is the reward of service which was condemned by Jesus Christ [18] and repudiated by St

---

[14] Just as the Sack by the Vandals in 455 may be regarded as the end of ancient Rome : see Villari *Le Invasioni barbariche in Italia* p. 122. This is a better date than Alaric's capture of the city in 410, although it may not be so well known.

[15] Cf. Inge's judgement on Ancient Rome in *Christian Ethics and Modern Problems* p. 291.

[16] Cf. the verdict of Tomasimo de' Bianchi *Chron. of Modena* IV. p. 392 on Clement VII : " May God pardon him his sins, but he has been a bad Pope for Italy and worse for his own soul ; for he was the cause of the ruin of Rome."

[17] Cf. Fabretti *Chron.* III. 120, 183 : cf. also 65, 70, IV. 294.

[18] Luke xiii. 1-5.

Augustine ; [19] none the less the tower of Siloam would seem at times to fall with discrimination.

It was Nicholas V who had begun the fatal work by which the Church became imbued with Renaissance ideals.   There had followed much outward show and brilliance ; but a decay of inward life and energy.   It might be said of the Renaissance Papacy that, like Hellenic civilisation, it collapsed through loss of nerve.   The religious foundations were almost gone, and culture was no substitute.[20]   For generations voices had been raised in protest ; but nothing short of the cataclysm of the Reformation, and the Sack, would have sufficed to rouse the Papacy from its obsession.[21]   The shock of the destruction of the hoarded treasures of the city, the harvest of long and diligent collection, shewed up things in their true light.   Those, too, who had been the instruments of the Renaissance, the artists and the scholars, were scattered.

There followed a wave of pessimism.[22]   So much that Effects of the men had valued had been destroyed before their eyes, and Sack the world away from Rome was almost equally staggered by the blow.   The pathos of life, the transitoriness of man and all his handiwork, stood suddenly revealed.   They had done well, from their point of view, to rejoice in their day, those children of the new birth ; for it was soon to pass. The rose of life might bloom ; but petal by petal it was falling around them ; its light and joy, its tenderness and pride, all were to vanish.   The world of make-believe like a fairy palace raised by the hand of a magician, was not to survive the clock-stroke of doom.[23]

Art itself found a new refuge in the security of Venice. Upon art

---

[19] In *De Civ. Dei.* Bk. I.

[20] If culture is no substitute for religion it is itself much more dependent on religion than many suppose ; see Christopher Dawson *Progress and Religion* pp. 232 sqq.

[21] Cf. Guiraud *L'Église Romaine etc.* p. 3.   " Il fallut le cataclysme de la Réforme pour enlever l'Église aux séductions malsaines de la Renaissance ".

[22] It is said that Vasari, who was but a youth at the time, then resolved to collect stories of the great artists and to write their lives ; that some record of their achievements might be preserved for an age in which their works might no longer exist.

[23] Cf. the comment of Monckton Milnes on the era of Louis Napoleon : " The grand theatricals in France go on.   I have always a feeling that 12 o'clock must strike soon and all Cinderella's splendour vanish into air " : *Life etc. of R. M. Milnes* I. p. 479.

Rome might still draw to it young artists, such as Vasari and his friend, Francesco Salviati, to copy the masterpieces of the Vatican ; but it was no longer to hold its place. Florence, too, was to suffer eclipse under the revived rule of the Medici. But if art survived, its spirit was changed. From a technical standpoint it might march on to fresh triumphs, but it had lost spiritual and moral force ; a lack of awe and grandeur soon became manifest and the coming of an era of sentimentality and sensuousness. From Fra Angelico to Correggio is a long step down.

End of medieval social system

But the sack was not merely the end of the Renaissance in Rome ; it was the close of a great epoch in the history of the West. The medieval social system had been a unity, based on the institutions of the ancient world as modified by Christianity. Its underlying motives were Christian, and it was held together largely by the ecclesiastical system. Now the age of universal things had perished, the universal Empire, the universal tongue, and the universal Church. Rome had found her task too great ; for centuries she had gone on " bearing on shoulders immense . . . the load of the too vast orb of her fate " ; now she had collapsed beneath it. She had drawn all things to herself ; but now she was to be no longer the sole bearer of the burden ; the centre of civilisation had shifted, it was no more to be the Mediterranean but the Atlantic—a new cycle of culture was to arise following an orbit of its own.

The Church and the new era

The Church faced the task of re-adjustment with stern resolution, avoiding alike the frivolity of the optimist and the despair of the pessimist. She had to find a place in a society in which the secular was to be supreme in law and government, a society which had turned away from the Church as the necessary leader and guide even in the moral life.[24] Never again was the Church to hold its unquestioned position, even in Italy.[25]

---

[24] In France it was left to Amyot's translation of Plutarch, with strength drawn from the Stoic law of nature, to attempt what neither the Catholic faith nor Calvin had been able to do, restore " mental and moral fibre to the nation " by " examples of lofty patriotism," and so " prepare the way for her regeneration " ; *Camb. Mod. Hist.* III. pp. 57 and 70.

[25] An example can be found in Ferrara which had suffered so much from papal ambitions, that though it had been a religious city it turned against Catholicism. Cf. the letter of Battista Stabellino to Isabella d'Este of 23 Mar.

The new life in the Church may be dated from the Council The Council of Trent of Trent (1545-1563). If it laid on the Catholic a straiter burden of doctrine, and curtailed liberty of thought in certain directions, this helped towards recovery. The Church had a definite system and a fixed belief as a basis for action.[26] The council also made a real attempt to abolish abuses which had been denounced, not only by those without its borders, but also by those within. After Trent, though the moral recovery might not have been so complete as some would have us imagine,[27] it was real, and public opinion was apt to be alarmed by events which before the Sack would have been taken as a matter of course.[28] But the problem of the immoral clerk was still with the Church ; and neither the secular ruler,[29] nor the curia could be acquitted of blame.

The Council gave to Catholicism a new sense of unity and stability ; whilst it quickened its moral sense. An unlooked for revival of ecclesiastical zeal, of which the Jesuits were the most prominent manifestation, followed throughout the Roman obedience. This led to aggressive measures, many of them of a political nature, against the advancing Protestants. There was a new hardness, the spirit of Ignatius and his Jesuits, diffused through the Church [30]—effort, rather than lazy acquiescence, became the order of the day. This saved the Church from further losses, and enabled it to recover

1581 : " Verily I can tell you that they will get little silver from here because among us there is not much belief in these ecclesiastical matters, and I think that it will not be long before we shall all be Lutherans, and shall believe sooner in the Mahometan faith and the law of the Turk than in the religion of the priests ".

[26] When the Protestants of Poland demanded a national synod to bring about a pacification the king was able to reply that this was unnecessary as Trent had settled the religious question ; *Camb. Mod. Hist.* III. p. 83.

[27] The Lutheran Sastrow, who was in Rome in 1546, found the moral condition still appalling. The lesson had not yet been fully learned, and Spanish influence, with its rigid puritanism, was not yet fully operative.

[28] When an upright Pope such as Sixtus V promoted his great-nephew, a youth of high qualities, to the purple, open censure was expressed.

[29] When Ariosto was ducal commissary in the Garfagnana in 1522-1523 one of his most difficult problems was how to deal with criminal clergy. He thought it would be " a holy work " to burn down all the presbyteries and churches in the country : see *Letters* xliv., lv., lxv., and cxxxi. Guicciardini had the same problem at Modena and Reggio : see *Opere Inedite* VII. p. 187.

[30] The Jesuits were the last flowering of Western Monasticism, which in them finally gained power over the Church. They were its masters rather than, as the earlier Orders had been, its tools.

24

much lost ground, especially in Central Europe, and among the Latin peoples who are for all time the natural upholders of the Roman religion.[31]

New type of Pope

With Pius V there began a new line of Popes ; his ascetic life, and the passionate sincerity of Sixtus V, were in immense contrast with Alexander VI and Leo X. Even Rome itself seemed to bear testimony to the new state of things ; for the pomps and splendours of the Renaissance Popes, with their pagan associations, were allowed to drop. The task of the new Popes was to apply to the Church the findings of the Council of Trent ; they were the founders of the Ultramontane system of to-day, and pioneers into a period which may have been " less rich, generous, and spontaneous than the early Middle Ages," [32] but a period which had noble compensations for these deficiencies.

Revival of Catholicism

At the beginning of the Reformation the Church had seemed to be dying, with all its faults and corruptions laid bare for the world to see. But it was not so. It was not to be left a splendid ruin of what had once been a habitation of God in the spirit, from which those who had found in it their spiritual home had long ago departed. The Church still stood ; its foundations might have been shaken, but the walls had not collapsed. Repair was possible, and if some fragile ornamentation had been shattered, perhaps that was all to the good.

The Church, to change the metaphor, was a living organism which cast off its old skin to begin a new stage of life. Its services were not yet ended, either to the West, or to the greater world which had been discovered beyond its shores. Even to the politician it was too useful to be allowed willingly to fall into nothingness ; for the time had not yet come, if it is ever to come, when the idea of a historic Church had been outlived by the human mind.

The need for re-union of Christendom

From the decline and fall of the middle ages the Papacy arose in a new form, purified and strengthened, and though

---

[31] Cf. Gregorovius *Roman Journal* p. 280. " The Papacy is a Latin institution and will only cease with the existence of the Latin races."

[32] Von Hügel claims that the period from the Reformation to the eighteenth century " is dominated by the Council of Trent—a period less rich, generous, and spontaneous than the early Middle Ages, yet which nobly eliminated, once for all, the danger of the Roman Church's enslavement to the Occamist conception " : see *Essays and Addresses* I. p. 245.

Western Christendom is still split and divided, it can hardly remain so for ever.   How healing will come no man can say ; perhaps the days will dawn, in God's good time, when the children will return to the Mother, richer for their wanderings, and bringing back new treasures of knowledge and of grace. But before that can happen Rome too must change.   One thing, however, is certain.   The greatest hope for re-union lies with that innumerable company, within each communion, of those who love the Lord Jesus in sincerity and truth, whose supreme object is to make His power rule in the world and in their own lives.   Through them the Church's true task is being accomplished, and in concentrating upon it the divided sections of Christ's army will be drawn nearer to one another, until at last they are one in Him.

INDEX

I. GENERAL

A

Aachen, 122, 125, 128.
Abailard, 74, 76, 78, 80.
Abbasids, The, 6, 38.
Adolf of Nassau, King of the Romans, 66, 120.
Adrian I, Pope, 236.
— IV, Pope, 32-34.
— VI, Pope, 338, 361 sq.
Adwert Academy, 318.
Aeneas Sylvius, *see* Pius II.
Aestheticism, 86, 259 sq., 320.
Agincourt, Battle of, 167, 198.
Agnello of Ravenna, 15.
Agricola, Rudolf, 261, 313, 318, 324 sqq., 329.
Alan of Lille, 88.
Alaric, 366.
Albert I, King of the Romans, 66, 120.
Alberti, Leo Battista, 273 sq.
Albertus Magnus, St, 69, 81 sqq., 86 sq., 319.
Albigenses, The, 102.
Albornoz, Cardinal, 114, 135 sq., 146, 285.
Albrecht of Brandenburg, Archbishop of Mainz, 323, 336 sq.
Alcalà, 321.
Alcuin, 73.
Alexander, Cardinal, 322, 338, 349.
— the Great, 246.
— III, Pope, 21, 33 sq., 105, 225.
— IV, Pope, 49.
— V, Pope, 172, 182, 242.
— VI, Pope, 216, 279, 293 sq., 297 sqq., 309, 370.
— of Hales, 87.
Alexandria, 9.
Alexius I (Comnenus), Emperor, 240.
Al-Farabi, 80 sq.
Alfonso V of Aragon (I of Naples), 192, 199, 286, 288.
— VI of Castile, 39.
— X of Castile, 52, 224.
— I of Naples, *see above*.
— II of Naples, 300.

A

Al-Khindi, 80.
Allemand, Louis d', Cardinal, 210 sqq.
Alvaro Pelayo, 10, 28, 118, 125, 130, 178.
Amadeus VI of Savoy, 247.
— VIII of Savoy, *see* Felix V.
Ambrose, St, 11, 19.
America, Discovery of, 264, 300.
Ammianus Marcellinus, 265.
Anabaptists, The, 334, 339.
Anacletus, anti-Pope, 31.
Anagni, 67 sq., 107, 156.
Anastasius, Emperor, 12.
Ancona, 197, 224, 286, 288.
Androin de la Roche, 185.
Andronicus II, Emperor, 252.
Angelico, Fra, 276, 281, 329, 368.
Angora, Battle of, 247.
Anne of Bohemia, 159.
Annibaldi, Theobald, 51.
Anselm, St, 18, 335.
— of Rheims, 24.
Anthony, St, 90.
— of Padua, St, 294.
Antioch, 7, 9.
Antonello da Messina, 320.
Antonino, St, 216.
Antonius Petri, 169, 185, 204.
Apelles, 279.
Appian, 117.
Aquinas, St Thomas, 69, 77 sq., 82 sqq., 87 sqq., 99 sq., 198, 295, 325 sq.
Aquino, 83.
Arabic Influence, 39, 79 sqq., 135, 227, 249.
— Language, 267.
Aragon, 61, 223.
Arezzo, 265.
Argyropaulos, John, 326.
Ariosto, 266, 369.
Aristophanes, 263.
Aristotle, 4, 76 sq., 79 sqq., 85, 90, 131, 175, 264, 276 sq.
Arles, 16, 213, 296.
Armagnacs, The, 163.
Arnold of Brescia, 32 sq., 141, 196.

II. MODERN WRITERS REFERRED TO OR QUOTED